SOCIAL CITIZENSHIP AND WORKFARE IN THE UNITED STATES AND WESTERN EUROPE

This book compares workfare policies in the United States and "active labor policies" in Western Europe that are aimed primarily at the long-term unemployed, unemployed youth, lone parents, immigrants, and other vulnerable groups often referred to collectively as the "socially excluded." The Europeans maintain that workfare is the best method of bringing the socially excluded back into mainstream society. Although there are differences in terms of ideology and practice, Joel F. Handler argues that there are also significant similarities, especially field-level practices that serve to exclude those who are the least employable or lack other qualifications that agencies favor. The author also examines strategies for reform, including protective labor legislation, the Open Method of Coordination, the reform of social and employment services, and concludes with an argument for a basic income guarantee, which would not only alleviate poverty but also provide clients with an exit option.

JOEL F. HANDLER is Richard C. Maxwell Professor of Law, and Professor of Policy Studies, School of Public Policy and Social Research at the University of California, Los Angeles. He is also Director of the Foreign Graduate Masters Program. He was awarded the American Political Science 1997 Kammerer award "for the best political science publication in the field of U.S. national policy," and the ACLU Foundation of Southern California, Distinguished Professor's Award for Civil Liberties Education, 1999. Recent publications include *Hard Labor: Poor Women and Work in the Post-Welfare Era*, co-edited with Lucie White (1999). He is co-author with Yeheskel Hasenfeld of *We the Poor People: Work, Poverty, and Welfare Reform* (1997), and author of *Down From Bureaucracy: The Ambiguity of Privatization and Empowerment* (1996); *The Poverty of Welfare Reform* (1995).

CAMBRIDGE STUDIES IN LAW AND SOCIETY

Cambridge Studies in Law and Society aims to publish the best scholarly work on legal discourse and practice in its social and institutional contexts, combining theoretical insights and empirical research.

The fields that it covers are studies of law in action; the sociology of law; the anthropology of law; cultural studies of law, including the role of legal discourses in social formations; law and economics; law and politics; and studies of governance. The books consider all forms of legal discourse across societies, rather than being limited to lawyers discourses alone.

The series editors come from a range of disciplines: academic law; socio-legal studies; sociology and anthropology. All have been actively involved in teaching and writing about law in context.

Series Editors

Chris Arup
Victoria University, Melbourne
Martin Chanock
La Trobe University, Melbourne
Pat O'Malley
Carleton University, Ottawa
Sally Engle Merry
Wellesley College, Massachusetts
Susan Silbey
Massachusetts Institute of Technology

Books in the Series

Law and Nature
David Delaney
0 521 83126 1 hardback

The Politics of Truth and Reconciliation in South Africa
Legitimizing the Post-Apartheid State
Richard A. Wilson
0 521 80219 9 hardback
0 521 00194 3 paperback

Modernism and the Grounds of Law
Peter Fitzpatrick
0 521 80222 9 hardback
0 521 00253 2 paperback

Unemployment and Government
Genealogies of the Social
William Walters
0 521 64333 3 hardback

Autonomy and Ethnicity
Negotiating Competing Claims in Multi–Ethnic States
Yash Ghai
0 521 78112 4 hardback
0 521 78642 8 paperback

Constituting Democracy
Law, Globalism and South Africa's Political Reconstruction
Heinz Klug
0 521 78113 2 hardback
0 521 78643 6 paperback

The New World Trade Organization Agreements
Globalizing Law through Services and Intellectual Property
Christopher Arup
0 521 77355 5 hardback

The Ritual of Rights in Japan
Law, Society, and Health Policy
Eric A. Feldman
0 521 77040 8 hardback
0 521 77964 2 paperback

The Invention of the Passport
Surveillance, Citizenship and the State
John Torpey
0 521 63249 8 hardback
0 521 63493 8 paperback

Governing Morals
A Social History of Moral Regulation
Alan Hunt
0 521 64071 7 hardback
0 521 64689 8 paperback

The Colonies of Law
Colonialism, Zionism and Law in Early Mandate Palestine
Ronen Shamir
0 521 63183 1 hardback

SOCIAL CITIZENSHIP AND WORKFARE IN THE UNITED STATES AND WESTERN EUROPE

The Paradox of Inclusion

Joel F. Handler

CAMBRIDGE UNIVERSITY PRESS

PUBLISHED BY THE PRESS SYNDICATE OF THE UNIVERSITY OF CAMBRIDGE
The Pitt Building, Trumpington Street, Cambridge, United Kingdom

CAMBRIDGE UNIVERSITY PRESS
The Edinburgh Building, Cambridge, CB2 2RU, UK
40 West 20th Street, New York, NY 10011–4211, USA
477 Williamstown Road, Port Melbourne, VIC 3207, Australia
Ruiz de Alarcón 13, 28014 Madrid, Spain
Dock House, The Waterfront, Cape Town 8001, South Africa

http://www.cambridge.org

First published 2004

Printed in the United Kingdom at the University Press, Cambridge

Typeface Goudy 11/13 pt.   *System* LATEX 2$_\varepsilon$ [TB]

A catalogue record for this book is available from the British Library

Library of Congress Cataloguing in Publication data
Handler, Joel F.
Social citizenship and workfare in the United States and Western Europe: the paradox of
inclusion / Joel F. Handler.
    p.   cm. – (Cambridge studies in law and society)
Includes bibliographical references and index.
ISBN 0 521 83370 1 – ISBN 0 521 54153 0 (pbk.)
1. Welfare recipients – Employment – United States.   2. Welfare recipients – Employment –
Europe, Western.   3. Marginality, Social – United States.   4. Marginality, Social – Europe,
Western.   5. Welfare state – United States.   6. Welfare state – Europe, Western.   I. Title.
II. Series.

HV91.H283   2003   362.5′84′094 – dc21   2003055127

ISBN 0 521 83370 1 hardback
ISBN 0 521 54153 0 paperback

CONTENTS

ACKNOWLEDGEMENTS

The preparation of this book took a long time, during which I had the help of many friends. I am grateful for their contributions: Yeheskel Hasenfeld, Dan Finn, Guy Standing, Alain Supiot, Ivar Lødemel, Claus Offe, Sigrun Kahl, Linda Bosniak, Maurizio Ferrera, Philip Harvey, Anton Hemerijck, Nanna Kildal, Jonah Levy, Tom Mertes, Jim Mosher, Martin Rhodes, David Trubek, Jonathan Zeitlin. Danielle Seiden provided valuable research assistance throughout the project, and I especially want to thank the research staff of the UCLA Law School library.

I dedicate this book to Betsy, and our family.

ABBREVIATIONS

ADC	Aid to Dependent Children
AFDC	Aid to Families with Dependent Children
ANPE	local employment agency (France)
ASS	solidarity unemployment benefit (France)
BIG	basic income guarantee
CCDBG	Child Care and Development Block Grant
CES	solidarity employment contract (France)
CME	coordinated market economy
COLA	cost-of-living assistance (Germany)
DGP	development guarantee program (Sweden)
EES	European Employment Strategy
EITC	Earned Income Tax Credit
ES	Employment Service (UK)
FDS	Flexible Development State (Ireland)
GAIN	Greater Avenues for Independence
HTW	help towards work (Germany)
JEA	Jobseeker's Employment Act 1998 (The Netherlands)
JOBS	Jobs Opportunities and Basic Skills Training Program
JSA	Jobseeker's Allowance (UK)
JSAg	Jobseeker's Agreement (UK)
LME	uncoordinated liberal market economy
MOE	maintenance of effort
NAP	National Action Plan
NSAF	National Survey of America's Families
OMC	open method of coordination
PES	public employment services
PPE	working families tax credit (France)
PRWORA	Personal Responsibility and Work Opportunity Reconciliation Act 1996
RMI	minimum subsistence allowance (France)
SA	social assistance (Germany)

SCHIP	State Children's Health Insurance Program
SPC	Social Protection Committee (EU)
SSI	Supplementary Security Income
TANF	Temporary Assistance to Needy Families
TMA	Transitional Medical Assistance
UA	unemployment assistance (Germany)
UB	unemployment benefit (Germany)
WIN	Work Incentive Program
YEA	Youth Employment Act 1992 (The Netherlands)

CHAPTER ONE

INTRODUCTION

> We have ended welfare as we know it.
>
> President Bill Clinton

> No one has a right to be lazy.
>
> Chancellor Gerhard Schröder

> Men fought for the right to live from their labor, not to be supported by the welfare state. Thus, progress demands reinventing the idea of the right to work, rather than shaping a right to income.
>
> Pierre Rosanvallon

> Insertion contracts are a load of rubbish, they don't guarantee anything.
>
> French RMI recipient

In the United States, welfare has "ended as we know it." In Western Europe, similar claims have been made – welfare states have been changed from "passive" to "active," "workfare" has spread in many countries. In some respects, these claims are too broad. In the United States, the Social Security pension system and Medicare are very much alive – each more than ten times larger than "welfare" at its height.[1] In Western Europe, there are large and expensive systems of health care, pensions, unemployment, and other benefits. Nevertheless, there are important changes in parts of the welfare systems, in both places, affecting significant populations.

---

[1] "Welfare" in the United States is the common term for Aid to Families with Dependent Children ("AFDC"), the program primarily for single-mother families, which has now been replaced by Temporary Assistance to Needy Families ("TANF").

This book deals with "welfare" in the United States, the program primarily for poor single mothers and their families, and "workfare" – or "activation" in Western Europe, the "active labor-market policies" that deal primarily with the long-term unemployed, lone parents, the unemployed youth, immigrants, and other vulnerable groups, usually lumped together as the "socially excluded." I explore the ideologies and practices that have led to these changes, comparing different views of social citizenship. The Western Europeans argue that their changes, although they resemble the US changes in some respects, are fundamentally different both in ideology and in practice. I raise questions about those claims.

The move towards workfare policies in Western Europe represents a fundamental change in both the meaning of social citizenship and the administration of social welfare. Social benefits are rights that attach by virtue of status – the status of citizenship. Under the new regime, benefits become conditional; *obligations* are attached to *rights*. Social citizenship thus changes from status to contract. What brought about this change? There have been major changes in global trade, finance, technology, and communication. There have been vast changes in populations – the growth of the aged, the decline in birth rates, the rise of lone parents, and immigration. There have been major changes in the labor markets – the demand for higher education and skills, an increase in part-time and flexible labor, the increase in female labor-market participation. These changes have brought both opportunities and risks – opportunities for more skilled work, for increases in employment, but also increases in lower wages and labor insecurity (European Council 2001). Gone are the labor-market assumptions of the traditional welfare state – the single, male, lifetime breadwinner.

Perhaps the most significant reason for the change in social welfare has been the decades – long sluggish economies and persistent long-term unemployment in several Western European countries – called "Eurosclerosis" (Huber and Stephens 2001). In most countries, practically every adult seeks employment, but, in contrast to the full-employment years of what is now referred to as the "Golden Age," the jobs are not there. Since the oil shocks of the 1970s, most European economies have been stagnating and suffering from extraordinarily high levels of unemployment. As of 2000, nearly 10 percent of the European workforce was unemployed; and millions of working-age people are not even looking for work (Boeri, Layard, and Nickel 2000: 2).[2] Although economies have improved somewhat, and joblessness has fallen, unemployment in several countries is 9 percent or higher. Low growth is expected in some of the largest economies, e.g., France and Germany (The Economist 2002a: 92).[3] Of increasing social concern are the growing numbers of economically inactive citizens of working age, particularly among the low-skilled, school-leavers, ethnic minorities, and the long-term unemployed (Hemerijck 1999). There is deep concern about "worklessness," the socially excluded. Welfare states are under great stress – from the unemployed, the aging population, rising health care costs – but governments are constrained by the European Monetary Union.

The economic establishment and most political leaders think that a major problem is the costs and inflexibility of the labor market, caused, in part, by an overly generous welfare state which discourages work and feeds a dependency culture. The traditional welfare states have not adjusted to the changes. Built during the era of full employment, they assumed that spells of unemployment would be short and that most of the unemployed would soon be re-employed and thus most active adults would work for a "normal" working life. Now, the welfare state is being blamed for the persistent, high levels of unemployment. The argument is that unemployment is caused by labor rigidity and overly generous social protection systems. Traditional solutions to unemployment have been "passive" – early retirement, generous disability, job protection, and generous income replacement, which support a dependency culture rather than provide incentives to encourage re-entry into the labor market (Supiot 2001: 5; Torfing 1999: 5–28). Labor, under the existing welfare state, has become too costly and inflexible. In order for employment to grow, labor must become more flexible and the welfare state must be changed from "passive" to "active."

Then, there are the overarching claims of modernity, of globalization, international competitiveness – the twenty-first century. "Globalization is portrayed as a force of nature with which we are compelled to come to terms – a historical necessity no less determined than the

---

[2] In Europe, only 61% of those between 15 and 64 years of age are working, as compared to 74% in the United States.

[3] Belgium – 11.6%; France – 9%; Germany – 10%; Italy – 9%; Spain – 11.7% (although unemployment has dropped considerably in Spain).

onward march of socialism once was for Marxists." " 'Social democratic government cannot resort to the traditional methods of demand stimulation and state intervention because the financial markets would not allow it' " (Dixon 2000: 2).[4] The new international capital markets create an "exit" option for domestic firms if domestic economic policies and taxes become unfriendly. The need is to create private sector service employment by lowering the costs of labor and reforming traditional labor protections so that labor becomes more "flexible" (Boeri, Layard, and Nickel 2000: 5; Ferrera and Rhodes 2000: 257–282).

There were moral arguments as well (Standing 1999: 255). The conservatives question social rights without obligations – the obligations that all citizens have (or ought to have). The "undeserving" are being treated too generously. Welfare should be made "conditional." European liberals also had complaints about the welfare state. There was the perception that it was ineffective in either protecting against risks or redistributing income. Despite the large costs, poverty and inequality persisted. The treatment of the so-called "undeserving" was arbitrary and unfair. The welfare state seemed to be perverse. Because the welfare state was based on steady, full-time employment, the regularly employed got most of the benefits rather than those most in need. The existing welfare systems, especially on the Continent, reinforced the "insider-outsider" cleavages. The existing privileges of a diminishing group of insiders – highly productive workers with high wages and expansive social rights – were safeguarded at the expense of a growing population of inactive outsiders (elderly workers, women, youth, immigrants) who remained financially dependent upon either the welfare state or traditional breadwinners (Hemerijck 1999: 15). But if governments tried to redress this outcome, they would risk losing political support (Manow and Seils 2000: 139–160).

An "active" welfare state will not only encourage job growth, it will also help bring the socially excluded back into the paid labor market and thereby restore true citizenship. It is a program of *inclusion*. In both the United States and Western Europe, the proponents of workfare believe that the surest, most stable path to inclusion is via the paid labor market. Lawrence Mead says that the employable poor want to work, but that the permissiveness of the US welfare system has led them astray. The poor need authority, the imposition of obligations.

---

[4] Quoting a Tony Blair intellectual, John Gray.

Mead is interested in helping, not punishing the poor (Mead 1986).[5] Pierre Rosanvallon, in his book, *The New Social Question: Rethinking the Welfare State*,[6] believes that the workfare contracts between the government and the client will *empower* the client. It is through the welfare contract that the capacities of the socially excluded will be developed and they will be included back into society, into citizenship.

The attacks on the welfare state in Europe began in earnest by the mid-1990s. The Economics Commission in Sweden claimed that the institutions and structures of the welfare state hindered economic efficiency with its one-sided concern for income safety rather than flexibility and incentives (Atkinson 1999: 1). They argued that the social security system was overburdening the economy. The European Union's influential document, *Growth and Employment: The Scope for a European Initiative*, after discussing the positive values of the welfare state, listed three major objections: rigidities in the labor market; increasing the size of government thereby risking inefficiency and tax distortions; and the prospect of cumulative deficits and public debt. Expenditures should be reduced and the welfare state made leaner and more efficient (Atkinson 1999: 2). At the same time, the Europeans were unwilling to follow the US example of increasing employment through the growth of low-wage jobs and increasing wage inequality and poverty. More jobs, to be sure, but they had to be "good" jobs. These conflicting demands have created what has been called the "service sector trilemma" – the need for employment growth, wage equality, and budget constraints.

While the public continued to support the welfare state – retrenchment has been incremental – there arose among the politicians of all parties a loss of confidence in "collective" public sector solutions in favor of either privatized or "marketized" social services. National leaders were also influenced by supra-national leadership on welfare issues. The IMF, WTO, and other economic elites heavily promoted free-market ideology (Ross 2000: 11–34). The OECD recommended the deregulation of labor markets, abolishing or lowering minimum wages, scaling back Social Security, and reducing progressive taxation (Hemerijck 1999: 21). The neoliberal rhetoric took hold. The arguments for the superiority of the "negative" economy over "positive" social rights began to appear convincing in the face

---

[5] Lawrence Mead proposes extensive amounts of supporting services – considerably more than is currently spent on welfare per person.

[6] (2000), Princeton U. Press.

of mass unemployment, the perceived failure of Keynesian macro-economic policies, and the alleged deficiencies in the implementation of the welfare state. The welfare state, it was charged, had not lived up to its promise, and, instead, weakened the moral fiber of its citizens (Hemerijck 1999: 9–10; Crespo and Serrano 2001: 295–322).

There were political demands for an end to "something for nothing" welfare. Labor-market policies should focus more on an active integration or re-integration and less on income support (Ferrera and Rhodes 2000: 4). As Germany's Chancellor, Gerhard Schröder, put it, "Germans had 'no right to laziness,' adding that those who reject 'a reasonable job' might lose benefits" (The Economist 2001a: 44). In the United Kingdom, Labour's new Minister of State for Social Security, Frank Field, said that the passive benefit system was now " 'broken-backed,' discouraged self improvement, thrift and independence and rewarded 'claimants for being either inactive or deceitful.' " New Labour began to adopt the rhetoric of "tough love" and "reciprocal" or "mutual" obligation which was popular in the United States and Australia (Finn 1998: 105–122).

"Tough love" captures the duality or ambiguity in workfare. From the earliest days of the Anglo-Saxon system of welfare, the attempt to separate the "deserving" from the "undeserving" poor was primarily concerned with making sure that those who could work would work. This policy was justified not only on saving costs, punishing the malingerer, and so forth, but also on a genuine concern about trying to prevent the slide into pauperism and permanent dependency. The moral concern for social character as well as the economic well-being of the poor was not cynical. Throughout welfare history, the most sympathetic, most charitable social reformers believed that the poor would be better off if they were self-sufficient. Today, in Europe, a large part of the change in policy is concern for the socially excluded. It is genuinely believed that the surest, best way to re-integrate the socially excluded, to restore their citizenship, is through the paid labor market. There is special concern at both the national and supra-national levels about the growing number of vulnerable people who are more or less permanently detached from the laborforce. They are the most vulnerable – youth, immigrants, the under-educated, lone parents. The lack of employment, it is argued, leads to a lack of connection with mainstream society. The 1994 EU White Paper (the "Delors paper") on *Growth, Competitiveness, Employment*, expressed concern about the development of a dual labor market resulting in a dual society. Those excluded from work are also excluded from the benefits of growth and social protection. A dual standard of treatment discourages new hiring and excludes the jobless from unemployment insurance. The White Paper called for "an economy characterized by solidarity," that is, solidarity between those who have jobs and those who do not, between men and women, between generations, and between more and less developed regions. The growing consensus, according to Hilary Silver, is "to turn a passive and precarious solidarity with excluded people into a contract that offers them real opportunities of both social and economic integration in return for a commitment to make an effort themselves" (Silver 1998a: 11).[7]

The result of all these pressures was a growing trend in several countries to give high priority to reducing public expenditures, increasing the selectivity of welfare benefits, and privatizing social policy. By the mid-1990s, the conventional wisdom held that industrialized countries could not afford extensive welfare states, that benefit systems were "inflexible," they "artificially increased unemployment" and there was a "dependency culture" (Standing 1999). The key to increasing jobs was labor-market "flexibility" (McFate 1995). These national tendencies were further institutionalized at the European Union level through the EMU agenda, the Maastricht Treaty's rules on national debt and borrowing, and the single currency. All provided a new rationale and legitimation for public spending curbs (Standing 1999). A dwindling minority supported the welfare state but by now, they, too, were put on the defensive. They agreed with the conservatives and the economic establishment – welfare states had to be reformed; in particular, labor was to be re-commodified (Standing 1999).

There have been attempts to reduce the costs to business, in particular non-wage costs (the "contribution-heavy" insurance systems), and search for different mixes of social security contributions and taxes to finance the welfare state (Ferrera and Rhodes 2000: 6–7). The emphasis has shifted to investment in human capital to meet international "information-based" competition. The new policies are to adjust to the markets rather than overrule them. The "Third Way" accepts a level of inequality and focuses, instead, on an "equality of initial endowments," the creation of equal opportunities rather than the de-commodification of labor, on successful market participation rather than on market outcomes. Social cohesion is to come about not through equal outcomes

---

[7] Discussing European Commission, *Modernizing and Improving Social Protection in the European Union*, COM (97) 102 final, Brussels, 12 March 1997.

but, rather, equal opportunities (Streeck 1999: 6,10). An "active" labor-market policy gives priority to training, placement, and rehabilitation. Individuals are encouraged to enter the labor market quickly. The emphasis is on improving the labor supply rather than the demand for low-skilled labor. There is more concern with welfare state "work disincentives" than on the growing wage inequality. Income support for the jobless is becoming increasingly conditional. By 1998, the favorite euphemism was "welfare-to-work." These programs should become a core of welfare systems (Finn 2000: 43–57; Standing 1999).

Guy Standing sums up the change:

> The end of the century of the laboring man. It began with calls for the *rights of labor* – the right to improved social status, dignity, security and autonomy. It was a call for freedom *from* labor. By mid-century, in the wake of the Depression and a world war, there was the demand for the *rights to labor*, seeking to ennoble the drudgery of being in a job and hinging everything on "Full Employment", which was the full-time employment of men. The century is ending with the libertarians and others advocating and introducing policies to strengthen the *duty to labor*, the state-enforced obligation to labor to obtain entitlement to be treated as a citizen and receive state benefits. In the process, governments are making it harder to survive without labor, without being in a job. (Standing 1999: 337)

"It may not be hyperbole to describe workfare as the great social experiment of the late twentieth century. Its success or failure will determine social and labour market policy in the early part of the twenty-first century" (Standing 1999: 314).

The thesis of this book is that inclusion through workfare obligations is contradictory. Positive acts of inclusion necessarily result in *exclusion* – those who cannot negotiate the barriers. Some barriers are structural, many of which are beyond the control of welfare departments. If jobs or training positions are unavailable in a particular locality, there is not much that the local welfare office can do. But many barriers are individual – health and mental health, substance abuse, lack of skills and education, child and other family care, transportation, and so forth. The importance of the deficits in individual capacities is obvious. The point that I want to emphasize is *administrative capacity* – an issue of critical importance – but that is often ignored or assumed away. Active programs make significant new demands on field-level administration. Workfare is administered at the local offices. Field-level workers are now required to make individualized discretionary decisions as to whether the obligations have been fulfilled, what counts as an excuse, and what sanctions, if any, to impose. Selectivity rules invariably are complex. In addition to the usual forms of bureaucratic disentitlement – delays, frustrations, unfriendly relationships, errors, and so forth – behavioral tests require officials to interpret, apply, and monitor rules and regulations, benefits and sanctions. Organizations are responsive to their political and social environments for support and cooperation and to avoid hostility. To manage these conflicting demands, and get through the day, officials stereotype claimants, sort those who are more likely to respond, defer or sanction those who are judged to be difficult. There is inevitably *exclusion* – those who cannot, for whatever reason, comply with the rules.

To be sure, there are significant variations in both ideology and practice among the Western European countries – some of which will be discussed in the following chapters. Different countries started from different positions and differ in their approach as well as the changes that have been made. In addition, it must be recognized that there is a great diversity of opinion on practically all of the issues discussed in this book which has produced a voluminous literature. For purposes of brevity, I have to simplify and generalize.

I frame the arguments in this book around the ideas of social citizenship. Citizenship commonly refers to a legal/political status within a nation state. The status has certain entitlements – the right to permanent residence within the state, to hold property, to use the legal system, and (with some qualifications) to vote and to hold office. Social citizenship refers to welfare state provisions – the supports that are designed to lessen the risks of sickness or disability, old age, unemployment, lack of income. States vary as to whether non-citizens can receive such benefits. Citizenship, then, describes concrete, positive, legal entitlements.

Social citizenship rights are commonly analyzed in economic terms – e.g., de-commodifying labor, protection against risks to earning capacity, reducing poverty. The core, though, of social citizenship rights, as with all citizenship rights, is fundamentally moral. Redistribution is an act of solidarity, of *inclusion*. The moral issues are multi-dimensional. They are captured in the Anglo-American concept of the "undeserving poor." Although ostensibly about work effort, these moral judgments involve race, ethnicity, gender, family responsibilities, sexuality, and various forms of deviant behavior (Forbath 2002; Gordon 1988; Higham

1988; Smith 1997). Thus, citizenship is also used in an ideological or symbolic sense – to distinguish people from others within the borders or from those who are outside the borders. It is often used as a term of exclusion, of moral superiority, a construction of the "Other."

One of the crowning achievements of the post-World War II era was the development of social citizenship in the Western European welfare states. The benefits of the generous welfare state were granted by virtue of citizenship alone. As discussed, Western Europe is experiencing increasing strains in solidarity from a number of different directions – the faltering economies and high unemployment in many of the countries, the presence of the socially excluded, and the huge volume of cross-border migration from all over the world (Bhabha 1998: 592–627; Tamas 2000: 42–46). With globalization and European market integration, nations have less control over their economies and social policies. There is increasing concern about transnational environmental issues, poverty, and human rights.

Thus, today, the concept of citizenship is much debated. It is argued, for example, that citizenship should be transnational or global rather than bound by the nation – "we are all citizens of the world." Within nations, it is argued that citizenship is ethnocentric and static, that citizenship should be plural or multi-national, that with the decline of class, it is a process rather than a status. There are various social movements on behalf of the socially excluded, environmental protection, raising labor standards in the underdeveloped countries, and so forth (Bosniak 2000: 963; Nussbaum 1996; Turner and Hamilton 1994; Falk 2000: 5–17; Evans 1999). Here, I will take the more traditional definition of social citizenship as developed in Western Europe in the decades following World War II. I contrast this definition with the concept of citizenship in the United States, which is based on contract rather than status. I then introduce the European "Third Way" which redefines social citizenship from status to contract in an effort to cope with the current strains on the welfare state. Social citizenship, at least for the unemployed, social assistance recipients, and the socially excluded, has changed from status to contract as the result of the spread of conditionality.

Chapter 2 provides an overview of what has been happening with the recent US welfare reform. There is a discussion of the ideas that have led to the current reform, particularly those of Charles Murray and Lawrence Mead, which are said to have been particularly influential in Europe.[8] Welfare has "ended as we know it" with the 1996 reforms. Among the several changes, there are strict work requirements enforced by sanctions and time-limits. The main focus of the chapter is on the implementation of workfare at the field level in several of the states. The welfare rolls have been dramatically reduced – by more than half – and of the 1.6 million parents still on welfare, nearly one-third are working. Everyone is claiming "victory." The chapter points out that while many ex-recipients are working, they are worse off than on welfare, and many are not working, or have unstable employment. Most welfare leavers still remain in poverty. In the low-wage labor market, they have difficult issues of managing family and work responsibilities. Inadequate child care and health care are particularly serious. Many recipients, especially those who remain, have significant employment barriers and are at a competitive disadvantage in the labor market. Most of the decline in the rolls is due to the economy, including income support (the Earned Income Tax Credit, which is not considered "welfare"), and not necessarily welfare "reform." And a significant part of the decline that is attributable to welfare "reform" is the result of sanctions and diversion (refusing to accept new applicants). The "positive" cost-benefit results are due primarily to the saving of government welfare costs. Many participants in workfare would prefer education and training for good jobs, which workfare does not allow. Nevertheless, they express satisfaction that they are at least better off than those who are excluded altogether. The chapter suggests recommendations to make welfare reform really work. They include reforming the low-wage labor market, income support, support for child care and health care, transportation, the separation of services from cash assistance, and the elimination of sanctions. There is a discussion of how welfare reform fits with the US notions of social citizenship – that it is a matter of contract, of obligations, not rights.

The chapter concludes with a discussion of some lessons from the US experience that *might* be applicable to Western Europe. A major challenge involves the implementation of "tough love" – the joining of both the conservative and liberal positions on welfare reform. In the United States, there is considerable empirical evidence showing that welfare offices, trained to tightly manage payments and reduce errors, have a difficult time in administering workfare programs which require

[8] On the influence of Mead as well as Charles Murray in the United Kingdom, see Clasen, Jacob (2002), *Managing the Economic Risk of Unemployment in the U.K.*, p.11.

individual judgment as to the suitability (i.e., moral characteristics) of clients. Workers screen and sort clients who contribute to organizational survival. They define the client problems and the alternatives; clients have few, if any, opportunities to influence the terms of the "contract." The fact that clients are herded into low-wage jobs, that they are often worse off than on welfare, does not matter to politicians, the media, and the public. The recipients are off the rolls; therefore, they (and the rest of us) are better off. Welfare policy in the United States has been and remains characterized by *myth and ceremony*. The myth is that once off the rolls, the family will become self-sufficient. Some do, in fact, improve. This is the ceremony that validates the myth, and poverty and inequality can be ignored.

Chapter 3 presents a survey of the Western European welfare states from the Golden Age to the start of the current reforms. This chapter is primarily addressed to a US audience. Here, I show that while there are considerable differences among the European welfare states, reflecting different histories, traditions, and politics, as a group they stand in sharp contrast with the US tradition. This was also true of the post-World War II welfare state in the United Kingdom, although under the Thatcher Government, it changed sharply in the direction of the US model. Hence, the United Kingdom can be comfortably linked to the United States as the Anglo-Saxon model in contrast to Western Europe.

Chapter 3 draws the contrast between a social welfare state where social citizenship is based on status as compared to the United States where social benefits are based on contract. It then discusses the significant changes that have occurred in Western Europe that are causing the present struggles over welfare reform – the decline in the European economies in the late 1970s and 1980s, the aging population, changes in manufacturing, international finance, globalization, growing deficits and budgetary restraints. At first, governments tried traditional Keynesian economics to stimulate demand but by the second half of the 1970s, these policies were considered a failure. Inflation, along with unemployment, became a major concern. Conservative governments then tried to cut back significantly on the welfare state. Because of the continued popularity of the welfare state, in most countries, they were replaced by Social Democrats. They, too, have promised to reform the welfare state but with a "human face," turning "vice into virtue." As the chapter points out, it has been difficult to roll back the major benefit programs, particularly pensions, disability, and health. In the meantime, there have been significant changes in labor. There has been a massive entry of women into the paid labor market, which is unprecedented during periods of high unemployment, and which has created new demands on the welfare state (e.g., child care). In several countries, there was at least some deregulation of labor, a decline in national, solidaristic wage bargaining, and increased cleavages between workers in the traded-goods sector versus the non-traded goods sector, between insiders and outsiders. High-skilled services expanded, low-skilled services stagnated. There is a growth in subcontracting and casualized labor. Union membership has declined but not necessarily union influence. This part of the chapter concludes with a discussion of the vulnerable populations, the socially excluded – lone parent families, low-skilled youth, the long-term unemployed, immigrants. There is growing "compassion fatigue" for the socially excluded.

While severe conflicts remain as to reforming the major components of the welfare state, the moral distinctions made as to the categories of welfare state beneficiaries have led to a more general agreement that assistance for those at the bottom should be changed. With the decline of Keynesianism, including the commitment to full employment, there arose a new faith in the market. Under the Social Democrats, now called New Labor or New Left or the New Social Democrats or the Third Way, active labor-market policies, or workfare, was adopted for the socially excluded. The chapter concludes with a discussion of Pierre Rosanvallon's *The New Social Question: Rethinking the Welfare State*, as one example of the New Left thinking. After criticizing the existing welfare state as inadequate to the current issues, Rosanvallon argues for contracts of *inclusion* – in return for benefits, recipients will enter into contracts with government workers for offers of education, training, rehabilitation, employment preparation, and, if necessary, public employment. These are called contracts of inclusion because it is through participation that the socially excluded will be re-integrated into society, families will be strengthened, and children will be properly socialized. New welfare is an act of solidarity. It is important to recognize that the Third Way ideology of workfare is broader than responding to the crisis of the welfare state; Norway, for example, has adopted workfare as the preferred policy even though there is no budget deficit or threatened welfare state. In short, conditionality has spread throughout Western Europe.

Chapter 4 describes in some detail workfare in the United Kingdom and Ireland (to a lesser extent), as representing the Anglo-Saxon tradition; Denmark, Norway, and Sweden as the opposite (Scandinavian); and the Netherlands, Germany, and France (Continental). I raise the issues that I raised in the discussion of the US workfare. How are dependent clients faring under the new systems? To what extent are the promises of re-entry into society being fulfilled?

There are some significant caveats. Workfare in most European countries is recent; policies and programs are still unfolding and, most likely, will change significantly in the course of time. Therefore, interpretations and conclusions are tentative. As might be expected, thus far there are some successes and what I regard as failures. I emphasize the negatives for several reasons. First of all, as in the United States, policymakers and other proponents of the changes very often only emphasize the success stories – the people who are getting jobs, the decline in the welfare rolls, and so forth. I do not mean to minimize the successes. After all, as Dan Finn has reminded me, even though the UK New Deal for Youth has helped primarily the most employable, those eligible have been out of work for at least a year. Nevertheless, it is too easy to ignore or even blame those who do not succeed, and these programs are for the more vulnerable members of society. Finally, in the United States, there is a strong collection of field-level empirical research. One can speak with relative confidence about many of the major issues of implementation. With some exceptions, this empirical research does not exist in Western Europe (Fafo Institute for Applied Social Science 2001). There are some important studies and bits of evidence that suggest that there are difficulties in implementation and that there may be disjunctures between what the various policies call for and what is actually happening in the local offices. But at this point in the research, it must be emphasized that this is more in the nature of questions rather than conclusions.

The principal impetus for workfare in most European countries was the high rates of unemployment. However, as stated, it is important to recognize that the ideology of activation was much broader. Norway and Denmark, despite good economies and no welfare state "crisis," reversed welfare state policies designed to encourage the disabled and the elderly to leave the labor market and adopted workfare for the unemployed and social assistance recipients. In all the countries, with or without high unemployment, the rights of social support have been changed from status to contracts of obligations, responsibilities, and re-integration into society through training, education, and paid employment. As mentioned, there are two sides to this major shift in the welfare state. One emphasizes anger and frustration about welfare abuses, but the other is humane – to bring the socially excluded back into society.

As expected, despite the overall similarity in ideology and basic approach, the specific policies and practices of workfare differ among the European countries. As stated, the United Kingdom and Ireland, along with the United States, represent the Anglo-Saxon countries. Sweden and Norway are the opposite. There, the basic welfare states are still intact. Denmark and the Netherlands (the "Dutch miracle") are cited as countries which most successfully met the challenge of high unemployment. France and Germany are struggling. They have rejected the US-UK model but have not yet found a way to reduce high unemployment.

Subject to the above caveats, and emphasizing the risks to the most vulnerable, there is substantial evidence that many of the negative practices found in the United States are also appearing in the administration of workfare in Western Europe. In general, workfare agencies are pressed for time and to achieve "positive" results. Rather than individually-tailored client conferences and contracts, discussions tend to be perfunctory, options are restricted, and beneficiaries agree in order to receive the assistance. There is little discussion of client needs. All programs are selective. Agencies "cream," that is, the "best" clients are selected for the "best" options (those closest to the regular paid labor market). Clients are often selected on subjective assessments of attitudes and behavior. Programs tend to favor clients who are younger, better educated, and with fewer social problems. In general, clients are not aware of the various options that may be available. In some agencies, desirable placements are only disclosed to favored clients. Sometimes, undesirable options are used as threats. Once placed, there is little contact with workers. Clients complain about disrespectful attitudes. In some countries, the more marginal clients are considered to be worse off as a result of workfare – they are offered "sink options" and further stigmatized. In several countries, significant portions of the target groups have not received contracts or placements or are otherwise not involved. At the same time, the workers complain about the lack of resources, the unavailability of employment opportunities, and the pressure to get results.

There is growing uncertainty in the low-skilled labor market. Although part-time jobs have increased employment and income, there is also an increase in job discontinuity for those who prefer more work. Gender discrimination and discrimination against immigrants remain

15

serious issues. In the Netherlands, for example, despite the very low unemployment rate, the unemployment rate for immigrants is over 30 percent. In general, labor law regulation does not protect those most in need, those at the bottom of the labor market. According to the OECD, as well as other studies, targeted programs are not reaching those most in need. Of the 10 million new jobs created, 70 percent have gone to new entrants rather than those on the unemployed registers. Activation programs typically do not reach those most affected by social exclusion. Thus far, the response of the Social Democrats has been defensive. They advocate tougher conditionality for the unemployed and the socially excluded.

Chapter 5, the concluding chapter, discusses various reform proposals. The chapter is divided into three parts. The first part reviews the possibilities for reform at the EU level. The argument is made that since the market has been integrated at the European level, so should Social Europe. Just as the various countries with their very different histories and traditions converged on a common market, free trade, and a common currency, they, too, can converge on a common labor and social policy. Some commentators, the neoliberals, believe this will happen but only in one direction – a dismantling of the social welfare state along the US and UK model. This is the direction that is supported by many of the political and economic elites, multi-national companies, financial interests, and so forth. Most commentators, however, think that this is not likely in the near future – there will neither be a uniform "race to the bottom" nor convergence, at least in terms of regulatory law dealing with labor relations and social welfare, especially as the EU is poised to expand eastward. The distinction is made between *negative* and *positive* integration, the former to remove trade barriers but the latter to enact substantive regulatory changes. A major difficulty with positive integration is what is called the "legitimacy deficit" – the current EU government lacks the popular legitimacy to enact laws that will tax and redistribute income and other benefits. Agreement thus far has been restricted to relatively non-controversial matters. With regard to welfare state reform, there are large differences among the nations in terms of ideology, institutions, regulation, and economic development.

On the other hand, in response to the difficulties of positive integration, there has been the development of what is called "soft coordination," or "open method of coordination" ("OMC"). With antecedents in monetary and economic policy, OMC was first developed for employment and has now spread to the reduction of poverty and social exclusion. Under OMC, governments exchange information as to "best practices" and engage in "benchmarking." The EC adopts annual guidelines for national action, and each nation files annual progress reports, which are then evaluated. Recommendations are not binding. Rather, the idea is that through a learning process about common problems and a dissemination of information about programs, states will have an incentive to institute reforms that are tailored to individual nations, while at the same time addressing the common problems of poverty and social exclusion. It is hoped that OMC – a kind of informal law by exhortation – will address the "legitimacy deficit" at the EU.

Not unexpectedly, the initial reports were problematic – e.g., lack of rigorous analysis and the reporting of relevant data, lack of specific, quantifiable targets, insufficient attention paid to gender and ethnic discrimination, etc. Some critics dismiss soft coordination as merely face-saving, a reflection of the failure of the EU to tackle tough social issues. Others take a different view. They think that OMC holds promise as a new method of cooperative regulation. It is claimed that OMC has been used successfully in some areas of employment, e.g., gender discrimination. At the minimum, it is believed that OMC will inhibit a race to the bottom and can lead to increased awareness of the need for positive reform.

Change, then, will come about at the national level, discussed in the second part of Chapter 5. Will there be convergence with welfare state reform or will the various nations continue their individual paths? Some commentators argue the former, and, repeating the arguments made at the EU level, because of the pressures of international markets, convergence will be along neoliberal lines. Most commentators, however, disagree; they believe that existing economic institutions, vested interests, and welfare states are too embedded, too resistant of major change. At the national level, there are two sets of proposals for reform. One addresses the labor market to encourage employment. The labor market has to be "recalibrated" to reflect the social and economic changes, including the large entry of women into the paid labor force. Jobs have to become more flexible and labor costs have to be reduced; at the same time, there must be new forms of labor standards and protections. There are new roles for concertation and collective bargaining. These reform proposals are called "flexicurity," and some countries seem to have moved toward this. At the same time, the welfare state has to continue to change to reflect the changing labor market. Recipients have to be encouraged to enter the labor market by the supply of good jobs as well as the opportunity to lessen or remove employment barriers and to improve their human capital. Different forms of work have to be recognized, as well as family caring functions. This package is sometimes referred to as "recalibrating welfare."

The third part of Chapter 5 deals with those who remain. Under the most optimistic scenario – revived economies, low unemployment, good jobs, flexicurity, etc. – there will still be those left out of the paid labor market – the most vulnerable. And, under more realistic scenarios, at least in the near future, the problems of social protection and the reduction of poverty and social exclusion will remain significant. The long-term unemployed and the social assistance recipients will be subject to workfare.

As discussed in Chapter 4, workfare is administered through individual contracts. The government will offer assistance through offers of education, training, and job opportunities. The clients have *rights* to these offers but, at the same time, they have *obligations*. If they do not fulfill the terms of the contract, they are subject to sanction. In this part, I argue that "rights" in welfare contracts are not the same as rights in ordinary contracts where the parties have equal bargaining power. In ordinary contracts, the relationship is horizontal; in workfare contracts, the relationship is vertical. The Third Way proponents of workfare contracts recognize the imbalance in power but argue that because the clients have rights and the government workers have obligations to fulfill these rights, clients will be *empowered*. I question this analysis. When people come to the welfare office, the field-level social service worker is to make an *individual* determination as to what conditions to impose on the client, to what extent have the conditions been met, if not, are the excuses valid, and if not, what sanctions, if any, to impose. Workfare reforms, as applied to unemployment and social assistance, contemplate a conversation between the line officer and the client. The officer is supposed to *listen* to the client and the two are supposed to work out a satisfactory plan for re-entry. I discuss the bureaucratic incentives and constraints on social service workers and clients, how power is exercised in human service agencies, and how, for the most part, dependent clients are not rights-bearing citizens. The pressures and temptations are to exclude those who, for one reason or another, cannot negotiate the barriers to the paid labor market. Despite the rhetoric, the government workers hold the cards, clients remain relatively powerless and dependent, and the evidence presented in Chapter 4 seems to bear this out. Targeting leads to exclusion.

The third part of Chapter 5 presents two reforms which address the imbalance of power between government workers and clients. The first is that there should be a separation of payments administration and services, which has happened in some countries. Payment offices are concerned with efficiency and accuracy, services with professional, individualized, discretionary decision-making. The tasks are very different and need to be staffed by specially trained workers. Payment offices can be monitored effectively; monitoring is much more problematic with the latter. In addition, there should be no sanctions. For over six hundred years, the specter of the "sturdy beggar" has bedeviled Anglo-Saxon welfare policy and has resulted in punitive, counterproductive, and largely failed efforts to separate the "deserving" from the "undeserving" poor. And now this shadow has fallen over Western Europe. There is little solid evidence that sanctions change behavior, and much evidence that they do harm. And there is evidence that human service agencies cannot do both – sanctions tend to drive out the patient, professional services that are needed.

The separation of services from payments will solve part of the dependency relationship in that services will have to have something to offer in order to get customers. Still, without income support, clients will be dependent. The second reform proposal is for a basic income guarantee. A basic income guarantee will not only relieve the suffering of the poor and help those who cannot fully support themselves in the paid labor market but will supply the all-important *exit* option for the dependent client. This, in turn, will dramatically change the worker-client relationship. In short, the worker will have to offer a desirable opportunity for the client to *voluntarily* enter into the bargain. Workers will have to listen to clients and address their needs. With an exit option, the vertical relationship will now be horizontal. Social citizenship will change back from contract to status.

CHAPTER TWO

THE US WELFARE REFORM: "ENDING WELFARE AS WE KNOW IT"

In this chapter, I sketch the historical development of the US welfare state. This will provide the background for the current welfare reform, and, in particular, American-style workfare. The major point of US welfare is to get families off of the welfare rolls and into the paid labor market. There is little or no concern about poverty or their well-being. It is simply assumed that with a job, they will be better off. I then present various reform proposals that address both the low-wage labor market and welfare support.

The chapter ends with two sections that serve as a bridge to the remaining chapters. One deals with the US conception of social citizenship, or, I should say, the social contract. This contrasts with the Western European conception of social citizenship developed in the post-World War II period which is now undergoing change in the direction of the US model. The concluding section discusses lessons from the US experience that *might* be applicable to Western Europe as they continue along their present path.

THE "UNDESERVING POOR"

Perhaps nowhere – at least among the advanced democratic societies – is the contradiction between the ideals of social citizenship and the reality greater than in the United States. The roots of this contradiction go back at least to the Middle Ages. The starting point is usually the Statute of Laborers (1349). During a period of labor shortage caused by the Great Plague, the statute was passed prohibiting the giving of alms to "sturdy beggars" (De Schweinitz 1947). The prohibition, however, was continued even when labor was in surplus. It was recognized that certain categories of the poor were outside the labor market – the aged, the sick, and the lame. At first, the "worthy poor" were given licenses to beg in designated locations; then, publicly gathered alms were provided so that they would not have to beg. The able-bodied, however, those who "be lusty or having limbs strong enough to labor," were kept in "continual labor." The various provisions were codified in the Elizabethan Poor Law (1601): the able-bodied must work, the family was primarily responsible for the welfare of its members, relief was for residents not strangers (settlement and removal), and was administered at the local level.

The foundational Poor Law distinction between the "deserving" and "undeserving" poor served a number of purposes. It was to save taxpayer money, never a minor consideration in welfare policy. It strengthened basic values. The failure of the able-bodied to support oneself and one's family – "pauperism" – was considered a *moral* failure. Pauperism was multi-dimensional. It was usually linked with other forms of deviant behavior – intemperance, vice, criminality, sexual promiscuity, illegitimacy, often with racial and ethnic overtones. The goal of the English Poor Law principles was to make sure that the able-bodied did not slide into pauperism. The English Poor Law principles significantly shaped welfare policy in colonial North America. By the mid-seventeenth century, several colonies had enacted Poor Laws patterned after English legislation (Katz 1986).

By the first decades of the nineteenth century, in both England and the United States, welfare was in one of its periodic "crises." There was the rise of pauperism, threats to the social order, rising public expenses, and concerns about the supply of labor. The problem, it came to be believed, was that welfare was too difficult to administer in the field and had become too lax. "Outdoor relief" was to be abolished. Henceforth, relief would only be given within the confines of the poorhouse. The poorhouse would deter the able-bodied by the loss of liberty and their miserable conditions. Those who could not work still had to go to the poorhouse. Thus, the "deserving" poor were held "hostage" in order to enforce deterrence (Katz 1986).

Eventually, the poorhouse reform failed and was replaced by "scientific charity." Charity, it was argued, had several advantages over public assistance. Assistance would not be a right but would be more uncertain, thus not weakening the work ethic. Moreover, charities were more resistant to political pressure to liberalize benefits and more effective in exerting "those moral and religious influences that would prevent relief from degenerating into a mechanical pauperizing dole" (Trattner 1999: 53). Although the proposed measures were clothed in new theory, the assumptions as to the causes and cures of poverty remained the same: the task was to keep the poor from starving without breeding a class of paupers who chose to live off the public rather than to work. Again, the goal of relief was not primarily to relieve misery but rather to preserve the work ethic (Handler 1995).

The "deserving"/"undeserving" poor distinction evolved into *categories*, which is a basic feature of the US welfare state: there are separate, distinct programs for specific categories of the poor. Categories began to develop in the nineteenth century with the start of separate state institutions for the blind, the deaf, and the insane. Then, institutions were created for poor Civil War orphans; they were not to be treated with the general mass of poor at the local level. This was followed by pensions for Civil War veterans, which grew into an extensive program before being abolished because of corruption by the Progressives by the turn of the century (Skopcol 1992). However, those who remained were the "unworthy" poor. The distinction was between those who were unable to care for themselves and the able-bodied (Trattner 1999). The former were poor, the latter paupers. The idle able-bodied were viewed as threats to themselves as well as to the community. They were either bound out as indentured servants, whipped and expelled, or jailed. Communities were willing to respond to the needs of friends and neighbors, but not strangers.

During the nineteenth century, poor single mothers and their children were considered no different from the general mass of undeserving poor, which meant that they had to work in the paid laborforce. Toward the end of the century, children began to be distinguished as a separate category and child protection laws were instituted to remove children from their "unfit" mothers. At the same time, however, there was a growing number of social reformers, known as the Child Savers, who claimed that if the mother was only poor but otherwise fit and proper, then perhaps it would be better for the children to support the mother than to break up the home. This idea was endorsed in a White House conference in 1909, and in 1911, when the first Aid to Dependent Children ("ADC") statute was enacted. By 1925, similar statutes had been enacted in almost all the states (Bell 1965).

ADC was primarily for "worthy" white widows; practically all others – African-Americans, immigrants (especially Southern Europeans), Catholics, divorced, deserted, unmarried – were excluded, and thus dependent on the paid labor market (Gordon 1988). They were part of the "unworthy poor." Thus, from its earliest days, ADC was an exercise in myth and ceremony. The myth was that poor mothers would be allowed to stay at home and take care of their children – hence the popular name "mothers' pensions." The ceremony was that a small number of deserving white widows were helped; this validated the myth. The reality was that, for most poor, single mothers and their children, at best, nothing had changed; at worst, they were stigmatized further by being excluded from the mother's pension program. In practice, ADC programs remained small. Relatively few families were enrolled; almost all recipients were white widows, and even these women had work requirements (Abramovitz 1988).

With the New Deal, President Roosevelt concentrated on pensions, unemployment, and work programs, not welfare. ADC, along with other state categorical programs (old-age assistance, aid to the blind), became grants-in-aid, supported in part by the Federal Government and administered by the states. Nothing much happened with ADC until after World War II.

Dramatic changes came in the late 1950s and 1960s. With the mechanization of agriculture, African-Americans moved north seeking jobs. However, there was significant unemployment, especially for the unskilled. Racial tensions exploded into urban riots. This was the period of civil rights activism, including welfare rights. The Democratic Party courted urban African-Americans, and, along with the civil rights revolution, there was a legal rights revolution. The federal courts and welfare rights activists forced open the ADC gates, welfare became a "right," and in streamed the previously excluded – women of color, divorced, separated, deserted, and, increasingly, never-married (Piven and Cloward 1977). Over the next three decades, the rolls went from 2 million to about 13 million. Expenditures rose from about $500 million to about $23 billion (Handler and Hasenfeld 1991). Welfare was now in "crisis." Eligibility was tightened; benefits were cut. Nevertheless, costs and numbers rose steadily and the program appeared out of control. Political and popular concern focused on the large number of African-Americans, out-of-wedlock births, single parenthood, and generational dependency (Abramovitz 1988).

Even though admitted to AFDC (the name was changed in 1962 to Aid to Families with Dependent Children), the new entrants did not shed their "undeserving" status. Instead, they now had to work. The Federal Government, in 1967, enacted the Work Incentive Program ("WIN"), which combined both incentives and mandatory work requirements. All adults and children over age sixteen, with certain exceptions, were required to register and be referred to state employment services for training and employment services. Overall, the program was a failure. In addition to high costs, only 2–3 percent of the eligible recipients obtained jobs through WIN. The vast majority were put on "administrative hold." Moreover, only 20 percent of those who were employed held their jobs for at least three months (Handler 1995: 58–59).

While the Nixon and Carter administrations each attempted to revive WIN through new initiatives, it was not until the Reagan years that welfare policies took a new course. This was the start of the "welfare queen" rhetoric: recipients labeled as inner-city, unwed African-American mothers, generational welfare, having children to stay on welfare, sexual promiscuity, drug addiction – in short, breeding a criminal class. The Reagan administration's principal changes were to restrict eligibility, cut back sharply on incentives, and encourage states to experiment with various work programs by reducing federal WIN funding. WIN funding declined, state funding increased, and more than half of the states adopted work requirements – the so-called WIN Demonstration Projects (Handler 1995: 63–88).

The most notable state program was California's Greater Avenues for Independence ("GAIN") Program (1985). GAIN was to move recipients from welfare to jobs by emphasizing job search and, if necessary, remedial education. In a 1994 Manpower Demonstration Research Corporation ("MDRC") study of the California GAIN program, Riverside County was considered the great success. Riverside County emphasized quick job entry combined with job development and post-employment support by the agency. Despite the publicity, the Riverside results were quite modest. The difference in earnings between the controls and the experimentals was less than 10 percent. Perhaps most important, at the end of the three-year experiment, about two-thirds of the experimentals were no longer working and almost half never worked at all during the entire experiment. But the program saved welfare costs, and became the model for proposed changes in California and the rest of the country (Handler and Hasenfeld 1997: 68).

For most of this period, the liberals opposed the work requirements; they argued that if non-welfare mothers were not required to work, it was unfair and punitive to impose work requirements on single, poor mothers. Conservatives thought otherwise. Single, poor mothers did not shed their historical "undeserving" status simply because misguided liberals let them into AFDC. They were morally different from mothers who were either man-dependent or self-sufficient. Thus, as always, they should be required to work. Both sides remained unhappy. Conservatives continued to attack the "entitlement state" on the grounds that there are *responsibilities* as well as rights in the social contract. Then, in the late 1980s, the liberals changed. Instead of arguing that it was unfair to require AFDC mothers to work, they now argued that AFDC mothers should be *expected* to work. Two reasons were given. First, social norms concerning female labor had changed. Now, the majority of non-welfare mothers were in the paid labor force, and therefore, it was reasonable to expect welfare mothers to work. Second, the families were better off, both materially and socially, when the adults were gainfully employed rather than continually dependent (Ellwood 1988; Garfinkel and McLanahan 1986). In 1988, the Family Support Act was passed, supported by both liberals and conservatives, designed to strengthen the work requirements. Not a great deal changed. The next change was the Jobs Opportunities and Basic Skills Training Program ("JOBS"), which went into effect in 1990. Compared to previous welfare-to-work programs, JOBS emphasized training and education, but these programs produced only modest employment increases (Freedman et al. 2000).

"ENDING WELFARE AS WE KNOW IT"

Throughout this entire period, welfare (AFDC, that is) remained a deeply divisive political controversy (Gilens 1999). Liberals joined conservatives in demanding stiff work requirements. President Clinton, during his campaign, promised "to end welfare as we know it." The promise was fulfilled with the passage of the Personal Responsibility and Work Opportunity Reconciliation Act of 1996 ("PRWORA") which "abolished" AFDC, and replaced it with Temporary Assistance to Needy Families ("TANF"). The legislation explicitly stated that welfare is no longer an entitlement. State authority, already considerable, was expanded by replacing the grant-in-aid funding with block grants to the states. Work requirements are to be strictly enforced through sanctions and time limits. Cash assistance is limited to a maximum of two consecutive years with a five-year lifetime limit (with exceptions for no more than 20 percent of the caseload). States were required to move an increasing percentage of welfare recipients into the workforce over the next six years, starting with 25 percent of the adults in the single parent family in 1997 and increasing to 50 percent by 2002. States are required to reduce grant amounts for recipients who refuse to participate in "work or work activities." These welfare-to-work requirements are to be enforced by funding cuts in the block grants. While the idea of work requirements is by no means new, the difference lies in the program's significant ideological and policy commitment to employment, enforced by the time-limits. Following the Riverside model, the "work first" strategy was adopted nationwide: any job is better than no job and by taking an entry-level job and sticking with that job, one would move up the employment ladder (Handler 1995:1–2).

In addition to the work requirements, there are a variety of provisions dealing with "family values." For example, the Act prohibits the use of federal funds for minor parents under eighteen years of age who are not in school or other specified educational activities or living in an adult-supervised setting. States are required to reduce a family's grant by 25 percent if they fail to cooperate (without good cause) with efforts to establish paternity. States may eliminate cash assistance to families altogether, or provide any mix of cash or in-kind benefits they choose. They can deny aid to all teenaged parents or other selected groups; deny aid to children born to parents receiving aid; deny aid to legal immigrants (since modified); or establish their own or lower time-limits for receipt of aid. States can provide new residents with benefits equal to the amount offered in their former states for up to one year (subsequently declared unconstitutional by the US Supreme Court) (*Saenz* v. *Roe*, 526 U.S. 489 (1999)). States may choose to deny cash assistance for life to persons convicted of a drug-related felony (which in many states can consist of possession of a small amount of marijuana).[1]

---

[1] The Act also modified other programs which will impact on the well-being and work effort of welfare recipients. For example, while the basic structure of Medicaid remained intact, welfare families will no longer be automatically eligible. They must apply separately. The Act also substantially narrowed the Supplementary Security Income (SSI) definition of disability for children. It is estimated that more than 300,000 children could be denied benefits by 2002. A previous law denies eligibility to recipients whose primary disability is alcohol and/or substance abuse. Recipients incarcerated for more than thirty days will be denied eligibility. The Act also reduced food stamps in a number of ways, including a general tightening of eligibility. As with

The welfare reform proposed by the Bush administration pushes for greater workforce participation: work requirements are to be increased by 5 percent per year until they reach 70 percent in the fiscal year 2007. Moreover, welfare recipients would be required to work a full forty-hour work week. Since child care spending would remain unchanged despite the increased work week, child care slots are likely to become even scarcer. There is little concern as to how a single mother can manage one or two jobs and take her children to child care and/or school without adequate transportation. Yet, as long as families are not on welfare, it is assumed that everything is OK. No one talks about poverty.

Not surprisingly, the current welfare reform is being hailed as "new," a fundamental change. But, as we have seen, the emphasis on work rather than welfare is as old as welfare itself. The cornerstone of US welfare policy has always been to separate the "deserving" poor from the "undeserving." The distinction is primarily – but not exclusively – in terms of attachment to the paid laborforce, a *moral* fault, which incorporates other forms of so-called deviant status and behavior. Hence, it becomes easier to blame the victim rather than address structural issues.

This is what welfare policy *purports* to do. However, as will be discussed, in many circumstances, especially with single-mother families, it is often less costly and less difficult administratively to provide welfare benefits (however meager) than to impose sanctions. Welfare workers, for the most part, are underpaid, overworked eligibility technicians, primarily concerned with error rates. The style was "myth and ceremony" – the myth was that welfare mothers were required to work, the ceremony was that a few actually did get jobs as a result of welfare-to-work programs. Most – about two-thirds of the welfare rolls, at any one time – would get jobs on their own. Thus, welfare policy is largely symbolic politics, the affirmation of values that serve to make majoritarian society feel better. At least that has been the record until now. What is new is the vigor of the ideology, enforced by the time-limits. Welfare reform today is still in the shadow of the sturdy beggar.

Medicaid, welfare families are no longer automatically enrolled. Funding was reduced or eliminated for child nutrition and meals programs, including programs in family day care, the Summer Food Program, the School Breakfast Program, and other meal services. Various child care programs are consolidated into the Child Care and Development Block Grant. Several provisions of the Act aim at trying to bolster current child support enforcement efforts.

THE "WORK FIRST" STRATEGY

The welfare rolls have fallen from 12.2 million people in 1996, when the new law was adopted, to 5.3 million (Pear 2002: A 24). And of 1.6 million parents still on assistance, nearly one-third are working, a three-fold increase from four years ago (Healy 2000: A12). Everyone is claiming "victory."

The heart of the welfare reform is the "work first" strategy. The assumptions are: (1) there are plenty of jobs for those who want to work; (2) by taking any job, even an entry-level job, and sticking with that job, a person will move up the employment ladder; (3) the problem with welfare recipients is that they do not have the motivation or the incentives to leave welfare and enter the paid labor markets; and, (4) the state programs have shown that recipients can be moved from welfare to work. The idea is to move not only current recipients but also applicants – before they get on welfare – into the labor market as quickly as possible rather than place them in longer-term training or education programs.

Prior to TANF, over thirty states had pending or approved waiver requests which imposed work requirements enforced by some form of time-limits. At least twenty states have time-limits less than five years; in ten states, it is only two years (De Parle 1997: A16). The reported experience of these welfare-to-work projects was used to justify the "work first" strategy. As discussed, one of the most noteworthy projects was the California, Riverside County program – considered the standard-bearer for the "work first" strategy (for a discussion of the Riverside program, see Handler and Hasenfeld 1997). The Riverside results were hailed as successful: welfare recipients who worked earned more than the controls, welfare payments were reduced, and the program showed a positive cost-benefit ratio. The unique features of the Riverside program make it particularly attractive to policy-makers. Led by a charismatic director, the staff were recruited and organized around the work program. The program emphasized the job search and quick entry into the labor market. The staff were evaluated and rewarded on the basis of successful placements. Most significantly, the agency engaged in job development. The staff actively sought out potential employers and encouraged them to use the welfare department to fill vacancies. The department could guarantee employers screened applicants who had received at least some training in job readiness and who had available critical services if problems arose with transportation, child care, or difficulties at work. In addition to these valuable services, employers were spared the costs of selecting applicants responding to public ads.

It all seems to fit together. A closer look, however, shows that the Riverside results are indeed modest. Riverside had the best positive results – the highest earnings and the greatest welfare savings. However, participants in the experiment averaged less than $20 per week more than the controls. A variety of research shows that most recipients supplement welfare with work and have monthly combined budgets of about $1,000 (Edin and Lein 1996: 253–266; Harris 1993: 317–352). Therefore, the difference between the Riverside experimentals and the controls (who are working off-the-books) was about 8.5 percent. Moreover, this difference came about because the experimentals were working longer hours rather than at higher wages. Perhaps even more significant is the fact that despite the great efforts of the Riverside County Department, about two-thirds of the experimentals were *not* working at the end of the three-year demonstration and almost half *never* worked during the entire three-year period. In other words, most recipients did not get jobs, and those that did earned very little more than those who packaged welfare with work on their own. Even with these modest results, replication is, at best, problematical. Florida, for example, was not able to replicate Riverside (Handler and Hasenfeld 1997). Charismatic leaders reorganizing local welfare agencies is not something one can take for granted.

The Riverside results are not unique. In a survey of 20 welfare-to-work programs, Manpower Demonstration Research Corporation found that earnings increased only about $500 per year more than the controls. Welfare payments were reduced by nearly $400 and food stamps by $100, thus resulting in welfare savings for the government (Michalopoulos and Schwartz 2000: 4, 7–8).[2] While earnings for the most disadvantaged groups (long-term, lack high-school diploma, three or more children, no recent work experience) increased, they still remained far below the more advantaged workers. Thus, despite the political claims for success, the gains for welfare-to-work recipients are very modest, and often fail to account for the costs of working – transportation, reciprocity in child care, missed days, and so forth. Most remain in poverty.

[2] The analysis excluded the Earned Income Tax Credit as well as work-related expenses such as payroll and income taxes, child care costs, and transportation costs.

Why these modest results? The reason is that the assumptions behind welfare-to-work programs are misconceived as to who welfare recipients are, why they are on welfare, and the characteristics of the low-wage labor market. First, we will consider the characteristics of the low-wage labor market; then, we will consider the match between the welfare recipients and the jobs. We will conclude by discussing what has been happening to ex-welfare recipients.

THE LOW-WAGE LABOR MARKET

The "success story" of the US economy is well known. Since 1990, over 20 million new jobs have been created. Moreover, until the current recession, unemployment was approximately 4 percent, and for a long time there seemed to be no sign of inflation. On the other hand, there has been stagnation in the real wages of the less-skilled, less-educated workers (Freeman 2000: 27–37). Over the past decade, there has been a tremendous increase in labor-market participation of less-skilled women. The earnings of single mothers grew, but the annual level remained low (at or below $7,000) (Blank and Schmidt 2000: 3). Despite the economic expansion and the rise in productivity between 1973 and 1993, the household income of the poorest fifth declined. The sharp growth in wage inequality and the sluggish growth of real wages for most people led to the rapid wage dispersion (Osterman 2001: 7).

Wages began to rise among the less-skilled workers after the mid-1990s. This slowed the growth of wage inequality, but the wage growth of the past few years has not made up for the large declines in the 1980s and early 1990s. Real wages in 1999 were below their 1979 levels for those with the lowest levels of education (Blank and Schmidt 2000: 7). For a while, the inequality in women's wages narrowed, primarily because of an increase in the hours worked *and* the significant decline in male earnings, rather than the increase in female wages (Mishel, Bernstein and Schmitt 2000: 134–135). The decline in real wages for the less-skilled, less-educated workers was especially pronounced for adults aged 24–35, with a high school diploma or less. Female dropouts earn only 58 percent of male dropouts (Katz and Allen 1999: 31–35).[3]

---

[3] "[T]he Educational Testing Service estimates that individuals with 'minimal skills' will qualify for only 10 percent of all jobs generated between now and 2006."

Jobs are increasingly contingent or short-term, and without benefits. Very few of the poor work full-time, at least at one job – in 1998, only 13 percent of the poor were fully employed (Osterman 2001: 2). The instability of employment is not confined to the low-wage labor market. A survey in California reports that four out of ten workers have been at their jobs for less than three years, and that just one-third fit the conventional mode – working outside of the home at a single, full-time job year-round as a daytime employee (Lee 1999: A1). Re-employed workers usually suffer a decline in wages. Employment instability continues to be a major problem for the less-skilled and disadvantaged workers. They experience frequent and long spells of unemployment (Katz and Allen 1999). Low wages and unemployment are most severe for young workers, minorities, single parent families, and those who lack a high school diploma (Burtless 1999: 31–35).

The "work first" philosophy of welfare reform emphasizes immediate employment over formal job preparation, and assumes that workers will be able to use the skills and knowledge gained in initial jobs to qualify for better paying jobs. However, employment mobility is also a myth. Whether or not true in the past, there is increasing evidence today that low-wage workers are not moving up the economic ladder (Mishel et al. 2000). Only one-fifth of the jobs held by less-educated workers are in "starter" occupations, which require little training or experience, and are associated with subsequent well-paying occupations. Most routes up the ladder are inaccessible to many less-educated workers (Kusmin and Gibbs 2000: 33). According to a recent study, the 1990s job expansion was mostly concentrated at the high end (20 percent) as well as the very low end (17 percent) of the job structure. Moreover, the study reports that it was "a racially polarized job expansion," as most of these bottom-end employment opportunities were dominated by minorities while the so-called good jobs were filled by whites. The very slow rate of growth of jobs in the lower-middle range of job quality makes it increasingly difficult for employees in the bottom tier of the employment continuum to move up to higher-quality jobs. In other words, even if welfare recipients and leavers gain work experience and receive on-the-job training there are few middle-range job opportunities to move up to (Alstott 1999: 967–1058; Wright and Dwyer 2001: 21–26).

Studies have suggested that staying with an employer is likely to yield returns for low-skilled workers (Gladden and Taber 2000: 160–192). Both in pre- and post-PRWORA periods, there is a weak positive association between length of laborforce participation and earnings (Cancian et al. 2000: 77). As a result, policy-makers and analysts concerned with the well-being of low-income families are emphasizing the benefits of sustained laborforce participation and lengthened job tenure. They tend to locate employment instability *within workers rather than workplaces*, emphasizing the need for "work supports" that help lower-skilled workers meet job requirements by overcoming "barriers" to employment, such as having young children (Danziger et al. 2000: 6–30). Lambert, Waxman, and Haley-Lock question this position. They argue that "work supports may not have their intended effect if, in fact, job tenure and earnings growth are driven as much by structural aspects of jobs and workplaces as by the personal qualities of workers" (Lambert, Waxman, and Haley-Lock 2001: 1). The researchers studied low-wage jobs in four sectors of Chicago's urban economy – retail, hospitality, shipping/transportation, and financial services. They examined multiple sources of instability in low-skilled jobs, which are defined as jobs that require no higher than a high school education and are not considered seasonal or temporary (Lambert et al. 2001: 3).[4]

Job instability is measured by turnover rates, number of hours worked, and scheduling of work hours. Turnover rates vary both within and across employers and industries. Of the 60 jobs for which they have specific turnover data, annual turnover rates range from 0 to 500 percent. Half of the jobs have an annual turnover rate exceeding 50 percent, and one-third over 80 percent (Lambert et al. 2001: 6). The striking part of the findings is the substantial variation in turnover rates among lower-skilled jobs *within* employers. These variation rates provide evidence of how the chances of job retention for TANF participants and other lower-wage earners are at least partially a function of the job (Lambert et al. 2001: 7). The analysis suggests that workers entering lower-skilled jobs often stand a low probability of remaining in a particular job for even a few months.

The number of hours worked also varies a great deal. In all the industries studied, the employers practice "workloading" or "workload adjustments" during off-peak seasons. Workers are given very few hours to work for weeks, even months at a time during off-peak time. Most workers don't apply for unemployment benefit during periods of

---

[4] The research combines multiple sources of data (administrative, interview, and observation) to develop an understanding of variations (across jobs, workplaces, and industries) in daily workplace practices.

"workload adjustment" because of fear of losing health insurance and seniority (Lambert et al. 2001: 12).

The temporal structure of work is another source of instability. For many lower-wage earners, work is scheduled along multiple dimensions: days of the week, time of the day or shift, and length of shift or time worked on a given day. Although an employee may hold a five-days-a-week job on paper, his/her life must actually accommodate seven. In general, in order to work a job that varies from 10 to 15 hours a week, employees must structure their time so that they are available to work the highest end of the range, even though they are rarely guaranteed that number of hours week-to-week. When schedules change frequently or with little notice, employees must absorb the impact of these fluctuations. Conflicts with family arrangements, other jobs or transportation can undermine an employee's ability to hold the job (Lambert et al. 2001: 13). Also shifting schedules may upset other work arrangements on which the employee depends for sufficient income – many low-wage workers have multiple jobs – and scheduling shifts may undermine some workers' strategies for making ends meet (Lambert et al. 2001: 15). When shifts change, seniority often governs the bidding process. New employees who are usually the least established members of the workforce generally fall to the back of the line in the process (Lambert et al. 2001: 16). In sum, although employers, caseworkers, and policy-makers may view job loss as employee-initiated, the high annual turnover rates of many lower-skilled jobs suggest that workers' chances of remaining employed are often slim. Furthermore, in lower-skilled jobs, the chances of job loss are highest among those most recently hired. The authors note that TANF does not take into account the variations in income that result from changing schedules and frequent job loss (Lambert et al. 2001: 19): turnover rates among new hires, scheduling practices that require child care almost "on call, and workload adjustment that may leave workers with a job but no pay" (Lambert et al. 2001: 19).

Given the characteristics of the low-wage labor market, it is no surprise that there are still millions living in poverty or close to it. In 2000, 11.3 percent (31 million people) were living below the official poverty line of $17,603 for a family of four (US Bureau of the Census 2001). Moreover, 13.8 million had incomes of less than *one-half* of the poverty line. Another 23.8 million are "near poor" – 150 percent of the poverty line (Heclo 1994: 420; US Bureau of the Census 1998). Despite the booming economy, despite the very low unemployment, and despite the fact that most Americans are better off, the bottom fifth of the population is *worse* off. The average after-tax household income of the poorest one-fifth of households, adjusted for inflation, has *fallen* 12 percent since 1977. The average annual income of this group is $8,800, down from $10,000 in 1997.[5] Thus, although more Americans are working harder, inequality and poverty remain severe among the working poor.

WORK EXPERIENCE OF WELFARE RECIPIENTS

Contrary to the stereotype, most welfare recipients are adults with small families (1.9 children, on average) and are on welfare for relatively short periods – between two and four years. Long-term dependency (five years or more) is rare – perhaps as low as 15 percent. Furthermore, it turns out – again contrary to myth – that the largest proportion of welfare recipients is connected to the paid labor market. Many packages work with welfare and the most common route off welfare is via a job. In other words, most welfare recipients have little or no problem with work ethic. However, those who leave welfare often have to return. The low-skilled labor market produces cycling back and forth between work and welfare.

Welfare recipients do not fare particularly well in the competition for these low-skilled jobs. Employers of low-skilled workers are looking for high school diplomas, work experience, and mainly social skills ("soft skills"). They often hire through networks, and, in general, prefer workers with similar ethnic backgrounds. African-Americans are at the end of the queue. Perhaps most significant, welfare recipients are often handicapped by being mothers of small children (Henly 1999: 48–75).

Reports are starting to come in about the employment of leavers – who finds jobs, what kinds of jobs, and how much do they earn (Loprest 1999: 10). Between half and two-thirds find jobs shortly after leaving welfare. Most of the jobs are in sales, food preparation, clerical support, and other service jobs. Moreover, despite the relatively high number of weekly hours of work, there are substantial periods of unemployment (Hamilton 2002: 24). The pay is between $5.67 and $8.42 per hour, and the average reported annual earnings range from $8,000 to $16,600, thus leaving many families in poverty (Grogger, Karoly, and Klerman 2002: 98). Increases in earnings are largely a result of working longer

---

[5] Discussing the recently published analysis by the Center on Budget and Policy Priorities.

hours rather than a growth in wages. Most do not receive employer-provided health insurance, paid sick or vacation leave. Employment loss is a significant problem (Strawn, Greenberg, and Savner 2001: 6–7). In addition, there are sharp declines in Medicaid and food stamps (Grogger et al. 2002: 104).[6] Most do not receive child care subsidies (Pavetti 1999: 48). Mandated work programs, in general, have little effect on income since they often result in a decline in welfare benefits (Hamilton 2002: 28). They did decrease poverty somewhat, but only for families just below the poverty line (Grogger et al. 2002: 229).

In a recent survey (2002) of over 8,000 respondents in Los Angeles County, California, only 26 percent of current welfare recipients and 29 percent of former recipients were employed at the time of the survey. Forty-three percent of the current and 44 percent of former recipients had worked during at least part of the past year. Almost half (44 percent) listed lack of child care during the day or night as a barrier to employment. Some of the other barriers listed were limited education (38 percent); limited job experience (37 percent); and lack of transportation (35 percent) (Flaming, Kwon, and Burns 2002: 1–2).

Assuming that a welfare recipient does find a job, she also has to compete in the child care market. The crisis in child care – especially for low-wage workers – cannot be over-emphasized. Millions of infants, children, and adolescents are at high risk of being compromised both developmentally and in health because of mediocre child care. Yet, the current welfare reform requires mothers of young children – in most cases, three-month-old infants – to enter the paid laborforce. Child care centers are at capacity, and even if there are vacancies, the cost is usually too high for welfare recipients (Children's Defense Fund 1998: 2–3).[7] Consequently, most welfare recipients use unregulated relative or family day care. Even here, costs are high, and expenses, as well as availability, vary as children are younger and the mother has to take shift work (White 1999).

Market-level child care costs between $150 and $175 per week (White 1999: 123). In New Jersey, the range is between $125 and $150 a week, which is at least 40 percent of the take-home pay of former

[6] About 65 percent of families leaving welfare stopped using food stamps.

[7] As of 1998, New York City lacks child care slots for 61 percent of the children whose mothers are supposed to participate in workfare. The state comptroller estimates that the New York state will need child care for 61,000 children by the year 2001, but only 27,500 slots are in the budget. There are currently 20,000 children on waiting lists for child care.

welfare recipients who are now working. The new federal law does provide more funds for child care, but according to the Congressional Budget Office, the amount is $1.4 billion short of what is needed (Clark and Long 1995: 1–2; Gormley 1995). Thus, working-poor mothers have to rely on cheap, low-quality, informal care. Many mothers do not pay cash for informal child care. Yet, as Katherine Newman has documented, they are expected to reciprocate through various kinds of services – child care, transportation, shopping, etc., all of which take time. There is also the problem of unreliability – which is also a significant problem in sharing transportation – especially when children are younger and the mother has to take shift work (White 1999). It is no surprise that most welfare recipients would prefer a formal child care arrangement if it were available, and if they could afford it (Newman 2000).

Along with child care, the problem of health care cannot be exaggerated. Poor health of either the parent or the children has an impact on the ability to work. Because of poorer health, low-income people tend to use more health care than higher-income people but they have greater difficulty getting health insurance and health care. AFDC/TANF recipients qualify for Medicaid, and under the new law – as well as several of the state reforms – Medicaid continues for a period but no more than a year. However, under the new law, welfare recipients no longer automatically qualify for Medicaid and food stamps and there has been a serious drop in enrollments (Greenberg and Laracy 2000: 10). Either welfare recipients may not be informed or applying at the Medicaid office may constitute an additional barrier. In the meantime, fewer low-wage employers are providing health insurance, especially for family members. The number of Americans without health insurance is now more than 40 million.

The decline in the use of benefits – primarily welfare and food stamps – usually leaves ex-recipients no better or even worse off than when on welfare but saves the government money. In a survey of 20 welfare-to-work programs, MDRC found that for most of the experimentals, there were higher earnings and lower welfare payments than for the controls, but the totals were very small – about $500 per year. On the other hand, since welfare payments and food stamps were reduced by about the same amount, these programs seemed to result in savings for the government (Michalopoulos and Schwartz 2000: 4, 7–8).[8]

---

[8] The analysis excluded the Earned Income Tax Credit as well as work-related expenses such as payroll and income taxes, child care costs, and transportation costs.

Evaluations of eleven state TANF programs show that employment is increased and welfare use is reduced, but net income is either largely unchanged or reduced. Increases in wages are off-set by declines in benefits. Few programs have generated substantial gains in incomes or declines in poverty (Blank and Schmidt 2000: 24).

Similar results seem to be true even for the programs that emphasize education and training. In a national evaluation of welfare-to-work strategies in eleven US locations where education and employment-based programs targeted employment and earning potentials, over the study's two-year follow-up period, 81 percent of the participants showed a marked increase in employment and earning rates that equaled or exceeded the results of work-first programs. Still, these programs are not able to lift the participants out of poverty. Even though most of the programs helped families rely on their own earnings rather than welfare checks, reductions in welfare, food stamps, and other benefits outweighed this positive finding. In other words, the family net incomes were roughly the same as before. The researchers find that the education-focused program does not produce added economic benefits relative to the job-search-focused program. Moreover, the job-search-focused approach is cheaper to operate, and moves welfare recipients into jobs more quickly than the education-focused approach (Hamilton 2001: 2). However, neither job-search-focused nor adult-education-focused programs have typically been successful in helping welfare recipients and other low-income parents work steadily and have access to higher-paying jobs (Strawn et al. 2001: 8; Brauner and Loprest 1999: 6).

More than one-third of the leavers are not working. Fourteen percent of this group rely on the earnings of a spouse or partner. Of the remaining 25 percent, more than a quarter say that they are disabled or sick or otherwise unable to work. Others report lack of access or lack of work supports, family responsibilities, transitions, etc. Of those not disabled, 69 percent say that they are looking for work. Only a small percentage receive unemployment benefits. Less than half are using food stamps and Medicaid. Almost three-quarters of all former recipients report receiving no private help in the first three months after leaving welfare. Former recipients report more economic struggles than low-income mothers – cutting down or skipping meals because of lack of money (33 percent), worried about lack of money for food (57 percent), ran out of food at the end of the month (about 50 percent), at times unable to pay rent, mortgage, or utility bills (39 percent), and having to move in with others because of lack of money (7 percent) (Loprest 1999). A rise in no-parent families was recently reported. Mostly, very poor inner-city mothers could no longer cope with the low-wage labor market and take care of the children. Rather than leave them with an abusive father or stepfather, the children were placed with a grandmother or other relative (Bernstein 2002: 1).

Many who have left welfare are not getting food stamps or Medicaid, even though they are eligible. Families who are no longer eligible or deterred from cash assistance may also think that they are no longer eligible for other programs or are not informed of these programs. The poorest 20 percent of families who left welfare lost an average of $577 a year primarily because wages did not make up for lost benefits. The next-to-the-poorest fifth of single parent families (incomes between 75 percent and 112 percent of the poverty line) had an average increase in earnings of $900 and an average EITC of $400 from 1995 to 1997, but these gains were off-set by the loss of means-tested benefits (the average loss was $1,460 per family). The decline in means-tested assistance was particularly severe for poor children. The reduction in means-tested programs is one of the reasons why poverty has not declined as fast as welfare caseloads. Only 40 percent of working poor families eligible for food stamps actually get them, and only one-third of the children eligible for Medicaid actually receive it (Greenberg and Laracy 2000).

It is not surprising that most recipients and leavers are in and out of the labor market. But why do they cycle back and forth with welfare? Because in most states, they do not qualify for Unemployment Insurance. Some do not satisfy the minimum hours and earnings requirements given the instability of many of their jobs. Many fail to satisfy the "nonmonetary" requirements (Gustafson and Levine 1998; Williams 1999). "Nonmonetary eligibility" conditions mean that the work separation was through no fault of the worker, excluding separations for misconduct or a voluntary quit, and the worker must seek and be willing to accept available work. In many states, "available work" means full-time work regardless of how many weekly hours the applicant worked in the last job. Most job separations are not because of job loss (which accounts for only about 25 to 40 percent of unemployment), and women, especially married women, are much more likely than men to have "voluntary" reasons for leaving a job – i.e., quitting a job because of child care and other family responsibilities and transportation difficulties (Gustafson and Levine 1998: 3).[9] In other words, for these women, welfare is the equivalent of unemployment compensation. In the past, when jobs disappeared or child care broke down, former recipients would return to welfare. Now, with the time-limits, this option will no longer be available.

What about the supply side of the labor market? How job-ready are welfare recipients? The rapid decline of the welfare rolls with record employment probably means that those still remaining on the rolls have the most serious barriers to employment. Nearly 50 percent of recipients have not completed high school, and "even in today's relatively robust economic climate, high school dropouts face an unemployment rate four times that of college graduates. [F]ewer than half of the recipients with the lowest skills are likely to be steadily employed by their late twenties" (Pavetti 1999). An analysis of the National Survey of America's Families ("NSAF") (Zedlewski and Loprest 2000: 7),[10] plus state surveys, showed that in 1997, three-quarters of the adults on welfare had at least one potential barrier to employment including very poor mental or physical health, limited education, minimal or no work experience, and family responsibilities such as caring for an infant or disabled child. All of these characteristics were found to significantly depress work activity. Various state studies confirm the pervasiveness of obstacles to work.[11] There is a relatively high incidence of physical and mental health problems among adult recipients, disabilities among

[9] In 1995, an individual working half-time for 26 weeks at $6 per hour met the eligibility requirements in forty-seven states (Gustafson and Levine 1998: 6).

[10] NSAF interviewed about 44,000 nonelderly families in 1997 and 1999. It oversampled the low-income population (under 200 percent of the poverty line), providing substantial samples of families on welfare or recently on welfare.

[11] Among recipients not working, about 20 percent (Florida, Tennessee, Utah) to over 30 percent (Idaho, Indiana, Minnesota, New Jersey, Texas, and Washington) reported limiting health problems. Eighty-five percent of the recipients not deferred in one Michigan county had at least one barrier, and two-thirds had two or more, and that study showed that the number of barriers was strongly and negatively associated with employment. A study in Alameda County concluded that the number with significant barriers may exceed the 20 percent exemption limit, and that many will need intensive or long-term support if they are to enter the paid labor market. Eighty percent of adults on TANF have at least one significant barrier to employment, and 40 percent have multiple barriers. Nevertheless, recipients have significantly increased their work effort since 1997 despite these barriers. Twenty percent of recipients with multiple barriers worked in paid employment in 1999, as compared to 5 percent in 1997, leaving 32 percent of the current recipients with multiple barriers and no

their children, alcohol and drug abuse, domestic violence, low education levels and cognitive abilities, and limited work experience. Not all of these problems prevent work, but most would require special services and supports if these recipients are to obtain and retain employment. SSI is available but only for the permanently disabled. Many of these recipients would not meet the strict SSI definition, but still may find it difficult to hold a job (Zedlewski and Loprest 2000: 4). A 1996 report of 15 major studies concluded that about 25 to 50 percent of the AFDC caseload would need special services if they were to work. Three out of ten recipients reported serious health-related conditions, and another third, modest health-related barriers. Many recipients had very low levels of education or basic skills. Despite the barriers, many on welfare did work, but work effort diminished with an increasing number of barriers. Continuous employment was not common among those with serious employment barriers (Zedlewski and Loprest 2000: 4).

The question is whether TANF provides states with sufficient flexibility and resources to serve the long-term needs of the most disadvantaged families. TANF allows states to exempt 20 percent of their current caseloads from the 60-month time-limit, and six states intend to provide their own funds indefinitely for these families. Some states have begun to target the needs of the most disadvantaged (Zedlewski and Loprest 2000: 4). To date, we know very little about what works for TANF families who face a diverse set of challenges that limit their ability to leave welfare successfully. About half of the states now require work activities for all recipients. Some states count a range of activities as satisfying this requirement, e.g., attending substance abuse or mental health counseling. Many states have temporary exemption for the disabled. Others, a wait-and-see approach. Often there is difficulty in identifying "hidden disabilities" – depression, learning disabilities, domestic violence – either because the recipients refuse to reveal them or because they are not easily identifiable. Repeated violations may be a clue; thus, there should be follow-up of sanctioned cases (Zedlewski and Loprest 2000: 17–18).

current work. Many in this group will need significant interventions to leave welfare successfully. And, there is about 17 percent of the leavers with no current work or disability income, nor a working spouse or partner. One-half of this group have multiple barriers. Thus, there is a high level of need among a significant share of families who are either currently or recently on welfare. And this is a conservative estimate (the authors allowed the presence of any work to serve as an indicator of some ability to move to independence).

The delivery of services for the disadvantaged is a difficult challenge for the states. They not only have to build their own organizational capacity but also develop the necessary linkages with other agencies that provide needed services, e.g., health care, substance abuse, domestic violence counselors, and so forth. Most programs serve only a limited number of disadvantaged recipients and there is little evaluation research. Most states just continue their "work first" strategies (Zedlewski and Loprest 2000: 18–22).

Once we fully recognize the life circumstances of welfare recipients, we understand why they have such a hard time competing even for the low-wage, entry-level jobs. They have low levels of education, major child care responsibilities, uneven or sparse work experience and are disproportionately of color. "Even if they do manage to find and keep jobs, the upper-bound estimate of their earnings should they work full-time-year round . . . is no more than $12,000–$14,000; given their family sizes, this level of earnings will not remove them from poverty. And this assumes full-time work. In fact, most recipients only find temporary jobs paying less than average wages. Indeed the typical former recipient earns about one-half of this 'outer limit' earnings level" (Burtless 1995: 71, 77).

ATTITUDES OF WELFARE RECIPIENTS

It is well known that most welfare recipients share the basic, majoritarian attitudes towards welfare. Although they recognize the necessity of welfare for themselves, they do not like being on welfare, they have negative attitudes towards those on welfare (e.g., lazy, dishonest, having babies to stay on welfare, etc.) (Rank 1994: 27–47; Seccombe, Delores, and Walters 1998: 849–865) but distinguish themselves – they are on welfare because of unfortunate circumstances and they will shortly get off welfare via paid employment and provide a better life for their children. How, though, do they view their own experiences with welfare reform?

In an in-depth, qualitative study of 80 TANF recipients in inner-city poverty areas in Cleveland and Philadelphia in 1997–98, Ellen Scott and her colleagues reported on the attitudes and aspirations of welfare recipients who were engaged in workfare (Scott, London, and Edin 2000: 727). All of the women in the study led "extremely disadvantaged lives." They had low levels of education, little involvement with the fathers, and were in and out of low-wage jobs – fast food, retail clerks, nursing assistants, custodial housekeeping, day care, and rarely, factory or clerical work. Many had additional barriers to work – mental and physical health, substance dependency, domestic violence, day care, and transportation.

In general, they had positive attitudes towards work. It would help them materially in terms of self-esteem and respect, and would help them be positive role models for their children even though they knew that they would have less time to manage the home and take care of their children. The women did not express anger or frustration about the workfare rules, including the mandates to go to work. Rather, they were optimistic about the future. However, their optimism was tempered by realism. The jobs they hoped to get were gendered, low-skilled, low-wage, and without benefits, or needed flexibility to take account of their families. Few jobs were expected to exceed the minimum wage, and some felt that it was inevitable that they would experience financial or other crises that, in the past, forced a return to welfare. "Not surprisingly, women's perspectives on their futures as working mothers were anchored in their own impoverished and disadvantaged life experiences and profoundly shaped by the structural constraints of class, gender, motherhood, and the labor market" (Scott et al. 2000). They knew that they were handicapped by their lack of education and skill. At the same time, they were aware that the new welfare rules would not permit education. Sometimes jobs or additional training were precluded by the cost of day care. "Although they dreamed of lives different from and better than the ones they lived on welfare, the jobs they aspired to and would likely be able to get were unlikely to provide them with the economic security and advancement that they want and expect" (Scott et al. 2000). Not surprisingly, many were worried about the uncertainty of the future and "fear about the welfare-to-work mandate." Similarly, another study reported optimism despite realism. Despite the high unemployment in this particular area (rural), some maintained that there were plenty of jobs "if women will get up and go look for them . . . If they say there isn't, they're just not looking, not checking their resources" (Monroe and Tiller 2001: 816–828).

How does one explain this apparent contradiction – a realistic and disappointing expectation of the workfare program, yet a generally positive, optimistic attitude? Joe Soss, in a series of in-depth interviews of AFDC applicants, addressed the "puzzle of subordination and satisfaction" (Soss 2000).[12] Observational studies suggest endemic degradation; but survey research shows that clients are, in fact, quite satisfied with their treatment. In surveys, clients usually describe workers as "courteous, considerate, prompt, efficient, helpful, and interested." According to Soss, AFDC applicants usually have quite negative attitudes about the application process; they report poor treatment and feel a lack of control. Clients complain about excessive waiting in uncomfortable settings. They feel "degraded, frustrated, and angry . . . that the agency does not highly value clients." The application process itself is viewed as intrusive, stigmatizing, and producing a sense of powerlessness. Pressed for time, the workers rapidly move through a range of topics without explanation; their job is to quickly sort the clients into "generic taxonomies," to impress upon the clients the realities of the bureaucratic relationship – the lack of time and resources to meet client needs, deference to worker decisions, the need for cooperation, and penalties for failure to comply. Most of the clients sense that they are categorized into welfare stereotypes. They feel that they are not allowed to explain their situation. At the same time, the standardized questions serve to buffer the workers from the harsh assessment of the agency. The clients blame the agency, rather than the workers. "Several women commented that the workers . . . seemed sympathetic or even apologetic as they asked for personal information" (Soss 2000: 106). Despite the negative feelings as to the application process, half the clients had positive attitudes towards the workers. One-third felt that they were able to explain their situation and did express gratitude towards the workers. Soss does not think that the positive attitudes represent false consciousness or self-deprecation; the clients clearly understood that they were being mistreated. Rather, the in-depth interviews reveal contradictions. Despite feeling degraded, they were relieved that their applications were accepted, and that things could have been a lot worse. "By making welfare claims, citizens can escape immediate and substantial threats to autonomy, such as domestic abuse, institutionalization, and homelessness. They can also enhance their abilities to fulfill social obligations and participate in social networks – to care for family members, assist neighbors, contribute to networks, and become involved in their

---

[12] The study is based on ethnographic field observations in welfare offices and in-depth interviews of twenty-five AFDC recipients and twenty-five social insurance disability recipients. The above discussion pertains to the AFDC recipients only.

communities . . . [T]he much maligned welfare system bolsters the security and engagement of citizens who would be far more vulnerable and marginal if it did not exist" (Soss 2000: 3).

The clients drew a distinction between the agency or the system and the worker. The workers were caught in a difficult work environment. The clients drew a distinction between the workers as individuals and the worker-client relationship. Blame was directed at the system rather than the workers. This allowed the clients to feel satisfied with the helpful and supportive demeanor of the workers. Thus, argues Soss, there are feelings of both satisfaction and subordination (Soss 2000: 123).

The attitudes described by Scott and her colleagues are consistent with Soss's interpretation. Dependent people in a variety of vulnerable settings invariably exhibit strong desires to remain in personal control (Maranville 2002). The respondents are those who have been selected by the agency workers. In contrast to those who have been denied welfare or sanctioned, these respondents have been told that they can succeed and given opportunities. However limited these opportunities may be, the clients want to shed the stigma of welfare – they are different from those "other" recipients – those who have been sanctioned or denied entry to the workfare program. "They" are going to remain dependent. Their optimism reinforces their sense of control – they are going to succeed – even though they are totally realistic about the low-wage labor market. After all, they have been there before.

DECLINE IN THE WELFARE ROLLS AND POVERTY

If employment is so uncertain, then what accounts for the decline in the welfare rolls and the poverty rates of female-headed households? Politicians – state as well as national – are, of course, claiming that welfare reform is "working" – despite the fact that rolls were declining significantly before many of the work requirements were enacted (De Parle 1997).

The poverty rate for female-headed households fell from 36.5 percent in 1996 to 30.4 percent in 1999, and child poverty has declined from over 20 percent to less than 17 percent. The proportion of children in severe poverty (incomes below half the federal poverty line) fell from 9 percent to less than 7 percent. The decline in poverty was due to large numbers of welfare leavers working. The proportion of income from earnings increased from 26 percent to 36 percent. Although work pays little (between $6.50 and $7.00 an hour), the poorest fifth of these women with children increased their average income from $7,920 in 1996 to $8,867 in 2000 (Corbett 2002: 3–10). While this is an improvement, it must be kept in mind that the federal poverty line is very low and seriously underestimates the cost of living for the poor (General Accounting Office 1997).

Most economists agree that the macroeconomy is responsible for a decline in the welfare rolls, but differ as to the relative importance of the economy versus welfare reform. Estimates as to the effect of welfare reforms, as compared to the economy, range from "trivial" to 30 to 40 percent (Figlio and Ziliak 1999: 4; Meyer and Rosenbaum 1999; Ellwood 1999).

A major difficulty involves what is meant by "welfare reform." When supporters of welfare reform cite the decline in the welfare rolls, the implication is that recipients are now working. As discussed, some are working, others are not. The question is how does welfare reform contribute to this change? There are a number of possibilities: the welfare-to-work programs (e.g., job preparation classes, job search, employer contacts, transportation and child care assistance, post-employment support); the time-limits; or the sanctions, or combinations of all three. The implication usually is that now welfare-to-work programs are serious. Sanctions emphasize the seriousness of the work programs. After all, just throwing people off welfare is not much of a reform.

Another complication arises from the use of discretion in administering these reforms. Not only the states, but the *individual* offices vary greatly in how they interpret and apply these rules. How does one take account of aggressive offices as compared to more lenient offices (Figlio and Ziliak 1999)?[13]

Then, there has been a significant increase in benefits to working families that provide strong incentives to work but are not considered part of "welfare reform." In the late 1980s, working families were eligible for about $5 billion (1997 dollars) in federal aid; by 1997, the total was above $50 billion. About half of this growth is with the Earned Income Tax Credit – a refundable tax credit of up to 40 percent of earnings for low-income families. By 1996, EITC expenditures alone exceeded state and federal AFDC expenditures (Ellwood 1999: 3; Figlio and Ziliak 1999; Meyer and Rosenbaum 1999). In fact, some scholars consider the Earned Income Tax Credit the single most important

---

[13] This has convinced some economists that they cannot look at data since 1996.

influence on the decline in welfare rolls (Meyer and Rosenbaum 1999). And low-income working families could have improved their financial situation even more if the government programs were more accessible. From 1993 to 1999, the poverty gap was reduced by US $16.9 billion, but the government aids (including social insurance and non-cash programs) were also reduced by US $13.8 billion within the same period (Haskins and Primus 2001: 6). Other factors could include the increase in the minimum wage in 1997, which could have off-set downward wage pressure from the entry of welfare recipients into the labor force. Some regions of the country experienced significant changes in population, which reduced the number of low-skilled workers in these areas. Finally, the recession of the early 1990s created a pool of unemployed low-skilled workers who were available to take new jobs when the economy began to recover (Stapleton et al. 2001).

The impact of sanctions
Welfare reform dramatically expanded the range of circumstances in which a family could have its welfare benefits reduced or canceled. Federal law requires at least a partial benefit reduction for families who do not satisfy work and child support enforcement requirements. States have the option to impose more stringent penalties and can expand the penalties to other parts of the program. In addition, TANF sanctions can affect food stamp benefits for the entire family and Medicaid coverage for sanctioned adults. Sanctions and time-limits have become a central characteristic of most state TANF programs (Kaplan 1999; Pavetti and Bloom 2001: 1).

Most states have chosen to implement strict sanctions. In thirty-seven states, the entire family loses its benefits if the adult violates work or other requirements – called the "full-family sanction." In fifteen of these states, the full-family sanction is imposed immediately; in the remaining twenty-two, the grant is initially reduced as a warning signal. In seven states, a lifetime ban may be imposed for continued or repeated violations. Only six states use the lesser sanction – eliminating the non-compliant adult only and continuing the grant for the children. In the remaining eight states, the amount of the sanction is increased but the whole family does not lose its entire grant, although assistance may take the form of vendor payments (Pavetti and Bloom 2001: 3).

As stated, federal law restricts using TANF money for assistance for ongoing basic needs for most families for more than sixty months. The clock starts with the enactment of the state's TANF program. States can set time-limits of less than sixty months, but may exempt up to 20 percent of the average monthly state caseload. States may use their own funds – called state maintenance of effort (MOE) funds – beyond the sixty-month limit. Other than child-only cases, which are exempt from the sixty-month limit, states can determine what categories of families are exempt. Again, there is great variation among the states. Twenty-six states have imposed a sixty-month time-limit, seventeen less than sixty months. Six of these have imposed a lifetime limit of less than sixty months; others have imposed fixed period time-limits – for example, a limit of twenty-four months of benefit receipt in any sixty-month period. And eight states have not imposed termination time-limits. Six of the eight states have "reduction" time-limits that eliminate benefits for adults but not the children. Two states have no time-limits at all. States can pursue these policies but have to use MOE funds for families who have exceeded the federal time-limit and the 20 percent cap on exemptions. Thus, states vary in terms of stringency. Twelve states have both stringent sanctions and time-limits; seven use a more moderate approach for both policies. In five states (California, Indiana, Maine, New York, and Rhode Island) which have the largest concentration of TANF cases (40.4 percent) both sanctions and time-limits are the most lenient. Finally, many states require "personal responsibility agreements" which contain additional requirements and sanctions (Pavetti and Bloom 2001: 3–5).

Families that are exempt from the work requirements are also exempt from the time-limits, though this is not true for eighteen states. Thus far, in these states, no one is exempt from the time-limits but this will have to be decided when the time-limit approaches. Deciding who is exempt can be a complicated process if there is disability in the family, especially, as will be discussed, with poor computer tracking systems. As noted, substantial numbers of welfare recipients have health and mental health problems but do not qualify for disability assistance. Exemptions can protect these families but also exclude them from needed services (Pavetti and Bloom 2001: 7).

Some of the states with no work exemptions allow activities such as substance abuse and mental health treatment to qualify as "work activities." However, most states are only beginning to develop services for those who have employment barriers in their work programs. Most caseworkers have neither the training, the skills, nor the time to handle these clients (Pavetti and Bloom 2001: 8).

Implementing sanctions

When the welfare rolls exploded in the 1960s, one of the charges was that the program was wracked with "waste, fraud, and abuse." Both the Federal Government and the states imposed strict quality control measures. The result was a change in the basic mission of the offices to a concentration on minimizing eligibility errors by requiring extensive documentation, including frequent reports of income and assets, birth records, Social Security numbers, and other eligibility data. When the 1996 welfare reform was enacted, some of its proponents recognized the changes that would have to be made in the offices to develop workfare plans, monitor progress, and impose sanctions. The "culture" of the offices had to be changed from being solely concerned with eligibility and compliance with rules to individual, service-oriented, intensive casework.

In a study of eleven local welfare offices, changes appeared to have been made or at least attempted. In Texas, cases managers are called Texas Works Advisers; in Michigan, Assistance Payment Workers are now Family Independence Specialists. Sometimes, jobs actually changed as well. Still, at the front line, the central tasks of eligibility determination and compliance with rules remained – getting the work done in a timely fashion, and eliminating fraud (Gais, Nathan, Lurie, and Kaplan 2001: 13–16). "The new emphasis on the 'work first' strategy did not change this 'quality control' culture; rather, it was added to it, further complicating the application process" (Gais et al 2001: 3). The result has been an enormous increase in the complexity of implementing welfare. Now, there have to be many separate contacts with clients over time to track families through the work processes. Often a variety of services are needed which involve separate, individual agencies, both public and private, complicated intake and processing systems, and, again, a tracking and information system. "When asked, many managers could give information on levels of eligibility, traditional cash benefits, number of cases, and some demographics. They had less information on work activities, support services (e.g., child care), reasons for exemptions, and barriers that clients were facing. Welfare information systems are weak, and managers are often unable to obtain data on individual recipients – where they are and how they are proceeding. In some states, there are no automatic clocks reporting how much time is left for individual clients. They could not tell clients how much time they had left" (Gais et al. 2001: 33–34). States have to decide who should be subject to the work requirements, who should be sanctioned, and the time-limits. This is a complicated process. The offices have to communicate the policies to the recipients, encourage them and make sure that the requirements of the program are met, and, if not, decide on the sanctions, and then, whether and how sanctioned families are to be supported (Diller 2000).

Under the previous law, states were required to take applications for all eligible applicants and act on the application within 30 days. Both requirements have been dropped. At least 31 states have implemented some form of diversion (Diller 2000). "A widespread practice is to require applicants to conduct job search while the application is pending. Requirements range from 2 to 6 weeks and from 2 to 40 employer contacts before benefits can start. The responsibility is on the individual rather than the program. In one Georgia County, applicants must search for a job for five weeks, contacting at least four employers per day. Every morning they are required to report their previous day's progress to the welfare office. If necessary, they will be referred to a Department of Labor satellite office (located across the street from the welfare office) for more job leads" (Gais et al. 2001: 7). "In a study of 30 local welfare offices, applicants had to first attend a general orientation program, a job search or registration for a job search, child support enforcement procedures where the applicants are required to cooperate in establishing paternity and securing child support, development of a personal responsibility plan, sometimes including alternatives to welfare, and, less commonly, an offer of diversion assistance, which can include a one-time cash assistance or loans, services, referrals to private charities, or entitlements to other benefits (e.g., Medicaid, food stamps). Few states conduct employability assessments; rather, they typically require applicants to seek jobs immediately unless categorically exempt. In other words, the market rather than the agency determines which cases are problematic" (Gais et al. 2001: 8). Another form of diversion is to offer a lump-sum grant of cash assistance rather than accept an application. In thirteen states, the minimum period of ineligibility is three months (Blank and Schmidt 2000: 13).

Diversion may be one reason for the decline in food stamps, Medicaid, and subsidized child care. When the focus is on keeping the front door closed and sending the applicants into the job market, the families may not receive the necessary information about what is available to the working poor. In the New York City Job Centers (formerly welfare offices), food stamp applications would not be accepted on the same day. Instead, "applicants had to complete a 'job profile,' wait for interviews for up to 6 hours, and be available for five separate appointments. These appointments consisted of a meeting with a financial planner, an employment planner, an intake worker, and an anti-fraud investigator (two meetings). In addition, caseworkers would visit the home of applicants. The acceptance rate fell from 75 percent to 25 percent" (Diller 2000). Many states contract out their "work first" administration to public or private employment agencies which may further limit the amount of information about other benefits (Gais et al. 2001: 10). When recipients become employed, they often do not bother to inform the eligibility worker that they are now off welfare and thus lose the opportunity for whatever post-employment benefits and services may be available (Gais et al. 2001: 9). In any event, in most states, post-welfare service systems are fragmented (Gais et al. 2001: 36). In response to the many complaints about the complexity of eligibility and verification rules of food stamps and Medicaid, some states have simplified the application processes, extended office hours, and use outreach workers (Golonka 2001: 4).

Sanctions and time-limits have to be communicated. With sanctions, the main message is that recipients have to participate in work in order to continue receiving benefits. Time-limits prove to be more difficult to communicate. Clients are often told about the time-limits when first applying or shortly thereafter because the officers use time-limits to motivate the clients. Clients may be told to hold off or "bank" their time or, if they continue on welfare, then to combine it with work to gain earned income disregards, which have been expanded in about forty states. Because information about sanctions and time-limits are combined with other information regarding benefits, reporting requirements, work requirements and opportunities, and so forth, it is often difficult to communicate all the relevant information. Recipients are focused on the immediate, short-term, pressing problems rather than issues that will arise in the distant future (Pavetti and Bloom 2001: 8–9).

In a recent study where local offices repeatedly explained sanctions, recipients did not understand them (Pavetti and Bloom 2001: 9). In another study, large numbers of recipients were not aware that they had been sanctioned (Hasenfeld, Ghose, and Hillesland-Larson 2001). Clients understood that they would lose benefits, but they did not know what was expected of them or what benefits they would lose and for how long. Other studies have found similar evidence of confusion (Pavetti and Bloom 2001: 9).[14] Many families who were sanctioned never appeared in the office, making it difficult to know whether they failed to comply because they were unwilling to do so or because they did not know what was expected of them or because they were experiencing personal or family problems. Some states have adopted strict procedures to review sanctions before they are imposed. Virtually all states have some form of grievance procedure where clients can appeal (Pavetti and Bloom 2001: 10–11).[15] In the past, the right of appeal in welfare cases was largely ineffectual (Handler 1986). Under the present regime, there is more confusion, more complications, and lack of awareness. Legal rights in welfare are another example of myth and ceremony.

As families begin to reach the time-limits, decisions will have to be made as to which families are exempt and who gets terminated. In states where time-limits have been reached, recipients who are employed have usually been terminated. There is more concern and variation for unemployed families. Since they have not already received a full family sanction, they probably have been looking for jobs without success. Connecticut, which has a shorter time-limit, grants a six-month extension for nearly all recipients who reach the time-limit with income below the welfare payment standard. In contrast, Massachusetts and Virginia grant relatively few extensions. Pavetti and Bloom report that some states have programs for alternative assistance for families who have been sanctioned or run out of time (Pavetti and Bloom 2001: 12–13).[16]

Thus, sanctions are playing an increasingly important role (Diller 2000; Haskins and Blank 2001: 24; Pavetti and Bloom 2001: 46–47).

---

[14] Lawrence Mead found that work programs that sanctioned many cases tended to perform poorly in terms of job placements and other performance measures. Offices that performed well made work expectations clear in more effective and informal ways. They threatened sanctions but rarely needed to impose them.

[15] Utah requires a "case staffing" to develop a plan to avoid the sanction. In Tennessee, a required review prior to termination reduced the number of cases sanctioned incorrectly by over 30 percent.

[16] In Cuyahoga County's (Ohio) Safety Net program, community agencies attempt to re-engage sanctioned families into work activities. "During the first 10 months of operation, 46 percent of sanctioned families were contacted, assessed, provided information, and almost all were able to participate in work activities and have their cases re-opened." Connecticut's Safety Net, a highly developed program, assists families whose time has expired in finding jobs and meeting basic needs – in some cases, using vouchers.

The number of families sanctioned is much larger than the number that has reached the time-limits. A recent General Accounting Office study (1998), found that an average of 135,800 families each month (4.5 percent of the national TANF caseload) received a full or partial sanction. Partial sanctions were most common, but still, an average of 16,000 families were cut completely. A US Department of Health and Human Services study (1999) reported an average of 15,000 monthly case closures due to sanctions. One study estimated that 540,000 families lost benefits due to full-family sanctions from 1997 to 1999, and that 370,000 remained off assistance at the end of 1999 (Hasenfeld et al. 2001: 11). Seven states reported that sanctions accounted for one-fifth or more of their case closures in 1999. Cohort studies have shown that sanction rates are quite high: one-quarter to one-half of families subject to work requirements are sanctioned over a twelve to twenty-four-month period. When New York City adopted a new, more stringent workfare program, over 400,000 people were dropped from the rolls. Last year, 69 percent of recipients in the work program were sanctioned and removed from the rolls for at least several months (Brito 2000). Other studies report similar results (Fein and Lee 2003).[17] Even though a great percentage of recipients in fact comply with welfare regulations, many are sanctioned because of bureaucratic errors. If the computer fails to record a required appointment, then the recipient is automatically sanctioned (Diller 2000). In contrast, the number of families that have reached time-limits is still relatively small – perhaps 60,000 nationwide; most are in three states: Connecticut, Massachusetts, and Louisiana (Pavetti and Bloom 2001: 19–21). Diversion, too, plays a significant role. A RAND report says, "Recent empirical work indicates that as much as one-half of the recent decline in the caseloads is attributable to declining rates of entry" (Grogger et al. 2002: xxv).

Who gets sanctioned? A number of states studies have shown that sanctioned recipients have several employment barriers – cognitive, health-related, and aspects of home life (e.g., lack of transportation, three or more children, child care problems, domestic violence) (Hasenfeld et al. 2001: 11–14; Pavetti and Bloom 2001: 21). Sanctioned families are disproportionately hard-to-employ. In Tennessee, 60 percent lacked a high school diploma or a GED compared to 40 percent who left welfare for work; 34 percent of the sanctioned families did not understand what they were required to do. In South

---

[17] Fein and Lee discuss reports from Montana, Kentucky, Minnesota, Utah, Michigan.

Carolina, 36 percent of high school dropouts were sanctioned as compared to 22 percent of high school graduates. Long-term recipients were overrepresented: in South Carolina, 38 percent of long-term recipients as compared to 21 percent of short-term recipients. Studies in Arizona and Minnesota report more than half of the families receiving full sanctions had an adult with less than a high school education. In Maryland, 41 percent of sanctioned families had no employment history, compared to 31 percent who left welfare for other reasons. According to a GAO report, sanctioned families had less education, more limited work experience, and longer welfare receipt. Many sanctioned families experienced personal or family challenges at a higher rate than other recipients, such as chemical dependency, physical and mental health problems, and domestic violence. These studies have been replicated in Utah, Connecticut, Minnesota, and Iowa. High incidents of chemical dependency among sanctioned families were found in Minnesota and Connecticut (Hasenfeld et al. 2001: 13). In general, state studies show that sanctioned leavers have lower employment rates than the average for all TANF leavers. In two states, there was about a 20 percent difference in employment rates. The federal five-year time-limit was reached on October 1, 2001. However, 60,000 families have reached the time-limits in seven states with shorter periods. Even though most observers thought that states would somehow extend benefits, most, in fact, have not and benefits have been terminated. Many of those who were terminated were working, but many were not (Haskins and Blank 2001: 25). The previously cited MDRC report on the health status of recipients and ex-recipients indicates – as might be expected – that those still on the rolls have multiple barriers. Yet, most were not exempt, and nearly one-third reported being sanctioned in the previous year. These were women who reported being highly depressed, having been physically abused, or having a child with a serious health problem (Polit, London, and Martinez 2000).[18]

An Office of Inspector General report (1999) stated that clients are seldom aware of "good cause" exemptions and often think that the sanctions for non-participation are more severe than they in fact are. Most sanctions are imposed because of missed appointments and deadlines. One state study found that sanctioned recipients with low educational

---

[18] Study of Cleveland, Los Angeles, Miami, and Philadelphia. In-home survey interviews with 3,771 women and in-depth ethnographic interviews with 162 women, during 1998–99.

levels were less likely to appeal the sanction and thus more likely to be dropped from the rolls (Zedlewski and Loprest 2000: 14–15). "Thus, they believe that they have been appropriately sanctioned when this may not be true which would, in turn, lead to a failure to seek redress. These results indicate the difficulty that welfare offices have in adequately communicating welfare requirements and sanctions to clients. Often this information is given along with other important information, thus diminishing its importance. It is the combination of cognitive barriers and poor communication that is a major predictor of sanctions" (Hasenfeld et al. 2001: 11–12).

Some states are just beginning to track what happens to sanctioned families. Most are coping, but the question is at what level. In the most thorough study of sanctions to date, Delaware's "A Better Chance" ("ABC") program, within eighteen months, 60 percent of the recipients had been sanctioned, and of these, 45 percent had their cases closed. Those who were sanctioned had more children, lacked transportation or access to public transportation, and lacked an understanding of the requirements. Local offices varied substantially. The average payment loss was a 60 percent reduction in the grant. These clients were less equipped to off-set the lost income through earnings due to less work experience, longer welfare dependence, and lower levels of education. Less than one-third (32 percent) eventually cured their sanctions; 45 percent remained non-compliant until their cases were closed, and 23 percent left the rolls before the sanctions progressed to class closure.

Do sanctions make a difference?

The evidence is contradictory as to whether sanctions are effective in encouraging compliance. Many agency staff firmly believe that sanctions "work" – they communicate the seriousness of the requirements. Some studies show that neither the threat of sanctions nor the imposition of sanctions change behavior. Several studies show that while stiff sanctions increase compliance, they also increase exit from welfare. Other studies show that severe sanctions are no more or less effective than moderate sanctions (Kaplan 1999: 7). Some believe that the "anticipatory" impacts of time-limits are quite large, but much of the evidence is anecdotal. One study estimates that time-limits may account for 16 to 18 percent of the recent caseload decline even though few people have actually reached a time-limit (Grogger et al. 2002). Other studies show no effects. At most, impacts are modest (Pavetti and Bloom 2001: 16). Summarizing the tracking reports of nine states, the

Children's Defense Fund says that employed families who were sancti-oned tended to work less and earn less than those who left welfare on their own (CDF 1998). According to caseworkers, recipients wait until the sanction is imposed before they take it seriously. However, it seems that most do not comply with the requirements even after a sanction is imposed. Pavetti and Bloom find that full family sanctions do not necessarily produce lower caseloads or increased employment. Other studies show that more stringent sanctions are associated with increased employment and caseload reduction. Indiana's experience suggests that full family sanctions may not be necessary to promote high levels of em-ployment. Taken as a whole, the studies suggest that sanctions are in-fluencing the behavior of many TANF recipients but not many others, even with the loss of all assistance (Pavetti and Bloom 2001: 15–16).[19]

THE FUTURE

Predictions as to the likely effects of major social legislation are always uncertain. Much depends on the state of the economy and the political climate. I will first discuss the likely effects if the law is carried out as presently written. Then, I will offer some predictions.

In light of the previous discussion about the state of the low-wage la-bor market, a significant number of welfare recipients will not be able to permanently leave welfare via work. However, how many will actually be cut off – whether under the two-year or the five-year time-limits – depends, in part, on the size of the rolls. For a long time, AFDC rolls were growing. And in the 1990s, for the first time in US history, wel-fare rolls have been declining. Whether rolls continue to decline, sta-bilize, or increase depends on two factors – the severity of employment deficits of those who remain on the rolls and the economy. Before the current economic slowdown, the decline in the rolls had been slowing, which is not surprising since those who are left face more employment barriers (Healy 2000: A12). Now, with unemployment rising, welfare rolls are rising in several states (Bernstein 2001: A1). How long the current slowdown will continue is anyone's guess.

Shortly, almost all of the time-limits will take effect. In California, if there is no net growth in the California TANF rolls, then of the

[19] Rector and Yousef find that states with an immediate full-family sanction had an average caseload decline of 41.8 percent (between January 1997 and June 1998) which was 24 percent higher than states which only deducted the adult's portion of the grant.

1.6 million children, approximately 36 percent will be long-term recipients.[20] If welfare growth resumes, in 2005, welfare will be terminated for 994,000 children. There are additional rules that can result in welfare terminations – paternity establishment requirements, additional children born to current welfare recipients. Children born to unmarried mothers will be denied benefits until the mother turns eighteen. The combined effects of the welfare cut-offs will affect 1,158,000 children.

What will happen to these children? Since the majority of welfare recipients are short-term and leave when they obtain work, we can assume that most of the long-termers will have the most difficulty in finding and keeping a job. Day care will be a significant problem.[21] Whether working or not, poverty will increase for this group, and poverty is the single most important predictor of poor outcomes for children.

One of the most serious problems is the potential impact of the cut-offs on the foster care system. The existing state foster care system is in crisis. So far, there has not been a significant increase in foster care as a result of the welfare reform, as the more stringent cut-offs have not really started (Sengupta 2000: A1). However, if only a fraction of the children subject to the welfare cuts enter the foster care system, the costs will skyrocket (Wolch, Sommer, Handler, and Stoner 1997).[22] And the consequences for children in foster care are not good. Foster care children have higher rates of both acute and chronic medical and mental health problems, higher rates of growth problems, and three times the national average for asthma. Infants and toddlers are more likely to manifest developmental problems such as motor, language, cognitive, and self-help concerns. The welfare reforms will certainly increase the poverty and hardship for hundreds of thousands, if not millions, of children. These children are already at high risk of failing to become successful, productive adults. The odds will now be increased (Wolch 1998: 8).[23]

---

[20] Data prepared by the Western Center on Law and Poverty, 1996 (on file with author).

[21] California already has a waiting list of 225,000 poor children for subsidized day care. Low-income working mothers have waited as long as two years to receive a subsidy for a toddler, and as long as one year for an infant.

[22] Assuming no change in TANF rolls, if half of the children who lose TANF benefits need foster care, the cost to the state would be $80 million additional funds per month. If only 10 percent need foster care, the cost would be $16 million per month. If 5 percent of these children are older and have to go to group homes, the cost would be $81 million in additional funds per month.

[23] Wolch predicts an increase of more than 15,000 additional children placed in foster care in Los Angeles.

As discussed, states can exempt up to 20 percent of their caseload from the work requirements, but it is not clear how many welfare recipients who face the "usual" employment barriers will be exempt. It is also problematic in the current welfare administrative climate that much help can be given to those who need services. Good programs, with well-trained workers, have very small caseloads. In public welfare departments, workers are only high-school graduates and have very high caseloads.

If the past is any guide, one would not predict dramatic changes in welfare. Throughout history, welfare policy has always been largely symbolic. Myths and stereotypes gain prominence; drastic reforms are enacted; but policy at the field level is usually decoupled from administration. There are many reasons, but usually the policies as enacted are too draconian and, more importantly, significantly more costly. More often than not, it is the states and local governments that bear the increased costs. Serious welfare-to-work programs – including community-service jobs – are more expensive than welfare, as are other alternatives such as shelter- and foster care.

Under the current law, the states have plenty of room to fudge. Welfare rolls have declined significantly, which reduces the number of recipients that states have to place in work programs. In addition, the states can decide what constitutes work or "best effort," and can excuse up to 20 percent of the caseload. So far the states have met their quotas, but even if they do not, serious federal penalties are not likely. Federal Government sanctions against states for not meeting quality control requirements are rarely, if ever, imposed. States always excuse their failures and their congressional delegations lobby against federal penalties.

Similar considerations may well apply within states. Counties and municipalities will resist state-imposed welfare costs. The usual practice in the face of these conflicting pressures is myth and ceremony. Some recipients will find jobs and leave welfare (whether as a result of the programs is another matter). Others will be sanctioned and everyone will proclaim success – as long as welfare does not remain a salient political "crisis." In many states, compromises are evident. On the other hand, as discussed, state sanctions are fairly severe and are having an impact.

The present situation, however, looks very different from past welfare reforms. Four kinds of changes have been occurring. One is a continuation of the recent past – the gradual erosion of benefits. Adjusting for inflation, the average welfare grant per recipient in 1970 was $676 per month; in 1996, it was $374 – a 45 percent reduction (House Committee on Ways and Means 1998: 402). It seems highly unlikely that welfare benefits will increase, at least in the near future.

The second change is the dramatic decline in the caseloads. The reduced welfare rolls and the seemingly high proportion of leavers who appear to be employed can cut two ways. In the past, those who remained dependent were further stigmatized. On the other hand, there is some evidence that now that "welfare has ended as we know it," there are increasing calls that more attention be paid to the plight of the working poor and, in fact, as noted, there have been substantial increases in aid to the working poor, primarily the Earned Income Tax Credit.

The third change has been the vast increase in *privatization*. Thus far, most of the privatization has occurred with specific parts of welfare – for example, the work programs, day care, child support collections, and Medicare. Over 30 states have entered into contracts for various services. Maximus, Inc., probably the most successful welfare contractor to date, runs welfare-to-work programs in nearly a dozen states and child care and Medicare for dozens of local governments (Hartung and Washburn 1998). The states, and, increasingly, private contractors are increasingly reluctant to either collect or disclose the information. As discussed, caseworkers have a great deal of discretion as to how to administer the work requirements. Applicants can easily be deflected without any record, which, as noted, seems to be going on (Swarns 1998: A1). With the increase in privatization of welfare, it will become even more difficult to gain access to what is happening. Private contractors have strong incentives to "cream" and to fudge the data. In discussing Lockheed's performance managing the child-support operations in San Francisco, the head of the system said, "We'd get slime data, which was incomplete or garbled. The system can't locate people. It can't produce forms" (Hartung and Washburn 1998). States can always reduce rolls on the basis of fraud.[24] Under previous law, if a state sanctioned a family, the state would lose the federal cost-sharing contribution. Now, the states make money when clients are dropped from the rolls under the block grant formula.

[24] As we have seen, most families supplement their income by off-the-books earnings and/or gifts from relatives and friends (including some child support). This vital, but extra, income is not reported; hence, all these families are vulnerable to sanctions for fraud.

This low-visibility sanctioning can become increasingly serious as states continue to privatize their welfare systems. Then, state governments and their contractors will be under even more pressure to show a positive cost-benefit ratio. This kind of welfare reform is particularly insidious because increasingly the victims have no redress. Although technically available, Legal Services was never able to handle the need, and now it is badly crippled.

The fourth change has been the economic slowdown. The welfare reform occurred during the booming 1990s. This allowed the welfare debate in the United States to be seriously distorted. The problem is poverty, not welfare, but very few people want to discuss poverty (Edelman 1988).[25] The debate over welfare reform equates the *absence* of welfare with *self-sufficiency*. Until recently, except for some occasional protests, no one seems to care that even when recipients leave welfare via employment, most remain poor; most are worse off than when they were on welfare. Now, there are large federal and state deficits. Unlike the Federal Government, the state governments cannot run deficits, and already cuts are being made in programs to help the poor – welfare, health care, child care, housing, and so forth. This will greatly limit the ability of the governments at all levels to cope with the rising rolls, the declining ability of welfare recipients to find employment, and to relieve the growing poverty of families who have been cut off from welfare. Welfare rolls are starting to rise in some of the states, and there are reported increases in family homelessness and the use of food pantries.

For a moment, the country was in a unique position. There was a projected federal budget surplus; in addition, the states had lots of money that was supposed to be earmarked for both welfare recipients and the poor (Greenberg 1999: 2; Greenberg and Savner 1999).[26] In general, most states did not do much. Some states banked the money and other states used the money to substitute for other state programs. A handful

---

[25] In Murray Edelman's terms, this would be the social (de)construction of "problems."

[26] Mark Greenberg pointed out that one of the overlooked features of TANF is that it created two very significant funding streams for the states: there is the state's TANF block grant and the state's maintenance of effort obligations (MOE). As discussed, when TANF was enacted, the block grants to the states were based on the higher levels of federal spending for AFDC. State MOE levels were set at 75 percent or 80 percent of state spending for AFDC and a set of related programs. Although it is hard to come up with precise numbers, Greenberg estimates that the combination of state TANF funds and MOE obligations total at least $27 billion.

of states made some, yet very modest improvements – such as small increases in benefits in the very poorest states.[27] A small group of states did spend considerable funds on helping welfare recipients. Consequently, about a quarter of the federal money – about $7 billion – remained unspent which could have amounted up to $22 billion when the law expired in 2002 (DeParle 1999; Greenberg 1999).

TANF regulations greatly expanded state flexibility. States can now provide benefits and services to low-income working families even if those families never received welfare and even if those families have incomes above the welfare eligibility level as long as the state is furthering the purposes of TANF. States can help working TANF families without having the assistance count for TANF time-limits as long as the state uses "segregated" state funds (Greenberg 1999: 8).[28] Some states have used their funds to help welfare recipients and other less-skilled women to obtain work, to provide child care, with education training, earnings disregard, and other problems (Haskins and Blank 2001: 17–19). States can provide refundable income tax credits, wage subsidies, work expense allowances, or other forms of direct help, post-employment education and training, supportive social services, incentives to employers to provide on-the-job training, asset formation (e.g., Individual Development Accounts), help a family buy a car or move (Greenberg 1999: 6).

Now that welfare "has ended as we know it," and former welfare recipients are in the paid labor market (so we all want to believe), attention turned toward helping low-wage working families, those who "play by the rules." The media changed. Whereas formerly the stories were about seriously dependent families – more often than not inner-city and of color – now they highlight the struggles that poor families (including leavers) have in surviving in the low-wage labor market (Greenberg and Laracy 2000: 12). And the country is usually a bit more generous – or less harsh – when times are good. Since 1994, the amount of money available to the working poor has increased from $6 billion to over $50 billion in 1999. Most of this is the EITC (now around $30 billion) and Medicaid. Now Medicaid requires the states to

---

[27] E.g., Texas raised the monthly grant for a family of three from $188 to $201, which still leaves Texas fourth from the bottom.

[28] An example would be a wage supplement which would fall within "assistance" and count against the federal time-limit unless the state uses segregated state funds.

provide coverage for all poor children (although the state responses are very mixed). The Federal Government also introduced a universal $500 child tax credit and a tax credit for child care costs (The Economist 2000: 28).

Congress is in the process of reconsidering TANF which was due to expire by March 2004 but has been temporarily re-authorized. No doubt the block grants to the states will continue, as well as many other TANF provisions. Some observers hoped that TANF would be improved along with a range of other programs that affect working families. Food Stamps and the Child Care Development Fund were re-authorized in 2002. Participation in both programs is low. Restrictions on legal immigrants remain very controversial. The House Democrats have introduced their proposals. They do not intend to tamper with the basic block grant structure, weaken the emphasis on work, or try to restore welfare as an entitlement. On the other hand, they propose an additional $20 billion over the next five years (or more than 15 percent) to reduce poverty. The block grants to the states would be increased to keep up with inflation. Bonuses would be paid to states that reduced child poverty. They would keep the five-year time-limits but would liberalize them by not counting the months when people were working and receiving welfare. The federal work requirements would be satisfied by training and education for up to two years rather than the present one year. Welfare benefits would be restored to legal immigrants who have not become citizens. House Democrats are also proposing a significant increase – almost 50 percent – in child care subsidies to the working poor whether or not they have been on welfare. Several Republicans have voiced opposition to these proposals and, given the size of the federal deficit, it is doubtful that additional money will be appropriated (Pear 2002: A24). The Administration is proposing, among other things, increasing the work requirements, even though there are fewer jobs and unemployment has risen, as well as the welfare rolls in some of the states.

RECOMMENDATIONS TO MAKE WELFARE REFORM REALLY WORK

There are many ways to improve the lot of welfare recipients, the working poor, and those who have fallen through the safety net. I can only briefly mention the direction that reforms should take.

Making work pay

Since the great majority of welfare recipients are presently working, have recently worked, are trying to work, and will eventually leave welfare via work, the most obvious reforms involve improving the low-wage labor market so that more jobs are available, and earnings and benefits are increased and there is less need for welfare. In other words, make present jobs better. Nationally, this means job creation where unemployment is still high or when unemployment begins to rise and jobs become less available (Alstott 1999; Harvey 1999: 497–504), continuing to support the EITC (Primus et al. 1999), modest raises in the minimum wage (Lazere 1998), providing health and child care benefits, and reforming unemployment insurance and disability. As will be discussed shortly, Americans must come to recognize that providing adequate health care and child care for the working poor is not only essential, but a major budget commitment.

If jobs are not available, no amount of welfare reform, education, and training, or simply denying benefits, will lead to employment. It is difficult to determine the precise extent of job availability since systematic data are not kept on job vacancies. Similarly, the data on job seekers are uncertain because of the difficulties of defining what constitutes participation in the laborforce. For example, persons who are working very few hours but would like to work more are counted as employed. Persons who have not looked for work in the past four weeks are not counted as unemployed. As a result, we lack good estimates of involuntary unemployment – that is, unemployment due to lack of jobs. The few studies that do exist suggest that many of the unemployed do not find jobs because they do not exist (Abraham 1983: 709–710; Newman and Chauncy 1995: 66–67; Harvey 1994; Carlson and Theodore 1995). It is estimated that for every 1 percent increase in state unemployment rates there is a 9 percent decline in the probability that welfare mothers will have earned income (Handler and Hasenfeld 1997: 99). Conversely, we find that when there is a labor shortage, the employment opportunities for the most disadvantaged improve markedly. Richard Freeman found that in a tight labor market (an unemployment rate under 4 percent) the employment opportunities and the hourly wages for disadvantaged young men improved considerably (Freeman 1991: 103–121; Osterman 1991: 475–491). If the poor and disadvantaged are to "play by the rules," then jobs have to be there, even if this means job creation. The right to a job has to be a real opportunity (Harvey 1989).

The EITC is the largest cash transfer program for low-income parents in the United States. A growing number of studies of the EITC have produced convincing evidence regarding its positive effects. During 1998, EITC was responsible for lifting more families out of poverty than all other means-tested programs combined. It has encouraged work among single mothers (Meyer and Rosenbaum 1999).[29] Recipients use the money they receive from the EITC for investments in education and savings as well as to help them pay for daily living expenses (Philips 2001: B27). The combined effect of the increase in the minimum wage and the EITC over the past decade has had a significant effect on income. The minimum wage with the EITC, with full-time work, puts a worker above the official US poverty line (Blank and Schmidt 2000: 17). In 2001, ten states and the District of Columbia provided their low-income working families with refundable tax credits that build on the federal EITC (Seiden 2001: 12). There should be a reduction of payroll taxes and refundable child tax credits. The marginal tax rates should be reduced as federal and state taxes are phased in and Medicaid and EITC are phased out (The Economist 2000: 29; Shaviro 1999).

Knowledge of the EITC is essential if all eligible, low-income parents are to receive the credit. According to the Urban Institute, nationally, nearly two-thirds of eligible parents know about the EITC. Very poor parents, those with incomes below 50 percent of the federal poverty level, are significantly less likely than higher-income parents to know about the EITC. Low-income Hispanic parents are much less likely to know about or receive the EITC than low-income non-Hispanic parents of any race, indicating that there might be a language barrier (Philips 2001). There are other problems with the EITC. The forms are overly complex. Of the approximately 19 million earners who received the EITC, almost 70 percent hired commercial tax preparers. In addition to paying the auditing fees, almost 5 million take loans to speed payments (the firms arrange electronic filing) at very high interest rates. In 1999, nearly half of the $30 billion in EITC was paid through these high-priced loans generating an estimated $1.75 billion in EITC refunds in fees for these services (Berube, Kim, Forman, and Burns 2002). Government audit rates are much higher than for the average taxpayer, largely because of errors in the returns and disputes over who is entitled to claim the children as dependents (Johnston

[29] Meyer and Rosenbaum, for example, believe that EITC expansions caused about 60 percent of the employment increase by single mothers between 1984 and 1996.

2002: C1). Thus, the forms have to be simplified and there needs to be more outreach programs (Seiden 2001: 10).[30] For many welfare recipients, financial work incentives have had impressive results. They have increased employment, earnings, and income, and have encouraged steady employment (Michalopoulos and Berlin 2001; Berlin 2000; Bos et al. 1999).

The time-limits clock should stop for working recipients. Policies that combine time-limits and earnings disregard send a mixed message: time-limits encourage recipients to leave the rolls and bank their lifetime-limited number of months; incentives encourage them to stay on the rolls and combine welfare and work. Implementing the two policies virtually guarantees that a substantial number of people will unwittingly exhaust their months of welfare eligibility.

The Unemployment Insurance system has to be reformed to take account of the changes in the labor market. This would include recalibrating the earnings requirements and the base period and a redefinition of the "involuntary" quit requirement to take account of family responsibilities, child care, and transportation needs.[31]

The Food Stamp program has to become more accessible – the forms have to be simplified, and the offices have to remain open so that working people can apply (Haskins and Blank 2001: 20–21).

Child care

There are two major issues with child care. The first involves the employability of the mother. Adequate, reliable child care is essential to enable poor parents to support their families with work outside the home. Formal day care center slots are not only in short supply and expensive, but many are not available outside of regular working hours. Almost half of the working poor, especially those in unskilled service work, are on changing, irregular, or unpredictable shifts. More than a quarter work weekends. "Yet only 10 percent of centers and 6 percent of family day care homes provide weekend care. These circumstances . . . may make it necessary for parents to patch together child care using multiple providers, sometimes of lower quality than they would prefer" (Wolfe and Vandell 2002: 106–110). As will be discussed

---

[30] One such program is the Los Angeles Campaign which created a webpage that lists IRS-sponsored sites in the Los Angeles area where low-income workers can receive free tax preparation and find EITC information in both English and Spanish.

[31] For an opposite view, see Lester 2001.

below, most low-income working mothers rely on unlicensed, informal care, usually relatives, which sometimes works, and sometimes doesn't. In Minnesota, a study found that lack of child care caused 14 percent of parents awaiting child care subsidies to leave their jobs and rely on public assistance. Conversely, the US General Accounting Office found that offering a child care subsidy to poor mothers increased the likelihood that the mothers would work by 15 percent. An Illinois study found that 20 percent of parents who left public assistance for work returned to assistance because of child care problems. Poor parents cannot work without reliable child care (Gong et al. 1999; Wolfe and Vandell 2002; White 1999).

A second reason is the impact on the infants and children. The problem here is the risk factors of mediocre or inadequate child care. A substantial portion of the working poor – perhaps as many as half – rely on family members (called "informal" care) (Wolfe and Vandell 2002: 110). Informal care-giving can be of high quality if the caregiver is a close relative or friend or has some other kind of close attachment with the child. However, if this attachment is not present, then there is a strong risk of poor quality care. Those who seek this form of low-wage work are more likely to be unable to compete in the higher wage labor market. These workers face the same kinds of stresses that other low-wage, poverty workers face – inadequate housing, health problems, depression, substance abuse, domestic violence (White 1999: 125). In addition to quality, there are often issues of reliability. As Katherine Edin has pointed out, informal child care is not "free." The mothers are expected to reciprocate, which means further demands on the low-wage worker, already struggling to make ends meet. But even with formal child care, either regulated home care or in licensed day care centers, there is a serious problem of poor quality. Ratios of children to caregivers is higher than recommended by health care professionals. In regulated home care, one-third of the providers had no schooling beyond high school, and only about two-thirds received any in-service training. And there has been a decline in the education and training of caregivers in centers for infants and toddlers, most probably because of the low wages.

The issue here is the impact of low-quality care on the development of these children. In most states, mothers are required to work when the infant is three months old. There is now a substantial body of evidence that a child's brain undergoes significant development during the first three years. Long hours of poor quality child care, without quality stimulation, may jeopardize neurological and psychological development

(White 1999: 126). Although sometimes reversible, low-quality child care is associated with poor outcomes in cognitive, language, and social development, and the reverse for high-quality care. Children who have had high-quality child care are better prepared when they enter school, they perform better in school and there is less juvenile delinquency (Wolfe and Vandell 2002: 108). Low-income working mothers are aware of these risks, but they cannot afford high-quality child care, even if slots were available. More and more children are entering day care at earlier ages and for longer periods of time (White 1999: 126–127). Considering the millions of infants and children now in low-quality child care, how their life chances are being compromised from the very beginning, it is hard to think of a more counterproductive, unfair national policy.

Improving child care – changing the adult-child ratio, the size of the group, and the education, training, experience, and turnover rates of the staff – is very costly. The single most important cost is labor, which is why, in the effort to keep the costs of child care down, labor is so poorly paid (White 1999: 123). The average amount that working families pay for child care is around $5,000 per year, which, it is estimated, puts almost 2 million people (including 1 million children) in poverty. This is up to one-fifth of the incomes of poor and lower-middle income families (Sawhill and Thomas 2001: 6). In a recent study of the impact of child care costs on welfare leavers, the authors estimated that if welfare rolls decline by half, and 60 percent of those who exit go to work, then child care expenditures will increase by 30 percent or more. Despite government subsidies, most of these costs will have to be absorbed by single mothers whose poverty rates will increase even if these mothers find above-minimum wage jobs, and receive the EITC and food stamps. The authors argue that government subsidies for paid child care must increase dramatically to at least lessen the poverty effects of these increased costs (Meyers, Han, Waldfogel, and Garfinkel 2001: 29–59).

Various child care programs have been enacted both at the federal and state levels. As part of the 1996 reform, several federal programs were consolidated into a single program, the Child Care and Development Block Grant (CCDBG), which increased state flexibility; the federal guarantee of child care support for welfare recipients was eliminated; and overall child care funding was increased (Adams and Rohacek 2002: 2). There were subsequent funding increases from $2.1 billion in Financial Year 1997 to $7.4 billion in FY 2000. States are authorized to use TANF funds for child care, and almost $4 billion has been spent by the states. The number of low-income children subsidized has increased from about 1 million in 1996 to about 1.9 million in 2000. The subsidies are usually in the form of vouchers, with about 71 percent of children in regulated settings (either child care centers or licensed family care) and 29 percent in legally unregulated arrangements (either relatives or non-relatives in the child's or caregiver's home). The states vary in terms of eligibility, reimbursement rates, co-payments, quality controls, favoring current or former recipients, or establishing a system for all low-income families (Adams and Rohacek 2002: 3).

However, "despite these major increases, many low-income families are still not getting help. One study of sixteen states found that no state was serving more than 25 percent of the families who would qualify for subsidies under federal income limits . . . and some were serving less than 10 percent" (Adams and Rohacek 2002: 4). "Although spending for child care has nearly quadrupled since 1996 in California, only one in seven parents is able to find a preschool or center-based care in the state" (Whitaker 2002: A9). Some states ration by setting eligibility limits lower than the federal standards (about $38,000). For example, a family of three earning $25,000 did not qualify in twenty-two states. Most states ration by limiting outreach efforts. Many families, especially those who were not on welfare, are unaware of the subsidies. Then, there are waiting lists, the difficulty of applying (during working time), supplying the requisite employment data (especially when there are frequent job changes). Thus, in addition to low usage, there are short spells of receiving the subsidy – the average is about seven months. There also remains the issue of quality. The CCDBG program emphasizes supporting work rather than improving the quality of child care. For example, nearly half the states set their reimbursement caps sufficiently low as to restrict access to the lower cost providers. Some providers are unwilling to take subsidized children because of the administrative paperwork. And now, with the economic downturn and the shrinking of state TANF funds, the funds available for child care may very well diminish. In the face of insufficient funds, many states ration in favor of TANF recipients as compared to low-income working parents in general, which creates perverse incentives – a family that desperately needs the subsidy will quit work and go on welfare (Adams and Rohacek 2002: 5–6).

The public sector already provides a significant amount of child care, although it is not counted as such – pre-kindergarten, kindergarten, and Head Start. All-day kindergarten is spreading, and there is support for providing free pre-kindergarten for four-year-olds. Barbara Bergmann says that by expanding these programs as well as before- and after-school care, the four- and five-year-olds of working parents would be covered, and, even with the problems of many of the public schools, the quality of care would be far higher than in a great many current settings (Bergmann 2001: 8). She notes that the present appropriation for CCDF covers only about 12 percent of the eligible children. She proposes additional funding to cover all eligible children, which would cost approximately an additional $15 billion. A sliding eligibility scale would cost about $50 billion. Parents would not be forced into cheap, unlicensed day care. Then, wages for workers have to be raised. In a recent paper, David Blau would provide a means-tested child allowance for up to two children in the form of refundable tax credit, subsidize the cost of accreditation, encourage outreach for high quality care, and means-tested vouchers for up to two children depending on the quality of care. He estimates that the net cost (the elimination of present programs) would be about $95 billion (Blau 2001).

Child support

To the extent that welfare policies favor one-parent families, they discourage marriage or co-habitation and push fathers aside. Many states still restrict eligibility of two-parent families. TANF appears to have reduced or eliminated most of these restrictions. However, because welfare is income-tested and tries to capture the economies of living together, there is an incentive for fathers with earnings and mothers without earnings to live apart (or at least appear to) (Garfinkel and McLanahan 1986: 19).

Under current law, states may retain child support payments while the mother is on welfare. In addition, once the mother leaves welfare, half of the overdue payments are retained by the states. Legislation has been introduced in Congress that would provide more of this money to go to the mothers and children. There are costs in administering the stronger child support enforcement system – federal and state child support offices, courts, prosecutors, and jails. In 1998, outlays on only federal and state direct administrative costs (including some indirect costs) reached $3.6 billion, or about 25 percent of the total collections (Lerman and Sorenson 2001).

Child support should not be disproportionate to the father's ability to pay. To prevent the growth of large arrearages, support obligations should be a percentage of the obligor's income and, thus, would automatically adjust with the father's income. States should also be forbidden from adding repayment of Medicaid or welfare to child support obligations (Garfinkel 2001: 15).

Irwin Garfinkel has proposed that Congress create a publicly financed minimum child support benefit payable to the custodial parent. In addition to reducing poverty and reliance on welfare, this will increase incentives to establishing paternity and securing a child support award. Garfinkel estimates that the cost of even a very generous minimum benefit is modest – in 1985, under $5 billion. On the other hand, there would have to be a sliding scale reduction in benefits to lessen disincentives on the father. But, says Garfinkel, there is no way to eliminate the incentive for living apart (or feigning it). The public benefit should not be too generous (Garfinkel 2001: 21–22).

Health care

Low-income people tend to use more health care than higher-income people, but they have greater difficulty getting health insurance and health care. As noted, welfare recipients no longer automatically qualify for Medicaid. At first, there was a serious drop in enrollments but lately, enrollments are increasing somewhat. States are required to provide one year of transitional coverage to families who become financially ineligible for regular Medicaid – called Transitional Medical Assistance ("TMA") – but this requirement expired on September 30, 2002. Welfare leavers tend to drop out of TMA as time passes primarily because of the requirement to file periodic, complicated forms (Ku and Park 2002: 4). Approximately one-third of the states extend health insurance to working parents with incomes at 100 percent of the poverty line or higher. In thirty-one states, however, the eligibility line is below, sometimes considerably below, the poverty line. In twenty-eight of the states, a mother with two children earning $7 per hour will not qualify. In addition, applications must still be made at a welfare office with a food stamp or welfare form which gives the impression that health insurance is still related to welfare. Many low-income working parents find it difficult to get to these offices during the working day (Kaiser Commission on Medicaid and the Uninsured 2002: 1–2). And now, federal cost-sharing for Medicaid is declining, and, because of deteriorating state budgets, a growing number of states will probably reduce their Medicaid costs (Ku and Park 2001; Ku and Rothbaum 2001). There are other sources of care for the poor – federal block grants for maternal and child health services, community health centers (providing primary care on a sliding-scale fee schedule), migrant health centers, and the Indian Health Service. In addition, hospitals provide a certain amount in "uncompensated care" (Wolfe and Hill 1995).

There has been an effort to provide health insurance to poor children, either under Medicaid or the State Children's Health Insurance Program ("SCHIP"). In forty states, eligibility is 200 percent of the poverty line or higher. Simplified application forms, including mail-in forms, are available. There have been outreach efforts to enroll more children in both Medicaid and SCHIP. As a result, poor children are twice as likely as their parents to have publicly-funded health insurance (Kaiser Commission 2002: 2). However, when SCHIP was created in 1997, with $40 billion granted to the states to expand coverage to low-income children, it stipulated that the funding would be reduced in FY 2002 and two subsequent years to meet the goals of the Balanced Budget Act of 1997. Unless these reductions are eliminated, it is estimated that 400,000 children will lose coverage between 2004 and 2006 (Park and Broaddus 2001a). In addition, under new waiver policies, states can reduce Medicaid and SCHIP coverage, increase co-payments, and eliminate certain services even though many states have unspent funds which they can now use for other state expenditures or tax cuts. It is estimated that up to 12 million low-income elderly and disabled, parents, pregnant women, and children will be affected (Park and Broaddus 2001b).

Contrary to the belief that the uninsured can get the necessary care from doctors and hospitals, the health status of the uninsured is considerably worse than the insured, adversely affecting both work effort and educational attainment (Hadley 2002: 6, 8–9). While many studies have documented extraordinarily high levels of depressive symptoms among welfare recipients, a comparison of the mental health of low-skilled welfare recipients and working single mothers found no difference in depression, stress, and sense of control. Not surprisingly, women on welfare, as compared to working and non-working leavers, had better overall access to health care, including health insurance and a regular health care provider (Duncan and Chase-Lansdale 2001: 28).[32]

---

[32] Only in the MFIP incentives-only group, for whom employment was voluntary, was there a significant reduction in depression. The New Hope participants showed no difference in depression, self-esteem, mastery, or financial worries. A likely reason for the general lack of improvement in mental health is the continuing difficulties inherent in combining child-rearing with employment in the context of economic hardship.

Nevertheless, the 20 percent limit has to be reconsidered as well as the definition and treatment of health and health-related barriers. Welfare policy has to be sensitive to varying degrees of employability. These families should not be made worse off by losing health insurance and food stamps when they leave welfare for work, or have to return to welfare to obtain such assistance (Greenstein and Guyer 2001: 1).

Access to health care for the poor is likely to get worse. Private insurance is increasingly resistant to cross-subsidization (that is, over-charging insured patients to cover the deficits of the uninsured), physicians are increasingly reluctant to take Medicaid patients because of the low reimbursement rates, there is a shortage of physicians in inner-cities and rural areas, preventive health care for the poor is declining, and with the tight budgets, counties and cities are cutting back on emergency room services which the uninsured poor use as primary care facilities.

At the present time, the difficulties of reforming the health care system for the poor are truly daunting. Some of the problems of the poor can be ameliorated by information, education, immunization, prenatal care, and so forth. Forms can be simplified, office hours can be expanded. Other problems are more intractable – time and wages lost, transportation, child care. The major problem by far is the issue of costs and financing. As discussed, Medicaid is already seriously inadequate. It covers fewer than half of those below the poverty line. Welfare recipients account for about one-quarter of the Medicaid enrollees, but the major cost increases are for the disabled, the blind, and the aged. A basic problem with Medicaid is its eligibility cut-off – one dollar above the limit and the family loses coverage, which, of course, creates a strong disincentive to increase one's earnings or even leave welfare. Other problems include variations in coverage and services among the states, lack of coverage of the working poor and adults who do not have dependent children, low reimbursement rates for providers, and the inability to combine Medicaid with private insurance (Wolfe and Hill 1995: 42–62).

Given the debacle of comprehensive health care reform proposed early on in the Clinton Administration, most politicians, as well as most Americans, are reluctant to think about systemic, costly reform even though there is no alternative if the country is to "make work pay" for the vast majority of low-income workers. They simply cannot risk the health of their families. The dilemma, of course, is that expanding health care coverage will dramatically increase health care costs, which are already steadily rising. Barbara Wolfe has proposed covering all children under the age of nineteen for a specific set of services. This "Health Kid" program would provide primary care in community care centers. Certain kinds of basic care would be provided free; others subject to co-payments on a sliding scale. There could be referrals for other kinds of services. Even though many would be left out (singles, childless couples), and children are relatively inexpensive health care consumers, she estimates the costs between \$40 and \$45 billion (Wolfe 1994: 253–288).

Given the vested interests, the rising health care costs, the political silence, and either the satisfaction or the bewilderment of most Americans, it is unlikely that there will soon be major reforms in health care. This is a severe problem for the low-income workers and their families. They must work, but they get sick.

Transportation

The work-first strategy imposes significant transportation needs on welfare recipients and welfare leavers – conducting job search, getting to and from jobs (which, as noted, often can have non-regular hours), dropping children off and picking them up from child care and school, household responsibilities, other appointments such as health clinics – yet, transportation is rarely mentioned as a significant barrier. Surveys have shown that as welfare recipients become employed, their travel patterns and problems are coming to resemble other low-wage workers (Ong and Houston 2002b). Large numbers of low-wage workers, especially minorities, live in communities which are spatially isolated from job opportunities (Stoll 2000: 417–452). Minorities, especially African Americans, have higher unemployment than whites even in tight labor markets. Part of this is due to discrimination, differences in skills, and so forth, but a large part is due to the fact that jobs are not readily accessible to inner-city residents (Stoll, Holzer, and Ihlandfeldt 2000: 207–231).[33] In Los Angeles, Black job seekers had to cover more geographical areas than whites or Latinos (Stoll 2000). Where public transportation is available and reliable, it helps, but often it is difficult, especially when welfare recipients have to travel to unfamiliar areas in order to fill a quota of job applications, while, at the same time, trying to manage their other demands. Not only is commuting time by public transportation far longer than by private cars, but often public

---

[33] The cities studied were Atlanta, Boston, Detroit, and Los Angeles.

transportation is not designed to serve inner-city workers working sub-urban jobs. Inner-city commuters often have to make two or three time-consuming transfers. In Los Angeles, a one-way trip from the central city to the white San Fernando Valley is approximately 2.5 hours and requires three bus transfers. Even then, access may be difficult. For example, in Atlanta, only about one-third of low-skill jobs in white suburbs were within a quarter mile of the public transit stop (Stoll et al. 2000: 217). And, then, add the burdens of dropping off and picking up children at child care and school. Transportation is mentioned by an overwhelming number of California county welfare administrators as a barrier in trying to move recipients off welfare (Ong and Houston 2002).

There are a number of policy responses to improving access to suburban jobs. One set involves attacking residential and employer discrimination. Another focuses on subsidizing commutes – van pools, improving public transportation, and cars. Employment problems are eased considerably with cars for all low-income workers, especially where public transportation is not well developed. But welfare policy still restricts recipients in their ability to own a car (Ong 2001).[34] There are also problems of affordable insurance and the cost of repairs. These policies should be changed. The asset limitation has to be raised or eliminated as unnecessary. Subsidies have to be provided for cars, repairs, and insurance, but, as with child care support, they have to be extended to all low-income workers on a sliding scale.

Immigrants
With some exceptions, immigrants who entered after August 22, 1996, are not eligible for most welfare benefits, including TANF, SSI, Medicaid, SCHIP, and food stamps until they have been in the United States for at least five years. The five-year ban applies after they become citizens. This includes "qualified" aliens – permanent residents, refugees, admitted asylum seekers, as well as some others. These so-called "non-qualified" aliens are only eligible for emergency assistance (especially Medicaid) (Fix and Haskins 2002: 2). On the other hand, children born to immigrants, whether qualified or not, are citizens and have the same entitlements as all citizens. The 1996 legislation also requires that most legal immigrants have sponsors with income over 125 percent of

---

[34] In about half of the states, TANF, food stamp, or Medicaid recipients cannot own cars worth more than $4,650.

the poverty line, and that this income is deemed available when calculating welfare eligibility, usually resulting in disqualification, and that the sponsors are liable for the costs of any welfare. Not surprisingly, the use of welfare by non-citizens has declined even more than by citizens, including United States-born citizen children whose parents are immigrants. On the other hand, the use of Medicaid and SCHIP has remained stable. Still, the percentage of children of legal immigrants who lack health insurance is higher than children of citizens (Fix and Haskins 2002: 2–3). The percentage of low-income immigrant children in Medicaid or SCHIP, which was low to begin with, has fallen substantially (Ku and Blaney 2000). Not surprisingly, there is more hardship, including rising food insecurity (Zimmerman and Tumlin 1999).

These restrictions should be lifted. Individuals who entered the country legally and otherwise meet eligibility criteria should have income support, food stamps, and health insurance, especially children, pregnant women, working parents, and those who have become disabled after coming to the United States (Greenstein and Guyer 2001: 14–15). According to Fix and Haskins, a complete restoration of benefits is not likely, given the present budget situation – food stamps, TANF, SSI, and Medicaid would cost about $25 billion over a five-year period. Current proposals are more limited – for example, expanding food stamps for children, non-citizens who are working, refugees, and the disabled. At the same time, given the large proportion of Latinos and Asians, there seems to be no inclination to make further cuts (Fix and Haskins 2002: 6).

The more difficult cases

As noted, many welfare recipients have multiple barriers to employment – low skills, cognitive limitations, health problems, language, addiction, and domestic violence. Some of these families need sustained and expensive assistance. Some are probably unlikely ever to become fully self-sufficient. Others may be able to do part-time, low-wage work. The 20 percent exemption should be changed to give the states more options in providing help for disadvantaged families (Haskins and Blank 2001: 19–20). There should be a division of responsibility between the two programs: TANF for those who are reasonably expected to work, and SSI as a non-time-limited program for those who cannot (Karoly et al. 2001: 17–19).

The more successful welfare-to-work programs are those that combine strategies – the "mixed strategy programs" which have a flexible, balanced approach that offers a mix of job search, education, job-training, and work activities. They have more individualized services, a central focus on employment, ties to local employers, and are intensive, setting high expectations for participants. Some of these mixed strategies have not only increased employment but also succeeded in helping welfare recipients find better jobs.

There should be increased attention to work supports – linkages to Medicaid, food stamps, child care, the EITC, and others. Most states (thirty-two) are providing post-employment support which includes transportation aid, purchase of work clothing or tools, payment of work-related fees. A few states offer short-term cash payments to help cover work expenses or emergencies. So far, there is little information as to how many welfare recipients are involved in these programs, but the numbers seem small (Strawn et al. 2001: 14–17). Education and job-training should count as fulfilling work requirements (Haskins and Blank 2001: 28).[35]

There should be community-based, employment-related organizations that would provide information, post-employment support, monitoring, and advocacy services for the working poor. Most employment is obtained through informal networks, and many welfare recipients lack these connections. In addition, poor single mothers often need post-employment support when there are breakdowns in child care or transportation or children are sick. As discussed, there is a need for information concerning the EITC, health benefits, the availability and quality of day care, and related programs, such as disability and unemployment insurance. Community-based agencies could provide this information, monitor health and child care services, and provide counseling and advocacy services for low-income working mothers (Handler and Hasenfeld 1997). It will be necessary to keep monitoring the changes in the welfare programs. Many decisions are of low visibility. Organizations serving the poor should engage in systematic data-gathering – tracking families who leave welfare, monitoring families needing shelter, food, etc. – and publicize the impact of the welfare changes.

These are some of the things that can be done for most of the welfare recipients. They are universal programs that will, at the same time, help the working poor. In addition, they will help the men who have to be brought back into the discussion if progress is to be made with poor

[35] This in Blank's proposal, not Haskins.

families. But then, there will be those who need more help. This population is varied. Some recipients will need relatively small amounts of training, help in networking, building self-esteem, and so forth. Others will need moderate amounts, and some will need considerable support. The success of service programs varies, of course, with the relative difficulty of their cases – the more ambitious the program, the more problematic the results.

Despite the success of some programs, we still know very little about what "works" and even less about how to replicate good programs. People with serious problems need patience, understanding, and resources. Above all, sanctions must be avoided. They rarely change behavior; they produce considerable harm; and they largely serve the function of making the rest of society feel superior and in control (Handler and Hasenfeld 1997).

SOCIAL CITIZENSHIP IN THE UNITED STATES

For almost four decades now, the United States has been fixated on welfare reform. What explains this fixation? It is surely not the costs. AFDC at its height cost $23 billion (both federal and state), less than one-tenth the cost of either Social Security pensions or Medicare. While US welfare policy is centrally concerned with the work ethic, it should be recognized that the stigmatization of the "unworthy" poor is much broader than failing to become gainfully employed. It encompasses race, gender, and other forms of deviant behavior. Who the poor are, whether they should be helped, and under what circumstances, are social processes that affirm moral norms of work, family, gender roles, and attitudes towards race and ethnicity. In a previous age, paupers were the code word for immigrants, Catholics, intemperance, promiscuity, crime, and other forms of deviant behavior. In more recent history, "welfare" is the code word for the inner-city, African-American young woman, most likely a substance abuser, having children to stay on welfare, and breeding a criminal class. This is the "underclass."

Given these attitudes towards the "undeserving poor," it is easy to see why the term "social citizenship" has no meaning in the United States As Fraser and Gordon point out, "while there is a rich discourse on civil citizenship – civil rights, individual liberties, freedom of speech; yet, almost a total absence of 'social citizenship.'" "[T]he expression 'social citizenship' evokes themes from three major traditions of political theory: liberal themes of (social) rights and equal respect; communitarian norms of solidarity and shared responsibility; and republican ideas of participation in public life." Why, then, the absence of "social citizenship"? Because, say the authors, "social citizenship implies entitlements. People who are 'social citizens' get 'social rights,' not 'handouts.'" "Citizens," they point out, "are entitled to equal respect, they share a common set of institutions and services designed for all citizens. In the United States, social provisions remain largely outside the aura of dignity surrounding 'citizenship.' Welfare is usually considered grounds of disrespect, a threat to, rather than a realization of citizenship . . . The connotations of citizenship are so positive, powerful and proud, while those of 'welfare' are so negative, weak, and degraded, that 'social citizenship' here sounds almost oxymoronic" (Fraser and Gordon 1994).

Citizenship in the United States, say the authors, is expressed in contractual terms. Contract theory presupposes an exchange of equals. In contrast, charity is a unilateral gift. The donor has no obligation and the recipient has no claim. With charity, "the moral credit goes to the donor; the recipient becomes increasingly stigmatized; the stigmatization, in turn, raises doubts about the wisdom of giving – the threat of 'indiscriminate giving.'" The ideology of contract is the more powerful. In the United States, the conservatives are also trying to incorporate welfare into contract. The emphasis is on "responsibilities" along with "rights." Under the present welfare reform, "responsibilities" means forced work in return for the grant – a far cry from the morality of free exchange – but this shows, say the authors, "how far the ideology of contract has penetrated social policy." Welfare has always been coupled with obligations, a contract. As Fraser and Gordon note, "it is not a formal, legal contract, but contract based on the *moral* obligations of citizenship."

Obligations are not exclusively in terms of work; they also include various kinds of family and social behaviors – for example, conservatives believe that welfare encouraged increases in deviant behavior, e.g. out-of-wedlock births and high-school dropout, and discouraged child support. Charles Murray, in his book *Losing Ground* (Murray 1984) argued that the Great Society programs of the 1960s were responsible for the rise in unemployment, crime, single-parent households, and out-of-wedlock births among African-Americans. The reason, he said, was that the liberals linked poverty to the faults of the system rather than the individual. This led to a rewording of the "undeserving" poor at the expense of the "deserving" (i.e., working) poor. Many people are poor because they choose that way of life. Social policies that try to induce them out of poverty actually reward their undesirable behavior. The undeserved poor must be coerced to participate in social programs to change their behavior – i.e., work. Murray advocated abolishing public aid programs altogether. Private charity would help the few who could not work.

Lawrence Mead, in his book, *Beyond Entitlement: The Social Obligations of Citizenship* (Mead 1986) argued that the welfare policies of the liberals failed to reduce dependency because they were based on entitlements without reciprocal obligations. They were too permissive. By not insisting on behavioral changes – primarily work – these policies were, at best, ambiguous, which resulted in an erosion of the work ethic. The poor want to work, want to be responsible citizens, but "it is something they would like to do, but not something they feel they must do at any cost. It is an aspiration but not an obligation" (Mead 1989: 162). Mead says that workfare is not coercive; rather it is an exercise in authority. What was needed was a firm imposition of authority requiring able-bodied welfare recipients to work for their aid. "Workfare should be seen in the broadest sense as a form of public education. Just as we require children to attend school, so we should require adults to do something to improve themselves if they are employable yet on welfare" (Mead 1989: 166). In the 1980s, the liberals also endorsed the obligation to work and proposed time-limited welfare to reduce dependency and enforce the work requirements (Ellwood 1988; Garfinkel and McLanahan 1986). And this is now the current US welfare policy. Welfare recipients have *obligations*, not rights. Contract (not a legal contract) is the moral definition of social citizenship. We return to this theme of social citizenship as contract when we discuss the Third Way in Western Europe, in Chapters 3 and 4.

SOME LESSONS FROM THE US EXPERIENCE THAT MIGHT BE APPLICABLE TO WESTERN EUROPE

There are great differences between the Western European countries and the United States (and the Anglo-Saxon countries), but there are also broad similarities – e.g., capitalism, religion, the Enlightenment traditions, ethical and moral philosophy, etc. In this next section, I draw out some important, general characteristics of the US welfare experience and ask, to what extent are these *possibly* issues for the Europeans. I emphasize that these are questions, things to keep in mind, and *not* answers.

Ideology: deterrence; reformation; inclusion; exclusion
The ideology of the US welfare state is two-sided. One side we know well – the continuous effort to separate the "deserving" poor from the "undeserving." This story is one of deterrence – to deprive the "unworthy poor" of assistance, to deter pauperism. As discussed, pauperism and now dependency are *moral* faults. The welfare system is to exclude the morally culpable (Gilens 1999). This view, however, is only one side of deterrence. The other side of welfare policy is *reformation*. This is a policy of *inclusion* – to prevent the poor from sliding out of mainstream society and to bring back in those who are already excluded. Then, as now, the principal method is through gainful, self-supporting work. Throughout welfare history, some of the harshest measures – forced work, the poorhouse, the abolition of outdoor relief, the denial of aid to the able-bodied – were supported by the most prominent social reformers and organizations of the day – the "best people." They were out to "save" the poor, not to punish them. "It is spirit the poor need, not soup," was the common refrain. The Mothers' Pension movement at the turn of the twentieth century was designed to *include* "proper" poor mothers into the middle class while excluding "unfit" mothers.

Over the next century, the US welfare system remained consistent – only help for the deserving. Workfare has the same double edge – include and exclude. The conservatives believe that the rigorous application of the work test, enforced by sanctions, is the most efficacious way to prevent dependency – reformation *and* deterrence. Now, the liberals have joined the cause. They, too, believe that paid work is the best way to re-integrate the welfare recipient back into society and to restore citizenship. And they, too, believe in sanctions. This is "tough love." Tough love will include, but it will also exclude those who do not abide by the rules. As we shall see, most of Western Europe has adopted both the conservative and the liberal position on workfare. For many, a driving force in welfare reform has been the spread of dependency – the abuse of the system. And for many, welfare reform is the surest way to re-integrate the socially excluded back into society. The carrot and the stick.

Welfare office strategies: moral typification; myth and ceremony
In promulgating these new programs, what is usually assumed away and otherwise ignored are issues of implementation. Welfare agencies and other human services agencies have to administer these programs. Workfare programs, as discussed, are complex administrative

tasks requiring professional knowledge, judgment, and discretion. After all, they are dealing with people, people who are in need and often have multiple problems. What are these agencies like? Are they capable of implementing the new programs? What lessons – and questions – can be drawn from the US experience?

In the past, work programs were never really enforced. Most recipients were deflected (put on administrative "hold"), few got jobs and it is questionable whether they got jobs as a result of the efforts of the welfare departments. The reason for the general failure of implementation was the lack of administrative capacity – an issue often ignored by policy-makers, as well as reformers. As discussed, in response to the dramatic changes in the welfare rolls – the size, the demographic composition, and the costs – welfare administration at the state and local level became highly bureaucratized. And it is these changes which seriously compromised the administrative capacity of the local AFDC offices to respond to the various welfare-to-work programs that have been imposed upon them over the past 30 years.

Two principal reasons are given for the failure to implement the work programs – the sheer volume of cases and the demands for program integrity, i.e. to reduce errors, increase compliance with rules, and the reduction of "waste, fraud, and abuse." These two pressures force routinization and bureaucratization so that field-level decisions can more easily be monitored for accuracy. But the drive towards routinization is broader than program integrity. All systems of administration must adopt a routine to handle volume and to meet performance goals, and welfare is no exception. To a large extent – never completely – management was able to assert control over the line staff by routinizing large parts of the program, instituting strict monitoring controls, and replacing the staff with eligibility clerks and technicians. The emphasis was, and still is, on strict adherence to eligibility and income-maintenance requirements. At the same time, local welfare offices have been hard hit. The staff is undertrained, underpaid, and overworked. In testimony before the General Accounting Office, welfare administrators from Cleveland described their offices in the following terms:

> [M]any human services departments cannot manage to answer the telephone, let alone conduct a civilized interview. They have been stripped of staff; the staff they have has been downgraded – some have only an eighth- or ninth-grade education; and they have been buffeted, blamed, and drowned in impossible regulations and requirements. (Schorr 1987: 18)

This is the context of the local welfare office. It is the culture of eligibility and compliance. Yet, it is rare for policy-makers to take these organizational constraints seriously; most of the time, they are content to make the political, symbolic gestures of reform and not worry about administration. This is especially true with the welfare-to-work programs. Bane and Ellwood were an exception. Just prior to entering the Clinton Administration, they argued that the recently enacted Family Support Act's goal of enabling more families to make the transition to self-sufficiency was doomed to fail because it was not likely to change the "organizational culture of welfare" (Bane and Ellwood 1994: 2). What they meant was that because AFDC was focused primarily on monitoring eligibility, work requirements were also viewed as "just another prerequisite for continued eligibility."

The path that welfare has taken is thus contradictory. It has kept its long-standing, moralistic, social control ethos. Applicants and recipients are viewed with suspicion. The emphasis is on moral reformation and the control of waste, fraud, and abuse. The former has resulted in the re-institution of increasingly strict work requirements which require intensive, close caseworker management. But the latter has resulted in bureaucratization, computerized rule enforcement, and the proletarianization of the workforce – in short, an organization that is administratively incapable of carrying out work programs which, at least in theory, are supposed to require individualized consultation and assessment, planning, contracts, implementation, supervision, and follow-up.

Faced with the basic incompatibility between welfare agencies and the demands of work programs, what are the survival strategies of the local welfare offices? When the state or the Federal Government decides that welfare recipients should be required to seek paid labor rather than welfare, the basic, enabling legislation sets the framework, and is in the form of mandates. If the program starts with the Federal Government, the mandates are to the states. But, whether state or federal, the mandates eventually go down to the local offices. In most states, these are county departments of welfare; in other states, they are local state offices. The term "welfare program," then, does not mean a single, uniform administrative system. Not only are there 50 states, each administering its own variation of a work program, but there are over 3,000 counties in the United States. Not all of them administer welfare programs, but in the larger, urban counties, there are several local offices. There are thousands of local variations in the actual, on-the-ground, day-to-day administration of the work program. States, counties, and local offices differ, sometimes in policies, and always in details.

Welfare-to-work programs require recipients to accept offers of suitable employment or participate in various kinds of pre-employment activities (e.g., job search, job preparedness classes, etc.); if, without cause, they fail to do so, they are subject to sanction. Within these seemingly simple requirements, lie volumes of rules, regulations, standards, and interpretations. There are scores of rules and regulations attempting to spell out just about every element in the work program. How is disability determined? Who decides when child care is inadequate and what are the criteria? When can a missed appointment or a class be excused? What happens when a recipient is fired from a job for misconduct? And so on, and on. There is an enormous amount of paperwork; everything has to be documented. But despite the quantity of rules, *a great many of the most crucial decisions require judgment or discretion on the part of the field-level workers.* The recipient who is claiming disability missed an appointment with a doctor because the bus was late. Does the worker believe the recipient is telling the truth? If yes, there is an excuse; otherwise, a warning or a sanction.

The work program is *an add-on* to the welfare office. The basic job of the welfare office remains administering the income-maintenance program, itself a formidable task. Now, the welfare office is directed to run an employment program, but it is not an employment service. It doesn't want to be an employment service, it doesn't have the expertise, and although it is often given additional resources, they are rarely sufficient. Complicating matters for the welfare department is that, in order to run a work program, it has to depend on other agencies in the local area. The success of any program is clearly dependent on local employers. If they are not willing to hire welfare recipients, there is nothing that the welfare agency can do. If the program provides for education and training, the agency will have to contract with other service providers in the community – for example, community colleges or adult education agencies. But while these other service providers are interested in acquiring the fees, they are not particularly interested in welfare recipients and rarely make adjustments for their special needs. This is particularly true for local education services; they are geared to working-class adults who are eager, paying customers, whereas many welfare recipients have had poor educational experiences and are doubtful, if not reluctant, about more education. It is not surprising that the participation of welfare recipients in education and training is problematic, and rarely shows positive results. There are differences in results when education programs are specifically tailored to the special needs of welfare recipients, but this kind of conscious adaptation is rare.

All organizations – welfare agencies, community colleges, adult education programs – seek legitimacy and support from their environments. They try to present themselves as efficient, capable institutions that are fulfilling their mission. Community colleges and adult education programs are interested in recruiting, educating, and graduating paying adults who want to take advantage of their services. Employment agencies seek to build a reputation as a source of reliable labor; they are interested in prime-age white adults, who are educated and have work experience. Welfare agencies are interested in clients who fit the rules, who follow the rules, and who don't cause problems.

There is a rich literature on the attitudes of welfare workers towards recipients. The workers practice what Yeheskel Hasenfeld has described as *moral typification*. The core activity of welfare agencies is to process or change people (Hasenfeld 1983). The very nature of selecting, processing, and changing people conveys a judgment as to the *moral* worth of the person. However technical or rule-bound the decision, somewhere along the line a value judgment has been made about the client. Cultural beliefs determine what values are legitimate and appropriate in working with clients. The welfare agency will attempt to select those clients who fit organizational needs and compartmentalize client needs into "normal" service categories. Other client problems will be considered irrelevant. Employment and training programs select and train the most promising students and somehow defer or deflect those who may need the services the most. Welfare agencies punish those who do not or cannot comply. Workers in human service agencies sort out and classify incoming clients according to preconceptions. They then screen out conflicting information and screen in confirming information. Client responses become self-fulfilling prophecies. Many welfare workers see themselves as but a short step away from welfare themselves; yet, they work hard, "play by the rules," and no one is giving them benefits and favors. Workers trained, socialized, and supervised in this manner will apply rules strictly, impose sanctions, avoid errors, and get through the day as quickly and painlessly as possible. Requests for change or required change consume scarce administrative time and run the risk of error. Clients with problems become problems (Hasenfeld 1983).

The social construction of the clients has important implications for client attitudes towards welfare. We have seen that welfare recipients participating in workfare have positive attitudes even though they are totally realistic as to their prospects in the low-wage labor market. The process of typification helps shape these attitudes. In many bureaucratic settings, the attitudes of dependent people are shaped by the professionals that they deal with. The professionals define the problems and the alternatives (Felstiner, Abel, and Sarat 1980–81: 631–654). As mentioned, dependent people want to remain in personal control (Maranville 2002). The attitudes of the workfare recipients reported by Scott and her colleagues are of those who have been selected by the agency workers. In contrast to those who have been denied welfare or sanctioned, these respondents have been told that they can succeed and given opportunities. However limited these opportunities may be, the clients want to shed the stigma of welfare – they are different from those "other" recipients. Their optimism reinforces their sense of control.

In the selecting, sorting, and processing of clients, the individual worker's field-level decisions are relatively immune from upper-level supervision. Field-level decisions are shrouded in factual assessments. It is difficult for supervisors to uncover the relevant information, assuming there is the will to do so (Hasenfeld 1983). Monitoring, especially from the top, is highly problematic, especially since the more important decisions are discretionary. Sometimes, out of frustration, administrators will impose strict rules on inherently discretionary judgments – for example, a welfare mother who is not satisfied with a day care offer can only refuse twice. There are categories of decisions which are routine, which field-level clerks can apply in a formulaic, mechanical way. Most of these decisions would involve financial eligibility and various accounting rules – for example, how work-related expenses are calculated, what is allowed or disallowed. But even here, one should not exaggerate the importance of mechanics. Rules depend on underlying facts. Sometimes "facts" are clear-cut – for example, rent receipts, employer pay stubs, and so forth. In other instances, they are not. In any event, for most of the rules that we are concerned with, both the underlying facts and the legal requirements are ambiguous.

At the same time, one must appreciate the working conditions of welfare field-offices. Workers have large caseloads, there are massive numbers of regulations and requirements. They are under great pressure to get the work out correctly. In large, urban offices, workers talk to clients from behind bars or metal screens. The job requires client placements in paid employment. Yet, the staff is confronted with clients of variable capacities and personalities as well as uncontrollable services (e.g.,

adult education) and local labor markets. Whatever the program demands, the staff response will be survival, and not necessarily service to
clients.

The confluence of the external and internal forces that shape the
implementation of work programs by welfare departments reveal their
inherent incompatibility. There is much talk about how a contract is
drawn up between the welfare recipient and the agency which spells
out the mutual obligations of both and makes them accountable to the
terms of the contract. Yet, the idea of the "contract" is also an exercise
in myth and ceremonies. In her study of the implementation of JOBS
in Chicago, Evelyn Brodkin showed how the state stacks the cards in
such a way that the clients have few opportunities to influence the terms
of the contract. The caseworkers use their discretionary power to force
the clients to comply with their interpretation of the contract. The
workers construct their own conception of the "welfare contract" which
"excluded a client right to help in job-finding and denied a state obligation to assure that decent job opportunities existed or could be found"
(Brodkin, Fuqua, and Thoren 2002). During assessment of the client
needs, the workers fit the clients into available slots and ignored information about service needs they could not respond to. Not infrequently,
caseworkers sent clients on job searches even though the clients did not
meet the required level of education or literacy proficiency. Workers
make judgments about "favored" clients in allocating education or vocational training. "The welfare recipients had little recourse in trying to
get the welfare department to meet its part of the contract. The ability
of the workers to redefine the needs of the clients, to ignore information
about client problems, and to interpret requests for additional services
as indications of noncompliance made it extremely difficult for clients
to exercise their rights" (Brodkin et al. 2002).

The findings by Brodkin are not surprising and are replicated in many
other instances. Yet, it is disturbing that current welfare reformers seem
to learn so little from history. As Alvin Schorr reminds us, social contracts were the social work strategy of the 1950s and 1960s (Schorr
1987). They did not work then primarily because of the bureaucratization of the office, the de-professionalization of the staff, and the pressure of managing accurately a complex income-maintenance program –
in short, for the same administrative constraints that Brodkin describes
over forty years later. For the average worker, the pressures are to
cream – to deal with those clients who will more easily fulfill the
program's requirements, and, above all, not cause any problems. This

means concentrating on the most readily employable. In the past, the workers would deflect the more troublesome cases. Now, they are sanctioned.

If the above is the general story of the welfare-to-work programs, what accounts for their continued re-enactment? Here, we are in the realm of symbolic politics. I raised the question before about the continued fixation on "welfare" despite the fact that it is a relatively small budget item and that a substantial majority of welfare families are not a "problem." The moral judgments that we (society) make about welfare recipients are really addressed to us. They affirm our values of hard work and proper moral conduct. They make us feel better by punishing the victim.

But if welfare-to-work programs are so ineffective, how can this satisfy our moral needs? Here enters the familiar concept in sociology of *myth and ceremony* (Meyer and Rowen 1991). The myth is that now we are going to get serious about making those lazy recipients get out of the house and get to work. And, from time to time, in various demonstration projects or experiments, this happens – recipients do get jobs, and do get off welfare. This is the ceremony that validates the myth. In the current welfare reform, one of the prime examples is the Riverside, California, demonstration project. This became the model for the welfare reform – the "work first" strategy. The program was hailed as a "success," despite its modest results, and of those who worked, almost all remained in poverty. It didn't matter, though. The country was determined to "end welfare as we know it." The "work first" strategy was clear, it was effectively communicated, and that is what the current US welfare reform is about.

We turn now to Western Europe where the effort is to change its welfare states into workfare.

CHAPTER THREE

THE EUROPEAN WELFARE STATES

The chapter starts with the contrasting conception of social citizenship in Western Europe, and then gives a brief history of the various welfare states. Because this story has been told, and told well, only the briefest summary will be presented. The chapter will emphasize a major common similarity – despite the varieties among the welfare states, they all depended on high levels of employment among the working population (Huber and Stephens 2001: 1). A relatively full-employment economy of decent jobs and a relative equality of wages allowed for the financing of the welfare state – that is, where most were contributing rather than drawing benefits – as well as for redistribution. The countries differed in how they accomplished high levels of employment, but they all managed to do so, and this enabled them to develop their social welfare states.

I then describe the subsequent, contemporary slowdown in the economies, the failure of traditional Keynesian policies, the deterioration of the labor market, the rising poverty, and the consequences for the vulnerable groups. The chapter discusses the dilemmas faced by the Social Democratic governments. They are caught between the strong pressures of globalization and changes in the economy and the labor markets on the one hand and domestic demands for social protection on the other. Thus far, changes in the major welfare state programs – pensions, disability, health care, the programs for the insiders – have been incremental. On the other hand, for the long-term unemployed, social assistance recipients, and the socially excluded – the outsiders – changes have been significant. Here, the welfare state is in the process of being changed from "passive" to "active." Eligibility has been tightened, benefits have been limited, and there is more means-testing. In all countries, for this group, social citizenship is being redefined in terms of *responsibilities*, called the Third Way. In the meantime, in most countries, the economies continue to remain sluggish, unemployment is unacceptably high, and conservatives are replacing Social Democrats. In the next chapter, I discuss how these changes – workfare – are being implemented in selected countries.

SOCIAL CITIZENSHIP IN THE GOLDEN AGE

Although continental Western Europe started from the same place as England (Braudel 1979: 75–76; Darnton 1999: 130–131; Kahl 2002a; 2002b),[1] its conception of social citizenship and the flowering of its welfare states could not have been more different. A common starting point, in the post-World War II era, is usually that of T.H. Marshall. In Marshall's formulation, *civil rights*, developed in the eighteenth-century, included free speech, access to the legal system, rights to a fair trial, and rights of contract and property. *Political rights* – the extension of the franchise, the secret ballot, the right to hold office – were products of the nineteenth-century (for men). *Social rights* belong to the twentieth-century – entitlements to Social Security when faced with unemployment, sickness, old age, and other kinds of hardship, that is, protections from the rigors of capitalist labor markets (Marshall 1950; Turner 1992).

In the immediate post-World War II period, the United Kingdom was in the process of constructing its social welfare state. Marshall was attempting to justify the national provision of social benefits. His concern was the contradiction between formal political equality and individual freedom, on the one hand, and significant social and economic inequality on the other (Turner 1992). The social entitlements of the welfare state would reconcile, or at least lessen the conflicts between, capitalism and civil and political citizenship. The cash/work nexus would be

---

[1] In discussing the "undeserving" poor, Friedrich Wilhelm, King of Prussia (Sept. 8, 1804), had this to say: "Whoever obstinately refuses to accept assigned work is considered a sturdy beggar and will be treated according to law." Translated by Kahl (2002b). Darnton (1999) reports on contemporary accounts of the poor and lower-working classes in eighteenth century France in terms of violence, crime, depravity – "dregs," "dangerous hordes of lackeys and low-life." Braudel (1979) describes the criminalization of the poor in medieval Europe.

weakened by the guaranteeing of social benefits not dependent on the labor market. There would be a universal right to a real income "not proportionate to the market value of the claimant" (Hemerijck 1999: 6). The central ethical principal was "equal social worth." Social rights, via the welfare state, would equalize "life chances" (Hemerijck 1999). Marshall's concept of social rights was expansive: "By the social element [in citizenship] I mean the whole range from the right to a modicum of economic welfare and security to the right to share to the full in the social heritage and to live the life of a civilized being according to the standards prevailing in the society" (quoted in Rees 1996). Social rights would give individuals a sense of security, which, in turn, would foster a sense of belonging and commitment to the political community; there would be a collective identity between the state and its citizens. He coined the term "social citizenship."

This was the theory (hope) of Marshall for dealing with the class/citizenship conflicts of capitalism. At the time that Marshall wrote, it was believed that capitalist exchange relations promoted the growth of a universalistic culture of individualism. At the same time, capitalism generated massive inequalities. Thus, the contradiction. The more capitalism develops in terms of class, the more it works against citizenship. Social citizenship rights, in Marshall's phrase, are "at war" with class.

Marshall's theory has been subject to a number of criticisms and modifications – British-centered, male gendered, evolutionary, complacent, insufficient attention to the impact of war, the variability among capitalist societies, the role of the state, and so forth (Turner 1992: 35–38; Bulmer and Rees 1996: 16–17).[2] It is claimed, among other things, that Marshall's theory cannot deal with persistent poverty and long-term unemployment social exclusion, immigration, and multiculturalism. As noted in Chapter 1, others claim that the issues of citizenship are now beyond the capacity of the nation state; citizenship is a universal project.

---

[2] For example, Britain is taken as paradigmatic of the welfare state, but this is not true. Other countries developed quite differently. For example, in Scandinavia, social rights were developed in a corporatist framework of assumptions and institutions. The French conception of citizenship is strongly assimilationist. In Germany, citizenship is a matter of blood and descent. Thus, it is expansive toward German immigrants but restrictive towards others. Naturalization in Germany is a slow and difficult process. Guest workers have a wide range of social and civil rights, but not political rights. The law has recently been liberalized to allow children of the foreign-born who are born in Germany to become citizens.

Marshall was writing at the start of what is now referred to as the "Golden Age." The economies of Western Europe enjoyed expanding growth and very low unemployment rates. It was during this period that the exemplary welfare states were created. Although the various countries took different paths, nevertheless, according to Gøsta Esping-Andersen, the common feature was the granting of rights – "social rights are given the legal and practical status of property rights" (Esping-Andersen 1990). Because these rights are based on "citizenship rather than performance, they will entail a decommodification of the status of individuals *vis-a-vis* the market." De-commodification is "the degree to which [the various welfare states] permit people to make their living standards independent of pure market forces. It is in this sense that social rights diminish citizens' status as 'commodities' " (Esping-Andersen 1990: 3).

The extent of de-commodification depends on both the adequacy and the conditions of the social benefit. There is not much de-commodification with last resort safety nets. In fact, the market is actually strengthened when benefits are low and means-tested. There is also not much decommodification when generous insurance-like benefits are based on employment contributions. "In other words, it is not the mere presence of a social right, but the corresponding rules and preconditions, which dictate the extent to which welfare programs offer genuine alternatives to market dependence" (Esping-Andersen 1990: 22).

According to Esping-Andersen, it was only in the late 1960s and 1970s that some states approached de-commodification – that is, where "citizens can freely, and without potential loss of job, income, or general welfare, opt out of work when they themselves consider it necessary." Although he calls this a "minimal definition," it is fairly "stringent." For example, a minimum proof of medical impairment would produce an entitlement to sickness insurance benefits equal to the normal wage for as long as the claimant thinks necessary. The same would be true for unemployment, pensions, maternity leave, and child care.

During the 1960s and 1970s, the economies of Western Europe enjoyed expanding growth, modest inflation, and very low unemployment rates. Under Bretton Woods, there was a system of fixed but flexible exchange rates which enabled governments to devalue their currency should inflation threaten competitiveness with a consequent risk of unemployment. Oil was the main energy source, and oil prices were declining. Increases in productivity and economic growth facilitated the incorporation of organized labor into industry-wide collective bargaining as well as national economic policy. The corporatist relationship between national unions and employer associations developed highly centralized systems of industrial relations. The unions would restrain wage demands in return for an expanded, more egalitarian welfare state, lower prices, and sustained economic growth. At the same time, governments could stimulate the economy through fiscal or monetary policies to maintain high levels of employment as long as wages were restrained. The expanding economies encouraged the importation of guest workers (Kitschelt, Lange, Marks, and Stephens 1999: 108).

It was during this period that the exemplary welfare states were created. In most countries, there were real increases in both wages and welfare state entitlements. While there were considerable differences among the various countries, the defining characteristic was the extension of social rights. The core idea was "social citizenship." Social rights were granted the status of rights. In theory, benefits are universal and solidaristic; they are not based on previous earnings or work performance. However, the practice never met the demands of theory. Except, perhaps, for pensions and disability, benefits are never high enough to offer a real alternative to work (Esping-Andersen 1990: 23). Welfare states required working-age beneficiaries to work. If benefits are tied to labor-market participation – for example, insurance contributions – people are required to work. There are no real alternatives to the market (Room 1999). As we shall see, Germany pioneered this form of social insurance. And today, Sweden offers very generous family benefits but in order to qualify, women have to have worked in the paid labor force, and the laborforce participation of women in Sweden is among the highest in Europe. The means-tested, restrictive Poor Laws, as well as the early social insurance programs, were deliberately designed to maximize participation in the paid labor market.

While social rights are intended to lessen the importance of class, Esping-Andersen brings out the important point that the structure of the welfare state itself creates a system of stratification. We have seen this quite clearly in the discussion of the US welfare state (Chapter 2). There, the process of categorization served to distinguish the deserving from the undeserving poor. Means-tested social programs, today, perform the same function. By the use of stigma, strict conditions, and low benefits, these systems perpetuate *social dualism* – a crucial issue when we discuss the future of the welfare state. Social dualism, however, is not just the product of means-tested benefits. The first social insurance programs, those promulgated by the conservative reforms of Bismarck and von Taffe (Austria) were "explicitly class politics." They were designed to forestall radical socialist demands. Working-class divisions were consolidated into distinct programs for different occupational status groups, each with their own set of rights and privileges, and designed to cement worker loyalties to the state. Bismarck and von Taffe built on the corporate, conservative, Catholic tradition which was always opposed to the commodification of individuals as degrading, corrupting, and atomizing. The developed social insurance programs of this state-corporatist model – which was adopted by Italy and France, in addition to Germany and Austria – contain multiple status-specific terms and conditions. They especially privileged the civil service (Esping-Andersen 1990: 24).

Social democratic labor opposed both the stigmatized means-tested poor relief and the state-corporatist model. They turned to universal, flat-grant benefits, financed by general revenues to achieve solidarity within and across the working class. This was the Beveridge program in post-World War II Britain. However, social dualism also appeared as parts of the working class became more prosperous and there arose a new middle class. Flat-rate universal benefits were simply too low, and the better-off turned to private insurance and bargained for fringe benefits.

In the United Kingdom, private subsidized welfare plans led to the erosion of middle-class support for the universalistic public transfer programs. The corporatist-statist countries met the demands for rising expectations of the new middle class by upgrading the existing system; status differences were maintained by moving from a contribution-based system to earnings-graduated benefits. Sweden and Norway, on the other hand, incorporated the new middle class by establishing an even more generous second-tier, universally inclusive earnings-related insurance program on top of the basic, flat-rate egalitarian one. While this created inequalities, it was all state supported. There was no private market. In these countries, there remained a broad political consensus on preserving the solidaristic programs even though financed by high taxes (Esping-Andersen 1990: 25–26).

Esping-Andersen divided the welfare states into his well-known three general types or clusters (Esping-Andersen 1990: 22): (1) liberal; (2) corporatist; and (3) social democratic. The *liberal welfare state* – the United States, Canada, the United Kingdom, Australia (although there are big differences between the United Kingdom and Australia, where there were Social Democratic parties, and the United States) (Esping-Andersen 1990: 75) – rely basically on means-tested assistance, modest universal transfers, and modest social-insurance plans. The concern is with the disincentive effects of welfare. Eligibility rules are strict, benefits are modest, and social assistance is stigmatized. The market is encouraged by the low minimum benefit and by subsidizing private social insurance programs. The modest welfare state is justified on the theory that poverty is the fault of the individual, not the system. Those who can work, should work. For those who cannot work, help is given by the family, religious institutions, or private charity. Means-tested social assistance is based on the principle of "less eligibility "(the conditions of aid always had to be less favorable than the wages of the lowest paid labor). Private insurance was the liberal preference. Public insurance was to be based on employment and contributions to encourage work effort. Business came to favor universal old-age pensions as a way to facilitate the replacement of older workers and to prevent a competitive advantage. Thus, even for liberals, social protections mitigated some of the adverse effects of the labor market (Esping-Andersen 1990: 41–44).

Under the conservative, *corporatist* regimes – Austria, France, Germany, Italy – the historic status-differentiated programs were upgraded both to meet the rising middle class demands but also to support the traditional family. Rights continue to be attached to class and status and redistribution is modest. The state intervenes only to help the family take care of its members. Women are discouraged from working. Social insurance typically excludes non-working wives; family benefits encourage motherhood. Both the conservative and liberal regimes favor a passive approach to labor-market regulation (Esping-Andersen 1990: 83–84).

Universalism, generous benefits, comprehensive risk coverage, and egalitarianism characterize the *social democratic* regimes (Scandinavia). Rights are based on citizenship. There is a deliberate attempt to minimize means-tested assistance. To counter the dualism produced by the rising middle class, benefits were upgraded. Benefits were still based on earnings, but there was substantial equality in earnings. Under this universal, all-inclusive scheme, there was no room for the private insurance market. Instead, there was a universal solidarity in favor of the state welfare system. All were dependent on the state. The Social Democratic regime also seeks to emancipate the individual from the family by socializing the costs of family. Grants go directly to children, child care, the aged, and the disabled. However, the most "salient characteristic" of the Social Democratic regimes is the importance of work. The Social Democratic welfare states are very expensive, especially in Sweden which relies so heavily on public employment (Esping-Andersen 1990: 80). Full employment becomes a practical necessity. There has to be a maximum of tax revenues and a minimum of social costs, that is, most people working and the fewest drawing state benefits. The trade unions, with the support of the ruling labor party, developed industry-wide bargaining. Wages were restrained in return for social protection (Esping-Andersen 1990: 28–29; 78–81).

Sweden was able to accomplish rapid economic growth, price stability, and growth in the welfare state (paid for with very substantial tax revenues). Other countries were able to accomplish full employment, growth, and a developed welfare state through other paths. Germany combined restrictive fiscal and monetary policies and a constant supply of foreign workers which reduced inflationary wage pressures. In the United Kingdom, there was full employment and inflation. The government instituted an incomes policy and wage and price controls, which the unions were incapable of opposing.

It is important to note that despite the strength of the trade unions, the left parties still had to form alliances or coalitions with other classes in order to establish a welfare state. In the Scandinavian countries, the initial alliances were between the working class and the farmers – full employment would be supported in return for agricultural price subsidies. In the post-World War II period, alliances had to be formed with the new middle classes which were not very concerned with full employment, and opposed to income equalization. In Scandinavia, the new middle class supported the state welfare system when they were incorporated into the system. On the Continent, middle-class loyalties were maintained by preserving the occupational status programs. In contrast, in the liberal welfare states, support from the middle class is tenuous, at best; these regimes depend on the loyalties of the lower class (Esping-Andersen 1990: 32).

While these are three general type clusters of welfare regimes, Esping-Andersen is careful to point out that there are no pure types. For example, the welfare state ideology of the liberal regime of the United States is strongly market-oriented, but its largest program is Social Security retirement. The official rhetoric of Social Security is contributory insurance; in fact, the program is compulsory, non-actuarial, and significantly redistributive. The continental conservative corporatist regimes have become less corporatist by incorporating both liberal and Social Democratic elements (Esping-Andersen 1990: 29). The most significant change is in the United Kingdom. Formerly, it was similar to the Scandinavian welfare states – universal, flat-rate benefit programs, national health care, and at least a rhetorical political commitment to full employment. Under the Thatcher government, the commitment to full employment was abandoned. The flat-rate benefits are an inadequate income replacement. There has been an increase in privatization, more targeting, sickness and maternity benefits have been transferred to employers, council housing has been sold, workers can opt-out of public pensions and purchase earnings-related pensions, and both private pensions and private health insurance have been aided via tax subsidies (Esping-Andersen 1990: 87–94; Arts and Gelisson 2002: 137–158).[3]

THE CHALLENGE OF UNEMPLOYMENT

Then came the oil shocks in the 1970s. The first response to the declining economies and growing unemployment was the traditional one. Governments either maintained or increased entitlements and welfare state expenditures (Huber and Stephens 2001: 207). By the early 1980s, the traditional economic policies proved ineffective. Bretton Woods collapsed and governments could no longer use fiscal and monetary policies to enhance economic performance. One of the most stunning reversals happened in France. Mitterrand, the socialist president, tried fiscal and monetary expansion to stimulate employment; instead, there was capital flight, an increase in imports which further depressed domestic production, three currency depreciations in two years, and then a complete reversal of policies (Kitschelt, Lange, Marks, and Stephens 1999: 1–8). The various countries experienced falling industrial profits and international trade. Labor was no longer willing to accept wage restraints; governments could not extract more taxes to pay for the expensive benefits or control the growing budget deficits, despite the increased demands for social benefits. All governments, both Conservative and Social Democratic, began trying to halt the increase in expenditures and increase revenues (Kitschelt, Lange, Marks, and Stephens 1999: 207, 219).

It was during this period that major structural changes in the economy began to develop – accelerating inflation, declining growth, and rising unemployment (stagflation), the decline in agriculture and

---

[3] For a recent review of the debate about Esping-Andersen's typology, see Arts and Gelisson 2002 and Hicks and Kenworth 2003.

manufacturing and the increase in services, the increase in the demand for unskilled labor from the developing world, the massive entry of women into the paid laborforce, and the growing technological innovations in production (Hall 1999: 125–163; Scharpf 2000: 30).

When the fiscal efforts in the second half of the 1970s failed to secure higher growth rates, Keynesian policies were abandoned. It was argued that because of the increase in trade, spending generated by deficits would go to imports. Inflation replaced unemployment as the major concern, and many of the European countries adopted deflationary policies. Rather than creating demand, market-based supply-side measures were to be used to tackle unemployment – manpower policies, technical policies, and deregulation – but these approaches were limited. With access to international capital markets, governments began to lose influence with domestic companies. In the meantime, the general enthusiasm for the market led to the Single Market initiative in the European Community (1985), then, monetary union, the Maastricht Treaty, further constrained deficit financing by the member states (Hall 1999: 153). Central banks became independent and they, too, adopted anti-inflationary policies. There was a move towards privatization and "marketization" in the public sector. Publicly-owned firms were re-organized along profit-making principles and market principles were introduced into public administration and services, where possible. Tax policies lowered rates and cut deductions, adopting the neoliberal arguments that high marginal rates become work disincentives. There was a move to abandon industry-wide collective bargaining. The most significant change occurred in Sweden where collective bargaining was decentralized to the industry-level. In other countries, the coordinated market structures remained intact, although there was pressure for more wage flexibility and changes in union composition. As a result of all of these changes, "governments found themselves with dramatically fewer options. Above all vigorous expansion of entitlements was off the agenda" (Huber and Stephens 2001: 221).

The conservatives were constrained because of the popularity of the welfare state; the Social Democrats because of the constraints of economic policies once high unemployment set in; in addition, low levels of growth prevented tax increases. Still, there were partisan differences in social and labor market policies. In some countries (e.g., Sweden, Denmark), as the economies improved, the conservatives favored more tax cuts, the Social Democrats restoring welfare cuts while retaining a smaller surplus.

Scholars differ as to the importance of various causes. Beth Simmons thinks that one of the most significant changes was the internationalization and integration of capital markets (Simmons 1999: 35–63). According to Simmons, starting in the 1970s, competing pools of unregulated capital began to threaten the fixed exchange rates, and capital controls collapsed. For a time, various countries used taxes and other incentives to channel capital flows but by the early 1990s, most major markets became completely unfettered. Added to the decline in restrictions was the technological revolution of instantaneous trans-actions. Local multi-national corporations demanded an end to con-trols; otherwise, they would be at a competitive disadvantage if they could not borrow and lend freely. The result, says Simmons, was a tremendous increase in relatively unrestrained capital flows. Foreign direct investment, particularly by the industrialized OECD countries and the United States, increased significantly. "Foreign investors pre-ferred service, high-technology, and mergers, acquisitions, and strate-gic alliances to raw materials, manufacturing or new enterprises. With the internationalization of the banking sector, liquid and volatile port-folio investment outpaced direct investment. Businesses invest in for-eign exchanges as readily as in domestic exchanges. There has been a convergence of interest rates." According to Simmons, the growth in cross-border capital movements during the past three decades has been unprecedented, and has been far more extensive and complete than the openness of the markets for goods and services. The developments in capital mobility have not only reduced the ability of governments to use monetary and fiscal policies to stimulate their economies, but they have also provided businesses with a credible "exit option" in bargain-ing over industrial relations (Simmons 1999: 38–40).

Simmons argues that the policy consequences are potentially pro-found. Governments can no longer simultaneously maintain capital mobility, monetary autonomy, and a fixed exchange rate (Simmons 1999: 63–64). Instead, capital now favors reduced government spend-ing, smaller budget deficits, and more limited fiscal policies. And it is the loss of fiscal autonomy that is one of the major causes of the dilemmas faced by the social democratic governments. While expansionary poli-cies alienate business and financial interests, welfare state reductions and changes in labor are opposed by the unions. On the other hand, since governments can no longer manage demand, they have less need for union cooperation, and unions, in turn, have less incentive to bar-gain collectively. Thus, argues Simmons, the liberalization of capital markets may have a more significant impact on social democracy than trade liberalization. Changes in trade often have only a sectoral impact, and adjustments can sometimes be made; this is less true with capital markets, which are much more volatile and can affect an entire economy (Simmons 1999: 64–69).

Several scholars think that the impacts of globalization are not primarily responsible for the pressures on the welfare state; rather, the pressures are generated primarily from domestic changes (Pierson 2001b: 3–4). Paul Pierson states:

> Changes in the global economy are important, but it is primarily social and economic transformations occurring within affluent democracies that generate fiscal strain. Slower economic growth associated with the transition to a post-industrial economy, the maturation of government policy commitments, and population ageing and changing household structures have all combined to create a context of essentially permanent austerity. At the same time, tax levels strain public tolerance, while payroll contribution rates appear to jeopardize employment. (Pierson 2001: 13)

Huber and Stephens argue that the primary cause of welfare state cutbacks in entitlements occurred when it became clear to political leaders that high unemployment was becoming permanent. This meant that welfare state financing and benefits could no longer be sustained (Huber and Stephens 2001: 225). They point out that the Golden Age welfare states were built during a period of open economies in Western Europe; in fact, the economies of these countries depended on exports. In the more recent period, direct foreign investment continued to flow into Europe (Huber and Stephens 2001: 227). The internationalization of capital did make fiscal stimulation more difficult. However, argue the authors, other factors were more significant in the growth of unemployment. They emphasize lower growth, the entry of women into the labor market (twice the rate that men have exited), and that many men exited involuntarily (Huber and Stephens 2001: 234). Another important factor in the more generous welfare states (the Netherlands, Scandinavia) is that "they had 'grown to limits'" (Huber and Stephens 2001: 237). By this, the authors mean that with near universal coverage, taxes were very high, and could not be increased (Huber and Stephens 2001: 224–225). On the other hand, Anton Hemerijck says, "Since the mid-1970s, European economies, with the notable exception of the Netherlands and Ireland, have experienced substantial employment decline in the exposed sectors, especially in agriculture, mining, manufacturing and transport" (Hemerijck 2002).

THE IMPACT ON LABOR

Through the 1970s, the average unemployment rate in OECD-Europe was 2.9 percent; by the 1990s, it had soared to 9.3 percent. Whereas unemployment had been a problem in the United Kingdom for a long time, it now occurred in the traditionally exemplary countries. No longer was Germany the economic miracle. The economy went into a slump and unemployment exceeded 11 percent (Powell 1996: 44). Sweden, too, was shocked by the unprecedented unemployment (Olsen 1996: 1–20). In France, the unemployment rate went above 12 percent; in Spain, above 20 percent. Not only did unemployment rise, but spells became much longer. In Europe, nearly half the unemployed could not find jobs in a year, as compared to only 10 percent of the US unemployed. The vast majority of the long-term unemployed were prime age workers. Among those who worked, in Europe they worked fewer hours than in the United States (McFate 1995: 5). Both unemployment and the fear of unemployment were affecting larger and larger segments of the population. Labor-market insecurity spread from the "secondary workers" to the prime age and older and male workers (Standing 1995: 163). In Germany, there was also wage stagnation. Wages increased only marginally over the previous 15 years, adjusting for inflation (Institute 1996: 4). Then, with unification, a growing number of East Germans went on means-tested public assistance (Lawson and Wilson 1995: 707).

Recently, European economies seemed to have bottomed out. Unemployment has dropped significantly in Sweden (3.4 percent), the United Kingdom (5.2 percent), Denmark (5 percent), and the Netherlands (3.9 percent). Still, in these countries, it is unacceptably high: Germany – 10 percent; France – 9 percent; Belgium – 11.6 percent; Italy – 9 percent; Spain – 11.7 percent (The Economist 2002b: 92). And, according to Huber and Stephens, the reductions in entitlements and expenditures were greater where unemployment was both highest and long-term (Huber and Stephens 2001: 6).

There has been a massive entry of women into the paid laborforce despite – and this is unprecedented – a period of high unemployment. In the 1960s, women comprised 30 percent of the Western European working force; in 1994, this had risen to more than 42 percent (Maruani 1997). Part-time work is increasing dramatically (Gobin 1997).[4] Most of the part-time jobs created in the last fifteen years have been in the unskilled and poorly paid sector of women's work. "[P]art-time jobs tend to receive lower hourly earnings than full-time ones and experience a lower incidence of employer-provided training than full-time workers" (OECD 1999: 35). While part-time work can be voluntary, in 1996, 1.5 million part-timers wanted more work. Women have a greater share of part-time jobs. While many say that they prefer part-time work, "in the case of women with children, many analysts have stressed that attitudes to part-time work may well depend upon the child-care arrangements respondents feel are available to them" (OECD 1999: 32). Women have the highest unemployment, the highest number of the young unemployed, and receive less unemployment benefits than men (Marauni 1997). Speaking of France, Margaret Maruani says, "We are now living in a society of rampant unemployment. With well over 3.5 million registered as out of work, unemployment has now turned into non-stop blackmail in the workplace: fear of redundancy, pressure on wages, threats to rates and hours of work. This has not reduced women's determination to stay on the job market. But it has started a trend towards the feminisation of poverty – and this time it is on this side of the Atlantic" (Marauni 1997). Finally, there are reports of extensive child labor, even in "socially progressive" countries such as Denmark, the Netherlands, and France, as well as illegal immigrant labor (Vaillant 1997).

The entry of women workers reflects, in part, the significant demographic changes that are occurring in Western Europe. Populations are aging, birthrates are falling. The result is that there is a declining fraction of workers supporting the welfare state – probably only two *potential* workers for each person under sixteen and over sixty-four in most Western countries (McFate 1995: 2). There are changes in the family – delayed marriages, declining marriage rates, increasing cohabitation, smaller families, more divorce, increasing numbers of children with lone mothers. Over 40 percent of children in Sweden are born out of wedlock, and 20 percent in the United Kingdom and France. Many are born to cohabiting couples, and paternity is legally established in 90 percent of all births, but a large proportion of these children will

---

[4] According to Levy (1999), approximately one-sixth of all jobs in France are now either part-time or fixed term.

spend at least some time in a single parent household (Lefaucher 1995: 257–289; McFate 1995: 11). The significant increase in the laborforce participation of women includes, of course, mothers, and those with very young children create an increase in the need for day care as well as other public social services (Lefaucher 1995; McFate 1995; Huber and Stephens 2001: 2).

Esping-Andersen says that the "changing role of women and evolving new household forms an intrinsic – possibly leading – part of the socio-economic transformation around us." In the Golden Age, the household, along with the full employment economy and the protective system of labor relations, formed the major pillars of the welfare state. The household performed a great many welfare functions. The unpaid domestic labor of women was a major source of welfare. With the dramatic changes in families, "the essential welfare contribution of the household is no longer available." He calls this "an emerging welfare deficit" (Esping-Andersen 1990: 49). The cost of private child care is now 23 percent of the income of poor households (Esping-Andersen 1990: 57). In most countries (with the exception of Sweden, with direct public provision; France, with subsidization and regulation; and the United States, with low-cost markets), most families with two small children lack access to day care (Esping-Andersen 1990: 64–65).

With the decline in manufacturing, large numbers of less-skilled men and women began looking for both full-time and part-time employment, but the European service sector seemed unable to provide well-paying, entry-level employment. The state of the European economies was tagged "Eurosclerosis." It was argued that the generous social benefits create a high reservation wage that traps people in unemployment or assistance dependency, imposes high labor costs on employers, a high, undifferentiated minimum wage forces out less productive workers, and job protections raise the costs of dismissals (Esping-Andersen 1990: 21–22).[5] There developed the belief that full employment could only be achieved by more inequality in wages, slower wage-growth, and less security for workers (Esping-Andersen 1990: 24; Teague 1999: 107–110).

---

[5] However, there are differences among the countries. For example, in Scandinavia, there are strong unions, but they emphasize flexibility, full-employment promotion, active labor-market policies, and welfare guarantees. In France and Spain, there are weak labor unions but strong protective practices (p.23). Esping-Andersen believes that the case for "Eurosclerosis" is rather weak. The service sector has grown. He thinks that the massive entry of women into the paid labor market is a much more significant cause of high unemployment (p.26).

There arose the demands for new forms of flexible production, called the "fourth industrial revolution" and the acceleration of international economic integration. It was argued that competitive pressures have increased and comparative advantages have been changed. Firms in developed countries can more easily invest in less-developed countries in labor-intensive manufacturing now that barriers to exporting back to the developed countries have largely been removed (McKeown 1999: 23–25). Countries did manage to protect particular domestic producers and blocs of voters with "nontariff barriers" that are low-visibility laws and regulations that deal with product standards, research and development, labor standards, occupational health and safety, product safety, and environmental standards (McKeown 1999: 26–32).

The balance of power shifted to capital. Governments began to reduce labor-market regulations (Hall 1999: 153–154). Pressure came from the European Community to deregulate labor markets. Deregulation and privatization, in turn, accelerated the breakup of worker enclaves. Union memberships declined sharply in some countries. The openness of markets tended to change the relative position of the traded-goods sector vis-à-vis the nontraded-goods sector. The import-competing sectors contracted and the exporting-sector expanded. These changes have different impacts on subnational geographic regions, political parties, and unions. Cleavages developed between workers in the traded sector versus the nontraded and public sector. The former pressed for upgrading skills and wage differentials. The unskilled felt the pressure of low wages from the less-developed countries. At the same time, the wages of the skilled increased in the developed countries, thus producing wage inequality, increasing strains on worker solidarity. Then, new modes of production – "flexible, on-time delivery," "niche" producers – also had differential effects on labor (McKeown 1999: 12–17). As a result, solidaristic wage bargaining came under pressure, and broke down in many countries; peak-level bargaining was replaced by sector-level or firm-level bargaining (Hall 1999: 154–156).

In the service sector, there is the dynamic "high end" – business, finance, insurance, professional, managerial. Then, there are distributive services – wholesale, retail, transportation, which accompany mass consumption and transportation. The latter services are now stagnant. Most growth is in the social services – particularly health and caregiving. There is a huge demand for health care in all countries because of the growth in the aging population. There has been a significant expansion of these services in Scandinavia – welfare state employment now accounts for about 30 percent of total employment, which is about twice as large as in other countries (the usual range is between 15 and 20 percent). These services are both skill-intensive (e.g., doctors, nurses, teachers) and low-skill. It is the latter that explains why there are more low-skilled jobs in Denmark and Sweden than in the United States (Esping-Andersen 1999: 105–106).

There developed what is called the "service sector trilemma" – employment growth, wage equality, and budgetary constraint are increasingly in conflict (Hemerijck 2002). Creating more private service sector jobs means lower wage and non-wage costs, thus risking greater inequality. Creating public sector employment is limited by budgetary constraints. But doing neither means continuing, if not rising, unemployment. The service sector trilemma is "regime-specific": In the Scandinavian countries, there is a significant service sector, primarily public, primarily female. There is a minimal social exclusion caused by poverty and long-term unemployment. The problem is the high cost. There is resistance to further tax increases, and, as a result, public employment has fallen, creating a need for an increase in private sector jobs. Thus, the "hard choice [is] between liberalizing private services, which entails more wage inequality, or a continued adherence to wage equality which, under conditions of budget constraint, implies more unemployment" (Hemerijck 2002: 13). The Anglo-Saxon model (United Kingdom) sacrifices equality of income for jobs and budgetary restraint. There has been a radical decentralization of labor regulation. There has been a marked increase in wage inequality, female employment (but with gender inequities) primarily in poor quality, part-time work, and an increase in poverty and social exclusion. Wage subsidies have been introduced for low-income workers (Hemerijck 2002: 14). In the continental countries, high fixed labor costs inhibit the growth of private service jobs. The emphasis has been on productivity, but this creates a "vicious cycle of raising wages and exit of less productive workers," called the "inactivity trap," primarily affecting the young and women, especially mothers. Anton Hemerijck says that while all countries face the service sector trilemma in one form or the other, some countries (e.g., Denmark, the Netherlands) have managed to increase service jobs, maintained wage equality, full employment, and fiscal restraint (Hemerijck 2002: 15–16).

Western Europe lags behind the United States in employment growth. In the sheltered sector of the economy, in Europe, 39.2 percent of the working-age population is employed, as compared to

54.2 percent in the United States. It is claimed that employment is higher in the United States because wages are low and employment is more flexible, but job growth in the United States is not just confined to the low-skilled (Ferrera and Rhodes 2000: 10–11). The move toward a knowledge-based society is likely to exacerbate risks of social exclusion since job losses continue to be concentrated among those with less than a secondary education or lacking vocational qualifications. The average unemployment rate for the low-skilled is two to three times higher than for the high-skilled. Spells of unemployment for the low-skilled increase in both frequency and duration. Long-term unemployed become stigmatized by employers – a person out of work for more than a year is perceived as "unfit" for work (Ferrera and Rhodes 2000: 11).

While countries differ, there is a growing use of self-employed, subcontracting, outsourcing which may be responsive to the new economy, or used to evade labor regulations and reduce costs (Supiot 2001). It seems to be more important for the creation of new jobs in the service sector in Southern Europe, Germany, the Netherlands, and Denmark (Supiot 2001: 70). The wide range of self-employment makes it difficult to formulate a legal framework and the laws in some countries (e.g., Italy, Germany) are incomplete (Supiot 2001: 6–9). Subordination is changing. In some countries, workers have greater independence whereas in others, subordination is increasing (Supiot 2001: 7). Large firms establish stable cooperative relations with subcontractors. The subcontractors are technically or financially dependent. There are advances in greater on-the-job independence, new technologies, enhanced training, new participative management methods, etc. Pay is linked to results. Thus, a growing number of wage-earners work under conditions similar to the subcontracted self-employed. Here, subordination becomes internalized. Alain Supiot calls this a "refeudalization" of labor through the "culture of contract" (Supiot 2000: 321–345). The new forms of subordination are mostly in the new kinds of casualized employment, the shift in jobs from large to smaller-sized businesses, subcontracting, outsourcing, etc. In most EU countries, small (under 50) or very small (under 10) companies account for most jobs. The result is a growing heterogeneity of employee-employer relationships, which, in turn, promotes the fragmentation of labor law (Supiot 2001: 15).

Thus far, subcontracting is poorly handled in European legislation. Most labor law is ineffective even though the principal may control the subcontractor's employees leading some to propose using financial dependence instead of legal subordination (Supiot 2001: 13). The debate is most fully developed in Germany where it is argued that the guarantee of fundamental labor rights should be expanded. The Nuremberg Labour Court adopted financial dependence in a case involving an outsourced insurance employee (Supiot 2001: 148). In the Netherlands, a bill is under discussion which provides that unless an employer can prove otherwise, persons working under "conditions similar to those that characterize employment relations" are considered to be holders of employment contracts. There is a "rebuttable presumption of the existence of an employment contract." The aim is to guarantee equivalent protection (Supiot 2001: 34–48).

Some countries (Denmark, the Netherlands, Portugal, northern Italy, southern Germany, and Austria) have combined high levels of new forms of labor protection with low and decreasing unemployment and vigorous economies. At the same time, in the United Kingdom, there is no real evidence that easing hiring and firing produces growth in employment; other factors were largely responsible for the decline in unemployment. Female employment has grown because women are more willing to accept non-standard jobs (Estevez-Abe, Iversen, and Soskice 1999).[6] Even without legal restrictions, there has been no significant shift from permanent to temporary jobs. Most companies use temps to cover staffing when regular employees are sick, on holiday, or on maternity leave rather than increase their workforce (Supiot 2001: 45).

There are new forms of organizing work and the expansion of the service sector. In the United Kingdom, the Netherlands, and France, there is a move to extend retail and service hours, which is opposed by unions in France, Germany, and Belgium. At the same time, the normal work week is being questioned. There has been a rise in non-standard jobs, holding several jobs, and the black economy. While the percentage of shift workers has increased, overtime and partial unemployment still play the main role in flexibility. This in turn increases the pressure to change flexible working time – e.g., the annualization of the employment contract, or even abolition of the legal working week (Supiot 2001: 72).

There are different responses. In Germany, the services are highly professionalized. High labor costs reduce private social services, there

---

[6] Estevez-Abe argues that women are more likely to invest in general skills because of child care issues, and that they tend to avoid "male jobs" because they are viewed as less desirable workers because of maternity leave and other family responsibilities.

is low female participation because of the absence of child care services, and not much employment for laid-off industrial workers or less-qualified women. The German labor-market strategies are early retirement or unemployment for industrial workers and discouraging female employment. In Sweden, there has been a significant upgrading of skills but a strong polarization in service work. There are very high levels of female employment in public sector jobs which are often low-skilled. In the United States, there is skill polarization in both industry and services. The emphasis is on low-skilled jobs; thus, the United States (at least until recently) is able to absorb immigrants, women, and redundant industrial workers (Esping-Andersen 1990: 107–111). Most countries allow wages to keep pace with general wage developments. This risks pricing these services out of the market. For example, laundries are ubiquitous in the United States and practically non-existent in Copenhagen and Stockholm. All countries subsidize some services – e.g., health, education, cultural. The three basic approaches: Scandinavia – they are state welfare jobs; in the United States – they are marketized; on the Continent, they are basically familialized (Esping-Andersen 1999: 111–114).

There also may be an intensification of work or hidden work. In France, there is a growing tendency for companies to demand after-hour availability of employees with no legal recognition of such over-time. There are other abuses as well. In any event, concludes Supiot, labor law can no longer govern working time with homogeneous rules (Supiot 2001: 219).

What has been the effect of the changing labor markets and labor law on unions? Despite the variation among the European states, there is general agreement on the historic importance of the labor movement for the growth of the welfare states and the political success of the social democratic parties (Western 1995: 179–201). Significant changes are occurring with labor and industrial relations. However, there are differences of opinion as to what these changes mean for the state of unions in the various countries (compare Western supra with Goldin, Wallerstein, and Lange 1999: 194–230). First, we consider the changing demographics of the laborforce and how that is affecting unions; then, we turn to the changes that are taking place in industrial relations and unions.

As mentioned above, the major changes in the laborforce have been the massive entry of women, the contraction of the manufacturing sector, and the rise of the service sector. The result has been a shrinking of working-class males, which have been the core constituency of the European unions as well as the Social Democrats. Today, the labor-force is much more diverse – increasingly women, increasingly service, part-time, flexible, all of which means an increasing diversity of interests. The question is how well unions can respond to this diversity. If they cannot, then the capacity of the Social Democrats to appeal to these groups that historically have mistrusted unions will be weakened (Klausen 1999: 261–290).

One view is that the unions have not been responsive. A prominent example is gender bias in the workplace which, in turn, is linked to many important political issues. It is claimed that in most countries, unions are trying to protect their core constituency and not mobilizing the new workers in the new occupations. Thus, the Social Democrats view unions as preventing them from reaching new constituencies. In the United Kingdom, unions lost almost half of their manufacturing members; now women in the service sector are the most important sources of new members. In Germany, women are not inclined to join unions. Sweden is the exception; women are organized – in fact, more organized than men – and women dominate the white-collar unions. Unionization is higher in the public sector, thus raising a potential conflict between the sheltered and export sectors. In addition, as confederated collective bargaining has declined, wage differences have grown. Practically all part-time workers are women.

At first, the official union position was to oppose part-time work even though many women prefer the flexibility. Now, some unions are trying to organize part-time workers and have succeeded; but others still refuse to accept part-time work (e.g., Germany, Austria). With the exception of Scandinavia, there continue to be wage disparities (women are disproportionately in low-skilled jobs); women are overrepresented among the unemployed but receive lower amounts of compensation. Sweden has a 50 percent quota on women in union leadership; unions in other countries have discussed quotas. German unions continue to define women as "a weak partner in need of protection, rather than as a group of wage earners with specific demands." While men in the competitive market sector tend to resent increased welfare state expenditures and think the public sector is overprotected, unions still strongly support the welfare state (Klausen 1999).

Bruce Western, among others, argues that the 1980s witnessed the start of the decline in European trade unions, thus diminishing labor's ability to check the conservative assault on the traditional welfare state's labor policies. The current decline of unions reflects the loss of political power of workers in these countries. To be sure, there were significant variations among the countries in terms of the decline of unionization. And in some instances, union density has remained constant, and there has even been union expansion – for example, white-collar workers in Sweden. Western argues that the principal reasons for the decline were the decentralization of labor-market institutions, primarily industry-wide collective bargaining, and the decline of social democratic parties. As a result, the capacity of unions to coordinate and advance organizing efforts at the national level was limited. In the highly organized countries (e.g., Belgium, Denmark, Sweden), labor-market institutions were decentralized and national bargaining was abandoned. The patterns were mixed in other countries with moderate levels of unionization. Decentralized bargaining, says Western, weakens unions for the following reasons:

> (1) Centralized bargaining extends union wages to nonunion workers, defusing employer opposition to unions, whereas decentralized bargaining focuses employer resistance. (2) Employers can co-opt unorganized workers by offering comparable wages and benefits. (3) Confederations of unions have less influence over macroeconomic policy – for example, employers began to dominate corporatist regimes in Germany, the Netherlands, and Switzerland and favored controlling inflation over full-employment when union density began to decline. (4) Under decentralization, interunion rivalry increases, top level coordination declines, and resources are spent on jurisdictional controversies. In Sweden, for example, after decentralization, there was increased competition between blue and white-collar unions. (Western 1995: 179)

While unions could not bring about welfare states on their own – they had to form coalitions with the middle class – they were clearly of major importance. In sum, Western claims that de-industrialization and the increasing employment in the service sector, by itself, does not explain the "novel and universal decline of unions in the 1980s." Rather, he argues, the new development is the result of "a fundamental reorganization of labor-market institutions and the declining success of social democratic parties," that is, "the erosion of class as an organizing principle, embedded in state institutions and highly centralized labor-market institutions, has driven union decline."

Miriam Goldin and her colleagues argue that this view of the state of unionism in Western Europe is overdrawn (Goldin et al. 1999). There have been changes, principally in corporatist bargaining. Ten years ago, authority was concentrated in either a small number of large industrial unions or in national confederations, whereas currently there has been a great deal of decentralization in wage setting in many countries. This change had led observers to conclude that unions were in decline; they were viewed as weak, decentralized, and with little power to affect industrial relations. Two reasons are offered for the decline – the change in production to smaller, more specialized units, and the increased integration brought about by globalization. Both reasons, say the authors, imply "a *widespread* and *permanent* weakening of unions since the causes are supposedly impersonal and uncontrollable forces sweeping advanced countries." This would imply convergence among countries (Goldin et al. 1999). But in fact, in looking at eighteen different countries, the authors find considerable divergence and the absence of a general decline in unionism. The authors looked at four characteristics: (1) union density – the share of work belonging to unions; (2) union coverage – the share of work covered by union agreements; (3) union concentration; and (4) authority, or the levels of union and employer organizations. It is true that in the 1980s union density declined, in some countries by more than 10 percent. This was due, in part, to the weak demand for labor and could change if employment improves. On the other hand, looking over four decades, in fourteen of the eighteen countries, the levels of density were either stable or increased. In some of these countries, the unions control the unemployment funds.[7] The biggest declines have been in the United States, France, and Japan. Nevertheless, there are substantial differences between countries, even in the 1980s; the recent declines may be temporary, and differences, rather than convergence, have increased since the 1950s (Goldin et al. 1999).

The percentage of the workforce covered by union agreements also varies among countries. In most, the coverage remains very high and stable, with the exception of the United Kingdom, and it actually increased in France despite the decline in union membership. In fact, say Goldin and her colleagues, France shows that union coverage (92 percent) can be independent of union density (10 percent in 1989), although coverage is uniformly higher once union density exceeds a certain threshold – about 40 percent. In general, throughout Western

---

[7] Non-union members can still get unemployment, but the advantage of union membership is the ease of administration.

Europe, union coverage is uniformly high despite the diversity in rates of density. This is not to argue that the effectiveness of unions has not changed, but only to point out that their institutional role in wage bargaining has remained intact (Goldin et al. 1999).

On the other hand, over the four decades, concentration has declined in six of twelve countries – Norway, Sweden, Denmark, Finland, France, and Italy. In the four Nordic countries, the blue-collar unions lost ground to the white-collar and professional unions, reflecting the changes in the laborforce. In general, where density has increased, it usually has been outside of the traditional unions – for example, the white-collar and professional unions in the Nordic countries (Goldin et al. 1999). Goldin and her colleagues argue that similar variation across countries applies to what they call union "authority" – "the extent to which central organizations (unions, employers) exercise authority over lower levels." The extent of authority does not necessarily depend on labor regulation. For example, in Sweden, there has been substantial devolution in bargaining without any legal changes.

The authors conclude that despite considerable changes and pressures in industrial relations, unions, so far, have proved to be quite resilient. In fact, dramatic changes have only occurred in the United States and the United Kingdom where governments encouraged the attack on unions. In no other country have authority relations substantially changed. However, as Sweden shows, there could be substantial decentralization in wage-setting despite formal authority. They argue for skepticism as to all general explanations for why unions appear to be declining. The only real changes have been in union membership, and this may be due to high unemployment rather than institutional changes (Goldin et al. 1999).

On the other hand, there have been significant changes in the collective bargaining systems which have had different impacts. Huber and Stephens argue that corporatist arrangements will only work when unions are strong and the social democratic party is an active participant (Huber and Stephens 2001: 24). The worst case scenario, according to Esping-Andersen, is where organizations are strong but neither centralized nor coordinated; here, they will privilege the insiders as against the outsiders. On the other hand, where unions are weak, there will be a rise in wage inequalities (Esping-Andersen 1990: 120–122). These changes raise the question of "insiders" versus "outsiders," and the rise of vulnerable groups.

VULNERABLE GROUPS: THE SOCIALLY EXCLUDED

Insiders, outsiders. Cleavages in the working population arise from a number of different sources. In the Golden Age, with the male bread-winner, there were generous rights, high labor wages and costs, and extensive job protection which produced a divide between the "standard" family and other working people (Esping-Andersen 1990: 18).[8] Within the labor market, there is considerable tension between the insider workers (and their unions) and the "outsiders"; the former are more interested in preserving their privileges than helping the latter. Many of the strikes and demonstrations against changes in the welfare state are to preserve the positions of the insiders. In terms of voting trends, the conventional political cleavages are still alive, but they vary. In the Nordic countries, the Social Democrats have growing white-collar support, especially from women; on the other hand, private-sector males are anti-public sector and favor the Right. The same is true in other countries with private-sector males. On the Continent, the working-class remains with the Left. Thus, in general, support for the Social Democrats has remained stable, at least until recently.

Esping-Andersen sees three distinct cleavage trends: (1) the United States and the United Kingdom, with weak welfare states and weak unions, have a significantly polarized economic structure; (2) Scandinavia has so far prevented employment marginalization, but has a heavily gendered sectoral employment cleavage; and (3) Continental Western Europe is now deeply divided between the employed core (the insiders) and a growing mass of excluded, marginalized groups (Esping-Andersen 1990). He detects an ominous trend in class labels to depict the outsiders – in Denmark, the "A-team" and the "B-team," (the "losers"), and now the "C-team" (those who are completely marginalized); the Germans speak of "two-thirds of society"; in the United Kingdom, the new underclass is called the "socially excluded," a term which is now spreading to the rest of Europe; in France, "société a deux vitesses." In France, those who rely on social benefits are identified

[8] Sweden took a different path. It actively promoted women's employment and created the double-earner, dual-career family. However, an unintended side effect was unusually strong employment sex-segregation. Women are disproportionately public employees.

as "RMIstes" (the acronym for social assistance) and "SMICs" (legislated minimum pay); in the Netherlands, as "benefit drawers" (Esping-Andersen 1990).

The future, according to Esping-Andersen, looks more like the growth of less qualified, routine service jobs. Skilled workers are declining faster than the unskilled, and sluggish growth and high wage costs provide no employment opportunities for laid-off manual workers. In addition, lifetime employment is now being replaced by the risk of repeated unemployment.[9] The new professional classes are organizing, which may create class closure at the high end. Exclusion appears to be hardening among the outsiders. There are indications that the "B-team" may be more and more identified with the vulnerable groups – youth, female, immigrants, low-skilled (Esping-Andersen 1990). Esping-Andersen does not describe the "outsiders" as constituting a new social class. They may be too varied, too amorphous to be a collective force. On the other hand, says Esping-Andersen, if the marginalized continue to be blocked, Europe could see the "rebirth of Disraeli's Two Nations" rather than a pluralist society (Esping-Andersen 1990).

Lone-parent families. Mostly headed by women, who are more likely to be in part-time work and, with the exception of Sweden, are more vulnerable to poverty and dependency (Garfinkel and McLanahan 1986). While every country supports lone-parent families, the type, amount, and anti-poverty effects vary considerably depending on earnings and transfers (McFate, Smeeding, and Rainwater 1995). Most social policies toward lone mothers in Western Europe are still primarily concerned with children and gender equity, but there have been changes (McFate 1995: 12–13, 17). In Sweden, many important benefits are tied to work experience; consequently, there are strong incentives for women to establish a labor-market connection, and very high proportions do work. Nevertheless, despite the strong emphasis on gender equality, Swedish women are clustered in a small number of occupations, mostly in the public sector; a large proportion work part-time, and have lower wages than men, even across occupations. Sweden has generous leave provisions – for example, the universal public child support system if the father fails to pay – but these are becoming increasingly controversial. Over half of lone parents receive money from this source. Nevertheless, while there is debate, major changes are not expected that would

[9] Sweden, again, seems to be the exception.

undermine the laborforce participation of lone mothers in Sweden (Gustafsson 1995: 291–325).

In France, lone-parent families are rapidly acquiring the negative stereotype of "problem families." Since the mid-1970s, there has been a dramatic rise in unemployment, poverty, and social isolation among this group, especially those who lack educational qualifications and/or are of foreign origin (Lefaucher 1995).[10] Despite the pressure to enter the labor market, lone mothers have a hard time. In France, for example, even with the high laborforce participation of mothers, because of the high unemployment and the lower wages, only about 31 percent of lone mothers were actually working, and, of those under twenty-five years of age, more than half were unemployed. Lone mothers who are never married are more likely to be less educated, and trapped in low-wage jobs (Lefaucher 1995: 274).

Despite the pressures and trends, France and Sweden do a far better job in reducing poverty and minimizing dependency among lone-parent families than in the United States. At least as exemplified in these two countries, work and social assistance are structured so that they reinforce each other. In fact, a great deal of the difference in comparative well-being is due to the returns from work of lone parents in Sweden and France, combined with good child care policies – both parental leave and high-quality, subsidized institutional care are *the* most important of the work-related policies. Conditioning these benefits to work encourages laborforce participation. On the other hand, this might make these families more vulnerable to deteriorating labor markets (Garfinkel and McLanahan 1996: 373; Casper, Garfinkel, and McLanahan 1994: 594–605).[11]

Young adults. Probably the group most affected by the deteriorating labor markets are households headed by young adults. Young adults tend to have higher rates of unemployment and lower wages than the general workforce. Poverty rates among young adults and household heads under thirty years of age have increased in the past decade. The

---

[10] In France, family allowances (CAF), historically a significant addition to family income, are becoming less universal; about half of transfer income is now means-tested. The other lone-parent allowance (API), also means-tested, with a majority of recipients never married, is being attacked as a disincentive to labor-market participation and marriage. Recipients of API are accused of cheating, having more children to qualify for aid, and so forth.

[11] On the importance of work, as well as transfers, in reducing the gender-poverty gap, see Casper et al. (1994).

OECD reports that the average youth unemployment rate was 13 percent in 1998, an increase of 3 percent since 1979. In most countries, it is in double digits (OECD 1999: 7). In France, the unemployment rate for those under twenty-five years old is 27 percent (The Economist 1999); in Sweden, youth unemployment is twice the national average. According to the OECD, there is a "hard-core" of young people who experienced prolonged periods of joblessness, interspersed with spells of low-wage work. They have multiple disadvantages – poor families, unstable families, they live in high unemployment communities, they do poorly in school and often drop out (OECD 1999: 7). The inequalities within the youth population have increased considerably within some countries, especially for those with poor educational attainment. The employment problems are most severe for those who lack good educational credentials. The unemployment rate is almost twice as high for those without a high school diploma. Almost one-fifth of unemployed youth live in households where no one else is employed. On the other hand, more young people are in school and the proportion of dropouts has declined (OECD 1999: 7).

In previous labor markets, the higher youth unemployment represented the usual sorting out process as young people settled into more stable jobs. In general, there was usually always a transition period of labor market adjustments, when youths move from job to job and eventually settle down, although paths vary by country. In the United States and France, for example, there is a high turnover in the secondary labor markets but eventual stable employment, at least for most. Now, however, the transitions from school to steady work are becoming more problematic. In addition to the high levels of unemployment, the spells of unemployment and low-wage work are longer. Those who are unemployed tend to become stigmatized and less attractive to potential employers, thus increasing the chances of a more permanent marginalization (McFate, Smeeding, and Rainwater 1995: 41–42).

In Italy, unemployment is mainly a problem for the young. Although adults under thirty years of age account for less than one-third of the workforce, they account for three-quarters of the unemployed. The length and severity vary with education, gender, and residence. While even most of the most vulnerable (e.g., dropouts) eventually find employment, many fail to find stable employment by the time they are thirty years of age (Osterman 1995: 391–393).

In Germany, there is the apprenticeship system which connects the young person with a firm. In the 1980s, the German system ran into considerable problems. There was a sharp increase in unemployment, large firms cut back on training, and, at the same time, large numbers of youth entered the labor market. Then, the situation eased. There was a declining youth cohort, and small firms continued to use apprentices, primarily as a source of cheap labor. But then these young workers aged into the regular labor market, and, at least now, are facing difficulties. In Paul Osterman's view, German youth are marginalized more subtly by being "confined" to the youth sector, that is, disproportionately apprenticed in small firms as low-wage workers. When they "age out" as young adults, unemployment rates go up. In other words, the effect of the German apprenticeship system is to delay entry (Osterman 1995: 387–414). Furthermore, even with its extensive apprenticeship system, about 10 percent of the youth cohort is outside the system – the most disadvantaged in the German youth labor market. Some are males who want to earn money immediately; others are women who are pregnant, or dropouts, or "psychologically disadvantaged" (problems with employers), or "economically disadvantaged" (local labor markets). "Foreigners" (especially Turks and former Yugoslavians) are disproportionately represented in all of these categories. They are more likely to be dropouts, to be victims of discrimination, twice as likely to leave apprenticeships prematurely. The plight of young foreign workers has become a matter of real concern in Germany, although programs, to date, have been marginal and incremental (Casey 1995: 415–437). In other countries, the situation facing young workers is described as "catastrophic" (Osterman 1995: 388–389).

At the present time, there is considerable variation as to how much help to give to households headed by young workers. In the Netherlands, France, and the United Kingdom, transfer programs lift about half of these households out of poverty. This is true for only about one-quarter of the households in Germany (McFate 1995: 18). In Italy, there is very little government support for unemployed youth. Training programs are desultory; there is no focus on increasing demand (Miongione and Pugliese 2000: 445–456).

Immigrants. Most of Western Europe is experiencing large increases in immigrants. Embedded in the welfare state is the concept of community, of citizenship. However defined, it somehow draws boundaries around the rights of "social citizenship." The presence of large numbers of "strangers" – again, however defined – strains the welfare state. As Morone and Goggin put it:

> Distributive justice presupposes some kind of bounded world, within which social solidarity is evoked by some shared principle, a common civilization . . . a unifying communal principle. Whatever the underlying logic, welfare states are built on and extend the sense of a common social identity. They are most powerful when they become a kind of universal public good – all contribute, all are eligible. Today, immigration poses a challenge to the traditional welfare state logic by reconstituting the communities that sustain them. (Morone and Goggin 1995: 562)

In the period following World War II, in most of the Western European countries, foreign "guest" workers were initially invited in during the labor shortages of the 1960s and 1970s. Attempts at repatriation were largely unsuccessful and most stayed on. At first, the largest group of workers came from Eastern Europe; then, from the rural eastern Mediterranean and from former colonies. In the 1960s and 70s, there was a growing Muslim and Asian immigration, and since 1989, again from Eastern Europe. Immigration flows depended on developing networks. Consequently concentrations varied – Algerians in France; Turks and former Yugoslavs in Germany; West Indians and South Asians in the United Kingdom; Italians in Belgium and Germany (Gordon 1995: 521–542). The differences in circumstances raised different questions of citizenship. Ex-colonials, for example, had varying forms of citizenship, rights of residence, political participation, and social welfare. "Guest workers" had none of these rights, and other migrants were illegal (Gordon 1995: 521).

Over the years, the urban ethnic and racial minorities have experienced increased segregation, discrimination, and hostility. In the view of Jacqueline Bhabha, "racial violence, discriminatory police behavior, and ghettoization have become rampant throughout Europe" (Bhabha 1998: 592–627; Daly 2002: A9). Richard Falk says, "In a situation of growing rivalry for jobs, there emerges a tendency to draw ever sharper lines between citizens and resident non-citizens, deny the latter social protection and full access to opportunities for health, education, and other services" (Falk 2000: 6). Immigrant labor is not only poorer but also perceived as "outsiders," leading to employer stereotypes, the use of recruitment networks, the creation of internal labor markets, reinforcing racist ideologies. In addition to becoming increasingly vulnerable to exploitation because of their uncertain legal and social status, immigrants have been restricted to concentrated occupational niches, resulting in both exclusion and marginalization. The immigrant enclaves became increasingly vulnerable to the transfer of labor abroad and the abandonment of full-employment policies (Gordon 1995: 525).

Concentrated joblessness and poverty, in turn, have increased the barriers to occupational mobility of succeeding generations. Racial and ethnic youth suffer from educational and skill deficits, further exacerbating their ability to obtain even low-wage labor. The general labor market insecurity has weakened the effectiveness of anti-discrimination policies (Standing 1995: 163). More and more minorities are thus forced into the informal or illegal economy, with high risks of unemployment and poor working conditions, reinforcing negative stereotypes, hostility and discrimination, and a decline in public support for social assistance (Lawson and Wilson 1995: 707; McFate 1995: 14–15).

In all of the Western industrialized countries, the "minority problem" means high rates of unemployment and poverty (McFate 1995: 19). As more of the immigrants in the urban enclaves are becoming more marginalized and segregated economically, there is growing persistent joblessness, material deprivation, and ethno-racial tensions. "French society is changing, with a growing rift between underprivileged masses surviving on welfare . . . and a prosperous, highly qualified minority. The proliferation of gated communities in France is an illustration of this" (Belmessous 2002: 62). There is tension between immigrants and native minorities (Miongione and Pugliese 2000). There is mounting concern about the "new poverty" and "immigrant ghettos." The marginalized immigrants are acutely aware of their stigmatized residential status and their diminished life chances (Wacquant 1995: 543–570; Cohen 2000: A1). At the same time, at least in France, there is "compassion fatigue" on the part of majoritarian society towards helping the minorities. Interest groups are fragmenting, national solidarity is declining (Body-Gendrot 1995: 571–583). In part, this may be due to the media. Says Hacene Belmessous, "Television news often shows cars burning and the police pelted with bottles and stones, and always against the same background, a low-income housing estate, its walls daubed with graffiti. The immigrant youths are always the same, too, and always filmed in a certain kind of action . . . under police protection" (Belmessous 2002: 63).

The effects of the presence of immigrants vary in terms of numbers as well as political response. While relatively small (at least by US standards) in several countries, nevertheless their presence provokes bitter charges of welfare fraud and crime. Those who favor markets applaud the open borders and the movement of labor. Others worry about the dilution of culture. The Left is concerned about jobs and social welfare, while others focus on human rights. These divisions cut across class lines, fractionalizing and ultimately weakening labor, responding to both right-wing attacks and mutually suspicious factions. Welfare becomes more problematic when identified with particular racial and ethnic groups. At the same time, given the demographic changes, it is argued that if Western Europe wants to maintain the ratio of older people to active workers, it will need 135 million immigrants by 2025 (Crossetts 2000). The racial and ethnic divisions in Europe have resulted in what Gary Freeman calls the "Americanization of European welfare politics" (Morone and Goggin 1995: 562–564).

There has been a rise of right-wing, anti-immigration political parties all over Europe – from Scandinavia to Spain. Europeans are worried about terrorism, the economy, their employment prospects, crime – all feeding into a backlash against open borders. In Germany, a hardline conservative, Edmund Stoiber, mounted a significant challenge to Chancellor Schröder in the re-election campaign. In Hamburg, a "fiercly conservative" local judge gained 20 percent of the vote. New conservative parties are making inroads in Denmark, the Netherlands, and Scandinavia. In Denmark, the anti-immigrant party is now the country's third largest party, doubling its seats in the parliament. In the Netherlands, the new party is called Livable Netherlands, and is sharply critical of immigration. A center-right government has taken over (Erlanger 2002a: A3). On the other hand, France's new government, reacting to the "excessive administrative zeal" of the previous administration (see, e.g., Maschino 2002: 44–53), is trying to strike a more balanced immigration policy (The Economist 2002c: 53).

The socially excluded. Of increasing concern are the most marginalized, those who are out of the regular labor market for the long term, now referred to as the "socially excluded" (Littlewood and Herkommer 1999: 1). The term is vague and can cover a variety of deviant social behaviors that are "beyond" economic behavior (Paugam 1998; Procacci 1998; Tsakloglou and Papadopoulos 2002: 211–225). Giovanna Procacci says, "'social exclusion' (as with the 'underclass') has come to identify all the problems of poverty with extreme poverty. Despite the diversity among the poor and the dependent, the concept is totally negative. This is a group that is apart from society." In her view, there is a connection between the concept of exclusion and the disappearance of the class struggle. "For while exclusion places the prob-lem 'outside society,' inequality inevitably raises the problematic issue of the attainment of equality . . . [E]xclusion focuses on the identifica-tion of typologies at the expense of the dynamic described by the class struggle" (Procacci 1998: 74). Anthony Atkinson says that "exclusion is both a *state* and a *process*." The reasons why a person is unemployed become as important as the fact of unemployment (Atkinson 1998: 69), but concepts such as the "underclass" and "social exclusion" turn pol-icy towards individual behaviors rather than structural reforms. There is an "army of low-skilled, marginal workers," a divide between the insid-ers and the outsiders. Unemployment, it is felt, leads to social isolation and estrangement. "It is an exclusion from consumption which leads to a weakening of social ties. Thus, an important conclusion is that avoiding poverty through transfers alone does not necessarily lead to social inclusion as long as the person is excluded from the labor market. Similarly, a worker can still be socially excluded if still in poverty" (Atkinson 1998).

Whether "social exclusion" is a class is subject to debate. Some claim that it describes a diverse set of the population which often has little in common (Paugam 1998: 41–62.) It encompasses a number of problems that may not be included in poverty – for example, divorce, separation, suburban strife, etc. "[A]n exclusion perspective combines economic and social problems, material and symbolic relations, distributional conflicts and identity politics, class and status order, social rights and human rights" (Silver 1998b: 2; Silver and Miller 2002: 1–14). It now refers to the large numbers of people increasingly dependent on social welfare. In France, for example, there are many marginalized, unem-ployed groups, living in rundown suburbs, and living on social benefits (the minimum RMI); they are both visible and stigmatized. According to Serge Paugam, the label "socially excluded" disguises the great diver-sity among this population as well as the process of social exclusion. For example, extreme deprivation is not necessarily irreversible. Poverty, it-self, can be "integrated," "marginal," or "disabling." "Different countries have different views of poverty – in Germany, and Scandinavia there is, essentially, denial; in the United Kingdom, moral fault; and in France, solidarity" (Paugam 1998; Whelan, Layte, and Maitre 2002: 91–105).[12] In the United States, there was the transformation of poverty into the

---

[12] Whelan et al. (2002) argue that there is no necessary connection between "persistent poverty and multiple deprivation."

"underclass, from structural causes to behavioral deficiencies. Poverty began to be measured in terms of the problems that produce the underclass – sexuality, family breakdown, dependency, criminality, drug abuse, etc. The underclass itself becomes the problem rather than the causes of poverty" (Procacci 1998: 63–78). However broad and various the meanings, the term has become increasingly prominent in the European countries as well as the EU itself (Littlewood and Herkommer 1999: 1–2).

The similarities between the underclass and social exclusion have come to dominate the research on poverty and social problems in Europe and the EU. The tendency is to identify all problems of poverty with *extreme* poverty. Because of the increase in inequality, social polarization, and the realization, in the 1980s, that the unemployment crisis was not a passing phase, the "exclusion from work" became the center of the relationship between society and the poor. According to Procacci, the concept is purely negative – a group apart, marginal, and separated from the rest of society. "This is not a new proletariat, there is nothing positive, they are simply outsiders. The focus is on individuals rather than collective identities, on behavior – as in the US. This transforms a process into a condition. Not only are these people separated from society but also from the processes that are responsible for their exclusion" (Procacci 1998). "Exclusion, thus, places the problem outside society. Thus, the rise of the concept of exclusion is linked to the disappearance of the class struggle, a refusal to recognize the collective nature of the problems that affect the poor. Instead, the focus is on individual rehabilitation. Inequality is then no longer a social problem. Poverty is reduced to the condition of the marginal minorities. And this accounts for the success of the idea of social exclusion – its 'social neutrality and pseudoscientific garb.'" Procacci warns that concepts such as underclass and social exclusion risk endorsing the isolation of the problem (Procacci 1998).

Class is usually defined in terms of common interests. Jon Elster, for example, defines class as "a group of people who by virtue of what they possess are compelled to engage in the same activities if they want to make the best use of their endowments" (Elster 1985: 330–331). Huber and Stephens's definition of class "excludes people without connection to the process of production . . . [B]ecause it lacks skills and connection to the process of production, it also lacks organization and power and thus is acted upon rather than being an actor in shaping the welfare state" (Huber and Stephens 2001: 18–19; Ormerod 1998: 23–40).

The socially excluded, in Ralf Dahrendorf's view, are the most tangible evidence of the loss of entitlements in the 1980s in Western Europe. The long-term unemployed, and the persistently poor disadvantaged ethnic groups, the uneducated and unskilled, the disabled – those who have fallen through the safety net – have lost access to labor markets, to the political community, and to networks of social relations. "The underclass," he says, "is, technically, not a class. Classes are conflict groups based on common interests. Because there is a mutual dependency among the members, a class generates and presses for its own solutions. In contrast, the 'underclass' is a mere category; it is a victim. While the victims have similar interests, they are not common interests. Self-organization is unlikely. If change comes about, it will be through outside agents or changes in values" (Dahrendorf 1994).

POVERTY

As in the United States, poverty in Western Europe is dynamic – many of the poor have short spells, with adequate incomes over the longer term; others experience persistent poverty. This is due more to changes in employment than the family (OECD 2001: 37). The OECD takes a somewhat optimistic view. Given the changes in the economies, and in particular, unemployment, there have been changes in poverty in the expected directions but they are modest, certainly as compared to the United States (OECD 2001: 39). However, the number of persons living in households with under 40 percent of average income was higher in 1999–2000 than in 1996–97 (Bennett 2002: 505–536). There has been a dispersion in earnings, inequalities have grown among the working-age population, the younger age (18–25) group has lost ground, youth and child poverty has increased in some countries, and the income position of single parents and persons in workless households has declined. The main cause of poverty is unemployment, especially for the young and single-parent families. The risks of poverty increase with female-headed households, the young, not finishing upper secondary schooling, or where no adult is employed (OECD 2001: 39). On the other hand, taxes and transfers have mitigated these effects to a considerable extent both for poverty spells and intensity, again especially for the working poor (Förster 2000; OECD 2001: 37).

Table 3.1 *Poverty rates, 1993–95 (OECD 2001: 45)*[a]

	Annual poverty	Permanent-income poverty
Belgium	9.8	5.2
Denmark	4.7	1.8
France	9.6	6.6
Germany	12.1	8.1
Ireland	8.2	5.3
Netherlands	7.8	4.5
United Kingdom	12.1	6.5
ECHIP average[b]	11.7	7.9
United States[c]	16.0	14.5

[a] Several more countries are included in the OECD table.
[b] European Community Household Panel.
[c] 1987–89.

Although there is variation among the countries, the poverty line in Western Europe is higher than the United States – one-half the median income. The annual poverty and "permanent-income poverty" rates are as shown in Table 3.1.

In Western Europe, except for the United Kingdom, Huber and Stephens conclude, "perhaps what is most impressive . . . for all countries . . . is how little the retrenchment and particularly the large increases in unemployment in the 1980s and 1990s have affected the levels of poverty and income distributions, which is a tribute to the effectiveness of the social safety nets in these countries" (Huber and Stephens 2001: 300; see also Castles 2002: 613–641). Interestingly, the picture in the mid-1990s is fairly similar to what Lee Rainwater described a decade earlier (Rainwater 1995).[13]

Others present a more somber picture, especially for the vulnerable groups (Atkinson 1998; Sainsbury and Morissens 2002: 307–327). The European Council of Ministers (1984) defined poverty in terms of "persons whose resources (material, cultural, and social) are so limited as to exclude them from the minimum acceptable way of life in the Member State in which they live." This definition addresses the issue of social exclusion. Using one-half the average income of member states, the EC estimated that 36.8 million were poor in 1975. Poverty

[13] In the late 1980s, the poverty rates were as follows: Italy 21.1; Spain 16.9; United Kingdom 14.8; France 14.7; West Germany 10.9; Netherlands 4.8; Denmark 3.9.

increased to 44 million in 1985, to 57 million in 1997 (using expenditures rather than income as an indicator of resources) (Atkinson 1998).[14] While poverty rates are higher in Southern Europe, two-thirds of the poor live in France, Italy, West Germany, and the United Kingdom. In several countries, a significant minority of the population is below the minimum level considered necessary to avoid social exclusion (Atkinson 1998).

Unemployment is increasing poverty. Either there are no transfers to the unemployed or insufficient transfers. According to Atkinson, even with firmly-based welfare states, the replacement rate (the ratio of unemployment and other benefits to post-tax income when previously employed) is substantially less than 100 percent. For example, in Germany, the unemployment benefit rate as a percentage of net earnings varies from 67 percent for those with children to 53 percent for those without children. The same is true for a number of European countries (Atkinson 1998).

Poverty statistics look at income. There are other ways of looking at the poor. Susan Mayer compares living conditions among countries – housing amenities (ownership, number of people per room, health and access to medical care, and consumer durables) (Mayer 1995: 109–151; Layte, Nolan, and Whelan 2000). She finds that although there are more poor people in the United States, and they are poorer than in other countries, they are not more likely to live with more material deprivation than the poor in other countries. The big exception, she finds, is with US African-Americans who live in much worse conditions than other US poor and the poor in other countries. They are much more likely to live in crowded housing, lack a complete bathroom and kitchen, and so forth. The reason she gives is that poor US African-Americans are much more likely to remain poor for longer periods of time than US poor whites or the poor in other countries. The lack of mobility of poor US African-Americans is also documented by Greg Duncan and associates (Duncan et al. 1995: 67–108). While, in general, they find a "remarkable amount of mobility" among the poor in all countries, except the United States and Canada, this depends on the fractions of the populations in poverty – the larger the fractions, the lower the escapes from persistent poverty. With the United States, the big difference is with African-Americans.

---

[14] The reports are the *Interim Report on the Second European Poverty Programme* (EC 1989), *Final Report on the Second Programme* (1985), and the *Eurostate* study (1997).

In sum, in all of these countries, there is an aging population, rising unemployment, especially among minorities and immigrants, and a growing number of lone parent households with limited earnings capacity (McFate 1995). The concentration of the unemployed among the least skilled and the increase in the long-term unemployed have led some observers to conclude that persistent high unemployment in Western Europe is "structural," that is, job loss is caused by technology and the ability of firms to locate labor-intensive work to cheap labor markets. Moreover, when firms who have shed workers rehire, they are more likely to hire less-skilled workers (McFate 1995: 6). Thus, even if unemployment is reduced, prosperity will not necessarily return. There are growing numbers of people who suffer long spells of joblessness or jobs that offer little security (McFate 1995: 8–9).

The result of these trends is that Western Europe is beginning to resemble the United States. Poverty is growing, and is disproportionately among the young, the less-educated, and racial and ethnic minorities. Racial and ethnic lines are hardening; there is a rising xenophobia and racism. According to Lawson and Wilson, people of color are not only suffering from material deprivation, they are also losing social status and moral dignity. They are entitled to social benefits, but the benefits are increasingly means-tested and administered grudgingly. While European minorities have not experienced the concentration, poverty, and segregation that is the experience of African-Americans in the United States, Lawson and Wilson think that the trends are in the direction of US-style ghettos. It is becoming increasingly difficult to sustain the more universal, integrative social programs in the face of the marginalizing tendencies of mass unemployment, the fragmentation of labor markets, and a means-tested welfare state. Citizenship is now being actively debated in terms of race, ethnicity, and cultural diversity (Lawson and Wilson 1995: 693–715; Bhabha 1998: 596).

The economies in some countries are recovering, but, on the whole, projections are mixed. Some countries (e.g., Sweden) are expected to continue a strong recovery; others (e.g., the United Kingdom) will probably experience no growth. France, for a while, experienced some gains and unemployment dropped below 10 percent. More recently, however, the economy seems to be slowing again. Germany, too, has suffered a setback. Recently, unemployment rose sharply, from 9.6 percent to 10.4 percent (Erlanger 2002b: A8). For the past eight years, the German economy has been the slowest in growth in the EU (The

Economist 2002d: 3–4). And now the deficit has exceeded the EMU limits (Andrews 2002: 5). Some attribute the slowdown to the US and global recession. Esping-Andersen, as well as others, however, thinks that the impact of the global economy has been exaggerated. He notes that several countries with very open economies also managed to have high employment – the Netherlands, Austria, Norway, and Denmark. Moreover, these countries have strong welfare states. As mentioned, he believes that changes in the household may have a more significant impact on national economies (Esping-Andersen 1990: 96–97; Huber and Stephens 2001: 223–241).

While transfers reduce poverty, all agree that the most important factor is income from employment. Here, the picture in Western Europe remains somber. Even with the improvements in the economy, as stated, unemployment is expected to remain a serious economic and social problem (OECD 1999: 15, 18, 19). What is particularly significant has been the growth of part-time jobs in most countries (southern Europe is the exception). Between 1987 and 1997, the growth of part-time employment was as important to the total employment as full-time employment. As discussed, although there is considerable variation both within and among countries, in general, part-time workers are paid less than full-time workers (the figures are lower for men than for women), benefits are lower, the differences in pay are smaller in those occupations which are low-paid for all workers (this may be due to the effects of the minimum wage), tenure is usually shorter, and part-time workers receive less training (even controlling for lower educational attainment). Most part-time workers prefer part-time to full-time; and less than half say that they are working part-time because they cannot find full-time work (OECD 1999: 21–26). There is a gender difference: men working part-time would prefer full-time (with the exception of Spain); women prefer part-time, and the higher the proportion of women who work part-time, the higher the proportion who prefer part-time. For example, in the Netherlands, where 65 percent of women work part-time, only 7 percent say they would prefer full-time, whereas in Italy, where 12 percent work part-time, 42 percent would prefer full-time (OECD 1999: 15, 18, 32). In France, 69 percent of men and 35 percent of women part-timers would prefer full-time. In Germany, 52 percent of men and 12 percent of women would prefer full-time. When asked why they are working part-time, 41 percent in France say because they cannot find a full-time job; these proportions have also increased in Germany and the Netherlands (OECD 1999: 15, 18, 33–34).

There are also variations between men and women and among the countries concerning the transitions from part-time to full-time. Generally, more men and workers who are younger and better educated and skilled move to full-time jobs. There is little movement in the Netherlands, Germany, France, and the United Kingdom. In sum, part-time work represents a growing share of employment in many European countries. Because of the differences in pay, benefits, and training, this raises significant policy issues for the high proportion of households where there is only a single adult where Social Security and pensions depend on lifetime earnings (OECD 1999: 34–35).

RIGHT, CENTER, AND LEFT: QUESTIONING THE WELFARE STATE

By the 1980s, the Keynesian commitment to full employment, as well as the corporatist regulatory framework, gave way to a new faith in the market (Mancur 1995: 22). Inflationary pressures, the globalization of labor, deindustrialization, technological change, and the fiscal crises among the various states, led the "economic establishment" – OECD, IMF, the World Bank – as well as most European policy-makers to argue that high taxes and interest rates impeded private investment and growth. It was argued that institutional approaches such as protective regulations and progressive redistribution, result in labor "rigidities" impeding employment flexibility, competition, and growth.[15] Global competition and new technology required "flexible" labor policies, both internally and externally. Labor rights were now considered "costs" or "burdens on business." Most significant was the rejection of public responsibility for full employment in favor of a "natural" rate. This meant the abandonment of policies to increase aggregate demand or the supply of jobs.

Huber and Stephens say that the rise of international neoliberal ideology contributed to the idea of retrenchment and the narrowing of partisan, political differences. The congruence of this ideology with the interests of capital, in turn, strengthened the influence of capital in dealing with governments and unions. Restraints on welfare policies were thus legitimized to the public at large (Huber and Stephens 2001:

---

[15] For a collection of essays arguing this position, see Esping-Andersen and Regini (2002). For an argument that this analysis is too overdrawn, and that while some provisions result in unemployment, others do not, see Nickell (1997).

240). Thus, the most significant welfare state cuts were, in the opinion of Huber and Stephens, driven by unemployment – "they were a pragmatic response to greatly rising burdens on welfare state programs and declining contributions to these programs from the working population" (Huber and Stephens 2001: 219). According to Guy Standing, it was this new market paradigm that contributed to the fragmentation of labor – "the worst legacy of the 1980s" (Standing 1995: 47–60; 153).

Paul Teague refers to the change in policies for unemployment as the New Keynesianism (Teague 1999: 110). Instead of wages, employment, and unemployment being able to be manipulated directly by expansionary monetary and fiscal policies, the New Keynesianism argues that labor market institutions in the wage bargaining process have a considerable influence on the level of unemployment. Trade unions, for example, can either contribute to disequilibrium or assist in its reduction. The historic example is highly centralized wage bargaining which can assist in job creation by balancing the trade-off between wage increases, inflation, and unemployment (Teague 1999: 110–112). As will be discussed, this approach seems to have been successful in some countries (e.g., the Netherlands) but in other countries, employers have abandoned centralized collective bargaining and unions have declined. Active fiscal and monetary policies are not only constrained by government deficits but also as threats to inflation. There has also been a growing concern with what is called "mismatch unemployment." This can be caused by the changing nature of the economy, but also by labor market institutions – that is, employee benefits may encourage employers to be more selective in hiring. These ideas would lend support for active labor market policies, including lessening the restrictions on more flexible labor, rather than traditional Keynesian policies (Teague 1999: 113–116).

The welfare state came under increasing attack. Europeans began to wonder: Has the welfare state become too generous? Are people losing their willingness to work? As Assar Lindbeck put it:

> The basic dilemma of the welfare state . . . is that the more generous the benefits, the greater will be not only the tax distortions but also, because of moral hazard and benefit cheating, the number of beneficiaries. This is a field where Say's law certainly holds in the long run: the supply of benefits creates its own demand. Indeed, moral hazard and cheating are, in my judgment, the weakest spots of the welfare state. (Lindbeck 1995: 9–10)

Lindbeck argued that a generous welfare state is only sustainable when the economy is healthy – high productivity and employment. Neither tax increases nor budget deficits could be used to finance the demands of the welfare state. The argument was made that countries can no longer afford the generous welfare state (Taylor-Goodby 1996: 116–126). Generous social benefits have made labor too costly, thus preventing job growth. There was the feeling, at least among many at the policy and financial levels, that somehow a generous social welfare state is no longer feasible for the global economies in the twenty-first century (McFate 1995).

The "cause" of the current crisis of the European welfare states varied with ideology. But the main cause – or at least the most influential arguments – was the incompatibility between economic growth and welfare state spending and regulation. European integration, economic globalization, and worldwide rising unemployment not only strained the individual state welfare programs but increased the demands for deregulation and retrenchment (Morone and Goggin 1995: 558–569). In Germany, employers increasingly complained about the burdens of indirect wages (Hinrichs 1995: 660). Germany began to question all aspects of its collaborative system – trade unions and corporate leaders on works councils – its banking policies, as well as its extensive labor market regulations (Powell 1996: 44–45). The idea was spreading that employment protection was impeding the growth of employment; that what was called for was new managerial strategies, "flexible production," cutting "non-wage" labor costs, all to meet the challenge of global competitiveness (Standing 1995: 164). In the Netherlands, Dutch employers became very much opposed to government interference on the demand side and began to prefer Eastern European workers over ethnic minorities (Veenman 1995: 607–628). Europeans were impressed by the growth in US jobs. Increasingly, there was the call in Western Europe for low wages and a "flexible" workforce (Freeman 1995: 16). There developed very little support for expanding welfare state benefits that are not tied to labor-market activity (Morone and Goggin 1995: 563–565).

Changes were made in the welfare states. The proportion of the unemployed who qualify for insurance has declined. The young and the new entrants – including both immigrants and returning mothers – often do not qualify, and the long-term unemployed exhaust eligibility. Those who do not receive unemployment benefits have to go to the next tier of social assistance, which is means-tested, less generous, often stigmatizing, and usually only available when claimants have exhausted their savings and assets (McFate 1995: 6–7). In general, the disentitlement to state transfers has increased. While the higher income groups have improved their position, the share of workers receiving work-related benefits has declined, especially with the increase in small firm and service employment (Standing 1995: 178–179).

At the same time, there has been significant resistance to change. The politics of welfare state retrenchment are different from those of welfare state expansion (Huber and Stephens 2001: 240; Pierson 1996: 143–179). In all of these countries (with the exception of the United Kingdom), broad coalitions resisted changes in the welfare state (Huber and Stephens 2001: 240). Proposed changes produced the sharpest conflicts and protest demonstrations in France and Germany in twenty years. After introducing its austerity plan, the French conservative government was resoundingly defeated at the polls four years after an overwhelming election victory (Pierson 2001a: 1).

The major part of welfare state expenditures are in pensions and health care, and these two areas provide significant political support for the welfare state which limits the possibilities for reform (Pierson 2001b: 410–456; The Economist 2002e: 41). Large numbers of the electorate rely on the welfare state for a significant portion of their income and "it is one of the basic axioms of political science that concentrated interests will generally be advantaged over diffuse ones" (Pierson 2001a). In addition to defending the status quo, voters usually react more intensively to a potential loss than to a potential gain. Then, there is what Paul Pierson calls institutional "stickiness." In most countries, there are formal and informal institutional "veto points." Minorities can block reforms. Institutional structures and other vested interests have a stake in the status quo. In practically all the countries, politicians have been unable to implement significant changes in the welfare state. Public support, the intensity of the current recipients, bureaucrats, employers have adapted to existing arrangements. This does not mean that change cannot come about, only that it is "bounded change." Thus, in Pierson's now famous phrase, this is "what happens when the irresistible forces of post-industrialism meet the immovable object of the welfare state" (Pierson 2001a).

Thus, despite the pressures for austerity, basically, the welfare states in fifteen OECD countries have remained largely intact – as measured by revenues as a percentage of GDP (Ferrera et al. 2002a). Transfer spending fell in only seven countries, and by relatively modest amounts.

Given the very large increases in unemployment in the 1980s and 1990s, the levels of poverty and income distributions were not affected that much, attesting to the effectiveness of the social safety nets in these countries (Huber and Stephens 2001: 230). Sickness benefits, disability pensions, and unemployment compensation experienced the major cuts; pensions remained largely protected (Huber and Stephens 2001: 302). Thus, argue Ferrera, Hemerijck, and Rhodes, support for welfare states remains high. Despite the predications, the authors say that there is hardly a "neo-lib" convergence (Ferrera et al. 2002: 2). Despite the supposed incompatibility between employment protection legislation and labor-market flexibility, there has not been much rolling back in this area (OECD 1999). Over the past ten years, many countries have liberalized significantly the regulation of temporary employment, but other protections, by and large, remain in place (OECD 1999: 88). At this time, it is hard to know how far European countries are willing to go.

The first response to these dilemmas came from the conservatives. In the United Kingdom, the conservative government, under Margaret Thatcher (elected in 1979), immediately tagged the unions as the scapegoat for all that was excessive in the welfare state. The government outlawed secondary picketing, weakened the closed shop, made membership more voluntary, and eliminated legal immunity. Union membership declined, weakening the Labour Party (Desmond and Wood 1999: 371–397). In the meantime, the Thatcher Government switched from trying to achieve full employment to reducing inflation, primarily by limiting public expenditure, controlling the rate of monetary growth, cutting public-sector expenditures, lowering interest rates and tax rates. There was a dramatic rise in unemployment, but voters were more concerned about inflation. Assistance was provided to firms to reduce production costs. The government promoted low-skilled flexibility in employment. Rights of part-time workers were reduced. Inflation was reduced. Unemployment benefits were shifted from providing security to emphasizing re-entry into the labor market. The unemployed under twenty-one were required to participate in youth training schemes, which in part consisted of supplying firms with temporary, low-cost labor – the British version of "workfare." The work requirement was extended to all the unemployed under the Major government collectively. There was a systematic shift towards labor deregulation (Desmond and Wood 1999).

The Thatcher Government was re-elected in a landslide (1983), helped no doubt by the Falklands war. Unemployment was largely in safe Labour seats, and the Social Democratic Party split the opposition. In fact, government expenditures increased during the first five years of Thatcher's government due mainly to the recession and unemployment, defense, and law and order. On the other hand, direct taxes were cut. Dismantling of the public sector had the effect of moderating wages in the sheltered part of the economy. The government was also helped by North Sea oil, the sale of council housing, and privatization (Desmond and Wood 1999). Extensive privatization reduced pressure for taxes and limited the ability of future Labour governments to re-establish these constituencies. The sale of council housing, for example, not only eliminated public sector unions, but served to establish "popular capitalism" which resonated among the upwardly mobile lower middle class who then voted Conservative. Both central and local governments were streamlined, independent agencies were created, areas of local responsibility were shifted from elected local officials to unelected, centrally-appointed, quasi-nongovernmental organizations ("quangos"). Market mechanisms were introduced in various government functions (e.g., trash collection, road maintenance) (Desmond and Wood 1999).

On the Continent, in most countries, the Christian Democrats were in office during the decades immediately following the Golden Age. They could not respond to the changing economic and social conditions (van Kersbergen 1999: 346–370). As distinguished from the United Kingdom, they were ready to moderate the harmful outcomes of the market and would support compensation for the loss of earnings but opposed financing a welfare state solely through taxation and providing flat-rate benefits. Instead, they promoted social insurance. Distributive justice meant that each class received its due, to preserve social status and the family. The Social Security system remained gendered – it was based on the "natural gender role of men and women" (van Kersbergen 1999). These policies soon reached their limits. While countries varied in terms of economic growth, budget deficits, and welfare cutbacks, the big problem was significant unemployment. Because the corporatist, transfer-oriented policies could no longer deliver, controversies over welfare spending intensified. "The Christian Democratic concept of the welfare state was exhausted" (van Kersbergen 1999). The reaction to the conservative failure was a sea-change in Western European politics.

The voters rejected the arguments of the financial establishment conservatives. The Left assumed power or shares of power in thirteen of the fifteen governments in the European Union.

THE "THIRD WAY": FROM STATUS TO CONTRACT

As with just about every issue in this period of rapid change, there is a difference of opinion as to whether the new Social Democratic governments represented a significant change in policy. Tony Blair's minister for welfare reform declared that the current conditions have undermined the post-war welfare settlement. Changing patterns of work and family life have challenged the traditional assumptions of Social Security (Driver 1998: 567–568). Anthony Giddens, Blair's favorite academic, in his book, *The Third Way: The Renewal of Social Democracy*, drew inspiration not even from the Clinton Democrats, but from Ronald Reagan, quoting: "we have let government take away those things that were once ours to do voluntarily" (Giddens 1998: 112; Przeworski 1999). He adds a moral tone to liberal capitalism, arguing that "no rights without responsibilities" should become a "prime motto for the new politics." According to Giddens, "no-one any longer has any alternatives to capitalism" (Giddens 1998). "Equality" is redefined by Giddens "to mean the redistribution of possibilities – through policies of social inclusion and investment in education – rather than the redistribution of income" (Klein and Rafferty 1999: 48). The state should help only those who are willing to help themselves; to assure the unemployed without requiring them to look for work would encourage them to be lazy (Przeworski 1999). "[G]overnment will tilt right rather than left when it confronts the question of what to do about employment" (Ryan 1999: 80). At a Labour Party conference, Blair proudly proclaimed the Third Way as "pro-business and pro-enterprise." Alan Ryan says that the old class structure is gone; "middle England" is now more worried about pensions, taxes, education, crime, and civility, thus, much closer to the US electorate (Ryan 1999). Echoing Bill Clinton, there is to be a "radical change" in the "culture of the benefits system" as New Labour's version of "workfare" was introduced. Employment is considered the key to welfare reform. All welfare recipients, including the disabled, must seek work, as will be discussed in the next chapter (Walker 1998: 533–542).

Blair's "Third Way" New Labour budget modestly shifted funds to health and education and work-and-training programs for the young and long-term unemployed (although there is no guarantee of a job, it is credited with substantially reducing youth unemployment). Programs were started to regenerate disadvantaged housing estates, schools, and communities. A Social Exclusion Unit was created charged with devising policies to avoid producing a US-style underclass (Klein and Rafferty 1999).[16] On the other hand, at the heart of the Third Way is controlling inflation; both parties are united on this (Driver 1998: 567–569). Control over interest rates was handed over to the Bank of England, overall spending limits have been imposed, benefits were cut for single parents and the disabled, education fees have been increased. It is claimed that the government encourages illiberal sentiments on crime, sex, and immigration. And privatization has continued.

Jonah Levy thinks the Jospin government in France tried to reverse the direction of welfare reform. Whereas the prior governments attempted to reign in public spending and balance the budget by raising taxes on wage-earners rather than capital, Jospin tried to redistribute income toward the poor without increasing public spending by taxing the rich and otherwise redirecting policies to the left. Jospin's political rhetoric emphasizes the "third way," a "moderate center" (Levy 2001).[17] During the campaign, there was the promise to create 350,000 public-sector jobs for the unemployed youth and, over strong opposition from employers, to reduce the work week to thirty-five hours without loss of pay by the year 2000 for all companies with more than twenty workers and for the rest by 2002. Bensaid has a less sanguine view. He says that "the Jospin government produced a series of U-turns and backsliding on its already modest electoral promises." He notes, among other things, the abandonment of a "progressive tax revolution," the acceleration of privatization and the dismantling of public services, undermining the

---

[16] According to Alan Ryan (1999), what Americans think about Blacks, unemployable young males, and teen moms, etc., is what Brits think about uneducated working-class boys and uneducated working-class teen girls.

[17] According to Levy (2000), examples of change include reforming family allowances and the child income tax credit, increasing taxes on business (slightly) and wealthy individuals, reforming the health care system by putting cost restrictions on physicians, pursuing privatization in a more socially sensitive manner, opposing the previous government pension reforms, re-introducing corporatism in planning for the thirty-five-hour week. On the other hand, the Jospin government has not faced the sharp spending cuts and tax increases needed to restore financial equilibrium in the social welfare system.

job creation prospects of the thirty-five-hour week proposals by granting concessions to employers, and eliminating any prospect of a thirty-two-hour week. In the meantime, the thirty-five-hour week rule has thus far only permitted employers to create part-time jobs; reform is promised for next year. Jospin announced plans to cut employer-paid Social Security contributions to those who create at least 6 percent more jobs but also enforce the thirty-five-hour week. Then, Jospin was replaced.

At the present time, the picture in Germany is far from clear – to put it mildly. During his election campaign, Gerhard Schröder promised to bring together heads of corporations, trade unions, churches, and government to create an "alliance for work." He courted the business community. There seemed to be a consensus on the need to create jobs – even if this means budget deficits and inflation. Germany (along with France) wanted to make the European Central Bank more accountable to ordinary citizens. They were less concerned with price stability. In the meantime, while the Schröder Government continued to struggle to define itself, Germany's six leading economic institutes predicted growth slower than anticipated, and that the expansion of the German economy was unlikely to have much of an impact on the job market (The Week in Germany 1998). At the present time, the German economy is flat (The Economist 1999). And most recently, as discussed, unemployment is on the rise.

The Netherlands is now being touted as a new "third way" – called the "Dutch Miracle." Over the last fifteen years, corporatist agreements have worked out wage reduction for a gradual reduction in working hours. Inflation is low, the budget deficit is shrinking, labor costs have fallen 30 percent in ten years, the economy is competitive in world markets, there is a trade surplus, and unemployment is low. On the other hand, the official unemployment numbers hide the true state of employment. As noted, there has been a huge spread of part-time work. In addition, there are large numbers who are on disability or early retirement. The OECD estimates this "disguised unemployment" to vary between 10 percent and around 50 percent. Thus, the percentage of the working-age population (15–64) in full-time work in the Netherlands is about 50 percent, down from 60 percent in 1970, and below the European average of 67 percent. The low employment disproportionately affects ethnic minorities and unskilled workers, which "takes away some of the shine of the miracle and points to unresolved problems of social integration and economic efficiency" (Visser and Hemerijck 1997: 11). Thus, "the present state of nearly full part-time employment may be judged a second-best solution only" (Hemerijck and Visser 2000). Employers, on the other hand, are pleased. In addition to wage restraint, taxes and social charges are lower, and jobs are more "flexible." As a result, in the 1990s, major changes were made in tightening eligibility, reducing the duration of benefits, and lowering maximum entitlements.

This chapter opened with a discussion of T.H. Marshall's conception of social citizenship. While there was variation on the Continent, the common theme was social rights by virtue of citizenship. This view was diametrically the opposite from the neoliberal market position where well-being rested on the sale of labor. As the discussion of the welfare states shows, the Europeans have come to the conclusion that Marshall's conception is no longer suitable for the changing world. On the other hand, the Social Democrats have rejected the neoliberal position. They have adopted what Tony Blair referred to as "the Third Way" – between the old left statist solutions and the conservative demands for a dismantling of the welfare state.

There are many expressions of the Third Way. I take as one example, Pierre Rosanvallon, *The New Social Question: Rethinking the Welfare State* (Rosanvallon 2000). Rosanvallon is an intellectual figure within the so-called "second Left" in France. The "second Left" distinguishes itself from the traditional, Jacobin left by its rejection of centralized, statist methods. Similar to the conservatives, the second left criticizes state solutions and bureaucracy. Instead, they seek strong associations – grassroots organizations, bottom-up politics, collective bargaining, and civil society – as the key to creating a progressive social and economic order. Rejecting neoliberalism, the second Left's agenda used to be a non-statist road to socialism; now it is a non-statist road to social democracy (email communication with Jonah Levy, 27 June 2001).

Rosanvallon presents a wide-ranging critique of traditional welfare ideologies and policies. In addition to the financial crisis of the 1970s, the 1980s were a decade of ideological crises. "The perceived inability of the state to manage social problems and the dissatisfaction with the welfare state bureaucracy led to a crisis of legitimacy. There was a disintegration of the traditional principles of solidarity and social rights as a framework for dealing with social exclusion and legitimate assistance programs." In the insurance society, solidarity was based on a sharing of social risk. Rosanvallon draws the analogy to Rawls's "veil of ignorance." "As long as people believed that there were common risks, they were willing to participate in the insurance system. The insurance society changed the focus from the subjective notion of behavior and individual responsibility to the objective notion of risk; probabilities and statistics replace judgments about individual behavior." According to Rosanvallon, "social insurance is a contract between the state and its citizens; benefits are an obligation, not an act of generosity. By becoming compulsory and universalized, insurance . . . produces solidarity and security; all become part of the whole, all are interdependent." Social insurance provides compensation rather than assigns blame; responsibility is socialized (Rosanvallon 2000: 10–16).

Our knowledge about the new social problems – long-term unemployment, social exclusion – increasingly questions the belief in the sharing of risks. He draws the analogy to medical science, particularly genetics. "With the knowledge of the predisposition for certain diseases or with certain behaviors (e.g., smoking), the risks of ill health are no longer common; rather, they are individualized, and thus, commonly applied insurance becomes '*redistribution.*' Similarly, knowledge now reveals the varied and individual nature and causes of social exclusion. Thus, the veil of ignorance is torn" (Rosanvallon 2000: 4–10). There is a change in direction – "in what might be called the American way":

> on all sides, "irresponsible" society is denounced, and individuals are called upon to take responsibility for themselves. Solidarity has to be re-thought in light of a clearer knowledge of individual risks. The acceptance of solidarity is now beginning to be accompanied by a demand for control over personal behavior. (Rosanvallon 2000: 18, 23)

According to Rosanvallon:

> the new factors creating disparities in France are first, the rise of long-term unemployment, the new poverty, and homelessness – the socially excluded. There is now a great divide between two worlds previously considered homogeneous. The second is the general destabilization of wages. There is a multifaceted weakening of wage earners, which can feed into the excluded. And third, there is a growing divide between the middle class and benefits that are increasingly concentrated on the excluded. There has been a significant growth in means-tested benefits and a corresponding feeling of unfairness in the number of households that are excluded from these benefits. Targeting is now fashionable in most industrial countries. (Rosanvallon 2000: 41–49)

The traditional welfare viewed risks as temporary. Now, with long-term unemployment and social exclusion:

the passive welfare state becomes pernicious. Compensation keeps increasing, unsatisfied needs keep multiplying, and one part of the labor force serves to compensate the exclusion of another large part. Thus, taxes on labor have to keep increasing, reducing employment, to deal with the excluded. It destroys solidarity by increasing the indirect costs of labor which eventually further reduces employment. With seven to eight million Frenchmen today living on the guaranteed minimum income, we have arrived at the "self-destruction of solidarity." (Rosanvallon 2000: 57)

Is there a way out? The insurance society will no longer work; instead, the welfare state will have to be a system of direct redistribution. The "logic of solidarity will have to rely on citizenship and citizenship, in turn, depends on a sort of moral covenant." What is the moral covenant? Now that the veil is torn, "what we now need is an approach of justice with knowledge of the differences among men" (Rosanvallon 2000: 31). Certain differences should be dealt with by social and political means – e.g., anti-discrimination, disability. But "the central problem revolves around *behaviorable* variables – the disparities that arise from voluntary actions which are both moral and psychological. Hence, justice requires both a political and circumstantial approach . . . The new welfare state has to deal with individuals" (Rosanvallon 2000: 31–32).

The basic challenge is unemployment. "The temptation is to keep paying wages for exclusion but this would assimilate them as socially disabled." This is the reason that Rosanvallon rejects a universal allowance or a basic income guarantee – social rights would end up supporting exclusion. "[I]nclusion through labor should remain the cornerstone of every struggle against exclusion . . . the principle of *mutual utility* that binds its members. Men fought for the right to live from their labor, not to be supported by the welfare state. Thus, progress demands reinventing the idea of the right to work, rather than shaping a right to income" (Rosanvallon 2000: 65).

Rosanvallon argues that there has to be "a new form of economic inclusion by reintegrating the unemployed with an expanded reunderstanding of social rights." By this, he means "changing payment for idleness to payment for work." This involves the right to work. The right to work has to be applied to the specific individuals. To be sure, he acknowledges, "there is a history of requiring work which runs the risk of controlling behavior." How are the negative effects to be avoided?

"A new conception of the social management of employment has to be created. This would build on the concept of inclusion."

Rosanvallon believes that the French RMI (minimum subsistence allowance) is a good example of this middle way – as well as the welfare reforms proposed by Clinton in 1993–94. "RMI (1988) is neither assistance nor Social Security. It is based on a mutual commitment of the individual and the collective. The excluded have a right to a minimum income to allow them to re-enter society but also a contract – the beneficiary's 'commitment to inclusion.'" The commitments are individualized rights (e.g., training, public works, rehabilitation). "RMI does supervise behavior; thus, it is not a right in the strictly legal sense, but it is also not 'legal charity.'" He calls RMI a "third type of society" – "neither traditional social aid (which takes care of the marginal) nor classic social protection which is mechanically distributed to beneficiaries." He says that this is the same with the current US debates about the direction of welfare. He discusses Mead, and then the Democrats joining in the Family Security Act (1988), and the Clinton proposals as evidence of the changes. Writing in 1995, he believes that the US workfare will soon become familiar in Europe. RMI and US workfare lead to the "same redefinition of society." "Neither the market nor the state can 'solve' the problem. In both cases, social rights are reinterpreted as a contract articulating rights and obligations" (Rosanvallon 2000: 84–87).

What is the nature of these obligations? Rosanvallon views the relationship as the "formulation of exchanges for social rights." "Social rights are enriched with a moral imperative: the right to social usefulness, considering individuals as active citizens, and not merely those who need help." "The obligation contributes to resocialization, individuals become full members of society. They not only have the right to live, but the *right to live in society*." The obligation is not only on the recipients, but a "positive constraint" on society. "Society is to take rights seriously." This is the "path of *mutual involvement*." "The subject is considered an autonomous, responsible person capable of making commitments and honoring them" (Rosanvallon 2000: 88).

Thus, the RMI contract "is not a contract in the sense of a legal right. It is a social contract, a contract of inclusion." The "accompanying obligation is not a restriction of freedom but an instance of constructing society, a radical reconsideration of the organizing principles of individualistic society" (Rosanvallon 2000: 88). "The modern individual is eager to escape dependency. But emphasizing the principle of autonomy conflicts with solidarity, the social contract. If begging is a right, then human rights can be a vehicle for social indifference. Thus, the way to avoid pure individualism or communitarian utopias is *contractual individualism*." However, Rosanvallon is careful to emphasize that there have to be effective proposals for work – "*there are no possible obligations without corresponding jobs*" (Rosanvallon 2000: 92). In the United States and the United Kingdom, the attempt at social inclusion is through low wages. Rosanvallon says that in France, "to conquer unemployment at the cost of massive increases in poverty is not a solution." "Democratic inclusion has to be based on equality, by contract."

Because the long-term unemployed are heterogeneous, "there will be different paths of inclusion that will take account of behavioral variables, particularly the attitude toward work" (Rosanvallon 2000: 97). The new social policies "target the social individual, aiming at the social impact of individual behavior, not moral correction." He recognizes the danger of "reviving archaic assistance" where local employment offices (ANPE) could resemble nineteenth century charity offices, "distinguishing good from bad paupers" (Rosanvallon 2000: 103). "Officials at ANPE are now aware that they must help a million different persons deal with their personal situation." While there is the risk of arbitrariness, there has to be individualized treatment. "The welfare state must become a service state providing individual means to change direction. This merges procedural right with justice – equity means equal right to an equivalent treatment, the equity of opportunity. But there has to be a guarantee for protests, a speedy appeal, to avoid a return to archaic paternalism. A new active welfare state will provide a renewed practice of solidarity" (Rosanvallon 2000: 107–108). As Barbier and Théret state, RMI reflects "the French state's orientation [which] stresses society's obligation to provide an individual with means, in order to become (and remain) 'integrated' within society" (Barbier and Théret 2001).[18]

Taking Mead and Rosanvallon as paradigmatic, a sharp contrast is drawn between economic support through paid labor market participation versus receiving a stipend more-or-less automatically under a conception of right or entitlement. It is only through the former that the person becomes integrated into society, becomes a functioning citizen. Many prominent liberals agree with this position – for example, Wilson (1987), Ellwood (1988), Garfinkel and McLanahan (1986),[19]

[18] The authors, however, argue that there are no obligations on the recipients.
[19] See also Harvey (2002).

among others, as well as the centrists, such as the New Democrats and the present Labour government in the United Kingdom. Welfare would no longer be an entitlement. The political mantra was to "end welfare as we know it." While there are many negative attitudes and stereotypes implicit in the recent welfare changes, this is not true of Rosanvallon, the Third Way, and many of the US centrists and liberals who now favor obligations. Rather, they believe that re-integration into the paid labor market is the one sure way of re-establishing social citizenship.

Nevertheless, there are many objections to this redefinition of social citizenship. Clients are to become integrated through contract. In theory, contract enhances the individual; it assumes independent, knowledgeable individuals contracting with each other. Both sides benefit. But this is not a legally enforceable contract; it is a contract of obligation. Rosanvallon calls attention to the state's obligation to respond to the beneficiary. Thus, the process of contract – as envisaged by Rosanvallon – empowers the beneficiary. It is here that the concern arises. Welfare recipients are dependent people; they are weak and in no position to bargain. I will discuss power relationships and the issues of contract in the concluding chapter after reviewing the experience of workfare, but note here that contracts, for the most part, are dictated by the field workers, not bargained. The staff has neither the time, the resources (nor probably the inclination), and the clients have no choice. Mead acknowledges this, but he believes that *imposing* responsibilities would have a positive effect on recipients. He analogizes welfare recipients to children who are required to attend school (Mead 1989). Rosanvallon acknowledges the risks, but believes that state workers will treat recipients and applicants as if they were equal. We will return to this issue more fully after we review the workfare experience in Western Europe.

In sum, the most significant attack on the Marshallian conception of social citizenship has come from several different directions – the neoliberal economic elites, the conservatives and the Third Way center. The new ideology of welfare is based on obligations and moral fault. The poor are responsible for their condition; social policy must support the work ethic and not subvert it by generous assistance. Inclusion comes through one's own efforts. With the decline of the Western European economies, neoliberal conservative and center governments argued for both the failures of the welfare state and the superiority of "negative" economic rights over "positive" social rights (Hemerijck 2002: 9). The welfare state (and Keynesian macroeconomics) not only failed to deal with massive unemployment and economic stagnation, but, by loosening the cash/work nexus, weakened the moral connection of reward through work. More is at stake than simply earning a living. Work, they claim, is necessary for social integration, the preservation of the family, and the socialization of children. In other words, in contrast to Marshall, it is *through* work that citizens become *included* into the community.

In the next chapter, we examine workfare – the Third Way in practice.

CHAPTER FOUR

WORKFARE IN WESTERN EUROPE

By the late 1990s, the response throughout Western Europe to the "passive" welfare state has been *active labor market policies* or workfare. Eligibility has to be tightened, benefits have to be made more conditional and there has to be active labor market policies to encourage people to enter or re-enter the labor market. Under the new regime, beneficiaries have *obligations* as well as *rights*. In return for benefits, beneficiaries must seek work or participate in work-related activities, including, if appropriate, education and training (Lødemel and Trickey 2001; Boeri, Layard, and Nickel 2000: 9–10). The duty to work – the "job first" principle – has spread throughout European unemployment systems (Ferrera and Rhodes 2000: 4). Workers must be prepared to change occupations, including accepting lower wages (Supiot 2000: 34). "[B]enefit conditionality [has] moved to centre-stage" (Clasen 2000: 89). The reason for this change, says Peter Taylor-Goodby, is that despite the differences in the welfare regimes, paid work continues to remain the most legitimizing basis for entitlement (Taylor-Goodby 2001: 133–147).[1]

---

[1] Peter Taylor-Goodby, on the basis of survey data, finds that across the three "ideal" types – the United Kingdom, Germany, and Sweden – there is broad public opinion support for activation in contrast to the conflicting views as to other welfare state reforms and growing lack of support to increase taxes to pay for the welfare state. Public support for activation, despite the welfare state, institutional, and political differences, accounts for activation as a common approach throughout Western Europe.

The legitimacy point raised by Taylor-Goodby calls attention to the fact that the ideology behind activation is broader than trying to revive the economy, reducing unemployment, and containing welfare state costs. Norway, for example, with no welfare crisis, has adopted workfare (Lødemel 2001: 133). After a considerable expansion of the welfare state, both the Right and the Left agreed that extensive rights to generous benefits threatened the ability to become self-sufficient and that individual responsibilities and obligations are more important than individual rights. The Norwegian Labour Party, the dominant party, came to the view that the welfare state had gone too far in encouraging exit from the labor market. The "work approach" would be substituted for the "social security approach." Means-testing, rather than "an unfortunate remnant of the past," would be more positively viewed as "targeting." This change was not the result of a conservative backlash against the welfare state. Rather, according to Ivar Lødemel, the Norwegian Labour Party reflected the contemporary Social Democrats in other countries that have endorsed the changes in the welfare state (Lødemel 2001: 134–136). So too, in Denmark. Despite a good economy and low unemployment, compulsory activation is based on the "principle that 'everyone with at least some work capacity to work should work'" (Cowell and Andrews 2001: C1; Fafo 2001: 11).[2]

There are three basic workfare components: (1) the state should reverse previous policies of encouraging workers to leave the laborforce; (2) it should place those on the margins of the laborforce in jobs (or training for jobs); and (3) the unemployed should be *obliged* to take and remain in such jobs. In general, those covered by unemployment schemes, after a certain period on benefits, have always been required to seek work and take a job. In several countries, these requirements have been increased. What is new are workfare measures applied to *social assistance recipients*. Social assistance recipients include those who have exhausted their unemployment benefits, those who have never entered the labor market (e.g., the young), and the socially excluded, including

---

[2] The New York Times reported the reaction of several European countries to the apparent adoption of Keynesian policies in the United States to cope with the downturn in the economy. France and Germany, as well as EU officials, rejected the US approach as inflationary. Prime Minister Jospin: "[I]t turns out the Americans . . . seem to forget the universal laws of the market." Chancellor Schröder thus far has rejected the advice of five economic research institutes that advise the government that Germany "should relax its adherence to the stability pact by accelerating tax cuts and certain spending programs."

those who may have significant barriers to employment. Compulsory work for social assistance recipients represents a *"fundamental change in the balance between rights and obligations in the provision of assistance"* (Fafo 2001: 46).

As previously discussed, in the United States workfare is usually accompanied by other objectives, such as reducing the number of unwed children and teenage moms. In Europe, too, the effort is to address the broader, social problems of the socially excluded. Historically and today, two themes prevail – helping the *deserving* and preventing them from sliding into the *undeserving* or helping re-integrate the *undeserving* (Standing 1999: 314). The rhetoric is sufficiently vague and inclusive – "social exclusion," "dependency," "rights and responsibilities" – that it appeals to all the major political parties, although, as will be discussed, there are significant differences in programs (Trickey 2001: 251).

While changes are occurring in all Western European countries, all countries cannot be discussed in equal detail. Somewhat arbitrarily, this chapter will discuss the United Kingdom, Ireland, Sweden, Norway, Denmark, the Netherlands, France, and Germany. In the range of welfare regimes, the United Kingdom and Ireland represent one polar position – the Anglo-Saxon, neoliberal state. Under the conservative Thatcher Government, the United Kingdom initiated the change from a passive to an active welfare state, and, at this point, is probably the furthest down the road. The United Kingdom is also important for ideological reasons. It was here, along with the presidency of Ronald Reagan, that the conservative, neoliberal policies were developed and have assumed a worldwide influence. As with the Democratic Party in the United States, the Western European social democratic regimes have become increasingly centrist as they struggle against this conservative influence. Finally, there is more ground-level empirical research on the impact of active labor market policies in the United Kingdom than elsewhere, and this will enable us to develop more precise questions concerning the other countries.

If the United Kingdom is at one end of the spectrum, then Sweden and Norway are at the other – long considered as the most developed, universal, "de-commodified" welfare states. Sweden went through a period of high unemployment, but, with modifications, its basic welfare state remained intact. Denmark and the Netherlands are the most frequently cited examples of countries that have successfully met the challenge of persistent long-term unemployment. The Netherlands is often referred to as the "Dutch Miracle." France and Germany are included not only because of their central importance in the European Union but also because each of these countries is struggling with trying to change its welfare regimes – but with a "human face." They have publicly rejected the US-UK Anglo-Saxon model of low-wage jobs and increasing income inequality, but have not yet found a way to reduce the persistent long-term unemployment as well as other high costs of the welfare state.

THE UNITED KINGDOM

After three decades of rising unemployment, the economy began to change in the 1990s, and by the end of the decade, unemployment dropped to 6.2 percent. There were significant changes in the labor market as a result of the decline in manufacturing, the rise in services and skills. Although employment increased, there was more unemployment for the less-skilled and less stable jobs for those who became employed. At the present time, almost one-quarter of the jobs in the United Kingdom are part-time with varying weekly hours. In 1980, 21 percent (42 percent of the female laborforce) were part-timers; in 1996, the figures rose to 25 percent (44 percent of women). Ninety percent of part-timers are permanent. The largest numbers are in service. There are growing numbers of families where the part-time wife is the sole support. The large entry of women into the paid laborforce off-set the large decline in the number of employed men. Economically inactive men now outnumber unemployed men. The United Kingdom has a high number of "workless" households – about 17 percent of working-age households in 1999 – with almost 20 percent of children, the highest rate in the OECD. Almost all of these families (90 percent) are poor. The United Kingdom has a high proportion of working-age people who are neither employed nor classified as unemployed. The number on sickness and disability has been increasing; working-age sickness is now the highest in the EU (Clasen 2002).

One-third of the unemployed are long-term. They are usually older (55 or more) with limited qualifications and in poor health. Short-term unemployment is high among the youth (under 24), especially for school-leavers (16–17). For this group in particular, there is a skills mismatch. This latter group has been of particular concern to the government and led to the creation of the Social Exclusion Unit in 1999. There has also been a rise in sickness and disability, especially in areas of high unemployment. Almost one-quarter of the unemployed report a health problem and a disproportionate share go on Incapacity Benefit. Finally, there is a high proportion of "workless households," where no adult has a paid job (Trickey and Walker 2001: 181–184).

As with the rest of Europe, the United Kingdom has increased conditionality and work-test rules, first under the Conservatives and continuing with Labour. Welfare reform was at the top of the political agenda of the New Labour Government (Finn 2000). Within a month of taking office, Prime Minister Blair stated that poverty would no longer be addressed by redistribution through taxes and benefits nor would Keynesian demand management or direct job creation be used to achieve full employment. Rather, jobs would be created through a flexible labor market, by restricting benefits, and upgrading the skills and education of the laborforce. There would be a strong emphasis on rights and responsibilities – "moral regeneration." New Labour continued the policies of the previous governments – mandatory activity for the young unemployed and extending the activity to other "workless" groups. Compulsory activity, eventually leading to compulsory work activity, is increasingly becoming accepted for the unemployed (Trickey and Walker 2001: 181). On the other hand, as part of the effort to provide fair minimum standards in a flexible labor market and to make a "deregulated" labor market less unjust, new union rights were established in the 1999 Employment Relations Act (Rhodes 2000: 181–182; Standing 1999).[3]

In the United Kingdom, the unemployed have always had to be available for work and to actively seek work. New Labour continued this supply-side approach to unemployment but would "modernize" the system. They promised to fight the "dependency culture," and reduce the "underclass" and the "socially excluded" (often meaning exclusion from work). The emphasis was to be on mutual obligations. The reform rhetoric emphasized "welfare-to-work," "making work pay," and "work for those who can; security for those who can't [work]" (Trickey and Walker 2001: 190–191). A series of "New Deals" for various target groups was established – for the long-term unemployed, lone parents, the disabled, for "partners of the unemployed," and for youth – specifying activity measures, and for some, compulsory work. Compulsory measures are directed primarily at the unemployed young (18–24).

---

[3] As Guy Standing has pointed out, neoliberal "deregulated" labor market is a misnomer. Labor markets are very regulated, albeit in different forms, under neoliberalism.

The appointment of Richard Layard as adviser to the Treasury and the workfare programs indicated a stronger stance for strict work tests and time-limited benefits (Clasen 2002: 22).

An important addition was the Working Families' Tax Credit (1999) (WFTC) – which is similar to the US Earned Income Tax Credit – for low-income families with dependent children. To avoid the stigma of claiming "in-work benefits", WFTC benefits are added to wages soon after work begins (Walker and Wiseman 2001: 12). The United Kingdom also established a minimum wage, proposed a national child care strategy to make child care more accessible and affordable, and a Disabled Person's Tax Credit which, among other things, increases the amount of work a disabled person can do without losing benefits. There is additional aid for low-earners without children and for pensioners (The Economist 2002f: 45). On the other hand, there is no assistance for those who cannot find a job even if no jobs are available (Trickey and Walker 2001: 191–194).

In the mid-1990s, in order to make benefits more closely tied to efforts to find work, Unemployment Benefit, which was payable for one year, after which the recipient would apply for social assistance (called Income Support), was changed to the Jobseeker's Allowance (Wright 2001: 3). One form of the Allowance was similar to the Unemployment Benefit but shortened to twenty-six weeks. A means-tested Income-Based Jobseeker's Allowance is unlimited. At the initial application for benefits, recipients are required to sign a contract, the Jobseeker's Agreement (JSAg), which states what they will do to try and find work – for example, check the newspaper want ads, or make periodic visits to the Jobcentre. They have to re-register every two weeks at the office – called "signing on" – with a log documenting their work search activities since the last visit. There are sanctions for failure to comply with the agreement (Wright 2001: 3).

In 1998, the United Kingdom established the New Deal for Young People, considered to be the "flagship of the welfare-to-work" policy (Trickey and Walker 2001: 199). Labour promised to move 250,000 young people (18–24) from benefits to work, eventually permanent, unsubsidized work. The emphasis is on integration, training, and skills. Each participant is assigned a "Personal Advisor" who draws up an "Action Plan" which is supposed to set "realistic achievable job goals." The gateway phase is supposed to be voluntary; however, there can be sanctions for "willfully and persistently" refusing to participate. Once the gateway is complete, the options are compulsory. Sanctions can be two to four weeks, depending on whether there was a previous sanction (Trickey and Walker 2001: 199–202).

The options are: (1) Subsidized work which is to be under the same terms and conditions as nonsubsidized work. Employers are to provide training and offer a nonsubsidized job at the end of the period (one year) if the participant has the "necessary aptitude" and "commitment." Existing employees cannot be displaced. (2) Grants for self-employment plans or training, with an allowance. (3) Those who are not "job-ready" may be required to work in voluntary or environmental jobs. This is the most "work-like" option. It is in return for social assistance benefits plus a small subsidy. In addition, there is full-time education or training for those without basic qualifications, but the education and training have to be likely to "result in immediate employment." The allocation of participants among the options varies among the localities (Trickey and Walker 2001: 202–204).

For the long-term unemployed – at least eighteen months – there is the New Deal for the over 25s. There is no gateway period. There are two options: a job (which may be subsidized for up to six months) or full-time education and training, for up to a year. This group is not subject to the New Deal sanctions – benefits will be withdrawn for refusing to participate in the training option, or from two to four weeks if dismissed from a training option because of misconduct. Even though this group is larger than the young and has more barriers, there is less funding. There are also voluntary New Deal programs for those over fifty, lone parents, the disabled, and partners of those participating in the New Deal (Trickey and Walker 2001: 202–204; Wright 2001: 3).

School-leavers (16–17) are ineligible for the New Deal. They are encouraged to remain in full-time education beyond sixteen. There are various training programs including the National Traineeships and the Modern Apprenticeships (MAs). The MAs are popular since they give the participants an "employed" status (Trickey and Walker 2001: 204–206).

The Employment Service (ES) was re-organized and given additional tasks of market-testing, contracting out, cost reviews, and annual performance indicators set at national, local, and sectional levels (Wright 2001: 4). In addition to monitoring and checking on clients, ES workers now have to enhance employment chances. The ES is required to work with local agencies and organizations to improve access to job vacancies and placements. There is a new generation of front-line ES personal advisers who have been given more flexibility to identify and deal with barriers and assist claimants with job search. A new program, ONE, (2000), creates a new agency which combines the functions of the Benefits Agency and the ES into a "single gateway" for almost all benefit claimants. The purpose is to "forge an entirely new culture by promoting a work orientation for all claimants" (Finn and Blackmore 2001: 8–9). In designated pilot areas, all claimants are required to have an interview focused on work. In 2002, a new Working Age Agency was established nationwide which will combine the Benefits Agency and the ES for all people of working age. These changes reflect a major organizational effort to "activate" the social benefit systems. "Government is institutionalizing the assumption that *all* able-bodied people on benefits should take a job" (Trickey and Walker 2001: 191).

The United Kingdom has encouraged the involvement of social partners and local community groups, and integrating and coordinating various services (e.g., vocational guidance, employment advice, welfare, social assistance) into "one-stop" or "one-counter" services.[4] Consequently, there is a large number of local NGOs for the development of local training, advice, employment initiatives, working with women, lone parents, refugees, ethnic minorities, the young, and the long-term unemployed. It is claimed that they have impressive job entry and progression rates. The ES is now required to work in partnership with these local agencies and organizations in an effort to improve its access to the job vacancy market and improve its job placements (Finn 2000: 47).

Finn and Blackmore report on field research with focus groups, carried out in 1997, in four areas of high long-term unemployment (Finn and Blackmore 2001: 1).[5] Overall, most respondents were doubtful about approaching employers, as they were now required to do by the ES. In general, they had a very critical view of the ES in terms of its ability to help them find work or improve their employability. They felt that the ES had the least attractive jobs and was inefficient in updating vacancies. Most felt that the staff did not have enough time or experience to deal with them as individuals. The primary goal of the staff was to remove the clients from the unemployment rolls rather than offer genuine help, and they were too rule-bound. Having completed the courses but still unable to find jobs, the clients doubted the value of

---

[4] As quoted in Finn (2000: 45), the OECD Local Economic and Employment Development Programme (1998) holds that local partnerships should be responsible for implementing national measures.

[5] The report is based on focus groups of just under eighty long-term unemployed and detailed interviews with over fifty street-level key workers.

training. According to preliminary evaluations, employers have been disappointed with the quality of the participants (Trickey and Walker 2001: 202–204).

The ES workers themselves pointed to a shortage of job opportunities as well as the tax/benefits poverty trap, but they also emphasized that the clients had often had significant personal barriers to employment: physical and learning difficulties, low education, mental health, substance abuse, poor social skills, lack of adequate transportation, and other basic facilities (e.g., telephones). In general, the workers favored more focused and selective job seeking – which was contrary to ES policy – otherwise, clients would become demoralized. The workers felt that they lacked the resources to do a difficult job, especially in areas of high unemployment (Finn and Blackmore 2001: 2).

As noted, the Jobseeker's Agreement (JSAg) is an individual action plan that is entered into at the start of benefits. All of the focus group participants were scornful of the JSAg – it was a ten-minute interview with a person "who knows nothing about you." The claimants sign to get the benefits – "the real issue." Several stated that commitments were inserted by the ES Adviser which were not, in fact, made. The terms of the participation contracts seem to be largely determined by the officers rather than the recipients. They agreed, in principle, with the idea that they should provide documentation of their job search activity. However, job searches were sometimes difficult to document, and there was a perception that the workers were inconsistent in applying the rules (Finn and Blackmore 2001: 4).

A survey of 1,800 clients found that less than 30 percent reported that their fortnightly job search review lasted no longer than six minutes, and 30 percent had interviews that lasted for two minutes or less. Forty-three percent reported that there was actually no discussion about job search, rising to over 90 percent in some offices. Overall, there was broad agreement that too many JSAgs are drawn up mechanically and too many people are forced into meaningless activities.

There were mixed attitudes toward compulsion. While there was agreement in principle, many said that in practice it is applied inappropriately and sometimes unfairly. What was most resented was compulsion without genuine choices. Clients felt that their own needs and goals were ignored because of the short-term agency outcome targets. They resented compulsory job search courses as a waste of time, especially when they were repeated. They attend only to prevent loss of benefits. Providers of compulsory courses complained of occasional disruptions and being undermined by those who resented having to participate. A common feeling among both claimants and workers was one of frustration – claimants at not being able to find suitable work, workers because of high caseloads and performance targets.

A large survey (nearly 1,500) of frontline ES workers, while positive about the new approach to work efforts, felt that the performance targets were counterproductive and "interfere with listening to job-seekers." The workers complained of a lack of time and resources to perform all the tasks, especially the fortnightly interviews for persons out of work for over six months which were supposed to take only seven minutes per person. There were complaints about lack of sufficient staff, paperwork, long lines, etc. Their problems were exacerbated because job seekers resisted taking low-quality jobs. Only one-third believed that sanctions and penalties were effective at enforcing compliance.

Sharon Wright, in a recent empirical study, reports on how the workers balanced the demands of administering benefits while trying to help clients in their search for jobs (Wright 2001).[6] The New Deal was to provide a personal service; the staff would build a rapport with the clients. However, within a short time, the demands of volume transformed the program. The fortnightly interviews, which were supposed to take between five and seven minutes, were to cover nine steps (e.g., explanation of purpose of interview, checking the client record for accuracy, reviewing the agreement, evaluating the client's job search activity, a computer check for suitable vacancies, benefit administration). Wright reports that the interviews were "perfunctory, usually lasting around two or three minutes and it was not unusual for the pleasantries of polite conversation to be dispensed with entirely." "There were no apologies for being kept waiting." Several of the required stages of the interview were omitted. The workers were "remarkably inactive"; they focused on benefits administration rather than trying to help people find work. Group sessions replaced the individual interviews. Similar to the Finn and Blackmore respondents, the staff complained about work pressures and time constraints. "The main purpose [of the interview] was to complete forms and windows in the computer screen . . . It is significant that the part of the work that was most likely to be neglected was the part that was not form-based" (Wright 2001: 6). "There were

---

[6] This is an ethnographic study based on seventy-four visits to one Jobcentre, analysis of interviews between staff and clients, informal interviews with forty-eight staff and semi-structured interviews with thirty-five unemployed clients.

always people waiting in front of the desks for interviews. More than twenty-two people had to sign at each desk in each hour of signing . . . [T]his equated to less than three minutes for each interview" (Wright 2001: 6). These pressures forced the staff to redefine their tasks. They had to ration – limiting what tasks to perform (e.g., especially omitting job search, facilitating access to jobs), in other words, processing instead of helping. Sanctions were rarely imposed because of the required paperwork. As one respondent put it, "It's a hassle."

Wright concludes, "[U]nemployment policy in practice is as much about what front-line staff do not do as it is about what they do" (Wright 2001: 7). Many felt that some of the clients had employment barriers that the staff was not equipped to help them with. When employers called in job vacancies, they would not be posted on the office boards. "Instead, the staff would reserve these slots for the more employable clients in order to both maintain good relations with the employers and meet performance targets. Information about available jobs was informally controlled so that only 'high calibre' clients were informed contrary to official policy. In fact, to meet performance targets, staff would make extra efforts to help the more employable clients." Critics of workfare have been criticized as being "alarmist," they say that clients are not as disadvantaged as feared. Wright makes the important rebuttal: "What is perhaps more concerning is that the procedures which were designed to protect clients' basic rights and those which are designed to enable them to find work were not necessarily implemented either" (Wright 2001: 7).

The Fafo Institute study reports that, in general, client attitudes reflected the relationship that they had with their personal advisers and whether they thought that the New Deal improved their chances for employment. If the clients felt that the advisers were concerned about their welfare, they tended to have a positive attitude and take an active, cooperative role. Those who did not have a good relationship felt that their advisers were trying to impose unsuitable jobs. All clients felt that there was some degree of compulsion, but they viewed compulsion as both necessary and fair for most clients. The respondents viewed most New Deal clients negatively – "lazy, unmotivated, untrained and needing an extra push towards work which compulsion provided." Many admitted that without the threat of sanctions, they would not have participated and benefited from the New Deal. On the other hand, they did not understand the sanction system or the appeals procedure very well. Few appealed either decisions or sanctions. From the advisers' perspective, cooperation is the key to success and cooperation is the responsibility of the client. There is a tension, however, between being a "social worker" and being a "civil servant," that is, "'policing' the programme." While they view the clients as considerably disadvantaged, the social work role is an add-on to their traditional duties. There is the conflict between meeting the needs of the clients and processing them within the short time periods and meeting placement targets. They felt that clients enter into options prematurely because the time allotted for advice-giving is both short and inflexible (Fafo 2001: 52–55).

Dan Finn has recently summarized studies of frontline staff and clients in four locations between 1999 and 2002 (Finn n.d.).[7] He reports that for most young people, there has been an increase in job search in order to avoid an option or a sanction. Nearly 10 percent of the young unemployed signed off before attending the first interview, and about 60 percent who attend the first interview leave before entering an option. Over 40 percent of leavers enter unsubsidized jobs, just under 30 percent enter other "known destinations" (e.g., education, other benefits), and nearly one-third are unaccounted for. Although the staff said that they were able to provide individualized service, there was "some evidence" that the staff worked more intensively with those considered most employable. The staff noted the difficulty in either helping or referring the more disadvantaged clients to needed services.

Client views were mixed. Some appreciated the support, others said that they were being "pushed" into things they did not want, others said nothing really took place. Workers said that they had to deal with unrealistic expectations on the part of the clients. There was little evidence, however, that clients were being compelled to take "'Mickey Mouse' jobs in the 'contingent' labour market." Finn found, as did Wright, that increases in caseloads, paperwork, program changes, and performance targets were beginning to take their toll on the ability to deliver an individualized service. Most young people move quickly into jobs. Two groups, however, did not – the "hardest to place" and the "hard core." The former had barriers, the latter (a "small but significant minority") "working the system" – e.g., working in the informal economy, "benefit surfing," etc. The staff resented having to work with this group at the

---

[7] Between 1997 and 2001, the author was an adviser to the national New Deal Task Force and the House of Commons Education and Employment Select Committee. The four locations were Manchester, Portsmouth, London, and Coventry. The data is based on interviews and focus groups with staff, providers, and clients.

expense of those more willing to work. They doubted whether sanctions would change behavior.

Views as to the options were also mixed. The employment subsidies were considered effective in moving clients into jobs. On the other hand, only about 20 percent of the leavers of the non-employer options went directly into a job. The providers pointed to client barriers. Some of the clients praised the non-employment options for giving them self-esteem, routine, and stability and were optimistic. Others were dissatisfied and complained about being forced to engage in unpleasant work (e.g., cleaning, gardening). They thought that they were being punished. Many providers thought that the performance targets impeded their ability to work with these clients. Sanctions have been increased under the New Deal – after a "third offence" benefits can be suspended for up to six months. Most agreed, both staff and clients, that sanctions were necessary to test the willingness to work. The staff complained, however, because of the complexity and paperwork involved. More than 3,000 clients were sanctioned in the last quarter of 2001 – either for failing to attend an option, or leaving without good cause – mostly the poorly educated and less motivated. A significant number of those sanctioned have disappeared. Finn reports that about one-third of those leaving the New Deal are at an "unknown destination." A national survey found no evidence that the most disadvantaged were disproportionately represented. About 43 percent were working, and 30 percent were unemployed. While the staff expressed reluctance to increase sanctions, they pointed out that the way the programs are structured (e.g., performance targets) the incentives discouraged spending resources on the "no shows" even though this defeats the policy of mandatory employment assistance (Finn n.d.: 13–14).

The sharp fall in unemployment has enabled more of the long-term unemployed, especially the young, to compete for jobs and ES morale has improved considerably. On the other hand, the ES is now encountering the unemployed with more barriers. The administrative tensions between the demands of the new "employment first" strategies and the more concentrated, individualized services and support for those who do not find work will increase (Finn n.d.: 16). Necessary services are often not available, public transportation may be inadequate, child care unavailable, especially for non-traditional hours or when children are sick. Work-based training opportunities for entry-level low-wage workers are limited. The greatest challenge is the "revolving door" – participants get jobs, but then a large number are likely to subsequently become unemployed (Finn and Blackmore 2001: 8–9). There is the difficulty of measuring performance, ensuring entitlements, and the disparity in resources. Local partnerships have to develop the necessary skills. In some places, the new partnerships and innovative strategies have been well received (Finn 1999). In other places, "partnership fatigue" is developing. There is "little hard evidence on implementation processes" (Finn and Blackmore 2001: 6–7).

The net employment effects of the New Deal are contested (Clasen 2002: 24–27). The government claims that 250,000 youth had been assisted into jobs by the end of 2000; by the end of 2001, more than a half million had found jobs through the various New Deals. More than 80 percent of these jobs lasted at least thirteen weeks. There is little information on the quality of the jobs, but there is a high degree of job satisfaction. There has been a significant drop in unemployment, especially the long-term (Finn n.d.: 14). How much of this was due to the economy and how much to the New Deals? The Fafo Institute says that while it is estimated that the New Deal has reduced long-term unemployment for youth by about 40 percent, perhaps half would have found jobs on their own (Fafo 2001: 55). While some studies conclude that the New Deals had a positive impact, others are less favorable. For example, about one-third of the young who participated failed to get a job, and 20 percent of those who did find work, re-entered the New Deal before thirteen weeks. "This problem is most acute for young black people and for those in many inner urban and depressed industrial labour markets where, it is suggested, the concentrated geography of unemployment leads to the 'recycling and churning' of participants" (Finn n.d.: 15). The government has responded with a "Next Phase of New Deal" to address the disparities in employment outcomes for ethnic minorities and "Step Up," temporary job creation for areas of high unemployment and for those who fail to get subsidized jobs (Finn n.d.: 15). At the same time, the United Kingdom is experiencing increasing immigration, especially asylum seekers, which is raising a hostile political reaction – a situation which, we shall see, is now becoming more common throughout the rest of Western Europe (The Economist 2002g: 57; The Economist 2002h: 49).

IRELAND

Ireland has become the "Flexible Development State" (FDS) (O'Riain 2000: 157–193). A new set of national, neocorporatist institutions developed "social partnership" agreements which negotiated wage restraint, public spending limits, and undertook some efforts to deal with social exclusion at the local level. The prime example is the software industry, which has become very dynamic and often cited as a model of industrial policy. Between 1986 and 1995, full-time employment increased by 2.5 percent for men and 24.4 percent for women, while part-time employment increased 24.4 percent for men and 36.6 percent for women. Many of the new jobs were good jobs. There was an overall upgrading of the occupational structure.

However, at the same time, there was a significant polarization of occupations and wages with a rapid rise in inequality – the most rapid within the OECD, and second only to the United States. The poverty rate of 15–16 percent remained, and there was an increase in "meager consumption" for the poorest 40 percent of the population. In other words, according to Sean O'Riain, spiraling inequality has become a dilemma of the FDS development model (O'Riain 2000: 159–162). Steady growth has enabled the government to reduce taxes, but tax reform still tends to favor the rich (Hardiman 2000: 815–842). There is a major gap between the middle and the top of the income distribution. Neocorporate wage bargaining allows for special local bargains. Many international firms exceed the national wage standards to retain employees. At the same time, there has been an expansion of low-wage, personal services, especially with the growing trend of two-earner families. In the face of high wages and profits, unions are reluctant to endorse wage restraint. Employers are resisting unionization as well as proposals to regulate the length of the work week, the rights of part-time workers, etc. The growing professional class, "deeply integrated into local and global technology and business networks," is increasingly uninvolved in the processes of national-level industrial relations and wage bargaining. According to O'Riain, there is "increasing fragmentation, which is the dark side of FDS" (O'Riain 2000: 162–183). In the meantime, economic growth has declined sharply, and "tax revenues have stalled" (The Economist 2002i: 52).

SWEDEN

The initial response in Sweden, as in the other countries, to the economic downturn was a series of countercyclical measures which were ineffective. A new conservative coalition took office in 1976 and, in an effort to preserve both employment and the welfare entitlements, tried both restrictive and expansive measures but without major reductions in welfare entitlements (Huber and Stephens 2001: 241). Budget deficits increased and some modest cutbacks were introduced in 1980 – e.g., one waiting day for sick pay – which resulted in a political backlash. The Social Democrats returned to office in 1982.

By this time, it was agreed that the welfare state had reached its limits in terms of coverage and taxes, and that expenditures had to be cut. The Social Democrats deregulated financial markets, instructed state enterprises to show profits, and introduced some privatization and market principles in public services. They also supported reducing the marginal tax rates in the higher and middle brackets down to 50 percent, agreeing that work incentives now took priority over redistribution, further devalued the krona, reduced the deficit, and persuaded the unions to accept wage restraint. This was called the "Third Road" (Huber and Stephens 2001: 242). The economy rose, unemployment and the deficits declined. The Social Democrats were returned to office in 1985 and, responding to the increasing influence of women in the Social Democratic party, additional reforms were enacted – parental leave and care for ill children was extended, and day care and preschool were expanded (Huber and Stephens 2001: 243).

Then, the economy deteriorated and unemployment rose significantly.[8] The groups most affected were men rather than women (many in public jobs), the young, immigrants, and the older unemployed (Boesby, Dahl, and Ploug 2002). In 1990, cutbacks were enacted and the Conservatives were elected the next year. By 1993, unemployment had risen to 8.2 percent. By now, all political parties favored reducing entitlements to increase employment. The pension system was reduced somewhat and changed to defined contribution, financed by equal contributions from both employer and employee. Early retirement due to unemployment was no longer allowed. There were increases in eligibility conditions and reductions in replacement rates in sick pay, disability, and unemployment. Huber and Stephens interpret these changes as a modest re-commodification of the Swedish welfare state and a modest increase in work incentives – a response to the rise in unemployment, and the large increase in the government deficit. Unions were fragmented and weakened by the decline in manufacturing, the rise in services, and the growth of white-collar workers. Previously, employers originated centralized bargaining to restrain wages; now they

---

[8] For a description of the 1990–99 period, see Palme (2002).

opposed it. Their major concern was wage flexibility. There was a dramatic decline in centralized bargaining. Then, the Social Democrats returned to office. There was a positive growth in the economy without inflation. Tax increases and budget cuts produced surpluses which, in turn, reduced interest rates, stimulated investments, and reduced unemployment. Now, with full employment (under 4 percent), there is some concern about wage inflation (Huber and Stephens 2001: 245–257).

There has been a huge expansion in temporary workers, but contrary to the experience in the United States, where part-time and contingent work has resulted in a dual labor market, in Sweden, temporary workers have been used to attack the dual labor market (Svensson 1999). In Sweden, parental leave, education and training, etc. do not interrupt the employment status. Part-time employment is considered the same as regular employment. Although there has been a rapid growth in the staff rental agencies (they were illegal until 1992), the proportion of temporary workers in Sweden is still far below other Western European countries and the United States. It is claimed that the staff rental agencies actually counteract labor-market duality (low-skilled, immigrants) by offering opportunities for experience along with job security. Employees of the staff rental agencies are represented by the Union of Trade and are entitled to most benefits.

At the same time, unemployment benefits have been tightened. Although Sweden has a long history of work requirements (Boesby et al. 2002: 17),[9] previously, the unemployed person (especially white-collar) was not asked to accept a job that did not correspond to his or her previous profession. Now, he or she has to accept any job equal to at least 90 percent of the unemployment benefit. There is a certain number of public-service-improvement "quota-jobs" for the unemployed – e.g., nature preservation, environmental protection, day care. If a recipient rejects a fair offer of activation during the benefit period (the first two years), he or she would lose benefits for four weeks; in serious and repeated cases, there would be a permanent loss of benefits. A rejection of a fair offer of activation during the activation period would result in an immediate loss of benefits. The recipient would have to go on to social assistance. Sweden, along with Denmark, Finland, and Norway, offer support for education and training of the unemployed as part of their active labor-market policies (Kuhnle 2000: 214). Those under

[9] "Active measures have been a central feature of the system since the 1950s."

twenty-five, if unemployed for six of the last nine months and without an education, were required to take eighteen months of education (Torfing 1999: 13).

A series of measures, culminating in the Social Service Act of 1998, the Development Guarantee Program (DGP), placed the responsibility for administering workfare for young people (20–24) with the municipalities. Those without work-like activity or training would be offered a place in the municipal work program or a competence-development scheme for up to twelve months. They are obliged to accept any offer or risk losing benefits. The work can be inferior to what is offered on the labor market; the pay is equivalent to assistance; there are no unemployment, sick relief, or pension benefits (Kildal 2000). The municipalities are not required to run these programs; they can contract with the state. Prior to this change, the unemployed youth were treated no differently than the adult unemployed. There would be an individual action place developed with the labor office, and the municipality was instructed to respect the wishes and qualifications of the unemployed. Now, after ninety days, the municipality, within ten days, is obligated to find suitable activity designed to achieve future independence. The activation period can last twelve months; however, if the unemployed cannot find a job in three months, the process can be repeated (Roche 2000: 31). Thus far, it is unclear what effects DGP has had on employment. Most (75 percent) of the participants left early. Many found work, but it was usually temporary. Longer term effects are still unknown (Roche 2000: 36–37).

Recently, the government has stressed that the quality of the action plans needs to be improved and that there should be continuous evaluation, and that the unemployed should be willing to accept a wider range of jobs as the unemployment period lengthens. A Ministry of Industrial Affairs commission recommended that action plans should be contracts. The Labour Market Board objected on the grounds that this would resemble a legally binding contract, and the government agreed. "Action plans are still considered as plans and not as contracts" (Boesby et al. 2002: 30). In any event, "all in all, it can be said that the active measures used in the 90s have had pretty limited effect on the chances of getting work for the unemployed. Nevertheless, the active measures might have prevented people from leaving the labour force" (Boesby et al. 2002: 31).

Sick leave continues to be high – an average of 10 percent of the workforce at any given time, double the EU average (Hoge 2002: A3).

More recently, there has been a rise in the number of "long-term" sick – the rates of increase have been more than 25 percent in the last two years. Sick pay is generous – about equal to one's earned income, after taxes. In response to the increase, the government has been pushing rehabilitation. The "passive" sick are now required to be "active," which includes compulsory rehabilitation. According to Antoinette Hetzler, "In many cases, especially for women, rehabilitation is actually returning to work but for fewer hours" (email communication with Antoinette Hetzler, September 3, 2002). The present government has announced extensive revisions for 2003. More of the cost will be put on the employers to discourage sick leave (email communication with Antoinette Hetzler, December 27, 2002).

Contrary to the supposed inconsistency between a generous welfare state and a market economy, Sweden, after almost three decades of a sluggish economy, has apparently rebounded *and* the welfare state has, basically, remained intact. Changes have been made – industries have been deregulated and systemwide corporatist bargaining has been abandoned. On the other hand, Sweden has invested a larger part of its gross domestic product in research, development, training, and education than any other developed country. Employment has grown and there is a shortage of workers in many fields. There has been a significant growth in public employment. It is disproportionately female, and very expensive (Andrews 1999: A1).

The Welfare Commission, established by the Swedish government, presents a more mixed view.[10] Reviewing the decade, 1990–99, which started with mass unemployment and then improved, the employment of those aged sixteen to sixty-four at the end of the decade was considerably lower than at the beginning of the decade. Neither women nor older workers left employment during this period, although there was a significant decline in manual workers. As discussed, there was an increase in temporary workers. Real wages rose but there was a decline in disposable household income for most of the period. There was a growing inequality of income; gender differences diminished only marginally, and remained considerable at the end of the decade. The circumstances of families with children worsened. Young adults, immigrants, and single mothers started the decade with lower incomes, higher unemployment, and higher proportions on social assistance, and they continued to be disadvantaged. Immigrants, mostly arriving

---

[10] The report is summarized in Palme (2002).

between 1992 and 1994, when unemployment was high, had a particularly difficult time. Despite the growth of active labor market policies during this period, they could not cope with the increase in unemployment. With the economy recovering by the end of the decade, the number of social assistance recipients declined; still, the number of social assistance recipients was higher at the end of the decade than at the beginning. The Commission concluded that the Swedish social welfare model has not been abandoned. "Universal social services and benefits, as well as earnings-related social insurance, still dominate the system." The challenges are inequality and social inclusion (Palme 2002: 344).

In the Scandinavian countries, public support remains high for the big universal programs – health care, health-related income transfers, old-age pensions – but there is less popular support for social assistance, housing benefits, and unemployment benefits. There has been a shift from passive benefits to active participation through education, training, and rehabilitation. In part, this shift was due to the budget deficits in the 1990s (except for Norway), and in part to high unemployment, but there is also the recognition that people should be regularly employed. While the basic, universal structure has remained intact and no one wants to dismantle the welfare state, all the Nordic countries are now more open to private schemes in health care, social care, and social insurance (Kuhnle 2000: 226–227). Nevertheless, the service sector trilemma has raised its head. "Since the 1980s, tax revenues as a share of GDP have been stagnant and, consequently, so has public employment. There is a clear need to expand private sector jobs to compensate for losses in public sector employment . . . [Thus] the Nordic countries have the hard choice between liberalizing private services, which entails more wage inequality, or a continued adherence to wage equality which, under conditions of budget constraint, implies more unemployment" (Hemerijck 2002).

NORWAY

Oil exports have sustained the Norwegian economy through the crisis periods experienced by the rest of Western Europe. The economy remained strong, with an unemployment rate below 2 percent. There have been some changes in welfare benefits. Eligibility has been expanded for unemployment benefits, but work conditions have been tightened for unemployment, disability, and sickness benefits (Huber and Stephens 2001: 257–259). Most of the unemployed are covered by the unemployment scheme which is nationally financed and administered by state offices at the local level. There is no means test, benefits are earnings-related, the replacement rate can be as high as 65 percent, and last up to three years. Entitlement can be renewed if the recipient gets a job or has temporary employment in an employment program (Lødemel 2001: 145). Benefits for lone parents have been shortened from ten years to three years, "to encourage – or urge – single mothers to seek (re)employment" (Kildal and Kuhnle 2002: 25).

Under the Social Services Act of 1991, for the first time in sixty years, local authorities were authorized to require work in exchange for social assistance benefits. There was a 5.5 percent unemployment rate but a 17 percent rate for the young (16–19), and 11 percent for ages 20–24. The higher rates of increasing dependence of the young became a major concern. (Today, there is a labor shortage.) The focus on the unemployed young was to instill responsibility in return for entitlements (Fafo 2001: 37). There were to be individually-based programs designed to achieve labor-market integration (Fafo 2001: 39). Social assistance, in contrast to the rest of Social Security, is locally financed. The local authorities have discretion as to eligibility, levels of benefit, and whether to impose a work requirement. Workfare is for social assistance recipients only, and is supposed to be a last resort, after other services have failed. The objective is to help the recipients, rather than discouraging claims. The national view is that workfare should be used especially for young recipients who have failed to successfully use other services; however, there is an absence of detailed rules and regulations. The minimum age is eighteen, entitlement is based on domicile and there are no time-limits. The local authorities have wide discretion to apply workfare to other social assistance recipients – e.g., refugees, asylum seekers, and single parents. Work is restricted to local authority services. It can be created work or work alongside regular employees. Training along with work is also discretionary. The work is in exchange for the social assistance benefits (Lødemel 2001: 145–146). There were a variety of other activation programs in Norway and coordination at the local level is said to be "problematic." The 1991 change was intended to cover a small, residual group, primarily the unemployed young. With a change in 1994, all Norwegians were entitled to twelve years of education. The emphasis was on vocational training. There was a guarantee for those sixteen to nineteen years of age of access to work, training, or education. The unemployed young (20–24), were to receive priority for government-sponsored training (Lødemel 2001: 146–147).

Given the existence of all these other programs, workfare provisions were intended to apply only to a small minority. Some local authorities, especially those with budgetary problems, used workfare to fill regular city jobs, at about one-third of the regular wage; others used it to discourage claimants. Still, less than half of the local authorities have used workfare. Most of the workers favored compulsion for the unwilling clients, although they stressed the positive aspects of workfare. Accordingly, sanctions were only used after repeated attempts to get the client to cooperate, and then, there would be a reduction in benefits rather than a complete cut-off. Under the Norwegian plan, workers are not required to offer recipients a place; thus, the workers emphasize client obligations to participate rather than client rights. All of the workers are trained social workers; thus the importance they attach to advice and counseling. On the other hand, several complained about administrative burdens and the lack of time.

The clients gave a different view. All said that participation was compulsory; if they wanted their full benefits, they had to comply. Clients who were more employable (higher education, a regular employment experience) thought that workfare should be voluntary and provide more vocational training. Those with less education, less employment experience, and significant employment barriers, were eager to participate. They agreed that there should be obligations as well as rights. In contrast to the experience in other countries, there is no creaming. Clients are selected according to need. In any event, there is very little difference in employment outcomes. "[T]he schemes can hardly be considered a success" (Fafo 2001: 40–43).

The result, according to Ivar Lødemel, is that Norway has created a "*social division of activation.*" Most who are in active labor-market schemes enjoy regular wages, regular working hours, and are given time for training. Those who are left – the residuals – are considered the least deserving, and they are subject to social assistance workfare. Recently, the central government has tried to promote more uniformity in standards at the local level. Differences remain between social assistance recipients and the rest of the unemployed but they may be diminishing. In the view of Lødemel, the Norwegian system resembles the United States rather than the other European countries (Lødemel 2001: 153–156).

DENMARK

Unemployment began to rise after the first oil shock and continued for two decades until it reached 12.2 percent in 1993. There were significant welfare cuts, but they only slowed the rise in expenditures. When returned to office (1993), the Social Democrats continued the cuts and increased active work policies – combining positive incentives (e.g., vocational and job training) with reducing the length of unemployment benefits and imposing the first two days of benefits on employers. Wage bargaining devolved to the sectoral level with a public mediator playing a strong role, which has restrained wage increases (Huber and Stephens 2001: 262–263).

Denmark tried unsuccessfully to raise employment through work sharing and reducing hours. The unions, which are very strong (about 80 percent of workers are members), then began to press for paid leave schemes so that workers could improve their skills and be replaced by unemployed substitutes – called "job rotation." In 1993, an expanded program was instituted (after several years of experimentation) of paid leave for education and training, and parental leave, to pursue well-defined goals (sabbatical leave, abolished in 1996). The jobs were to be temporarily filled by substitutes who would otherwise have remained unemployed. They were also eligible for these benefits. The substitutes would get work experience and extend the time for unemployment benefits. While they were working, the government would save on unemployment benefits and this would pay for those on leave. Starting in 1994, the take-up rate was very strong, especially for education and parental leave. About half were employees and half were unemployed, which greatly reduced the official number of unemployed (Coompston and Kongshoj Madsen 2001: 117–132). At the same time, dismissal rules have been relaxed permitting flexibility and competitiveness, access to unemployment benefits has been tightened while the maximum period for benefits has been reduced from nine years to five (of which three must be spent in active labor market activities) – which is still very generous (Hirst 2000: 6). In the mid-1990s, the economy began to grow, there was a budget surplus in 1998, and unemployment fell to 6.5 percent in 1998 (Huber and Stephens 2001: 264) and 5.1 percent in 2002 (The Economist 2002j: 84).

Rejecting the workfare strategies of the United States and the United Kingdom, activation in Denmark consists of training and education, and improving skills and work experience of the unemployed. The benefits are generous. It is more inclusive than just the unemployed. There are also wage supplements, grants for special costs, and wages while in job training. On the other hand, social assistance could be denied to those who rejected a fair offer of activation (Torfing 1999: 17). In 1998, about 74,000 participated in activation. The largest number was in subsidized employment in the private sector. Within a year, a little over half (51 percent) of the short-term unemployed found regular employment as compared to less than 20 percent of the long-term unemployed. Job placements in the private sector were the most successful in producing regular employment, which may have been the result of creaming in the activation placements. Both recipients of unemployment insurance and social assistance had a favorable reaction to activation. More important than improving specific job opportunities, was the increase in self-confidence and motivation (Roche 2000: 40–41).

Despite low unemployment and high laborforce participation, there were still large numbers on unemployment benefits, social assistance, early retirement, and sickness benefits. There were pockets of unemployment and questions began to be raised about the efficiency of job search and the unwillingness to change jobs. Youth unemployment remained high, there was an increase in social assistance, and middle-class youth used social assistance for summer vacations, which became a national issue. Soon, part-time work and workfare were supported by all political parties (except the extreme Right). Reflecting the policy shift to work-test a wider range of recipients, along with the desire to avoid the dangers of idleness, the policy developed that "everyone with at least some capacity to work should work" (Rosdahl and Weise 2001).

Successive governments established what was called an "Active Line" designed to provide activities for the "workless" to help them enter the paid labor market. Workfare was to be "offensive" rather than "defensive." This meant "activation rather than reductions in benefits and wages; improving skills and work experience of the unemployed rather than increasing their job-search efficiency; emphasizing training and education rather than work-for-benefits; empowerment rather than control and punishment; and more inclusive than just targeting the unemployed" (Torfing 1999: 17). Hence, "rather than punishing the unemployed, the Active Line explicitly states that the beneficiaries must take responsibility for the offers that are being made. The goal is empowerment" (Torfing 1999: 17; Cox 1998: 397–414). Both the state and the private sector have an obligation to provide opportunities for inclusion as well as long-term strategies to reduce unemployment and social barriers for the "highly marginalized." Private enterprise should be willing to hire people with "reduced working abilities," the "weak groups." The various schemes are financed either completely by the national government or shared between the national, county, and local governments. There is a division of responsibility between the Ministries of Labour and Social Affairs and local authorities. The municipalities fund half the costs of social assistance. Coordination, however, can be problematic (Rosdahl and Weise 2001: 167–168; 170).

Social services were separated from income transfers and employment. The age limit was raised from twenty-five to thirty. All recipients under thirty years of age were required to be activated within thirteen weeks. The activation period was either six or eighteen months. At the completion of the activation period, the client had the right to a new activation offer within another thirteen weeks. There was no specified length of activation periods for those over thirty. In response to protests, a complaint system was established (Torfing 1999: 17).

A significant proportion of activation offers are work, which is expected to become increasingly important.[11] Applicants for social assistance have to demonstrate that they do not have a "suitable work offer," which is decided by the local authority. The previous wage is not relevant. Recipients must also accept a "reasonable" activation offer. Social assistance families receive 80 percent of the maximum unemployment insurance benefit, the young 40 percent if they are living alone, and 20 percent if they are living with their parents. Generally, there is no time-limit for benefits. There are exceptions – illness, pregnant women or women with children less than six months of age, women with children where child care is not available. Subject to national minimum rules, the local authorities have discretion as to who will be activated and the terms of activation.[12]

A recent study finds that the vast majority of the insured unemployed have individual action plans and that 85 percent are satisfied. Almost all (90 percent) want activation. Large majorities claim that

[11] According to Fafo (2001: 45–46), there are even suggestions that the work principle will be applied to early retirement and disability with the work offers tailored to the individual's reduced capacity to work.
[12] According to Fafo (2001: 47), there are minimum rules set by the national government – e.g., there are various time-limits for different groups after which there must be activation.

activation has provided them with new qualifications, improved their self-confidence, and their job chances. Twenty percent say that activation has been limited. High economic growth combined with the active labor market policies have benefited the unemployed. As many as 60 percent get a regular job. For a time, activation lowered the incomes of the unskilled, but this was remedied with tax reform (Barrell and Genre 1999: 82–89).

According to the Fafo study, the workers report that activation "trajectories" are based on an estimation of the client's abilities. However, they said that the clients must have decent options. Some clients feel compelled, but it is rare for a full sanction to be applied. The clients, on the other hand, do not think that options are available, but most have a positive attitude and think that they have benefited. A small minority, especially younger people, has negative views; they think that workfare is unfair and a waste of time. Those with more skills and abilities are more satisfied and benefit more than those who have more barriers. Activation in private firms (subsidized jobs) is the most successful in securing regular employment (Fafo 2001: 48–49).

There have been implementation problems. The quality of the plans and the offers are uneven. There is creaming for the well-qualified unemployed into long-term education plans. It is not clear whether the short-term plans are effective. There are difficulties in activating weak and marginal groups. The Labour Exchanges are reporting that they are now left with the hard-to-activate. At the local level (where the activation is administered), about one-third of the social assistance claimants have difficulty in activation because of serious social problems. This group will have to receive some kind of early retirement pension, or, if the government is willing to pay the cost, sheltered "flexi-jobs" in the private and public sector (Torfing 1999: 21).

As employment increased, and the pool of recipients has become less skilled and less suited for job training, the trend has been more towards individual job training (in special projects with other recipients rather than the regular labor market) and a greater use of workfare as a requirement for social assistance. It came to be increasingly accepted that unemployment could be "voluntary" and local authorities began to use workfare as a work-test. Because of the shared funding, there are strong incentives on the local authorities to reduce the number of social assistance recipients and the local authorities use the Youth Allowance Scheme to deter social assistance applicants. Although there is variation, strategies include placing employable recipients in unattractive slots so that they will seek employment in the regular labor-market or help in locating jobs or education and training. By 1997, nearly two-thirds of all activated recipients were in workfare. With low unemployment, those who remain on social assistance have more significant barriers. At the same time, activation to address the broader social problems has proven difficult to implement. Questions are being raised as to whether the goals for this group should be labor market participation (Rosdahl and Weise 2001: 175–179).

Despite the efforts, there remains a large group of marginalized unemployed. According to a recent study, only one-half of those on activation were actually looking for work. Many claim that they have been put in low-pay, low-quality activation. The Social Democrats were re-elected in 1998 promising to make special efforts on behalf of those difficult to activate. They plan to create 40,000 flexi-jobs for those not sufficiently disabled to be excluded from the labor market and put on social pensions. There are no plans to cut benefits or minimum wages but there are plans to increase work incentives through tax reductions (Torfing 1999: 23).

In the meantime, public employment has grown to 30 percent of the laborforce, and is heavily concentrated in services – e.g., day care (which is widely available), public transportation. Most citizens consume high levels of high quality public services and universal benefits. There are no insiders and outsiders. This supports low-income workers and a willingness to pay high taxes. The Danish system is paid for primarily by current taxes. Governments have been able to restrain budgetary growth and cut back on entitlements when necessary. With equality, inclusion, and solidarity, there are reasonable expectations of fairness (Hirst 2000: 7–8).

Thus, Denmark has high levels of both passive income support and active labor market programs. Labor markets are flexible. There is a good deal of frictional unemployment – "resting" – but not much long-term unemployment (in fact, the lowest in the EU). The unemployed are not marginalized. Most of the long-term unemployed are married women. Wages are negotiated by the unions at the national level and are growing. Labor markets remain tight throughout the economy, which keeps wages high in the lower segments (email communication with Sigrun Kahl, November 4, 2001). Denmark has the highest levels of income equality in the OECD. The absence of social exclusion makes the unemployed more easily employable. Dual-income families and readily available benefits mean that people are not forced into low-wage work (Hirst 2000: 6). On the other hand, there are suggestions that there may be significant "hidden unemployment." A proportion of activated people move from one program to another and do not enter the labor market (Barrell and Genre 1999: 95). Still, the poverty population is low and the unemployed, in general, do not differ significantly from the rest of the population. It is claimed that the Danish strategy preserves the universalistic welfare state in that it has prevented widespread marginalization and polarization (Torfing 1999: 18–21).

In the meantime, there appears to be a dramatic shift in politics. In the November, 2001 elections, the Liberal Party out-polled the Social Democrats, which may force the Social Democrats to rely on the anti-immigration Danish People's Party for a parliamentary majority. The campaign expressed concern that immigrants are exploiting the welfare system. The Liberal Party leader "pledged to crack down on foreigners trying to cheat the system. 'Denmark must not be the social security office for the rest of the world'" (New York Times 2001a: A6).[13] The People's Party leader exploited fears about Muslims (after the terrorist attack in New York City). There are 5.3 million people in Denmark; 5 percent are foreigners, which is a smaller proportion than in many European countries (New York Times 2001b: A17).

THE NETHERLANDS

A key example, which everyone cites, is the Netherlands – from an economy of falling productivity, high unemployment, and an expensive, dysfunctional welfare state to a competitive economy, low unemployment, and a leaner, more active welfare state – from the "Dutch Disease" to the "Dutch Miracle."

In the 1970s, labor costs rose, there was a significant rise in unemployment, an expansion of the welfare state, and an increase in government spending (Hemerijck and Visser 2000: 235). Unemployment benefits were high and without work requirements. The less productive, expensive workers (mostly older) were dropped by the firms. Large numbers of unemployed workers went on disability or early retirement. The economy continued to decline in the 1980s and unemployment rose to 12 percent. The Conservative Government made further reductions in entitlements. Among older workers (60–65), the laborforce participation

---

[13] For the escalating struggles over immigrants in Denmark, see Cohen (2000).

rate fell from about 70 percent in 1973 to 22 percent in 1991. Between 1970 and 1986, the proportion of unemployed who had exhausted their benefits and had to rely on social assistance rose from 3 percent to 67 percent. There was a decline in manufacturing jobs and union memberships (Huber and Stephens 2001: 280–281). The economy was no longer competitive. Government deficits were large. Inflation and unemployment rose along with the tax burden (Teague 1999: 123).

By the end of the 1980s, disability had become, in effect, a generous unemployment allowance. Nearly one million were on the program, which was 14 percent of the laborforce, two or three times higher than in neighboring countries (Hemerijck and Visser 2000: 241–242). By 1986, working age (55–64) disability recipients outnumbered workers (Hemerijck and Visser 2000: 239). For a while, the percentage of workers on disability slowly declined, but then it started to increase and is now at the same level as in 1980 (Hartog 1999). Between disability and early retirement, only about 31 percent of fifty-five to sixty-four-year-olds are in the labor market, which is significantly lower than other EU countries. If all economically active people were included in employment measures, the unemployment rate would have been 27 percent instead of the 5 to 6 percent claimed by the Dutch Government. This was the "Dutch disease" (Teague 1999: 125–127).

Change started in 1982. The government and the leading labor and employers' federations at the national level decided that the low level of employment was due to the extensive, passive system of social protection. There was agreement on the need for wage restraint, reduction in working hours, government control of expenditures and the deficit, and Social Security reform (Hartog 1999: 7). In return for a modest reduction in weekly and annual working hours, lower taxes and employer Social Security contributions, collective bargaining at the sectoral level produced wage moderation which made Dutch exports competitive, stimulated economic growth, job creation, and improved public finances. For the next fifteen years, a series of wage agreements have kept wage increases down, lower than rises in productivity (Teague 1999: 123). To improve competitiveness and reduce the budget, there was retrenchment – a lowering of the minimum wage (Becker 2000: 224),[14] payroll taxes were reduced for low-wage workers, Social Security contributions were raised, and eligibility was tightened for social

---

[14] At first the minimum wage was frozen for a year, then reduced from two-thirds of the average income to half.

assistance and disability (Ferrera and Rhodes 2000: 263). The wage restraint is considered the most important factor in turning the Dutch economy around and restoring international competitiveness (Hirst 2000: 10, relying on Hemerijck and Visser 2000).[15]

There still remained excessive inactivity. In addition to some effort to reduce fraud and abuse, there were reforms in sickness and disability – new eligibility, lower benefits, shorter duration for full benefits, and stricter conditions for accepting alternative employment. There was a reduction in the rolls but also significant political opposition leading to a change in government. However, the Social Democrats remained in favor of the reforms (Huber and Stephens 2001: 283).

In 1993, a left-liberal coalition, following the recommendations of a parliamentary committee representing all the parties, implemented significant changes. There was to be more government involvement and supervision of the administration of the Social Security schemes that were administered by employers and unions. Unemployment was tightened. Sickness benefits were transferred from the state to employers, thus giving employers an incentive to reduce absenteeism and seek private insurance (thus privatizing sickness insurance). In 1998, a similar scheme was applied to disability (Huber and Stephens 2001: 284).

Unemployment was significantly reduced (declined to 5.8 percent in 1997 and then 2.5 percent in 2002 (The Economist 2002k: 84)) by the creation of part-time jobs, which accounted for two-thirds of the net new jobs, primarily in the service sector. Many of the new jobs have very limited and irregular hours and with few career prospects (Visser and Hemerijck 1997: 11). On the other hand, the part-time jobs, according to Jelle Visser, do widen alternatives "beyond the traditional choice between 'all or nothing'" (Visser 2002: 36). Older workers were replaced by younger, cheaper, and more flexible and skilled workers. Of all the part-time jobs, 75 percent are held by women. Thus, a large part of the growth in the laborforce was due to the massive entry of women (van Oorschot 2002: 402). Sixty-three percent of all women in the paid laborforce are part-time workers. There are high levels of part-time work among men (16 percent) and youth (25 percent) (Hemerijck 1999: 17). There has also been a big growth in temp agencies. Now, collective bargaining agreements for workers come through

---

[15] Says Paul Teague (1999: 123), "Overall, the national pay deals have been the single most important factor for improved economic competitiveness."

these agencies. There is also protective labor legislation for part-time employees.[16] With the increase in women in the laborforce, they also constituted the largest part of new union members. Unions then began to take up issues such as child care and sexual harassment. However, there still remains extensive gender-discrimination in the labor market (Huber and Stephens 2001: 285–286).

With part-time work becoming the key to the growth in jobs (Hemerijck and Visser 2000: 243, 251), the Flexibility and Security Act of 1999 was enacted both to increase flexibility and strengthen the legal coverage of the "flexiworkers" (Spies and van Berkel 2001: 115).[17] Restrictions were removed on hours for retail stores, business licenses, temporary jobs agencies, working time, and dismissal laws. Comprehensive Social Security attaches to part-time work. On the other hand, many part-timers work fewer than ten hours per week which reduces their social security protection (Teague 1999: 124–125). Concertation was revived with unions and employer groups agreeing on the "normalization" of temporary work, e.g., pension protections after four consecutive contracts or twenty-four months of service, removing discrimination on the basis of working hours. The unions began to emphasize jobs over income. There was an increase in wage inequality but it was modest (Huber and Stephens 2001: 282, 285).

There still remains a great deal of hidden unemployment. The total laborforce participation is still low (Huber and Stephens 2001: 284–285). According to Wim van Oorschot, there are large shortages in the Dutch labor market; at the same time, there are 230,000 registered unemployed, which he interprets as a "serious mismatch" between what the employers want and the qualifications of the unemployed (van Oorschot 2002: 403). The most important programs for reducing unemployment were lowering taxes and Social Security contributions for

---

[16] For example, workers on call have to be paid for at least three hours, the contract with the temp agency is now considered an employment contract, after twenty-six weeks legal rules for a sequence of temporary employment contracts apply (e.g., entitled to a tenured position after three temp contracts with the same employer). Collective bargaining rules can set additional rules.

[17] Labor contracts would clarify employment relations. Stand-by workers were to be paid for at least three hours; there were shorter probation periods for short contracts; automatic fixed term contracts where short contracts are repeated three times; full labor contracts after twenty-six weeks of employment. In return, the employer's period of notice was shortened to between one and four months depending on the duration of the contract.

employers who hired the long-term unemployed; creating regular jobs in the public sector – primarily public security, health care, child care, education, social services; creating temporary subsidized jobs (with a maximum time-limit of two years); a subsidized "Jobpool" in the public sector for the very long-term unemployed (unemployed for more than three years and considered to have no chance of finding regular employment); the Youth Employment Scheme (supplementary subsidized jobs); and Social Activation (municipal programs of unpaid activities, both voluntary and obligatory, to combat social exclusion) (Spies and van Berkel 2001: 117). As an incentive to hire the unemployed, there would be combination wages – i.e., low wages (below the minimum wage) topped with state subsidies. The demand for such employees has increased but not the wages, which might indicate that regular jobs are being replaced (email communication with Sigrun Kahl, November 20, 2001).

As to nondisabled unemployment, the Dutch Scientific Council for Government Policy (WRR, 1987) decided that social policy must change from its focus on "care" to providing activation opportunities for self-sufficiency, complemented by increased surveillance and stricter sanctions. Individuals were to be explicitly held to be co-responsible for their status. This policy was re-affirmed three years later. The Dutch Scientific Council (WRR, 1990) report affirmed the essential role of work not only for creating solidarity and preventing social disintegration but for the health and development of individuals. "*Work, Work, Work*" became the major political slogan, with widespread popular support. In the 1998 political campaigns, all of the major parties emphasized the importance of job creation (Spies and van Berkel 2001: 113–114).

The Dutch activation policies are a mixture of Scandinavian and Anglo-Saxon ideas. There is the institutional commitment to full-employment – education and training projects, job creation, rather than passive benefits – and obligations on the part of the employees. The labor market would be deregulated. Government would stimulate both unions and employers to create more entry-level jobs. Retail hours were to be extended, and employment made more flexible. A bill is being considered that would guarantee the virtual right of employees to move to part-time work, within certain limits (Spies and van Berkel 2001: 111).

Other changes were made to discourage opting out of paid work. Eligibility for unemployment insurance was raised – the applicant must have worked in four of five years prior to applying instead of three of five – and benefits were reduced from twenty-six of thirty-nine weeks to twenty-six weeks of fifty-two weeks, and the amount from 80 percent of the previous wage to 70 percent. Social assistance was fixed rather than indexed to the average wage. "On average, being unemployed now means lower benefits, for shorter periods" (van Oorschot 2002: 48). However, while unemployment insurance costs went down, disability pensions remained high. The Disablement Act was still used as an "opting-out" alternative for older workers (Spies and van Berkel 2001: 111).

In addition to stimulating flexibility in regular employment, subsidized and created employment was used for the unemployed. In 1997, 180,000 were in subsidized jobs, which was 3 percent of the working population. This included sheltered employment for the disabled (Spies and van Berkel 2001: 117). Social assistance recipients are now expected to accept a job, the unemployed have to actively seek work, and there has been a start in the privatization of Social Security (Becker 2000: 226). Monthly unemployment benefits would be cut if recipients refused an offer of a training place considered necessary by a local authority official (Spies and van Berkel 2001: 117). In the Netherlands, along with Finland, Sweden, and Denmark, the young unemployed are subject to more activating measures – more obligatory, more of a workfare nature – than other groups of unemployed, for example, older unemployed, women, and ethnic minorities (Roche 2000: 30; van Oorschot 2002: 406). Van Oorschott thinks that part of the reason for not including these groups as targets for activation may have been to avoid stigma, especially for women and ethnic minorities (van Oorschot 2002: 406). Public employment was to be reorganized and administered by regional employment boards. Competition between public and private employment services was introduced. There were to be 400,000 permanent public sector jobs for unemployed youth and the long-term unemployed. Additional job programs were planned to provide jobs for 1.5 million workers. A total of 60,000 jobs, mainly low wage in the public sector, are being created for the long-term unemployed (OECD 2000: 5).

In response to the high youth unemployment in the 1980s, the Youth Employment Act (YEA) was adopted in 1992 providing that all young people (19–22) who were unemployed for six months were required to take a job in order to continue receiving benefits (Fafo 2001: 29). In 1998, YEA, as well as other activation programs, were consolidated under the Jobseeker's Employment Act (JEA). There are three principal programs: subsidized employment with a regular employer, either for profit or non-profit; subsidized municipal employment; and training or "social activation," which can be combined with subsidized employment. Placements can be sequential. Subsidized employment contracts, designed for low-skilled workers, have to be at least six months but no longer than two years. Working conditions are covered by sector collective agreements. The hours are generally about thirty-two per week; the wages are a little above the minimum, but income is enhanced with welfare. Whereas subsidized work with regular employment has proved to be a successful path to employment – a 50 to 70 percent chance of a regular job – it is expensive and used less in recent years. Subsidized municipal employment is supposed to lead to a regular job but, in practice, has become an "end station." For the young, this alternative ends at age twenty-three, with a return to welfare; there is no time-limit for older workers. Jobs are covered by labor contracts and typically include school caretaker, filing, zoo cleaning, maintenance, and construction. The jobs pay a minimum wage and are considered most helpful for the young. Those in training and activation remain on welfare. The income is below the minimum wage; for the young, it is very low. Training and activation are to help find a regular or a subsidized job. It is mainly for people who are ready for employment but have a specific barrier – e.g., language, substance abuse (Spies and van Berkel 2001: 119–121).

Under the JEA, the young in subsidized municipal work have to work for the minimum income. The rights and obligations of these workers differ significantly from regular workers in terms of conditions, earnings, and content of work. The work is partly superfluous, considered "second rate," but is required in order to receive income. Training and social activation is also compulsory for the young, but voluntary for the older, long-term unemployed (Spies and van Berkel 2001: 121–122). All municipalities are required to run the JEA. They are obliged to offer every young person up to age twenty-three a placement after six months of unemployment. However, the differences between the younger and older unemployed may become blurred at the field level (Roche 2000: 32).

JEA offices have been partly transferred to local government in an effort to provide more flexibility. Thus far, cooperation between social services and employment offices has "not been optimal," especially with respect to the "hard core." The employment offices generally "cream." But the social services have to rely on the employment offices for

175

subsidized placements. Recently new Centres for Work and Income have been created to integrate intake, diagnosis, information exchange, client monitoring, enhanced job search, and combine benefits with activities to improve employment. It is hoped that cooperation will improve with the "single counter," but this remains uncertain. Measures have been instituted to limit local differences – e.g., "measuring rod" to categorize and then match strategies, computerized data collection, and so forth (Finn 2000: 51–53). According to the Fafo interviews, there still remains considerable confusion as to the allocation of responsibilities between the local agencies, the local governments, and the national government (Fafo 2001).

Although workers tend to favor compulsion, especially with the favorable employment situation, they think that existence of opportunities is more effective in motivating clients than the threat of sanctions. In addition, they cite other reasons to avoid sanctions – the increase in paperwork, the high caseload, the possible overruling by the "back office" (Fafo 2001: 33–34). According to the Fafo report, the recipients give a different view. Although originally motivated by the opportunities that may be available, their positive attitudes begin to change over time. The longer they stay in the program, the more prominent the threat of sanctions become. Many feel that their individual needs and problems are not taken into account and that they are treated bureaucratically. They do not like their YEA jobs which are not to be substitutes for regular jobs. They find them boring, often have nothing to do, receive lower wages than regular workers for the same kind of work, and are looked down upon by regular workers (Fafo 2001: 34).

The selection of the young unemployed suggests that there is creaming based on prior social background, and that dismissal and sanctions are counterproductive in terms of social exclusion. There is a serious dropout problem. In 1996, 54 percent of YEA (now JEA) leavers found regular employment; 8 percent went back to school; 25 percent dropped out and lost benefits; and 13 percent left for other reasons. The dropouts, who generally have more problems than the other participants, are considered serious risks for "severe marginalization." It is estimated that about half of the dropouts are from either single-parent families or families headed by an unemployed or disabled person. Many (about 40 percent) are in trouble with the police. Yet, they are "entirely on their own" (Spies and van Berkel 2001: 124–127).

Research on JEA is not yet available. Under the Guaranteed Youth Employment Act (GYA), which in 1998 became part of JEA, municipalities are required to offer a contract even though placement opportunities may not be available. In 1996, about 20 percent of the vulnerable groups (low-education, immigrants, no work experience) were on "empty contracts" – that is, not placed in a job. The "full-coverage" objective was never met, although there has been an improvement between 1992 and 1994. Those who leave for regular employment do so more because of general economic conditions rather than the program (Fafo 2001: 33). The participation percentages only include the young unemployed who had registered at the employment agencies; they do not include those who are outside the official systems – e.g., drifters, young migrant women workers who are not allowed to do paid work, etc. (Roche 2000: 37). In a study of Rotterdam, the young who do not enter and are not registered at employment agencies have very problematic backgrounds. Thus, according to Maurice Roche, those who would most need the program, benefit the least (Roche 2000: 37–38). Research on dropouts, who then lost their benefits for three months, suggests significant marginalization – in some cases, criminal activity (referred to as "other" solutions). "Although the threat of sanctions may contribute to . . . participation of clients – and in that specific sense can be said to contribute to inclusion – actual sanctioning leads to exclusion" (Fafo 2001: 35).

In the mid- and late-1990s, Dutch policy was changed to require lone mothers on social assistance with children over five years of age to seek work (Knijn and van Wel 2001: 235–251). By the early 1990s, they began to be considered a social problem. The composition had changed from largely widows to mainly divorced and unmarried. Widows received a separate pension. There was an increase in the number of lone mothers on social assistance – from 60,000 in 1978 to 103,000 in 1991, and, because benefits were no longer linked to the average wage growth, an increase in poverty. Activation policies were introduced for lone mothers, but implementation remained ambivalent. Child care, particularly after-school care, was not developed and remained of poor quality. Municipalities were given the responsibility of implementing the activation policies but given no criteria. Lone mothers on welfare had disproportionately more barriers to employment, especially in education, training, and work histories. To benefit financially, those who lacked employment qualifications needed full-time work, but would qualify only for lower-wage, part-time jobs. In addition, there was resistance to work because of the perceived inadequacies of child care. The municipal caseworkers, in turn, also resisted the policy. They were trained as payment officers. Putting lone mothers in various activation categories would significantly increase their tasks, and they were not sure how to treat this class of social assistance clients as compared to other groups. If a particular lone mother was exempted as "not available for the labor market," she would not have to be re-interviewed for eighteen months. A majority of lone mothers was exempted from the activation requirements (Knijn and van Wel 2001: 241–242).

In 1999, in response to a labor shortage especially in education and care, it was argued that it was unacceptable for so many lone mothers to be on social assistance with so many vacancies. New subsidies for child care, education, and training, and tax reductions were provided. Still, the local governments continued to be ambivalent and not optimistic, especially for the lone mothers who had low levels of education and training. "They did not want to force lone mothers to work full-time which would not improve their income, conflict with their beliefs as to the importance of child care, and create more work for their caseworkers" (Knijn and van Wel 2001: 242–249).

The apparent economic and employment transformation in the Netherlands – now referred to as the "Dutch Miracle" – has been attributed to the changes in the welfare state. There is some dispute about this conclusion. Instead, it is argued that wage restraint and harmonious relations between labor and capital are the most important explanation for the increase in employment (Becker 2000: 219–239). Still, despite the fall in unemployment, long-term unemployment has remained high. There were various explanations – the mis-match between jobs and skill levels, the overrepresentation of immigrants and workers with low skills and education, the decrease in manual labor, the growth in part-time, "flexiwork," and the re-entry of women into the labor market after initial years of child care (Spies and van Berkel 2001: 111). Moreover, as noted previously, the unemployment rate does not reflect the true state of the Dutch labor market. The Netherlands full-time employment rate is lower than neighboring countries. This is mainly due to part-time work (Hartog 1999: 14; OECD 2000: 1–6; van Oorschot 2002: 412).[18] And because employment growth was due primarily to part-time work, the number of hours worked is low (van Oorschot 2002: 412).

---

[18] The actual hours worked per year have dropped to the lowest level in Europe: 1,452 per year in 1993 vs. EU average of 1,669.

According to Uwe Becker, the welfare state is still largely passive "despite the Purple Government's slogan, 'work, work, work'" (Becker 2000: 227). Despite the reforms, a high percentage of working-age adults (55–64) are retired, and a large percentage are still on disability – still nearly 14 percent of the economically active population. With the exception of Italy, the Dutch proportion of those on disability is more than twice as high as any other comparable country. This is the safety net for nearly a half million long-term unemployed. Thus, the redistribution of work was not only to part-timers but to the younger and healthier workers (Becker 2000: 234–235).

As is true in all the countries, it is difficult to separate out the impact of activation measures on the increases in employment and the decline in social assistance beneficiaries. As in most other countries, reducing wage costs for employers appears to be the most effective measure for re-employment. Job creation results in very few moving on to regular employment. And, as stated, there still remains a large number of long-term unemployed, social assistance beneficiaries, and those with employment barriers. The privatization of sickness benefits and the premium differentials in disability have resulted in more stringent screening by employers. In short, according to Oorschot, "the reintegration of the most vulnerable groups is 'stagnating'" (van Oorschot 2002: 414–415).

And, again according to Becker, ethnic minorities in the Netherlands are not sharing in the employment boom. In fact, quite the opposite. Islamic males from Turkey and Morocco have six times the unemployment rate of Dutch males; males from Surinam and the Dutch Antilles, four times, and other cultural minorities five times. Ethnic females do better, but employment rates are still low. The overall unemployment rate of immigrants (including Westerners) is three times the Dutch indigenous rate. In France and Germany, the immigrant employment rate is 60–70 percent higher than the Dutch rate (Becker 2000: 235–236; van Oorschot 2002: 416). Van Oorschot concludes, "Clearly, the activation policies of the 1980s and 1990s have not been able to alter existing patterns of exclusion" (van Oorschot 2002: 416). In sum, the "present state of nearly full part-time employment may be judged a second-best solution only" (Hemerijck 1999: 19–21).

Now, a new center-right, largely conservative government has been elected with the promise of cutting back on the welfare state and restricting immigration (New York Times 2002: A6).

FRANCE

As with almost all the other countries, the initial response to high unemployment was to remove the older workers from the laborforce (Palier 2000: 122; Levy 1999: 5).[19] Costs rose, and there have been some reforms.[20] But pension reform remained politically difficult (The Economist 2002k: 48). Pensions are very fragmented – each "professional category" has its own scheme. Unless changes are made, the French pension system will become insolvent in 2005, and there will be massive deficits between 2015–40 (Levy 2001: 21).

Most unemployment benefits are based on contributions and are earnings-related. There are two traditional unemployment benefit systems – one, managed by the social partners (AUD), and a "Solidarity" system (ASS) tax funded and managed by the state (Enjolras, Laville, Fraisse and Trickey 2000: 48). When unemployment benefits are exhausted, there is the "Solidarity Benefit" (ASS, 1984), which is means-tested and pays about half of the minimum wage. The number of ASS beneficiaries trebled between 1985 and 1994, from 157,000 to 449,000. Women, older workers, and those under twenty-five have been especially vulnerable to unemployment and precarious jobs (Enjolras et al. 2000: 48; Barbier and Théret 2001).

Initially, there was no job search requirement. Then, in 2000, employers and the unions signed an agreement that if an unemployed worker turns down two job offers, benefits are reduced by 20 percent; after three job offers benefits are suspended, and after four job offers, benefits are withdrawn permanently. On the other hand, unemployment insurance payments will no longer decrease every six months as they have since 1992. As long as the beneficiary keeps searching for a job, he or she keeps full benefits (email communication with Jonah Levy, July 12, 2001).

There were various regulatory attempts to provide both flexibility and employment protection. Modifications can be made for a legitimate business reason, but, then, the employer is under an obligation to

---

[19] The retirement age was lowered from sixty-five to sixty, then fifty-five and in some cases fifty, all with full pensions. Consequently, the laborforce participation in France among those aged between fifty-five and sixty-four dropped to just over 40 percent, which was the lowest in Western Europe.

[20] The qualifying period for the full pension was extended from thirty-seven and a half years to forty years, the salary period from the best ten years to the best twenty-five years.

train the employee, or if dismissed, to assist in the search for a new job. There is remuneration for a certain period called "conversion agreements." If the employee refuses to accept the training plan, he or she can be dismissed. In 1996, nearly 3 million held part-time jobs. Most part-time employees have the lowest level of training, and are either non- or low-skilled. The vast majority are women, most over forty years of age. Parental leave, education, and training, etc., do not interrupt the employment status. In this respect, part-time employment is considered the same as regular employment (Supiot 2000).

French law tries to encourage job sharing. There is a reduction in the workweek, with employer rebates of Social Security contributions. In 2002, this provision was extended to companies with fewer than 20 workers. This law attempts to link the reduction in working time to hiring new employees or safeguarding existing jobs (Supiot 2000). With the recent change in government, there are suggestions to "soften the effects" of the thirty-five-hour working week (The Economist 2002l: 49).

Several major changes have been made in various parts of welfare. First, means tests were introduced in a variety of programs – family allowances, child care subsidies, and income supplements for single parents. Second, and most significantly, a guaranteed minimum allowance was established in 1988, called RMI (*revenue minimum d'insertion*) which replaced a variety of local and targeted social assistance programs. Until RMI, there was no central government transfer system for those not covered by unemployment insurance. Social assistance was available on a discretionary basis, and highly variable. RMI is governed by the principle of *subsidiarity* – a last resort for those who are unable to take care of themselves. Eligibility is based on the inability to work. RMI, it is claimed, "transformed the institutional landscape." It provides the right to a minimum income and a right to *insertion*. The insertion contract is not restricted to work; rather, re-integration can also be accomplished by improvements in health, housing, the education of children, and so forth. As discussed in Chapter 3, Pierre Rosanvallon describes the RMI contract as follows: "While the [client] must make an effort at integration and must respect the contents of the contract, the public employment services and the social services also theoretically have an obligation, together with the local authorities, to propose integration offers" (Rosanvallon 2000). It represents a compromise between the Right which favored a minimum condition of participation in "collective activity" and the Left which wanted no conditions

(Enjolras et al. 2000: 49). According to Barbier and Théret, RMI "entitlement is explicitly associated with the state's obligation to provide beneficiaries with opportunities to 'integrate' . . . without obliging them either to be 'available' or to 'actively seek work' " (Barbier and Théret 2001: 157).

RMI is means-tested. Administration is complex. The cash benefits are funded at the national level; the insertion program is largely funded and administered at the regional level by the departmental authorities rather than regions or other local governments. New partnerships between state, regional, and local authorities are to coordinate the delivery of complex employment and insertion programs. There are required local matching funds for certain insertion programs. It applies to all citizens and long-term residents over the age of twenty-five. While job placement is one of the objectives, there is no job search requirement. The RMI pays about half the minimum wage; there are supplements for a couple (50 percent) and per child (30 percent). The insertion contract is between the individual and the "commission for insertion" which sets forth the objectives and strategies. The commissions are at the department level and are composed of representatives of agencies likely to help, including representatives from municipalities, various state agencies, voluntary organizations and social workers. In addition to employment, insertion contracts may cover social and family life, health, housing, and vocational training (Enjolras et al. 2000: 50).

In theory, all recipients are entitled to an insertion contract, but work-based placements are limited. One-third were oriented towards "social autonomy" (health, daily living, etc.); one-third were jobs in the public and voluntary sectors, and one-third of recipients were looking for work. The degree of obligation is ambiguous with varying interpretations at the local level. Sanctions for refusing to take a job are few. The Right wants to strengthen the conditions. The Left is now divided – some want to make RMI unconditional by removing the insertion requirements (Enjolras et al. 2000: 51). Many RMI recipients are unemployable or hard-to-employ – older, unskilled, have mental health problems, or alcohol or drug dependency. Nevertheless, RMI has been criticized for creating a "poverty trap" – with earned income from low-wage, part-time work not equal to the benefits. For a full-time minimum wage job, the effective tax rate is estimated to exceed 60 percent (Levy 1999: 9–12).

RMI does not apply to the young unemployed. As administered for adults, it was considered too passive and there was the fear of generating a "culture of dependency" (Fafo 2001: 16). Instead, the Jospin government expanded the insertion programs originally designed for RMI to the young, non-RMI recipients. As a result, the insertion programs increasingly target the young. The young are more likely to work outside of the regular labor market in return for benefits. In France, this is considered "workfare" (Enjolras et al. 2000: 52–59).

There were three main objectives of the French youth employment policies: (1) improving vocational training, especially for those who left school with no qualifications; (2) increasing job opportunities in the private sector by reducing labor costs; and (3) experimenting with new jobs outside the private market such as local services and unmet social needs. In the private market, there were exemptions from Social Security contributions for apprentices, who would be paid between 25 percent and 75 percent of the minimum wage, depending on age and length of service; there were to be bonuses for hiring apprentices; qualification contracts for fixed terms (between six and twenty-four months) for at least one-quarter time, again at a reduced wage; and adaptation contracts, either fixed term or permanent, for the young (16–25) to acquire training and experience, also at a reduced wage. In the non-market sector, the "Travaux d'Utilite Collective" (TUCs) provided part-time (three to six months) work for sixteen to twenty-five-year-olds in local authorities, public institutions, and non-profits (Roche 2000: 52–53).

TUC was replaced by Solidarity Employment Contracts (CES) in 1989; again, part-time (eight month average) for the young, the long-term unemployed, and RMI recipients. CES was extended to the long-term unemployed and older adults. Costs were held down by limiting work to twenty hours per week. Wages were about one-half the full-time minimum wage. Like the TUC, it operated only in the public and voluntary sectors. Jobs were typically in caretaking and upkeep of community areas. Yet another youth employment program, the *Emploi Jeunes* was created in 1997. The goal was to create 350,000 jobs in the public and voluntary sectors. The emphasis was on job creation. Employers were to be subsidized to create "real" jobs. The program applied to anyone, aged eighteen to twenty-six, out of work rather than just disadvantaged youth, as long as they were not registered for unemployment insurance (Enjolras et al. 2000: 52–65).

There has been an increase in the number of young participants. Over 200,000 full-time jobs have been created, two-thirds of which are apprentice contracts and assisted employment (TUC, then CES) in the non-market sector. However, it is claimed that a large number of these jobs would have been created anyway. On the other hand, the training courses and the subsidized jobs have countered unemployment, at least in the short-term, for several hundred thousand of the young. Insertion, however, is problematic because of the growing lack of secure working conditions, resulting in a lower level of wages for the young (Roche 2000: 61–62).

There are also provisions to supplement earnings. *Le mécanisme des activités réduites* provides that insured job seekers who take a lower paying job can keep part of their unemployment benefits for a period of up to eighteen months while they are looking for a better job. Under a 1998 law, welfare recipients can receive part of their benefits as they re-enter the labor market for up to 750 hours per year for a period of twelve months. In 2002, the government introduced a tax credit, *prime pour l'emploi* (PPE) for low-income households, which is similar to the UK Working Families Tax Credit. PPE was fully phased in in 2003 and should equal one month's wage for a person earning the minimum wage (Daguerre and Palier 2002: 9, 17, 18, 23).

There are mixed reviews of the French record thus far. Jonah Levy says that it is often possible to enact controversial changes when blame is shared through tripartite "social pacts" – unions, employer representatives, and the state. In France, this approach does not look promising. Corporatist groups have been marginalized and fragmented as a result of the *dirigiste* state. The traditionalist statist mode of decision-making continues. Despite the Jospin government's slogan of "treating the French as adults," it is still top-down. There continues to be confrontation over unemployment funds, health reform, and pension reform. The government has been thwarted by public employee protests (e.g., teachers, hospital workers) (Levy 2000: 22–26).[21] The average salaried worker is paying more in payroll taxes and receiving slightly less in benefits, pensions, and health care reimbursements. While the poor and the disadvantaged have gained from the state, they have lost more from the market – there are higher levels of unemployment, inequality, and social exclusion. For a time, it looked like the economy was beginning to recover, and with predictions of growth, proposed

---

[21] Even a "whiff of prosperity" may be something of a "mixed blessing." In 1999, 30 billion more francs were collected than expected, and in 2000, 50 billion. There have been fierce public battles as to how to spend this windfall – tax cuts, subsidizing low-wage workers, more money for teachers and hospital workers – even though France continues to have a large budget deficit.

austerity measures would be even more resented (Levy 2000). Under the *cohabitation* of Chirac and Jospin, the French economy grew – almost 3 percent a year, capital investment and employment increased, and unemployment began to decline (9.1 percent, 2002) (Hall 2002). Nevertheless, the last election revealed extensive discontent. Even though Chirac won the presidency and his party has a majority in the National Assembly, the combined vote for Chirac and Jospin was only 36 percent, and a record 40 percent did not bother to vote for the legislature. With predictions of growth, proposed austerity measures would be even more resented.

The Jospin government tried to create a concertational approach to policy-making. The difficulty is that French unions are weak and divided and unable to match the employers. On the other hand, if the state intervenes, it undermines the credibility of the corporate process. The government had to intervene (and provide more subsidies) to save the thirty-five-hour week proposal from being completely one-sided. But now, the employers' associations have hardened their stand on both pensions and health care reforms.

It is too early to tell whether the structural reforms will succeed and restore financial equilibrium to the Social Security system. The health reform has barely started and already it has been circumscribed and is deeply in debt. As noted, the pension system will become insolvent in 2005 or shortly thereafter. A commission has recommended gradually raising the minimum years of contributions for retirement, but the government did not respond. In France, it remains politically dangerous to cut public employee benefits. The government relies heavily on early retirement to ease the transitions involved in restructuring.

In the meantime, the welfare state has continued to expand. Many of the most significant commitments of the early 1980s required new spending – reductions in the retirement age from sixty-five to sixty (in practice, much closer to fifty-five), creation of a universal guaranteed minimum income ("RMI"), plus health insurance for the indigent, jobs for youth, the thirty-five-hour week. But the spending on health and pensions are the big runaway items. Public expenditures are now at an all-time high, and the French voters want more, not less, state intervention in the social area (Levy 2000).

According to Bruno Palier, the re-insertion policy (RMI), a new social tax, and new power distributions within the system, amount to a new logic or direction – that of means tests, taxation, and more state autonomy in the construction of welfare policy (Palier 2000: 128–129).

As discussed, RMI is the most important change. There are seven other minimum social incomes, enrolling more than 10 percent of the population. There are a number of new policies dealing with the excluded, including employment contracts and re-insertion. There is a high degree of devolution to local authorities with the idea that they would handle a range of problems (poverty, housing, vocational training) in an integrated manner (Palier 2000: 129–130). There has also been a shift in financing. There is a move toward state-run, tax-financing of health care, family benefits, and poverty reduction. With the new tax in 1990 (CSG), the government is increasingly replacing contributions with taxation. Most health care contributions have been replaced. Another reform was the means-tested CMU (*couverture maladie universelle*), which provides free health care to those who could not afford the co-pay under the regular health care program (Levy 1999: 9–12). In 1999, CSG provided more than 20 percent of all social protection resources and 35 percent of health care. Palier says that these reforms are not marginal. They deal with a significant portion of the population and increase the state's ability to intervene (Palier 2000: 130–134).

The various employment programs have very mixed results. Progress in employing older workers has been described as "meager"; the impact of programs that target young people "remains modest" (Daguerre and Palier 2002: 24). It is claimed that employers are substituting subsidized placements rather than creating new jobs. The reduction of Social Security contributions or a subsidy equal to the unemployment benefit seems to have produced no real rise in employment. The programs seem to have had little impact on the participants; rather, clients tend to move from placement to placement within the subsidized sector, thus increasing job insecurity. For many RMI beneficiaries, these jobs are considered "bad jobs" – poorly paid with poor prospects for permanent, regular jobs. The differences between the skilled and unskilled youth have not been lessened; instead, the programs enhance traditional labor-market selectivity – the more skilled get into the better programs and get the better jobs. Nevertheless, although most RMI leavers are dissatisfied with their jobs, they have a positive view of RMI (Fafo 2001: 19). It is argued that the programs continue because they act as a "*substitute*" for the absence of social programs for the young. That is, since social assistance is not available, the social activation programs prevent the youth from falling into poverty (Enjolras et al. 2000: 60, 65; Daguerre and Palier 2002: 24).

In theory, the French social protection and insertion policy is conditioned on reciprocal obligations. The practice seems to be very different. There is a great deal of local variation. Overall, the insertion contract rate is about 50 percent but this rate tells nothing about the content of the contracts. According to survey data, one-third of the beneficiaries had never heard of the insertion contract. Many receive help from the local employment agency (ANPE) without signing a contract. Clients are not always familiar with the contracts and what they are supposed to do; they are sometimes unclear as to their rights and responsibilities. They view the contracts as a necessary step in order to obtain benefits rather than as an opportunity to improve employability. The Fafo Institute quotes one respondent: "'insertion contracts are a load of rubbish, they don't guarantee anything. They are not going to make companies take anyone on'" (Fafo 2001: 15–17). Several of the Fafo respondents were unaware of the insertion contracts. And many of the workers take the view that the "right to integration is partly illusionary while there are no 'real' jobs available for clients" (Fafo 2001: 61–62). "[A] majority of participants are in the insertion sector for a long time and . . . only a minority (20–25 percent) of participants experienced these schemes as a kickstart for a return to the regular labor market" (Barbier and Théret 2001: 173). The policies are ambiguous in terms of objectives and implementation. The role of the commissions is unclear. For the young, the theory is that these programs are voluntary, not part of welfare benefits. The breach of conditions rarely leads to sanctions, either for adults or the young (Enjolras et al. 2000: 66–67). According to qualitative interviews conducted by the Fafo Institute, the RMI clients rarely mention the insertion contracts. Rather, they speak of "real work" or "bad jobs" (Fafo 2001).

RMI has turned out to be a very loose form of constraint. Most workers favored keeping the penalties as a way of maintaining the credibility of the program and said that sometimes the threats of sanctions did result in a signing of the contract. However, most workers thought that the penalties were marginal. The main problem was the lack of suitable opportunities, and the workers were not willing to impose a sanction if they had nothing to offer. Of the clients interviewed by Fafo, few had been threatened and none sanctioned, and few were familiar with the sanction procedures (Fafo 2001: 15–16).

Survey data indicate that the lack of work ethic assumptions of the RMI are doubtful. Three-quarters of the RMI recipients who are unemployed are as active as the rest of the unemployed in looking for work. Most RMI recipients leave the program via a job, many without signing an insertion contract, but the jobs are very insecure. The insertion contracts help in obtaining a subsidized job but not a regular, full-time job. Insertion contracts as well as social worker selectivity tend to concentrate on the most employable. "In short, the sociological profile of beneficiaries plays a decisive part in their chances of leaving the scheme for a job, and the 'insertion contract' does not really reverse the order of the job queue in favour of those further from the labour market" (Fafo 2001: 17–18).

Levy says that there continues to be confrontation over unemployment funds, health reform, and pension reform. "By all accounts, the 'insertion' dimension of the RMI has remained woefully underdeveloped, and there is no hint of conditionality. Benefits cannot be withdrawn from the 'undeserving poor' unless they are employed" (email communication with Jonah Levy, July 12, 2001). In light of the positive economic developments, Levy argues that there are two possible scenarios. The pessimistic one is that if there is economic recovery, the government will abandon its efforts to restructure the welfare state, even instituting the most elementary spending controls. The optimistic view is that there will be sustained, gradual, negotiated reform. With a better economy, side payments can be offered to the "losers" of proposed reforms, facilitating trade-offs and compromises (Levy 1999: 20–21).

In the meantime, French immigrants, especially from North Africa and the Middle East, including children who were born in France, suffer discrimination which further diminishes their chances for labor-market success. A great many are confined to squalid housing estates and are greatly disadvantaged in the competitive education system. Many fail to obtain the secondary school certificate which is considered necessary to obtain a reasonable job (The Economist 2001b: 50–51). In describing the conditions in a housing estate in Grigny, 30 kilometers south of Paris, Rabah Ait-Hamadouche says, "[M]ore than one in four is unemployed, half of the population is under 25, one in four of foreign origin and hundreds of tenants are under threat of eviction. The reputation of the 'estate of fear,' as some call it, is abysmal. Life here means unemployment, casual labor, insecurity and exclusion" (Ait-Hamadouche 2002). "According to opinion polls, almost two-thirds of French adults believe that there are too many Arabs (and therefore Muslims) in France" (The Economist 2001b: 50).

GERMANY

The German economy fluctuated until unification. Prior to 1973, unemployment was below 1 percent. The economy then began to decline and unemployment rose to 8 percent by the mid-1980s, which was then followed by a recovery with a decline in unemployment to 4.2 percent in 1991. Reunification brought on a severe recession; by 1996, the unemployment rate was 10.3 percent. The first responses, in 1977, by the Social Democrat-Liberal government, was to reduce expenditures by changing pension rules, raising contribution rates, reducing health benefits, and tightening unemployment benefits. When the Christian Democrat-Liberal government took office in 1982, these changes were increased. This proved to be particularly controversial with social assistance. Both the replacement rates and the duration of unemployment benefits were reduced. After one year, recipients had to go onto means-tested social assistance, which was locally monitored and stigmatizing. At the same time, welfare state policies continued to favor the male breadwinner and discouraged women from working. Two-thirds of the unemployed were women who could not combine work with family care (Huber and Stephens 2001: 265–268).

Manufacturing collapsed in East Germany, and, although one-fifth of the population, they accounted for almost one-third of the unemployed. Demands for social expenditures, tax increases, and wage increases came into serious conflict with the Bundesbank which imposed very restrictive monetary policies. This resulted in a severe recession in 1993, further increasing unemployment. By 1998, unemployment rose to 11.6 percent even though there was a slow economic recovery (Huber and Stephens 2001: 265–271) and then declined to 10 percent in 2002 (The Economist 2002m: 92). The incidence of long-term unemployment is over 50 percent, well above the OECD average of about 30 percent (Adena, Gray, and Kahl 2001: 5).

The first response to rising unemployment was to encourage early retirement. Eligibility was reduced to sixty if the claimant was out of work for at least a year. Large companies used this change to reduce staff. The unemployment pensions did ease labor market pressures with the reduction of workers aged fifty-five to sixty-five but proved to be very costly. Access to early retirement is in the process of being restricted, but it is being slowly phased in and is still significant. In the East, early retirement is widely used and the laborforce participation of older workers is very low. In the meantime, unions continue to defend real wages, costs continue to rise, and unemployment remains high (Manow and Seils 2000: 142–150).

Reducing the work week through work sharing has been a major goal of unions who are willing to accept a proportionate decline in pay. The Volkswagen agreement (reduction from thirty-five to twenty-eight hours a week) is being followed by other companies; flexible work time is spreading in collective bargaining agreements. Rising social insurance contributions are particularly problematic for low-wage workers and since part-time jobs (under fifteen hours per week) are not subject to Social Security contributions, many (an estimated 1.1 to 3.3 million workers) hold part-time jobs. Presently, about half of the 40 million workers in Germany are in precarious jobs (including public work programs, occupational retraining, and part-time work) (Supiot 2000).

The unions have been urged to strike a balance between high wages and loss of jobs, that is, while protective of the "insiders," they have to become more aware of the trade-offs. At least, the employers so argue. The unions often agree that the unemployed should get subcontracted jobs which pay substantially lower wages. Of similar effect is the new combination wage – that is, low wages supplemented with social assistance or benefits from the national employment office or direct wages subsidies to employers. One effect is the substitution for regular jobs (Kahl 2002a: 41–44). Another development has been the growth of part-time, often temporary jobs (under fifteen hours per week) – called "minor employment." In 2001, there were about 2,543,000 people working in minor employment (Adena et al. 2001: 32). About 80 percent of these workers are women, often mothers with child-care responsibilities (Streeck 2001).

The social insurance system dominates the German welfare state covering all major risks – unemployment, sickness, disability, long-term care, and old age (Adena et al. 2001). The unemployed are eligible if they have made contributions for at least one year prior to claiming benefits. For those under forty-five years of age, Unemployment Benefits ("UB") last only for one year, and are about two-thirds of the previous income. When UB is exhausted, the next tier is Unemployment Assistance ("UA") which is not time-limited; benefits are about one-half of previous income. Both programs are administered by federal offices at the local level. These offices are also responsible for job and training placements and job search assistance (Voges, Jacobs, and Trickey 2001: 73–75).

The Federal Social Assistance Act of 1961 ("SSA") established a national legal entitlement to social assistance. Social assistance is intended to cover basic needs – e.g., food, housing, heating, personal needs – but also to allow for participation in social and cultural life. The amount varies with family size and it is considered to be a last resort safety net. There is some variation between East and West Germany. Social assistance is financed and administered by the local authorities. There are two parts. One, "Assistance in Special Situations" is for the ill and disabled who need costly care; benefits are usually in kind in the form of personal services. The other, "Cost-of-Living Assistance" ("COLA") is for people who lack sufficient income (Voges, Jacobs, and Trickey 2001: 75).[22] This program contains a high proportion of single mothers and the long-term unemployed. The COLA is based on the social assistance standard rates which are defined by the Federal Government.

There have been significant changes in the social assistance rolls – the growth of unemployment (especially since unification) and the decline in unskilled work. Although never intended to provide benefits to the employable, social assistance is increasingly relied upon because of the high rate of the long-term unemployed; in fact, almost half of the caseload is the unemployed (Adena et al. 2001: 5, 7). Within the unemployed, the social assistance recipients are the most poorly qualified. Over three-quarters have been unemployed for at least nine months as compared to less than one-third of the other unemployed. Mothers returning to the laborforce are at a higher risk of remaining on social assistance. Higher proportions of younger social assistance recipients have more severe personal barriers, including substance abuse. Other causes of the increase in social assistance have been the growth in low-income single person households, as well as refugees and asylum-seekers, who, until 1993 were not permitted to work (Voges, Jacobs, and Trickey 2001: 78).

Since the early 1980s, Germany's asylum seekers have been increasingly viewed as the "undeserving poor." Welfare policies began to deter asylum seekers from receiving social assistance by granting only reduced

---

[22] In addition, there are programs for income support for specific groups that are considered compensatory payments – e.g., victims of war, military, crime, publicly-supported vaccinations. These benefits are usually not based on need and are designed to compensate for low wages rather than maintain individual standards of living. There are also grant programs for education, vocational training, housing, and children's allowances, which are means-tested.

entitlements and cutting housing benefits altogether. The situation for asylum seekers worsened again with the enactment of the Asylum Seekers Benefits Act in 1993. Asylum seekers and foreigners residing in Germany were now completely excluded from receiving social assistance; only permanent residents retained their eligibility rights. In order to establish some kind of public assistance program for ineligible foreigners, the government created a new benefit scheme for those without full citizenship rights. Generally, the benefits are about 20 percent below the social assistance benefits. In 1999, about 435,930 persons received benefits from the Asylum Seekers Benefits Act, which amounted to a total expenditure of DM 3,950 million (Kahl 2002b: 19).

As a result of the growth and changing character of social assistance, changes have been made to make the system more "active." Starting in 1981, there have been several reductions, mostly in the form of delays or denials of adjustments for inflation as well as a tightening of eligibility. Since 1988, social assistance has been tied to the net wages of the lowest income groups, rather than the cost of living. In particular, the wage replacement rate for both UB and UA has been cut several times since 1984 (Kahl 2002b: 22). These changes were designed to provide stronger work incentives, leading critics to claim that the social assistance level is too low to alleviate poverty (Kahl 2002a; 2002b).

Lone mothers have been considered "truly needy" and acknowledged as reproductive workers. Since 1985, there have been several increases in their benefits. The Conservatives have sought to upgrade the value of family work and uphold the noncommodified status of caretaking by creating a new occupational image (*Berufsbild*) of the mother and housewife. The Christian-Democrat Government introduced the National Child Raising Benefit to reaffirm the woman's traditional role as housewife. Women are granted compensation for their work in the home until their child reaches the age of two. As part of the condition, recipients are only allowed to work fifteen hours outside their home. Despite these limited work provisions, however, single mothers receiving the Child Raising Benefit in conjunction with Social Assistance have incomes that equal their income in unskilled work (Kahl 2002b: 7). Following the pattern set by the Conservatives, the 1996 Social Democrat legislation expanded support for mothers by extending financial assistance to all teenage mothers regardless of their parents' income (Kahl 2002a; 2002b). Still, lone mothers and their children, together with immigrants, are considered most at risk for social assistance. In 2000, about 4 percent of German households were on social assistance with more than one-quarter being lone parents. Young children are especially overrepresented in social assistance households (Adena et al. 2001: 29).

Varieties of work schemes have a long history in Germany (Voges, Jacobs, and Trickey 2001). The Federal Social Assistance Act ("SAA"), enacted in 1961, required social assistance recipients to accept an offer of work as a condition of receiving aid. Implementation is at the local level. Previously, during periods of low unemployment, social assistance recipients were considered unable to work and the work requirement was not enforced (Fafo 2001: 21). The present workfare program was pioneered in Berlin, between 1982 and 1984, where up to 23,500 people were put in workfare programs, mainly cleaning. The main objective of these programs was to "test the recipient's will to work" and to improve the work ethic (Kahl 2002b: 46).

As a reaction to the large numbers of unemployed, Germany, at least at the federal level, is now committed to active labor-market policies. There has been a rise in workfare. In part, this is due to the rising costs of social assistance for the local authorities and, in part, intended to provide a greater "work-testing" of the unemployed. Other reasons include a desire to re-integrate, to increase local level employment, to reduce poverty, and to help local charities with community service jobs. The public favors work in return for benefits. The Schröder government is committed to providing work and training for the younger unemployed (Voges, Jacobs, and Trickey 2001: 88).

Serious debate on reforming unemployment protection in Germany did not come until the late 1990s. Part of the reason for this late start was that one of the promises of reunification was not to change the social protection system (Reissert 2001: 11). When the debate did come, reflecting the changes that occurred in the rest of Europe, it centered primarily on activation measures, specifically increasing responsibilities for the unemployed and stronger incentives to return to work and protection and promotion for more flexible work, rather than unemployment protection (Reissert 2001: 14–15). Changes in activation were made. All unemployed recipients who are considered employable are in principle required to participate. Activation for UI recipients is usually mandatory and focuses on re-integration and rehabilitation; activation for SA recipients is more focused toward direct job placement in the low-wage sector. Able-bodied COLA recipients are supposed to be sent to the local federal employment office for job-seeking, and are required to accept any job that is offered either through the unemployment office or the local authority social assistance office. The primary goal has been to place the recipient in a real job. Social Assistance benefits are to be cut if the recipient refuses to accept any job (Kahl 2002b: 24, 32). In addition, a "jobs package" would be offered in which local authorities would provide jobs for some long-term unemployed receiving social security payments. If they refuse a job, benefits are cut. There are exceptions if the work is "overtaxing," or endangers the future pursuit of a previous occupation, or endangers child-rearing (Voges, Jacobs, and Trickey 2001: 76–77). This was described as a "welfare-to-work" program. In 1993, about 50,000 social assistance recipients were in workfare projects (Standing 1999: 314).

In 1996, in an effort to curb rising social assistance costs, the Federal Government demanded that local administrations of social affairs create more workfare positions in order to "test the will to work." By eliminating abusers of the system, it was argued that the truly needy would be helped. The reform was to provide "incentives, support, and sanctions" to encourage work. Starting in 1999, welfare benefits were to be at least 15 percent lower than the net wages of the lower income groups. It was also mandated that recipients who refused a workfare assignment would have their benefits reduced by at least 25 percent. A parent with a child under three years of age would be exempt, and, if day care was not available, the exemption would continue after the age of three. Employer subsidies were available if social assistance recipients were hired. And recipients could receive extra money for the first six months of regular employment. Between 1995 and 1996, the number of new social assistance recipients declined by more than 50 percent. Currently, about 400,000 of the 800,000 social assistance recipients considered able-bodied and employable are in workfare projects (Kahl 2002a; 2002b).

By the late 1990s, all the political parties were in favor of workfare, although there were differences, primarily over the issue of compulsion. The Christian Democrats favored "work testing"; the Social Democrats and the Greens emphasized support rather than sanctions (Fafo 2001: 24). In 1998, with more than 400,000 under age twenty-five unemployed, the government adopted a "Cornerstones of Action" program which was a combination of work training and wage subsidies. There was job creation for those not ready for regular jobs. Local authorities were given more money from the Federal Employment Office as well as the European Social Fund to expand and tailor their programs (Voges, Jacobs, and Trickey 2001: 97). The local social assistance offices are supposed to send all the unemployed to the local employment offices to register. These offices, in turn, are supposed to maintain contact with the unemployed and help with placement (Voges, Jacobs, and Trickey 2001: 84).

The local authorities have become increasingly reluctant to continue supporting Social Security claimants, especially the long-term unemployed. They introduced a range of "activation" policies (Clasen 2000: 95, 103). The new program is called "Help Towards Work" (HTW), which, as distinguished from PES programs, emphasizes a "strong 'work-for-benefit' element" (Adena et al. 2001: 39). There are two forms of work requirements. For the most employable, there is work under an employment contract which carries standard wages and is incorporated into the social insurance system. These jobs are time-limited. If the worker is not hired permanently, he or she is eligible for unemployment benefits, which reduces expenses for the local authorities. For those with major barriers to work, there are "specific work opportunities." These are individually-tailored work opportunities and are considered "social activation." These jobs can be "real" or what is called "noncontract" pursuant to an employment agreement between the local authority and the recipient. The wages may be at a reduced level. The noncontract employees continue to receive social assistance, with a supplement for work expenses, and are not covered by standard employee rights. However, these work opportunities are declining in importance because of the high costs to the local authorities (Voges, Jacobs, and Trickey 2001: 83–84; Adena et al. 2001: 41).[23] In addition, local authorities may provide vocational training and education. All unemployed recipients are supposed to register with the local employment offices which, in turn, are supposed to maintain contact with the clients while on benefits (Fafo 2001: 22).

Now, nearly all local authorities have created HTW jobs, although there is considerable variation in terms of targeting, contracting versus noncontracting, and implementation especially as between the East and the West (Voges, Jacobs, and Trickey 2001: 81). In the West, some local authorities offer activation measures for volunteers; others require participation after a certain period on benefits; others permit recipients to reject workfare altogether. In the East, Leipzig attempts to offer workfare to all social assistance recipients, including the disabled.

---

[23] It is estimated that the cost of a work placement is about €23,000 per year as compared to the cost of a single person on social assistance of €6,600 per year.

Most other cities in the East lack the capacity to implement workfare on any significant scale (Fafo 2001: 23). More women participate in East Germany than in the West, reflecting differences in previous work patterns. Gender differences in assignment are also present – in the West, women tend to be assigned to the service sector; in the East, more to construction.

In general, there are two types of job-creation – a "contract work" scheme and a "work-for-benefit" scheme. About 40 percent of social assistance recipients participate in either of these two schemes. These are "non-market" jobs, designed to benefit the community; they are not to displace permanent workers, but this is considered "almost impossible" to achieve. The community jobs include street and park cleaning, sanitizing contaminated soil, cleaning waste dumps, etc. Thus, "it is not surprising that these schemes have a low chance of helping clients in achieving long-term independence from benefit support." The main benefit to municipalities is that even though a contract work job is a lot more expensive than social assistance, the worker qualifies for unemployment benefits, which will last until retirement. While this system benefits the municipalities, "this structure does not necessarily help clients to regain their self-supporting capacity. Indeed, the system may well contribute to prolonged public assistance dependency" (Adena et al. 2001: 40–41, 46).

There are also differences in sanction policies. In Berlin and Leipzig, there is more of a willingness to sanction; other West German cities believe sanctions are counterproductive. Worker attitudes towards sanctions reflect the differences in practice – in the East, they view sanctions as necessary for workfare. The workers complain about the relatively small amounts of time that can be spent on each client resulting in low professional support (Fafo 2001: 23, 25). In any event, the new rules for social assistance claimants, as well as the application process, "give a clear signal to prospective clients about the undesirability of being on social assistance and the stigma that may be attached to it, and their reliance on relatives" (Adena et al. 2001: 23). Stigmatization and social control, says an OECD Occasional Paper, may be responsible for a non-take up rate of between 33 and 63 percent. Many are unaware of entitlements (Adena et al. 2001: 23).

With the persistent high unemployment, there continues to be concern about the re-integration of social assistance recipients, especially the young, into the regular labor market. The local authorities have received greater federal attention and funding. In 2000, a law was passed to improve cooperation between employment offices and social assistance. The law provides for the merging of SA and UA, with one uniform activation system for both programs, with an emphasis on direct and quick job placement. In other words, UA recipients will now be required to participate in the SA activation programs. All recipients are to be immediately offered a job or be placed in a work program. Local UA offices and SA offices are to set up cooperative contracts to place the unemployed SA recipients in jobs. The two offices are to establish a single common office responsible for both sets of recipients, that is, both sets are to be subject to direct job placement as the first strategy. The local authorities may get federal funding for model projects. It is expected that while the two programs will be more closely linked in the short run, they will be merged in the long run. There is legislation, which became law in 2002, that mandates that with the beginning of unemployment – whether UA or SA – an individual re-integration plan has to be entered into, and recipients have to meet their obligations or will face a complete cut-off from their benefits for at least twelve weeks (Kahl 2002a: 46).

Until 1993, local authorities used their discretion not to impose sanctions. Since 1993, they are now required by federal law to sanction after a threat by a social worker. Up to one-quarter of the benefits are to be cut for the first refusal. For continual refusal, the recipient would lose his or her portion of the household benefit. It is reported that now social workers sometimes refuse to issue a threat to avoid having to impose a sanction. There is no clear evidence as to the proportion that refuses to participate, although it is clear, at least at the present time, that a majority of local authorities do not sanction (Voges, Jacobs, and Trickey 2001: 86–87). Because the long-term unemployed tend to be concentrated in the fifty years and over group, they are well-trained, with long work histories, and receive insurance-based benefits, the workers feel that it is harder to justify mandatory activation programs. And, it is easier politically to encourage exit than promote entry (The Economist 2001c). Lone parents are exempt until a child reaches four years, or up to ten years with two or more children. In practice, lone parents are exempt until the child reaches the mandatory school age, which is six to seven years (Adena et al. 2001: 28). Thus, despite the federal legislation and despite the position of both national political parties, it is claimed that the majority of local authorities do not sanction (Clasen 2000: 95). According to a recent OECD Occasional Paper, sanctions were rarely applied prior to 1996. "However, in 2000, of all clients who were offered a job or placement in activation or public works programme, about 10% were sanctioned for refusal" (Adena et al. 2001:17). It is said that sanctions for social assistance recipients will increase. There is the strong commitment to activation at the federal level. The basic problem at the local level, it is said, is not necessarily an unwillingness to sanction, but the lack of sufficient work and training opportunities. Many of the specific active labor market policies are new, with local authorities experimenting with what works. In the meantime, the Federal Government is increasing its monitoring and tightening national guidelines (Kahl 2002a: 34).

Most local authorities do not monitor HTW results. Some cities, because of inadequate data collection systems, do not know the number of workfare clients in their programs and the kinds of problems they have (Fafo 2001: 26). Thus, it is hard to generalize as to how HTW is being implemented. The few studies that do exist report that there is considerable "creaming." Costs to local authorities have been rising with the increase in unemployment. By concentrating on the most employable, they can more easily be placed in contract jobs, which are then covered by social insurance in case the worker becomes unemployed instead of the local authority social assistance budget (Voges, Jacobs, and Trickey 2001: 72). Based on interviews, the Fafo Institute reports that most recipients volunteer for the HTW program; in the East, they feel that they have to participate as a condition of benefits. Still, most of the recipients, both West and East, have positive attitudes towards HTW. On the other hand, there are extremely negative stereotypes of non-German recipients, especially in the East (Fafo 2001: 25).

As in other workfare programs, it is difficult to evaluate impacts. One summary of the evaluation studies concluded that training and direct job placement were more effective in reducing caseloads, although information on recidivism is lacking as between municipalities that use a work-first approach and those who use longer-term activation (Reported in Adena et al. 2001: 44). The OECD Occasional Paper concluded, "The group of clients that face multiple barriers to social and labour market integration . . . does not appear to benefit from common activation programmes. These 'hard to serve' clients are in need of targeted assistance, but are often neglected by [the local offices]" (Adena et al. 2001: 44).

For those on unemployment benefits, new legislation was enacted in January 2002, called "Job-AQTIV." The focus is to shift from training to quick entry into the labor market through mandatory profiling of all new clients as soon as they register with the PES. Caseworkers are to complete forms on education, qualifications, work experience, etc., which may trigger more in-depth assessments, to be followed, in turn, by intensive job counseling. Clients would be classified in terms of immediately employable, favorable, or limited prospects. A recent OECD Occasional Paper considers this legislation "largely aspirational in practice . . . PES-staff consider that since caseworkers are already overburdened, introducing this elaborate scheme is currently impossible to achieve" (Adena et al. 2001: 36–37).

The latest proposals come from an official commission on labor-market reform, set up in response to a report that the Federal Labour Office had greatly exaggerated its success in finding work for the jobless. The commission recommends that the 181 regional labor offices be turned into temporary-employment agencies. Anyone still without work after six months would be hired by the office for short-term work (at union rates) or have benefits reduced. In addition, unemployment payments would be changed from being calculated on the basis of previous earnings to three levels of flat benefits for six months and then gradually reduced to the basic social welfare level. With the economy struggling and unemployment a major political concern, Chancellor Schröder has expressed cautious interest (The Economist 2002n: 51; The Economist 2002o: 8). In the meantime, with the possibility of another recession, the government is floundering and there has been a significant decline in popularity (The Economist 2002p: 45).

RISKS FOR THE SOCIALLY EXCLUDED

As to be expected, the record thus far with active labor market policies is mixed – or, as will be discussed shortly, *appears* to be mixed. None of the goals can be accomplished quickly. The issues, though, that I want to conclude with in this chapter are the *risks* involved in pursuing inclusion through workfare. I do this because government officials, policymakers, and other proponents of workfare emphasize the positive – those who find employment, the decline in the unemployment rolls, the numbers who are actively engaged in work and training, and, invariably, a positive cost-benefit ratio. These are important accomplishments, and I do not mean to minimize them – after all, those included in workfare, at the minimum, have had a considerable spell of unemployment and many have various employment barriers. However, the workless and the socially excluded are a diverse group, some more employable and trainable than others, some with fewer barriers than others, and it is the most vulnerable who run the greater risks. Programs of inclusion based on contract necessarily exclude those who cannot negotiate the entry points and conditions of participation. Workfare programs are evaluated on the positive outcomes, and thus, there are pressures to cream. Programs that target the most vulnerable will, inevitably, have higher failure rates. But the political leaders and public want to hear about success, not failure. In emphasizing the positive, there is the tendency to ignore, or even blame, those who drop out. For these reasons, I call attention to the negative side.

It should be emphasized that, with few exceptions, the empirical evidence at the field level is uneven. A recent report by the Fafo Institute for Applied Social Science (Norway) evaluating workfare in France, Germany, the Netherlands, Norway, Denmark, and the United Kingdom concluded that the results are, at best, "suggestive rather than conclusive." Most of the studies were not well designed to answer the basic question of whether the participants benefited from the programs or were worse off (Fafo 2001: 73–74). To give one illustration of a key issue: workfare contracts are to be *individually* formulated, tailored to what the claimant needs to re-enter the labor market. How are these contracts, in fact, carried out? Do the agency workers have the resources, the time, and the inclination to listen to the claimants and carefully assess their needs and desires? Are the claimants willing and able to participate? What are the organizational constraints on the agency workers? Are options available to meet the needs of claimants? What pressures are on the agencies to fill quotas and meet targets? And so forth. The agency worker-client relationship is not only discretionary but also of low visibility. Careful field research, as conducted in the United Kingdom and Sweden, has not provided much evidence that these contracts are individually tailored. Instead, agencies merely offer brief sessions, with the officers restricting the options and the beneficiaries agreeing in order to accept the benefits (Roche 2000: 43). For the most part, this kind of field-level research is lacking for the other countries, although there are suggestions of similar practices in the other countries as well.

The Fafo Institute summarized its (suggestive rather than conclusive) findings as follows: (1) Many studies show that workfare has had positive effects on employment, as measured by earnings. However, in France, as previously noted, a majority of RMI participants do not have a contract even though it is a legal requirement. Those with contracts tend to be younger and better educated. Only about 25 percent of recipients leave RMI for work. The net employment effect of the Dutch JEA program is about 18 percent, but this number is uncertain. In Germany, it is not known whether participants are more likely to find a job as a result of participation. With the Norwegian compulsory programs, there was no significant improvement either in employment or earnings. (2) Those who benefit the most tend to be younger, with better education, and fewer social problems. This was true for France, Denmark, the Netherlands (including non-immigrants), and the United Kingdom. The French CES, on the other hand, was more effective for people with low skills as compared to higher skills. (3) In several programs, participants who were more likely to be successful tended to be selected by the offices. Thus, they would have been more likely to find jobs on their own. On the other hand, Norway attracted people with less experience and more problems. (4) Most participants expressed satisfaction with the programs, but a significant portion was negative. Satisfaction was quite low in the Netherlands ("boring, a waste of time") and there was evidence that the program was harmful to the most vulnerable. In the United Kingdom, the more disadvantaged tended to have negative attitudes. "It is noteworthy that the most disadvantaged people benefit less and tend to be most dissatisfied with the programmes, and that some participants, namely in *the Netherlands* – are worse off after the programme than before" (Fafo 2001: 71–73).

According to the workers, the delivery of options depends on the state of the economy, what is available locally, the nature of the political support for the programs, and client awareness. In general, clients are not aware of the various options that might be available. Clients are primarily interested in improving their employability but also their social status – they do not want to be considered "second rate people" (Fafo 2001: 60). They want to be treated with respect. In some of the countries (the Netherlands, Norway, and the United Kingdom), they resent "second rate jobs" although the workers may view these jobs as "stepping stones." While many complain about the lack of individually-tailored options, the workers say that they are hampered by bureaucratic procedures, the pressure to hold down expenses, the lack of available options, differences in the cultures of the social service agencies and the employment offices, and the variations among the clients. In the United Kingdom, for example, workers say that the emphasis in the New Deal has changed from a client-centered approach to labor-market placements, driven primarily to reduce costs (Fafo 2001: 60–62). While all the programs have sanctions, their use varies depending on worker discretion, staff attitudes towards the clients, the impact of the sanctions (i.e., whether sanctions would make no difference or make matters worse), how much paperwork would be increased, and so forth. In the United Kingdom, there has been a marked increase in the use of sanctions, and "the most socially excluded are more likely to experience sanctions . . . [despite the fact] the previous research has provided no evidence that the experience of sanctions has any positive influence on behaviour, whether of the person sanctioned or other jobseekers" (Training & Employment Network 1999: 2). As noted, clients have a right to appeal, but there is both a lack of understanding and the resources to pursue this right (Fafo 2001: 65).

In general, the workers favored compulsion. They considered it necessary because many recipients would not participate even though contrary to their best interests. In addition, "compulsion would reduce fraud, provide a work test, it is a fair bargain in return for assistance, it is justified if decent options are offered, and there is an improved economy." In some countries (Norway, Denmark), workers mention clients who would not have otherwise participated and have benefited; on the other hand, the workers either do not mention the dropouts or dismiss them as the clients' responsibility. There are some workers in France and the United Kingdom who oppose compulsion. Client attitudes towards compulsion are usually related to the quality of the offers. There are those who have positive attitudes towards the programs and say that compulsion not only helps some, but minimizes fraud. Other clients feel that compulsory participation is unjust. For these clients, the offers are considered degrading and unjust, especially if the work pays less than regular wages (Fafo 2001: 62–63).

All of the programs are selective. The workers pick from a variety of options, although the clients are generally unaware of the various options. Sometimes undesirable options are used as threats (e.g., "you'll be digging canals"). Clients are ranked to match the desirability of the options – "on the basis of their 'aptitude' or 'inaptitude' for the options."

> Intuition seems to play an important role in the street level bureaucrats' categorization of clients. Street level bureaucrats seem to focus on clients' attitudes and behaviours more strongly than may be expected on the basis of official policies, which often emphasised more objective features . . . The subjective factors often involve making distinctions between co-operative and unco-operative clients, between genuine clients and hard core unemployed clients, and between clients with realistic and

unrealistic ambitions . . . In practice, clients close to the labour market are often defined in neutral, objective terms . . . leaving subjective aspects more implicit. Whereas clients more distanced from the labour market are usually defined in terms of their subjective shortcomings (psychological or social handicaps, unstable lives, inability to deal with authority relations and so on). (Fafo 2001: 66)

It follows that the "best" clients are selected for the "best" options (those closest to the regular labor market – e.g., subsidized employment) which leaves the rest for the least desirable social activation options (e.g., the Environmental Task Force or voluntary service in the United Kingdom) (Fafo 2001: 67).

Because of high workloads and bureaucratic regulations, communication with clients tends to focus on meeting bureaucratic targets and placing clients in options without much discussion about client needs. Once placed, there is little contact with the workers. Clients are sensitive to this kind of treatment which they consider disrespectful (Fafo 2001: 67). Workfare conditions go both ways – they can result in a loss or a reduction in entitlement, or providing new resources designed to help labor market integration. Opportunities have increased and extended to people who had few labor-market prospects. On the other hand, in liberal countries, such as Denmark and the Netherlands, large numbers of people are not active, especially those considered to have more employment barriers, lone mothers, and ethnic minorities (Lødemel 2001: 295).

Flexibilization of employment has increased jobs and income for many, especially those who prefer part-time work. In some of the countries, comparable benefits and extensive labor rights now apply to part-time and temporary work (Svensson 1999). In other countries, flexible labor policies have led to an increase in job discontinuity (Supiot 2000). Countries vary on how they treat discontinuous employment. In general, protection against dismissal and the safeguarding of existing jobs has eased, but there is variation (Supiot 2000). Many prefer full-time work. Many workers – e.g., in Germany – are now considered to be in precarious jobs. In some countries – e.g., the United Kingdom, Ireland – there is considerable income inequality. In the Netherlands and Denmark, despite the very impressive employment gains, there remain considerable numbers of inactive and marginalized unemployed.

On the demand side, programs provide subsidies to private employers to hire disadvantaged workers (Supiot 2000). While the number of subsidized jobs has increased significantly in most countries, the importance of subsidies and the number of people that benefit vary considerably. So far, subsidized jobs are less effective in creating additional job opportunities. Usually, there is one new job for every five subsidized jobs. There were complaints that subsidy programs to private employers to hire disadvantaged workers produced windfall profits and were only "effective" when firms were going to expand anyway. The consensus was that overall employment did not improve. Most countries now rely on tightening unemployment benefits (McFate 1995). Another key component of active labor market policies is supposed to be public employment services ("PES") – to both reduce frictional unemployment and help disadvantaged workers gain skills and access. Except for Sweden, however, few job openings actually come through these offices.

The main trend has been to push more people onto means-tested and behavior-tested social assistance (Standing 1999: 265; Behrendt 2000: 23–41). The right to benefits is increasingly emphasizing earning capacity rather than previous occupation (Supiot 2000). In all countries, the take-up rate for social assistance is well below 100 percent. Moreover, of those who do receive benefits, many still remain in poverty. The general failure to alleviate poverty is due to a lack of coverage, low benefits, and low take-up rates (Behrendt 2000: 30–36).

Gender discrimination remains a serious issue throughout Western Europe. Almost half of all women are in the paid laborforce (as compared to two-thirds of all men). According to a survey of EU member states, more women than men work part-time (32 percent vs. 5 percent). With the exception of the Netherlands and Scandinavia, a high proportion of these women indicated that they would prefer to work full-time. There persists a significant amount of occupational segregation and discrimination in wages (Supiot 2000: 131). Pay differences are narrowing but still remain large. Female hourly wages average only 83 percent of male hourly wages (EXSPRO 2001: 7). Women continue to face discrimination in terms of the benefits and conditions in the standard labor contract. The hourly wage rate for part-time is lower than full-time (e.g., 85 percent in Sweden, 71 percent in France, 60 percent in the United Kingdom) and has not led to a redistribution of family responsibilities (Supiot 2000). Anton Hemerijck says, "[W]ith rising education women's preferences have changed dramatically. But . . . the institutional environment has remained 'frozen' in the traditional male breadwinner mold. In brief. Overall job stagnation is worsened by the severe incompatibilities that women face when they opt for a career" (Hemerijck 2002). Growing female participation has not led to an increase in union membership, in employers' associations, and collective bargaining. Even where women's union membership is high, they are underrepresented in executive bodies. While many EU community action programs purport to address this issue, they are weakly formulated and there are no binding obligations (Supiot 2000).

Several countries have succeeded in getting youth to stay in school longer, have tried to improve school-to-work transitions, and are emphasizing practical training in companies to bridge the gap between schools and employers (Supiot 2000). At first, the German apprenticeship system was the model, but now German employers are less inclined to train young people, they are seeking shorter apprenticeships, and are no longer willing to offer permanent employment to all apprentices at the end of the training period. In most European countries – as in the United States – there remain large disjunctures between general education, vocational education, and the labor market, particularly as labor markets are changing (Supiot 2000).

According to the OECD, targeted programs, by themselves, do not do much in helping young people as long as unemployment rates remain high (OECD 1999: 8). The OECD thinks that there are a number of things that can be done to help youth employment – for example, prevent school failure, raise school standards in terms of employability, early intervention for at-risk youth, a re-appraisal of the vocational stream, a better integration of academic and vocational education, and better coordination between education and employment. For disadvantaged youth, there should be a range of individually tailored, supportive services. Short-term programs do not work (OECD 1999).[24]

In some countries, the social inclusion programs are regarded positively by most target group clients. However, many difficulties have been noted. The professional and occupational culture of employment service offices has difficulty in sustaining a client-centered approach rather than an employment placement-centered approach (Roche 2000: 77). Creaming seems to be widespread. In Germany, as noted, the local authorities have a strong financial incentive to get the most employable into nationally-covered jobs and thus save local authority

---

[24] For example, perhaps as many as 25 percent of students completing upper secondary education are not sufficiently prepared for stage employment according to the International Adult Literacy Survey. The "dual" apprenticeship systems in Austria, Denmark, Germany, and Switzerland appear to have a better record in integrating non-college-bound students into the labor market (OECD 1999).

expenses. So far, the record on workfare concerning the socially excluded that has been evaluated is not particularly encouraging. Most policies to help the long-term unemployed, such as training, subsidized work contracts, and insertion in the social economy, have had modest effects on re-employment while offering employer windfalls. Positive outcomes are sometimes counterbalanced by perverse policy effects that contribute to new exclusions (Silver 1998b: 20). The most motivated and skilled workers disproportionately reap the benefits of subsidy and training programs. The EU White Paper expressed concern that, of the 10 million new jobs created during the 1980s, only 3 million were taken by those on unemployment registers. New laborforce entrants rather than the socially excluded took most of the jobs (Silver 1998b: 12). Hence, the workers who most need income protection – part-timers, services, domestics, homeworkers, flexiworkers, the black or shadow economy, etc., are usually not affected by regulatory schemes (Standing 1999: 293–298; Supiot 2001: 35).

The considerable variation in the design and implementation of the European programs appears to be related to the perceived characteristics of the target groups. In the more universal and generous programs (e.g., Nordic), groups with more barriers and risks become included, some are stereotyped as more deserving, others are not. Recipients of different options within social assistance have different rights and are subject to different attitudes (Lødemel 2001: 324–330). Under this view, Heather Trickey argues that compelling clients to participate in unproven programs is questionable. Under some conditions, compulsory programs can even be more damaging for those who fail; they face even more social exclusion (Trickey 2001: 287–288). While all programs have a range of options, the selection of options "inevitably mirrors the selectivity of the regular labor market." This leads not only to creaming but also to "exclusion trajectories" or "sink options" where clients are recycled. With the more decentralized programs, most of the disadvantaged who live in the areas of low labor-market demand may simply be ignored (Trickey 2001: 288–289). Case management is on the increase, which gives rise to tensions between social work and enforcement, between meeting targets for getting people off the rolls or into work. These tensions become most problematic for clients with multiple barriers. In the Netherlands, research has shown that compulsion has led to an increase in marginalization and social exclusion (Trickey 2001: 289–290). The use of sanctions is uneven. In Germany, thus far, several local authorities are still not inclined to use sanctions, especially for the more experienced, older workers. On the other hand, in the Netherlands, it is claimed that sanctions are used on the basis of officer-perceived negative social background characteristics (Spies and van Berkel 2001: 124–127). While creaming may well be taking place, there are no new anti-exclusion policies. In the Netherlands, a substantial number of the young unemployed, especially those with personal and/or social problems, are not involved even though the policies claim "full-coverage." In time, a "hard-core" group of unemployed will be left (Roche 2000: 43).

A major issue in all countries involves immigrants – an issue which will continue to grow in importance as the EU expands. Most countries are facing increasing anti-immigration problems – increasing ghettoization, race murders (even in Norway (Cowell 2002: 1)), even race riots. In some countries, there has been a rise in anti-immigration political parties – most recently in Denmark, which, in comparison with other Western European countries, has a relatively small immigrant population. Unemployment among ethnic minorities is considerably higher in all countries. Even the Nordic countries, which are most successful in dealing with social exclusion, are less successful in integrating immigrants into the labor market (EXSPRO 2001: 19). According to the EXSPRO report, "Dealing with excluded immigrants is . . . an area that needs to be confronted soon" (EXSPRO 2001: 3).

Inclusion of the socially excluded, especially those who have multiple employment barriers, involves income poverty, but it is broader. It includes developing *capabilities*. As the EXSPRO report states, "Social policy now has to support not only the 'freedom from want' but also the 'freedom to act,' for instance the freedom to combine career and child rearing or to engage in life-long learning" (EXSPRO 2001: 14). Finding a job depends on effort but also human capital, place of residence, networks, health, access to transportation, etc. The socially excluded are not likely to benefit from a more flexible Social Security system and more flexible labor markets. "Flexibility as such is not a strategy of social inclusion" (EXSPRO 2001: 3). Activation programs also have their pitfalls. Access to jobs, services, and training may be denied based on *a priori* perceptions of employability as field-level offices strive to become more "efficient." Thus, in the opinion of the EXSPRO report, "activation typically does not reach those most affected by social exclusion . . . Activation is most successful for those just above or just below the income or deprivation poverty thresholds, not those in the lower strata" (EXSPRO 2001: 20). Although it may seem both efficient and equitable, targeting social and employment policies on the most disadvantaged may further stigmatize those who are already excluded. Universal welfare state programs enjoy the most political support, while taxpayers suspect that means-tested benefits encourage malingering, even though they now require active contributions by the recipients in return for the benefits. Mandatory workfare programs – because they are stigmatizing – may actually contribute to the loss of motivation to work. Sanctions may thus accomplish the opposite of what is intended, namely, re-integration. Similarly, job creation programs that rely on deregulation also promote labor market dualism, which can contribute to those who lack "real" jobs (Silver 1998b: 17). In describing workfare tendencies in the Scandinavian countries, as Nanna Kildal says, "The new policy is less concerned with justice than personal morality. The basic normative challenge of workfare policy is it ignores the fact that non-humiliating and just institutions matter" (Kildal 2000: 18).

Labor market insecurity will continue for the foreseeable future – among the employed, those working at the margins of the flexible labor markets, the unemployed, and those outside the laborforce. Thus far, the social democratic response to the erosion of the legitimacy of the welfare state has been defensive. They have tried to resist the decline in the legitimacy of the welfare state by strengthening the "productivist" or "labourist" character of welfare. They have joined those advocating tougher conditionality in entitlement and less "generosity" for those not in jobs (Standing 1999: 289–290).

In the next chapter, I will discuss the implications of active labor-market policies for social citizenship.

CHAPTER FIVE

SOCIAL EUROPE: ALTERNATIVES? SOLUTIONS? CONCLUSIONS?

Despite the argument that the Western European welfare states are largely intact, there has been a major shift. Social citizenship has been redefined from status to contract. In place of the Marshallian concept that social rights are based on legal citizenship alone, entitlements have been replaced by rights and obligations. True, for the large majority of the population not much has changed. They earn their living in the paid labor market; they pay taxes; they contribute to the basic insurance systems – health care, unemployment, pensions, and disability. When they get sick or retire, the social welfare state is available. The change has occurred for the more marginal people – the long-term unemployed, the socially excluded. To obtain welfare benefits, they are required to engage in workfare.

At the conclusion of the last chapter, I raised the issue as to how successful these policies are so far, based on the available evidence. In this chapter, I turn to various policies and proposals designed to reform both the labor market and the welfare state. Social exclusion is both dynamic and multi-dimensional. Certain structural conditions have to be met. The socially excluded cannot be re-integrated into society via the paid labor market unless there are jobs, primarily in the private sector but also public jobs if necessary. These jobs have to be good jobs, not the US low-wage jobs. They have to pay a sufficient earned income, or, more likely, they must be supplemented by public funds (e.g., the Earned Income Tax Credit in the United States, the Family Tax Credit in the United Kingdom, etc.). There has to be employment protection, either through reforms in regulatory labor law or collective bargaining agreements, or both. There has to be health care, child care support, access to transportation, and housing. In Europe, there is also the children's allowance.

A good labor market will, no doubt, substantially reduce the number of unemployed, but there will be many who remain outside the labor market. Why, and what to do about those who still remain, is both multi-faceted and complicated. The term social exclusion covers a large variety of people. Some are disabled, others have family care responsibilities. Many suffer various kinds of employment barriers – health and mental health problems, substance abuse, insufficient education and training, and so forth. Moreover, these conditions are not stable. A mother might be well employed, but then a child or a parent falls ill. People get sick and get well. In most countries, people move in and out of poverty. The same is true with social exclusion.

Therefore, it is important to emphasize that many of the various alternatives and proposals are *cumulative* and not *exclusive*. Some issues can be addressed by changes in the law, others by increasing funding for certain programs, others by the establishment of norms and goals and what is called benchmarking, others through collective bargaining, and still others by new forms of worker/client relationships with employment and social services agencies.

Chapter 5 is divided into three parts. The first part looks at the potential for reform at the European Union level. The argument is made that since there is extensive integration with the market at the EU level, it should follow that labor law and welfare state reform should also be at the EU level. This would harmonize employee benefits and protections across nations and prevent a race to the bottom in welfare state reform. With minor exceptions, however, it has proved to be very difficult to enact cross-border "positive" regulation, that is, the establishment of rights and the redistribution of benefits, as distinguished from the removal of trade barriers, called "negative" integration. In the face of these difficulties, the various member states have developed what is called the Open Method of Coordination. Starting with employment law, and now social protection, the member states agree on general principles or goals of reform. Each country is committed to filing a yearly progress report – called National Action Plans (NAPs) – which not only specifies the extent of unemployment, social exclusion, and poverty, but also the policies and programs for reform. The idea is that the "benchmarking" will result in the dissemination of "best practices" and lead to reform at the national level. The process is called "soft law." The first part discusses the experience of OMC thus far.

The second part is concerned with reform at the national level. The first topic is whether the various member states will "converge" in the changes in labor law and the welfare state or continue on their separate ways, called "path-dependent." Some argue that there will be convergence; moreover, it will be the dismantling of the welfare state along neoliberal lines rather than the spreading of more uniform labor and welfare protections. Others believe that the various national traditions of employment and welfare protection will be maintained, but that extensive reforms will be necessary. In light of the vast changes in the economy and demography, the labor market and the welfare state have to be "recalibrated" to provide "flexicurity." As the name implies, employment has to be both sufficiently flexible to adapt to the changing conditions but, at the same time, basic security and opportunities have to be in place for the workers.

The various proposals are designed to improve employment and provide protection and security for those who enter the paid labor market. But there will be some number of people who, for one reason or another, do not become employed. This is the subject of the third part. As discussed in Chapters 3 and 4, the response of both the conservatives and the Social Democrats is contracts of inclusion; in return for benefits, the clients have a "right" to a contract of inclusion from the government. The socially excluded will be *empowered* through these contracts. The third part analyzes the nature of rights and contracts when one of the parties is a dependent person. I explore the risks involved for the socially excluded under a contract regime. Contracts are usually entered into voluntarily by people of roughly equal means. When the bargaining relationship is unequal, interventions are often considered necessary. The major example is labor relations. I discuss what is meant by a contract regime given the imbalance of power in the client-agency relationship in social welfare. I show how power is exercised in a social service dependency relationship, which explains why workfare has increased the risks of the most vulnerable. I develop the client-agency relationships that are needed to make a contract regime work. The task is to make the employment services and social services accountable. The incentives for the workers in the services have to be changed so that they serve the needs of the clients. I recommend that the services be independent of payments, and that sanctions be eliminated. Still, the clients will be dependent if for no other reason than that they need assistance. I conclude that there should be a basic income guarantee. A basic income guarantee will not only reduce poverty but also provide clients with an *exit* option. Therefore, service workers will have to offer opportunities that are tailored to individual client needs if they are to recruit clients into their programs. The contractual relationship will become horizontal. Social citizenship will be a status.

SOCIAL EUROPE: CONVERGENCE VS. PATH-DEPENDENT; NEGATIVE VS. POSITIVE INTEGRATION

Which way is Social Europe going? One view is that since nations no longer control major parts of the economies, especially monetary and fiscal policy, Social Europe will track market integration. Change and *convergence* among the various social welfare states will come at the EU level. But change in what direction – less social protection or more social protection? Others dispute both predictions. They argue that change in welfare states will be primarily at the national level, called *path-dependent*. Change here can also be in two directions – more social protection or less social protection.

Hooghe and Marks describe the differences in approach to welfare state reform as follows. The *neoliberal project* attempts to combine market integration with a minimum of government interference or regulation. The *regulated capitalism project* accepts the market but seeks to create welfare social protections through European political institutions. The Center-Left tends to support regulated capitalists, and thus are supra-nationalists. The Right supports neoliberalism. They resist supranational authority since national governments are limited in regulating the market. Neoliberalism will be furthered not only by competition among firms but also among governments. In other words, there will be convergence among nations – not on social issues but on neoliberal capitalism (Hooghe and Marks 1999: 75–76).

The neoliberal project has broad support among political and economic elites, multi-national companies, employer associations, financial interests, conservative research organizations, various pressure groups, and conservative parties. It also has strong support in several of the directorate-generals of the European Commission, particularly those that are responsible for implementing the internal market. The OECD recommends common objectives in social protection. In its

Green Paper, *Options for Europe* 1994, the OECD says that notwithstanding a variety of historical traditions, EU countries share the same "social model"; therefore, it is reasonable to expect similar responses; and that European nations should go along with this process through the dissemination of intervention as well as occasional legislative interventions (Ferrera 1998: 81–96; OECD 1994).

The neoliberals, according to Hooghe and Marks, have appealed to political democracy at the national level to block regulation at the European level. It is easier to defend the status quo since positive regulation requires an extensive legislative process (Hooghe and Marks 1999: 77–86). Viewed from this perspective, Adam Przeworski sees convergence along neoliberal lines:

> While the degree to which neo-liberal ideas permeated different social democratic parties is not the same – to cite just one example, French Socialists are successfully pursuing a rather orthodox program of job creation – policy convergence is again apparent. The dominant policy regime of our times is the neo-liberal one and, while the neo-liberal ideas softened as a result of some evident fracases, social democrats, in government and in opposition, are abandoning even some of their remedial policies. (Przeworski 1999)

Neoliberals also raise the conflict between national citizenship and welfare state solutions at the EU level. The social contract is considered to be central to the concept of citizenship and neoliberals question the idea of EU citizenship rather than national citizenship (Closa 1998: 266–283). They point out that even with EU integration, the member states retain full discretion in determining who their nationals are even for the purposes of EU law. Hence, the argument goes, as long as EU citizenship depends on nationality, it is untenable to think of EU citizenship as a new basis for social rights (Closa 1998).

Others, too, think that convergence along neoliberal lines is the more likely possibility. Wolfgang Streeck argues that because of the pressures for coordination at the international level and competition at the national level, industrial relations are becoming more "voluntaristic." By this, he means that unions and governments are relying less on sanctions and more on incentives to meet employer concessions. Rather than excluding labor, employers seek to change the terms of inclusion. Streeck calls this "concession bargaining 'in the shadow of exit.'" Employers still want to include unions – they remain strong, and the risks of conflict are uncertain; and, in addition:

most unions more or less want to be included in the restructuring processes that are now going on. The unions are interested in protecting
the core workers, but this is a declining share of the workforce. A rising number of workers are no longer part of the union constituency and
thus outside of union social protection. Thus, increasingly, countries are
moving toward a *"functional convergence"* of "flexible" employment relationships. (Streeck 1998)

Streeck questions whether unions and governments will succeed in
their efforts to defend national social protections from international demands of financial orthodoxy. In a number of countries, there have been
alliances between government, business, and unions to conform to the
Monetary Union. Labor has been asked to make large sacrifices in the
face of pressures for national deregulation. Other pressures come from
the fragmented system of wage-setting. Efforts to provide minimum participation rights to workers of multi-national companies (the European
Works Council Directive, 1994) vary considerably. The Social Protocol
(1993) appended to the Maastricht Treaty which gave business and
labor a formal role in social policy legislation at the European level,
has so far produced only two agreements – on parental leave and part-
time work – but neither has had much impact on the member countries although they may prevent a country from lowering its standards.
The Posted Workers Directive which provides for "equal protection for
posted workers from low-wage countries, at the same time, refrains from
intervening in the internal affairs of national systems of industrial relations and social protection. What a country chooses to have and thus
apply to posted workers is up to that country" (Streeck 1998).

An example Streeck gives is what happened with the German
construction industry after unification. "Employers were able to push
through a low-wage category with growing numbers of unskilled workers, especially in the East, assigned to the new category. Employers in
East Germany refused to join the association of West German employers, and the unions were unable to defend their wages. They were weakened by the increased market access of foreign firms, and they were unable to organize the workforce in the East, primarily because of the high
unemployment" (Streeck 1998). Streeck concludes that the ability of
national systems to resist the international pressures will diminish, but
while this will lead to more structural diversity within national systems,
there will be more functional convergence along neoliberal lines. Labor
and capital will increasingly emphasize a joint interest in company competitiveness (Streeck 1998).

Although Anton Hemerijck believes that path-dependency is the more prominent force, he gives an example which may indicate convergence along neoliberal lines. With the high unemployment, and the increase in the costs of health care, pensions, and poverty since the mid-1970s, taxes should have increased, but they have remained more or less frozen. Instead, government have chosen deficit financing, which Hemerijck interprets as the effects of tax competition (Hemerijck 2002).

Bill Jordan, too, thinks that there will be convergence along neoliberal lines. Welfare, he notes, requires a commonality, a collective concern, but the tendency over the past twenty years is for fragmentation into smaller, narrower, often antagonistic groups, and this tendency will continue to grow stronger. The balance of power between capital and labor has shifted making collective solutions more difficult. Jordan thinks that the real danger is a new social contract based on the US model, which has already taken hold in the United Kingdom. This will intensify and institutionalize social divisions and exclusion. Nor, thinks, Jordan, are the prospects good for mobilization redistribution among the irregularly employed and the unemployed. Politicians are more interested in programs of enforcement that are directed against marginal members of society. He points to the spread of workfare. "As welfare becomes more stringent, the poor search for scapegoats rather than mobilize" (Jordan 1998).

There is substantial opposition to the neoliberals. Those who favor regulated capitalism argue that markets can be more efficient if the necessary collective goods are provided – for example, transportation, communications, workforce skills, research and development, and so forth. Helping the poor and the unemployed will increase economic productivity. In view of the globalized economy, they believe that a European welfare state is more feasible than national ones. Thus, they seek to enhance democracy at the European level (Hooghe and Marks 1999: 86–88, 94).

In any event, so far there seems to be a consensus that the transnational approach is not a solution if one is talking about *positive* social welfare measures (see, e.g., Closa 1998; Scharpf 1998; Streeck 1998).[1] Some common provisions flow from market integration – for example, the free movement of labor, perhaps occupational safety standards

---

[1] Hooghe and Marks (1999: 97), are less certain as to how European integration will evolve.

(although this is doubtful), but not major industrial labor protections and redistribution. Fritz Scharpf says that there are two basic interrelated reasons: one is the difference between the removal of various restrictions that distort competition – e.g., trade barriers, restrictions on the flow of capital, etc. – which has been the primary focus of the various European Union treaties, called *negative* integration; and *positive* integration, sometimes referred to as "market correcting," which includes the regulation of working conditions, social and environmental protection (Scharpf 1999: 45). Aside from some decisions by the European Court of Justice (Scharpf 1999: 47),[2] positive integration depends on directives which are proposed by the European Commission, and passed by the Council of Ministers often with the European Parliament. Directives are binding orders on the member states. Although in some areas, a qualified majority is all that is required for a directive, for some topics, unanimity is required. Accordingly, directives have been most useful for building the single market where uniformity was an agreed-upon method to ensure the free movement of capital, goods, and services (Trubek 2002). "Positive interventions" says Scharpf, "require not only fundamental changes in governmental structures, decision-making processes, and claims to legitimacy, but citizen solidarities across borders. The post-war welfare states differ so greatly in terms of institutional embeddedness that there is no single 'European social model.'" To be sure, the welfare states are changing but in path-dependent ways, "if change is to be distinguished from dismantling." Scharpf believes that "in fact, the only solution that could be uniformly imposed would be the Anglo-American form of deregulated and disembedded capitalism, that is, neoliberalism, but not a common model of (reconstructed) embeddedness" (Scharpf 1999: 191–193; see Streeck 1998).

The difficulties involved in positive integration, according to Scharpf, are numerous. There is the question of governmental capacity, of democratic legitimacy. Again, there is the difference between negative and positive integration (Scharpf 1998: 157–177). Negative

---

[2] The ECJ decides, with the acquiescence of national courts, whether national health, safety, and environmental protection regulations are "reasonable" in their impact on free trade. Other decisions include free trade (the removal of customs duties, quantitative restrictions on imports and exports, and barriers against non-members); customs unions (the harmonization and quantitative restrictions with non-members); the common market (the free movement of goods and services, capital and labor); economic and monetary union (a common currency), that is, policies to eliminate frictions between member nations.

liberalization has been extended without much political attention, at least until recently. Positive integration, on the other hand, must take place in the more visible institutions – the Council of Ministers or the European Parliament. Since the Luxembourg Compromise (1966), all Council decisions must be unanimous. This was modified in the Single European Act of 1986, where there is a rule of qualified majority voting for some issues. Nevertheless, vetoes threaten any decision which involves important interests. Since the mid-1990s, there has been a growing reaction to the central authority of the EU. Scharpf says that because these "institutions lack political accountability, the legitimacy of their decisions depends on unanimity." "Positive integration proposals cannot survive mass opposition; success is usually restricted to non-controversial, win-win solutions" (Scharpf 1999: 23–25). And there are many areas of conflict – ideological; economic self-interest (e.g., environmental regulations would destroy the Portuguese economy); institutions (e.g., differences in tax systems, welfare state financing) – that would make agreement at the European level extremely difficult (Scharpf 1999: 72–83).

There has been some consensus on health and industrial safety, environmental risks, consumer protection, and employment rights. Scharpf interprets this to mean that there can be positive integration as long as conflicts are not too intense. There are many areas where there are sharp differences in ideology, regulatory approaches, feasible security, and the value of environmental measures. The costs of social or environmental regulation cannot be paid for through higher taxation in the poor EU countries; at the same time, the wealthier countries are not willing to compensate the poorer countries for the costs of harmonization (Scharpf 1998).

While Scharpf doubts that the EU decision-making capacity will greatly increase any time soon, he argues that certain areas should remain within the control of the member states to resist the pressure towards negative integration. These would include union organization and collective bargaining, education, culture, the media, social welfare, health care, industrial relations, political and administrative organization.

> There would be an explicit dualism which, if provided for under treaties, would force the European Court of Justice and the Commission to balance the claims for market integration against the legitimate claims for the maintenance of national institutional integrity. Such constitutional

changes would protect or re-establish the powers of national govern-ments to take certain sectors out of the market altogether or to organize them in ways that modify the market. (Scharpf 1998)

Scharpf acknowledges that even this division would have limitations. There will still be the pressures of transnational competition, in-cluding the mobility of capital and business. "The dilemma is that Europe needs a common market with common rules, but also needs au-tonomous problem-solving capacities at the national and subnational levels. Then, it will be able to combine the efficiency of the larger market and the preservation of national and subnational democracy" (Scharpf 1998).

Scharpf believes that there are possibilities for positive regulation under "regulatory competition." "With certain products, such as bank-ing and the regulation of stock markets, there is a 'race to the top.' This can also be true with certain product standards." Access to cer-tain national markets may depend on complying with environmental or product safety requirements, as is the case with many foreign drug companies that want to sell in the United States. GATT and WTO al-low states some forms of protections. So far, environmental regulations seem to be immune to downward competitive pressures. The same may apply to health and safety regulations. On the other hand, there is cross-national competition to keep taxes down (Scharpf 1999: 91–95).[3]

With regard to social regulation, Scharpf would distinguish "bad jobs," child labor, and hazardous work on the one hand from Social Security, health care, and other welfare transfers and services financed through the payroll taxes on the other hand. The latter he considers highly vulnerable to international competition. But most types of so-cial regulation, he believes, are between these two extremes. He would include in this "middle position working hours, vacations, conditions, security, sick leave, maternity leave, collective bargaining, codetermi-nation of worker rights. While they change the nature of the employ-ment relationship, they are seen as having the effect of increasing costs and thus vulnerable to the exit option. So far, though, a race to the bottom has been resisted by the political commitments of the national governments" (Scharpf 1999: 100–101).

As Scharpf points out, the areas of negative integration and global economic forces that most reduce the problem-solving capacities of

---

[3] The example he gives is auto emissions standards in California. Manufacturers wanted access to the California market and not to produce cars with different standards.

nations are those that are most closely identified with democratic legitimacy – e.g., the Golden Age welfare states.

> Thus, citizens expect government to prevent mass unemployment and forcing people to live below socially acceptable levels. In most member states of the European Community, citizens consider these achievements as constitutive elements of a legitimizing social contract. If revoked under pressures of economic globalization or the asymmetry of negative and positive integration in the European Community, there is the danger that rising political dissatisfaction will undermine the political legitimacy of democratic governments or the political commitment to economic integration. . . . There has to be a search for options to deal with mass unemployment, the crisis of the welfare state, and rising inequality. These options have to be pursued nationally even in the international economy. (Scharpf 1999: 121–123)

In the meantime, the Treaty of Amsterdam did little to increase the institutional capacity for positive integration. The President of the Commission as well as the European Parliament have been strengthened, but there was no agreement on changing the Council of Ministers. In fact, even countries such as Germany and France, which previously had favored majority voting, are now becoming concerned as a result of the plans to enlarge the Community. On the other hand, even though the Amsterdam agreements have been criticized as a compromise on the lowest common denominator, Scharpf thinks that there was some agreement on certain principles that may hold some promise. Article 125 commits the members to "work towards developing a coordinated strategy for employment"; Article 126 calls for "promoting employment as a matter of common concern" (Scharpf 1999: 159). This is called the Open Method of Coordination, which will be discussed in the next section.

There are some limits being placed on negative integration. There is a public service exemption (e.g., public-service broadcasting, public-service banks) from European competition law. Council directives can limit the impact of negative integration – for example, as previously mentioned, the Posted Workers Directive. The European Court of Justice, too, is beginning to respond to limits on negative integration and European competition law, again especially in the public service area. Scharpf thinks that there is a "new awareness of the direct, legal effect of negative integration on national problem-solving capacities" (Scharpf 1999: 167–169).

Scharpf proposes that Europe should consider what he calls "differentiated integration," that is, not all countries have to have the same, uniform levels of protections. There could be a "two-tiered Europe" providing for temporary exemptions. This kind of flexibility should improve chances of agreement. There could be a minimum floor as a percentage of GDP (Scharpf 1999: 176–179). To reduce the heterogeneity of social policy among nations, he suggests a two-step process. There should be an agreement "in principle" to assure high levels of employment with protections against involuntary unemployment, sickness, and poverty. There could be a "combination of basic earned income support with health insurance and (funded) pension schemes financed through individual contributions, part mandated by law and part subsidized for low-income groups. Instead of uniformity, policy-makers should consider the various welfare state 'families' that could coordinate reform strategies" (Scharpf 1999: 181–193).[4]

A report to the EU president proposed different welfare state floors under a new EU coordination role. This would allow different levels of social protection linked to varying levels of labor costs and social spending, and would prevent the poorer member states from vetoing upward harmonization. However, all members would be subject to a threshold. Floors could be supplemented by groups of states – for example, Sweden, Denmark, Germany, and Austria. There are at least two obstacles to such a plan. The poorer members may resist a two-tier European social policy; they would fear a permanent consignment to a second-class club, and thereby reduce the pressure for implementing EU legislation already enacted. Second, it would not make implementation any easier among wealthy members. Germany, for example, is a principal opponent of further supra-national social protection regulation. Nevertheless, the authors of the report think that the idea of an agreed welfare floor is good, much in keeping with EU tradition and practice. The new European Works Councils can play a role in keeping firms in

---

[4] Scharpf identifies four such families: (1) Scandinavian – the welfare state is financed mainly from general tax revenues, generous income replacement, universal high-quality public services, including health care; (2) Continental – relatively generous income-maintaining social transfers and health care, financed from employment-based social insurance contributions, a relatively low commitment to social services; (3) Southern systems – less comprehensive, less generous versions of the continental model: (4) UK, Irish – egalitarian and tax-financed basic pensions, unemployment benefits, and health services; other forms of income replacement and service to private firms and the family.

the bargaining process. Incentives have to be provided to keep unions to productivity-linked wage increases. These, in turn, can be linked to national pacts and the European social dialogue. There can be EU-level coordination with regard to minimum wages, human capital standards, reforming welfare/work nexus, etc. And there can be diffusion of "best practice" policies (Ferrera et al. 2002a: 63).

However, even with a multi-level problem-solving approach, Scharpf remains skeptical. There remain the three major legitimacy deficits at the European level: "the lack of a pre-existing sense of collective identity; the lack of a European-wide policy discourse, and the lack of an institutional infrastructure that could assure accountability." Furthermore, because the Amsterdam agreement to broaden the membership did not address constitutional reforms, there is even less likelihood of agreement on important transnational issues. He thinks that it will now be even more difficult to institute majority decisions in the Council as well as reducing the size of the Commission since governments previously in favor of these moves now worry about being outvoted (Scharpf 1999: 191–199).

In any event, in light of the considerable differences between the nations with regard to social regulation, ideology, and economic development, most scholars doubt very much there will be much convergence (see Kitschelt et al. 1999). As we have seen, even in the more developed states, there are major differences in their welfare systems. Thus, "there would be strong pressure from those vested interests that would lose through harmonization. A uniform system of European social protection would be revolutionary in some countries – for example, the difference between a tax-supported national health system and insurance for private providers. The same difficulties apply to industrial relations and the harmonization of capital and business taxes. So far, all attempts have failed" (Scharpf 1999: 112–114).

Thus far, despite the international pressures as well as the reduced capacity of governments to regulate their economies, there has not been a race to the bottom (Scharpf 1999: 194). Nevertheless, to deal with high levels of unemployment, nations will have to expand the sheltered sectors of their economies. It is here, thinks Scharpf, that the continental welfare systems encounter a major challenge. Transfers and payroll taxes have to be reduced. "Thus, it is not the size of the welfare state that is so important; rather, it is the particular construction of the welfare state. Welfare states have to become 'competitive.'" By this, Scharpf means increasing private service sector employment but not the costs of production and not dependence on revenue from mobile tax bases. "Benefits have to be restructured to increase opportunities and work incentives, but at the same time, maintain common commitments to solidarity and integration." At the same time, Scharpf urges that "the problem-solving potential of the legal integration should be expanded to protect national decisions. There has been an expansion of human and social rights; there could be constraints on 'social dumping'" (Scharpf 1999: 112–114). "What is needed is negotiating a new social contract" (Rhodes and Mény 1998).

"Soft" law: the open method of coordination (OMC)

By the 1990s, it came to be recognized that positive integration, while important for some issues (e.g., fundamental rights), would not progress very far in addressing the issues of welfare state and labor market reform (Scharpf 2001: 1–26). Europe then began to move toward a mixture of "hard" and "soft" law (Scott and Trubek 2002: 1–18). One of the more promising approaches, first applied with employment law, is called the "Open Method of Coordination" (OMC) or "soft law." OMC consists of common guidelines and national action plans which are then subject to peer review, evaluation, and recommendations. The recommendations are not binding. Rather, the idea is that through a "bottoms up" learning process about common problems and *benchmarking*, the member states will have an incentive to adopt *best practices* tailored to individual nations but addressed to the "common concern" of all the members so that "each citizen can count on a basic floor of rights and resources for participating in society" (Ferrera et al. 2002b). The aim would be a convergence of goals, rather than harmonization (Jacobsson 2001: 1). Under this method, the Council is to adopt annual guidelines for national action, member states are to submit annual reports on the implementation of the guidelines, and these reports, in turn, will be evaluated by a permanent committee of high-level national civil servants and by the Commission which may then propose specific recommendations to the Council (Scharpf 2001: 19). The OMC, with national action plans and benchmarking, contemplates "a multilevel process of common monitoring, self-evaluation, learning, and goal setting, the pooling of problem-solving experiences, comparing pragmatic solutions, which then trigger a learning process which serves to benefit participants engaged in separate, individual decisions" (Héritier 2001: 4; Dorf and Sabel 1998: 267–473; Sabel 2000; Gerstenberg and Sabel n.d.).

This process – called by the British and the Swedish governments, a "third way between intergovernmentalism and supranationalism" (Jacobsson n.d.: 7) – it is believed, will solve the "democratic deficit" at the European Union level, that is, "makes possible joint action in areas where the Community lacks legal competence or where the political support for a binding decision is not present" (Jacobsson 2001: 4; Scharpf 2001: 19). It is "a kind of informal law by exhortation" (Kenner 1999: 58). It "provides a pragmatic rather than a principled answer to the Achilles' heel of the EU – legitimacy" (Hodson and Maher 2001: 722). By this route, the EU will gradually assume a distinct coordinating role in a number of policy areas. It can rebalance "softly" and "from below" the structural asymmetry between negative and positive integration. Targets, progress reports, and voluntary agreements can avoid the cumbersome legislative process, although the threat of legislation may increase the willingness to act voluntarily (Héritier 2001). Kerstin Jacobsson argues that soft law can be viewed as a first step in the enactment of hard law when a particularly controversial area has been "softened up" (Jacobsson 2001: 4). Maurizio Ferrera and his colleagues claim that the "soft law" approach is clearly visible with regard to gender policy. In the 1990s, they say, there was a real blossoming of initiatives for both gender equality and equity (Ferrera et al. 2002a).[5]

OMC had its antecedents in the Economic and Monetary Union (EMU) multilateral surveillance system, and was then extended to the Cologne process on macroeconomic policy, the Cardiff process on structural policy, and the Luxembourg process on employment. Prior to the Luxembourg Council, the Commission's 1988 report, *The Social Dimension of the Internal Market*, noted some important gains but said that the changes brought about through technology and international competition required a "more flexible and pragmatic policy with different ambitions" (Kenner 1999: 33–60). The EU encouraged its member states to improve the employability of the young. Efforts began to be made to increase the transparency and coordination of the labor market initiatives of the member states. In 1993, the European Council endorsed a strategy to promote employment growth. Employment reports have been issued to help a more informed debate about what the various countries are doing. The 1996 Action for Employment encouraged the member

---

[5] For instance, there were new standards for equal treatment in wages, Social Security, pensions, and a wide range of programs to promote female integration into the labor market.

states to adopt initiatives to improve employment. At the 1997 Madrid summit, the member states agreed on youth and long-term unemployment goals as well as equal opportunities (Teague 1999).

Still, the member states were unwilling to concede social and industrial policy to the Union. Faced with the neoliberal demands that the welfare state had to be rolled back and the workplace made more flexible, the proponents of what developed into a European Employment Strategy (EES) recognized that the Social Model had to be "recalibrated" (Trubek and Mosher 2001: 5). At the Luxembourg meeting (1998), the Council approved nineteen guidelines which were organized into four pillars: (1) Employability – policies to make unemployment systems more active and increase the skills of workers; (2) Entrepreneurship and Job Creation – to encourage new, smaller, innovative businesses and make tax systems more employment friendly; (3) Adaptability – to increase the flexibility of workers and employment arrangements; and (4) Equal Opportunity for men and women (Trubek and Mosher 2001: 9–10). The EES provides for the coordination of national employment policies using "management by objectives" (Ferrera et al. 2002b: 64). The EU institutions are to draw up guidelines and monitor implementation with regard to the diagnosis of problems and evaluation. There is to be "EU-wide priority setting, the identification of good practices for benchmarking; the involvement of national policymaking systems with regard to national plans, specific national targets, monitoring and policy evaluation through peer review mechanisms, plus the possibility of issuing recommendations" (Teague 1999).

As Kerstin Jacobsson describes it, the new system of governance is based on five principles: Voluntarism: pressure will be generated on member states to engage in more systematic monitoring and peer review. Subsidiarity: the EU identifies common objectives but national and subnational levels decide concrete measures. The relationship between the EU and the member states is intended to be "complementary rather than competitive." Flexibility: rather than a uniform model, the aim is flexible coordination between various national policies. Inclusion: legitimacy will be increased by the inclusion of social partners, and other relevant actors. Policy integration: additional policy areas, such as economic, structural, social, and education will be integrated to pursue the same goals (Jacobsson 2001: 13–14).

By the mid-1980s, EU policy discussions began to recognize other policy areas, including social protection, combating poverty and social exclusion (Ferrera et al. 2002b). In 1992, two Council Recommendations noted that social exclusion was becoming a significant problem and that growth alone was not sufficient for re-integration. Members were encouraged to recognize the problem, exchange information, engage in mutual learning, exchange best practices, and engage in peer review. In 1997, the Commission said that national welfare states had to be recalibrated to combat social exclusion. This did not necessarily mean downsizing; rather, strong levels of social protection would enhance social cohesion and economic progress (Ferrera et al. 2002b). The Amsterdam Treaty (1997) authorized the Council to adopt measures to encourage cooperation and facilitate coordination among the member states in the fight against social exclusion. In 1999, the European Parliament adopted a resolution inviting a process of voluntary coordination among the members addressing the problem of social protection modeled on the European employment strategy. This, in turn, was followed by a recommendation of the Commission which included promoting social inclusion as one of four key objectives of a common strategy (Ferrera et al. 2002b: 6). At a series of European Council meetings (Lisbon, March 2000; Nice, December 2000; Stockholm, June 2001), a commitment was made to promote "sustainable economic growth and quality employment which will reduce the risk of poverty and social exclusion as well as strengthen social cohesion in the Union between 2001–2010" (European Council 2001: 6).

At the Lisbon Council meeting (2000), OMC was specifically introduced along with an enhanced coordinating role for the Council. To combat social exclusion, the aim of the OMC was to develop EU guidelines and timetables, establish indicators and the benchmarking of best practices, translating the guidelines into national practices, peer review, periodic monitoring and evaluation and the development of a mutual learning process (Ferrera et al. 2002b: 7). The Commission proposed quantitative targets, as was done with the employment strategy, but this approach was rejected by the Council. Instead, there were to be "qualitative objectives" which were subsequently agreed to at a Council meeting in Nice, which launched the social inclusion process. Among the objectives in the fight against poverty and social exclusion were facilitating participation in employment and access to resources, rights, goods, and services, preventing the risk of exclusion, and helping the most vulnerable. Members were invited to submit national action plans (NAPs), covering a two-year period, which would set forth indicators and monitoring mechanisms measuring progress. The Commission would then present a report summarizing best practices and identifying common approaches. Recognizing the diversity of policies among the members, the first round, then, would emphasize "'good features'" rather than evaluations as a first step (Ferrera et al. forthcoming: 9). In 2002, there was to be a five-year EU action program dealing with social exclusion (Eurpoean Council 2001). The hope, as Ferrera and his colleagues put it, was that, "If well designed and calibrated, open coordination policies against social exclusion could thus lead to a virtuous mix of external spurs for 'puzzling' about problems and internal efforts for identifying (and implementing) adequate solutions" (Ferrera et al. forthcoming). Jacobsson says, "To start a 'toothless' cooperation, like information exchange, has in the history of the EU allowed the Commission to get a toe-hold in contentious policy areas" (Jacobsson 2001: 11).

The goal of combating social exclusion was formally adopted at the Treaty of Nice. A Social Protection Committee (SPC), composed of two members of the Council and one from each member state, was formalized and given the responsibility to promote cooperation on social protection policies. The SPC developed a list of commonly agreed social inclusion indicators, which was then adopted by the Council (2001) covering financial poverty, employment, health, and education. The indicators would be used by the member states in their NAPs in the second round of reports starting in 2003 (Ferrera et al. 2002b: 10–11).

The first round of the NAPs was submitted in June 2001 which was followed by a Joint Report on Social Inclusion (European Council 2001: 6). The Joint Report noted that this was "the first time that the European Union endorses a policy document on poverty and social exclusion." The Report documents what is happening across all the member states, and identifies the key challenges, thus "strengthening the European social model." It claims that "It is thus a significant advance towards the achievement of the EU's strategic goal of greater social cohesion in the Union between 2001–2010" (European Council 2001: 5). The Report says that it shows that the member states are actively involved in the process of developing a more rigorous and comprehensive system of monitoring and evaluation of various policies. Thus, it "gives a concrete reality to the open method of coordination on Social Inclusion agreed at the Lisbon Summit in March 2000." It furthers the European Social Agenda that was agreed upon in Nice as well as the goals of the European Employment Strategy (European Council 2001: 5).

The Report noted that although there was sustained growth, including job growth, in the EU between 1995 and 2000, unemployment still remains high, and there are large numbers of people "experiencing high exclusion and poverty risk." The NAPs considered long-term unemployment the most important risk factor for poverty and social exclusion. Other risk factors included low income, low quality of employment, homelessness, poor health, immigration, lack of education, gender and racial discrimination, disability, old age, family break-up, substance abuse, and living in high risk areas (European Council 2001:7).

Accordingly, there was agreement that the labor market had to be inclusive, that employment had to be a right. Employment policies must be responsive to individual needs. There had to be a guaranteed, decent income and access to education, including lifelong learning, strengthening families, protecting children, improved housing, and so forth (European Council 2001: 26). While the importance of employment was emphasized by all, members with high employment focused on improving the participation of specific groups (older workers, immigrants, the disabled) and members with low employment and high levels of persistent unemployment emphasized job creation and improving the employability of the long-term and the young (European Council 2001: 33). Measures to promote a more responsive labor market included reducing employer costs, especially for the low-skilled, promoting education and training, preparing action plans to improve ethnic diversity, "social clauses" in public employment contracts to require the employment of the long-term unemployed, and so forth. There should be insertion measures, e.g., counseling, training, subsidized employment, active support, and improved targeting. Insertion measures should be individualized, and supportive, not punitive. Services should be decentralized and integrated with local employment and social services (European Council 2001: 35). However, there have to be disincentives to accepting welfare rather than work. There is widespread concern about reducing avoidable dependency and promoting activation to "make social benefits a springboard for employment and not an obstacle" (European Council 2001: 43).

The Report identified a number of weaknesses in the NAPs, including the lack of a rigorous evaluation of existing policies, thus making it difficult to identify best practices; a concentration on existing policies rather than on new initiatives; the lack of cost estimates; a lack of specific and quantifiable targets as a basis of monitoring; a "limited visibility" of gender issues; and what appeared to be a limited role for social partners and nongovernmental organizations.[6] Growing immigration has led to increases in discrimination, racism, and xenophobia. While most member states recognized that ethnic minorities and immigrants are at high risk of social exclusion, and that this is "likely to be a growing challenge for many member states over the next few years as the number of foreign workers and their dependents will increase," there is a "generalised lack of data and common indicators for people from these vulnerable groups" (European Council 2001: 20, 24). The Nice conference emphasized access to rights, but only a few NAPs mentioned access to legal services and justice, and developing laws and mechanisms to counter discrimination and promote equality (European Council 2001: 58). However, it was noted that similar deficiencies were also present in the early rounds of the Luxembourg process national action plans on employment. The Report concluded that the first round on the social exclusion plans was considered "successful in that it provided a great deal of information on what the member states thought were important aspects of their policies, they indicated an institutional building capacity, and allowed national policy-makers to identify weaknesses in their policies" (Ferrera et al. 2002b: 12–13). Still, the members are a "long way from a common approach to social indicators allowing policy outcomes to be monitored and facilitating the identification" (European Council 2001).

The European Anti-Poverty Network report on the 2001–03 National Action Plans was more negative. Several networks are "not fully convinced of the practical serious intent of their governments" although many networks "anticipate improved participation and content in future Plans." Among the deficiencies mentioned were lack of clarity as to implementation and funding. In all the countries but one (the Netherlands), the poor and disadvantaged were excluded from the process. The networks expressed concern about the emphasis on responsibilities rather than rights (Duffy 2001).

Are all these efforts "empty shells"– only voluntary efforts? Several commentators believe they are more (Ferrera et al. 2000: 65). OMC

---

[6] Jacobsson (n.d.: 18), also noted that with EES, conversations were mainly between a "limited number of officials at national ministries, often working in international offices mediating between national capitals and Brussels."

is praised by some who see it as a "creative breakthrough" from the current impasse (Biagi 2000: 159). Ferrera and his colleagues recognize that the fight against social exclusion is "an area jealously guarded by Member States" and that while all politicians may champion the fight, priorities are determined by a wide variety of factors which "makes anything but an 'open method' a political non-starter" (Ferrera et al. 2000: 14) and that "in the absence of sanctions . . . or even guidelines (as in the European Employment Strategy), the whole process could conceivably degenerate to a biennial ritual of 'dressing up' existing policies, at least on the part of governments with little inclination to direct energy and resources to this policy area." Still, they think that there are real opportunities in the preparation and peer review of the national action plans. "They will raise the awareness of policymakers and other interested groups as to possibilities and pitfalls, identify gaps in information, and help structures of coordination and monitoring" (Ferrera et al. 2002b: 14–15). The OMC "processes create trust and cooperative orientations among participants and tend to encourage learning dynamics. It is in this sense that the OMC has a strong potential for actually influencing policy developments – at least if compared to [the traditional methods of OECD efforts at cooperation]" (Ferrera et al. 2002b: 227–239). Anton Hemerijck is optimistic "because no government wants to be seen to perform badly." Thus, "OMC can potentially stimulate 'learning ahead of failure'" (Hemerijck 2002: 43; see also Begg and Berghan 2002: 179–194).

Others think that abandoning mandatory, uniform social and employment standards will further weaken the European Social Model. According to Adrienne Héritier, in the area of social policy, formulating precise targets has been highly contested. Member states prefer vague formulations which obfuscate progress where there are contested goals. "Vague targets make monitoring, combined with voluntariness and the choice of instruments, a duller weapon than was originally planned." Thus, she says, the employment goals decided upon at the Lisbon summit in 2000 – "lifelong learning," "increasing employment in services," "modernizing social protection," and "promoting social inclusion" are "rather fuzzy." On the other hand, "there is some indication that the pressure from these measures – as soft as they may be – may help overcome domestic resistance to starting the reform on these deeply entrenched policies." She believes that there is a rather limited willingness to learn from member states. "Learning seems to be restricted to minor points among countries with basically similar systems and to problems

229

of coordination where all stand to win from promoting the common good. In general, social policy has been notoriously resistant to the influence of Europeanization." Against this background, it is difficult to assess the significance of target setting and publication. It will only be over a longer time that one can say whether this is a first step toward legislative European policy-making or a new policy mode in its own right (Héritier 2001: 9). Streeck, too, is skeptical. The unwillingness to impose binding obligations on the member states and the high degree of voluntarism to address controversial social problems, such as redistribution, reflect, in his view, the bias towards the market (Streeck 1996: 77).

As expected, the impacts on national social and economic policies are mixed. The Commission and the Council believe that the EES has created a new climate of coordinated responses and that one can detect a cycle of "ongoing structural reforms." On the other hand, implementation across the four pillars has been uneven (Trubek and Mosher 2001: 13). "At this stage," say Hodson and Maher, "it operates as a form of negative co-ordination, with monitoring and peer pressure ensuring compliance of national policy instruments through agreed commitments, rather than as a form of positive integration with agreement on a specific policy approach at the EU level" (Hodson and Maher 2001: 739).

According to Paul Teague, benchmarking has revealed some best practices examples in Portugal and Spain for promoting the re-entry of women in the paid labor market. But benchmarking has also uncovered large gaps in equal opportunities across several states. Only Belgium, Austria, Sweden, and the United Kingdom have taken steps to close the gender gap. Wide variation was also found in the EU with regard to child care. Teague says that the early returns from benchmarking show the "lack of coherence to national labor market strategies and the lack of coordination across the EU." Diversity among the member states makes adherence to the benchmarking "best practices" hard to operationalize. However, many of these policies are relatively new. It may be that more progress will be made as member states learn from each other (Teague 1999: 121–122). Trubek and Mosher argue that the EES cannot significantly affect the balance of power in the member states, but they believe that "it can serve as a learning process by providing information and arguments for those political leaders who favor moderate reform – those who believe that choices can be made other than preserving the status quo or rolling back the welfare state."[7] There are ways to combine security and flexibility, to adjust benefits to changing demographics, to serve previously excluded groups (Trubek and Mosher 2001: 23–24).

In other areas, intergovernmental bargaining has diluted major initiatives (Ferrera et al. 2002b: 60). For example, the European Works Council directive has not spread the German co-determination system to the rest of Europe. EU social citizenship rights remain underdeveloped. Trubek and Mosher say that while there are "positive" industrial citizenship rights and freedom of movement, there is no definition of fundamental citizenship rights (Trubek and Mosher 2001: 17–19; 23–24).

Ferrera and his colleagues suggest additional measures to improve the Open Method of Coordination for combating social exclusion. There has to be closer coordination between national action plans on employment and social inclusion. Labor has to be made more flexible but at the same time, social protections and safety nets have to be made stronger. The new term is "flexicurity." Social partners and nongovernmental organizations have to participate in the development of national action plans. This would include representatives of the poor and the socially excluded. In response to the charge that the appeal of social exclusion rests on its vagueness, they argue that national action plans have to be made accountable by improving the quality of relevant information. There has to be accurate and comparable statistics. And, despite the differences in national welfare states, there has to be continued efforts to provide a guaranteed minimum income at a decent level and access to health care, housing, and lifelong learning (Ferrera et al. 2002: 15–16).

The most recent report on the EES, reviewing the experience of five years, is quite favorable. The Luxembourg process has resulted in "'multilateral surveillance' . . . which has stimulated a 'stress of convergence' towards the best performers in the EU." The peer review has been able to evaluate the "transferability of good practices." The report notes that there has been an overall improvement in the labor market – e.g., more than 10 million jobs have been created since 1997, 6 million of which were taken up by women, laborforce participation has grown

---

[7] For a more detailed discussion on the idea of EES as a learning process, see Trubek and Mosher (2001: 17–19).

by nearly 5 million (largely by women) – and, while acknowledging that one cannot separate out the impact of the EES from the overall economic improvement, the report does note that "there have been significant changes in national employment policies, with a clear convergence towards the common EU objectives set out in the EES policy guidelines." The changes emphasized are the move towards an "active and preventive approach," more employment-friendly taxation (the rising trend in the overall tax burden on labor was reversed), closer adaptation of education and training systems to labor market needs, modernization of working time arrangements and more flexible work contracts, improvements in lifelong learning, "gender mainstreaming" with various measures taken to close the gender gap, including improving child care and reconciling work and family life, and fostering coordination of the social partnerships. On the other hand, there remain "serious employment challenges." Almost 13 million (2001) remain unemployed, of which 42 percent are long-term. There is a widening gap in access to training between those with higher education and those with low skills. School dropout rates remain high (over 19 percent). The employment of disadvantaged people (disabilities, ethnic minorities, immigrants) remains weak. While the gender gap in employment has declined, it is still significant. Improvements have been made in the security of workers with flexible jobs, but these workers are still disadvantaged and are more likely to experience frequent spells of unemployment. Most flexible workers have negative views of their jobs. More and better jobs have to be created, clearer objectives have to be established, governance by social partners has to be improved. There is still a widespread reluctance to set targets and reveal budgetary aspects.[8]

In sum, Ferrera and his colleagues conclude that there has developed something of a multi-tiered policy system which, some argue, may at least serve to resist regression. There have been important substantive developments (Community legislation, European Court of Justice case law); procedural rules and innovations (expansion of qualified majority voting, social partnership provisions of the Maastricht Social Protocol and Agreement); methods of enforcement (strengthened by the empowerment of the ECJ to fine dilatory member states). There has been a reduction in the autonomy of member state social policy vis-à-vis European regulations and market compatibility requirements (largely freedom of movement) which has begun to break down the

[8] For a generally favorable review, although with reservations, see Zeitlin (2002).

borders of welfare state development. The implications of this move are that member states may no longer limit social benefits to their own citizens, may no longer require benefits to be consumed on their own territories (except that unemployment benefits are exportable for only three months), and in a limited number of instances, they are losing control of how people within their own borders should be protected (e.g., controlling entitlement to disability, invalidity benefits established by an authority in another member state). Thus, there is a web of enforceable regulations resulting from EU legislation (Ferrera et al. 2002b: 60).

Anton Hemerijck agrees. He thinks that "across the European Union we observe a clear convergence of employment and social policy objectives over the past decade. All member states are explicitly dedicated to raise employment, promote social inclusion, invest in the productivity and skills of future workers, and enhance innovation in the pursuit of a competitive knowledge-based economy" (Hemerijck 2002). Although welfare reform will take place primarily at the level of the nation, he argues that they are constrained by the EMU, and increasingly, supranational regulations and policies. The Employment Strategy treaty was a "positive breakthrough", a "new model of cross-national policy making through monitoring and benchmarking" which has the potential for developing into new modes of governing. It can help safeguard against the "race to the bottom" and its successes will "likely enhance the legitimacy of the EU as a social union" (Hemerijck 2002).[9]

Nevertheless, for the immediate future, the most significant social and economic policies will be determined at the national level.

REFORM AT THE NATIONAL LEVEL

Convergence? Path-dependent?

The direction of reform at the national level mirrors the debate at the European level – will there be convergence among the member states, and if so, along neoliberal or social democratic lines, or will the various states continue along their individual paths (*path-dependent*)? The neoliberals argue that because political interference with markets is inefficient, those countries that conform (along neoliberal lines) will succeed and therefore there will be convergence. Most analysts disagree. They give two clusters of reasons: the politics of welfare reform,

---

[9] For a less generous view, see Lemaigre n.d.

and the organization of the principal economic actors. As noted, in most countries, there have been only modest changes in the welfare state.

Herbert Kitschelt and his colleagues say that most voters remain unconvinced that significant change is necessary. Party competition has become more complicated because of the growing inequality between skilled and unskilled workers, insiders and outsiders, sheltered and exposed workers. Interest groups and social movement groups are now challenging party loyalties and the core constituencies are a declining proportion of the electorate (Kitschelt, Lange, Marks, and Stephens 1999; see also Hemerijck 2002). Countries differ in terms of the organization of business, government, and a variety of other institutions that impact welfare state reform (Kitschelt et al. 1999: 57–60). The differing combinations of business, labor markets, and government constitute a country's "production regime, a framework of incentives and constraints deeply embedded and relatively impervious to short-run political manipulation." They call this, "embedded diversity." Thus, "despite international competition, there will always be space for sheltered, local production regimes; countries will try to specialize in terms of the particular production regimes; the relevant actors in various countries will view the competitive pressures differently and respond differently." In their view, "Most importantly, the impact of international competition on domestic policy and institutions is refracted by the domestic status quo – that is, the relative strength and organizational capacities of producer groups, political parties, electoral rules, laws and regulations, bureaucracies, and so forth." "Institutions are not just a 'dependent variable.'" "Different countries will respond differently to the challenges, even if the choice is not necessarily the most 'efficient' adaptation." Where institutions are more deeply embedded, as in the continental countries, there will be less convergence. For example, where unions control unemployment funds, higher levels of unemployment will increase union membership (Kitschelt et al. 1999). Scandinavia has been able to maintain efficient production and international competitiveness while still maintaining coordinated market economies. "The 'consumers' of the welfare state – e.g., female workers in Scandinavia – have defended the status quo" (Kitschelt et al. 1999). However, the authors are careful to emphasize the instability of the current picture. They think that "neither the present national or sectoral coordinate market economies nor the liberal market economies are that stable. There are deep political conflicts, especially arising from the dual labor markets. Nonetheless, path-dependent diversity is likely to continue, at least for the immediate present" (Kitschelt et al. 1999).

David Soskice, too, draws attention to the importance of the *production regime* – "the ways in which companies, customers, employees, and owners of capital organize and structure their relationships (the 'rules of the game') that are embedded in market-related institutions. These include the financial system, industrial relations, education and training, and relations between companies" (Soskice 1999: 101–134; Hall 1999: 135–163).[10] Previously, in comparing the political economy of countries, the focus was on unions. Now, says Soskice, it is on "employers and employer organizations and their capacity to adjust to the changing economies. The most important determinate is the extent to which companies are coordinated outside of competitive market institutions – that is, through interlocking boards, associations, and so forth." In countries where coordination is at a high level (e.g., Germany, Sweden, Switzerland) – "coordinated market economies" (CMEs) – there are "industry-wide unions, the transfer and diffusion of technology, vocational training, the encouragement of long-term financing, cooperative industrial relations and coordinated wage bargaining, and standard-setting cooperation" (Soskice 1999: 106–107). With "uncoordinated liberal market economies" (LMEs – e.g., Anglo-Saxon, Irish), the emphasis is on "deregulation, competition, and short-term profits." With CMEs, generally there are long-standing relations with skilled employees and suppliers, employer associations, and coordinated wage-setting fosters cooperation. LME companies, with minimum constraints, emphasize innovation. Increasingly, unions are excluded from decision-making. Even though insiders tend to be privileged with CMEs, in almost all countries it is now easier to hire temporary workers and youth. Nevertheless, according to Soskice, not much has changed. In Germany, even though contracts have been deregulated, not many temporary workers have found employment. The same is true in the rest of the Continent. In Scandinavia, there has been considerable employment flexibility, but wage and income inequality has increased; however, the increasing cost of direct public service employment (now one-third of all employment) has become significant. "So far, different responses in the different countries produce different winners and losers" (Esping-Andersen 1990: 148–153). Thus, changes in the welfare states have to take account of their diversity.

---

[10] Sometimes referred to as the "new institutionalism."

Instead of a predicted convergence, Soskice maintains that there has been a "*bifurcated* convergence along these two models" (Soskice 1999: 122–124).

Looking more specifically at welfare regimes, Maurizio Ferrera says that there are fifteen national systems of social protection. Although one can detect some signs of convergence – for example, Southern Europe is moving towards a guaranteed minimum income – nevertheless, there are four distinct types of "social Europe" which "differ significantly in terms of access, benefit formulae, financing regulations, and organizational-managerial arrangements." In addition to the three clusters previously mentioned (Scandinavian; Anglo-Saxon; continental – Germany, France, Benelux, Austria, and Switzerland), he includes Southern Europe – Italy, Spain, Portugal, and Greece. Targeting is widespread in the United Kingdom but not in Scandinavia where means-testing is considered "an injury to the social fabric." While there have been cuts in benefits, universalism remains intact. On the Continent, there is opposition to universalism (e.g., French unions). Southern Europe has mixed systems, but here, targeting becomes problematic because of "poor administrative capacity and an easily manipulated state" (Ferrera 1998; Przeworski 1999). Despite similar pressures, countries will respond differently – for example, the United Kingdom could deregulate and privatize basic sectors and public enterprises but Germany could not. The French failed to institute the German apprenticeship system because of a lack of institutional networks at the local and sectoral levels. "The capacity of firms to adjust will vary, depending on existing institutional infrastructures. Since nations differ in the degree to which producers are organized, adjustment paths will differ as well" (Hall 1999: 160–163).

"Recalibrating" the labor market and the welfare state: "flexicurity"

Within this diversity, there are common proposals for reform. Ferrera, Hemerijck, and Rhodes, in a Report for the Portuguese Presidency of the European Union, *The Future of Social Europe: Recasting Work and Welfare in the New Economy* (October 26, 2002) (Ferrera, Hemerijck, and Rhodes 2002), put forth the requirements for a "*competitive, employment-friendly, equitable welfare state*." Although there is no "one best way," the "elements of an optimal policy mix" are: (1) A robust macroeconomic policy is "a necessary (but not sufficient) background condition for limited damage control." (2) Wage moderation and flexibility. (3) Employment-friendly and efficient taxation. The authors argue that tax and other social policies should pursue redistribution rather than an egalitarian wage policy which distorts market wages. As Denmark and the Netherlands have demonstrated, "social spending *per se* does not predict employment performance." (4) "Flexicurity" – the most discussed innovation – is to provide flexible working conditions without creating a working poor. To ease the employment barriers facing women, there has to be shared working time for both men and women. Part-time work is most extensive in the Netherlands. For the most part, these jobs are stable, well paid, and have basic Social Security benefits. In the Netherlands, "the legal position of part-time and temporary workers was strengthened in exchange for a slight liberalization of dismissals among regular, full-time employees" (Hemerijck 2002). Consequently, in contrast to other countries, part-time work is preferred by most women (Ferrera et al. 2002b: 49).

The authors then set forth six policy strategies to establish flexicurity (Ferrera et al. 2002b: 50): (1) "Increase the demand for low-skilled work through methods such as wage subsidies, either using tax credits (Ireland, UK), or exemptions from social contributions (the Netherlands, France and Belgium)." (2) "Expand part-time work by making working hours more flexible through a mix of incentives, including a lower tax burden for low-income workers but with standard social and job protections." (3) "Labor market desegmentation (Spain), which involves relaxing the employment protection for the full-time core workers and linking new standards of protection for the part-time workers. This will help contain the growth of precarious jobs and narrow the gap between insiders and outsiders." (4) "Increasing use of activation policies, tightening eligibility for unemployment benefits." (5) Reconciling work and family life – for example, "expanded child-care facilities and increased parental leave and education and training which do not interrupt employment status." (6) Social drawing rights. The idea here is a savings account and an autonomous decision by the holder to pursue certain social goals, such as child-rearing, elder care, training, and education. The authors say that this would be a "new method of fighting poverty and social exclusion, as well as lessen the risks of inequalities between dual and single earner families, the latter mostly led by women. Social Security systems have to be redesigned to prevent the disentitlement of women and part-time, temporary workers. They have to guarantee access to skill acquisition and social services at any point in the life cycle" (Ferrera et al. 2002b: 52, 56).

Other areas have to be recalibrated as well. The welfare state has to be more evenly divided across the social structure. In addition to the especially large differences in the continental systems, "there is a growing gap between DINK families (double income, no kids; insider jobs) and SIMK (single income, many kids – or single parent, one child – outsider job or unemployed)." In some countries, there are marked distributional inequalities not only between insiders and outsiders but also among insiders. "Though less visible than in the US, there is an American-style underclass already in some regions, falling outside the reach of social insurance – workless households, lone parents, ethnic minorities or (illegal) immigrants" (Ferrera et al. 2002b: 71).

There is a need for a "normative" recalibration (Ferrera et al. 2002b: 71). Here, the authors call for a shift from a "static notion of equality centered on material resources to a more dynamic notion, centered on capacities and empowerment. The knowledge-based economy is likely to create a new cleavage line unless there is life-long training and education." More attention has to be paid to the lack of equality of opportunity, especially for the worse off. "In many trades and occupations in Europe, family backgrounds rather than talent are the most important determinant" (Ferrera et al. 2002b: 72).

There has to be "*politico-institutional*" recalibration. The authors argue that Social Europe already appears more integrated than normally assumed – *de facto* functioning, as compared to its modest formal "constitution." They believe that "soft co-ordination is a promising mechanism for mitigating the undesirable effects of 'negative integration,' diverting tendencies for regime competition into a possibly virtuous game." Nevertheless, there is "both a need and an opportunity for re-launching a 'hard' agenda, resting on more binding legal instruments, including the formal recognition of some fundamental social rights in the treaties" (Ferrera et al. 2002b: 72).

The authors believe that state intervention and social protection are feasible in the generous corporatist-continental type welfare states because, as compared to the liberal states, there remains considerable cross-class solidarity. "Through a process of adaptation, the essence of the European social model can be sustained – extensive basic Social Security for all citizens, a high degree of interest organization and coordinated bargaining, and a more equal wage and income structure. While there is variation among the countries, there is a commitment to implicit guarantee for all citizens, and so far, resistance to a 'race to the bottom.'" The examples of Denmark and the Netherlands show that a generous welfare policy does not necessarily inhibit economic progress (Ferrera et al. 2000: 3).

Gøsta Esping-Andersen, on the other hand, thinks that there has to be a major overhaul of the welfare state. He bases this judgment on the fact that youth and young families are now at the highest risks of poverty, unemployment, and entrapment. The welfare state has to be recast to help these groups. Consequently, to lower the risks of marital instability, childhood poverty, and inadequate skills, welfare states have to become more woman-friendly by improving child care, work incentives, and income support (Esping-Andersen 1990: 179–183).

Reforming the low-wage labor market

Proposals to improve the low-wage labor market are more controversial. In many countries, they are strongly resisted by employers, central banks and other financial institutions, and by the leadership at the European Union. On the other hand, they are favored by the Social Democrats (Ferrera et al. 2002b). In Scharpf's opinion, the problem of high unemployment on the Continent is in the low-wage service sector (rather than in the exposed export sector); in particular, the high costs to employers that discourage the creation of jobs for low-skilled people. To avoid the US solution, Scharpf argues that "what is needed are strategies that are able to combine 'work with welfare'" (Scharpf 1999). The most comprehensive reform would be an income supplement along the lines of the negative income tax. Scharpf, however, thinks that this kind of a reform would "require too far-reaching a restructuring of the various forms of taxation, social assistance, social insurance, pensions, and wage-setting. A more modest, less costly alternative would be job creation in the form of income subsidies to low-wage workers. Unions would have to agree on the creation of new wage scales. So far they have resisted, fearing an erosion of the present wage structure." Another alternative, which does not require union cooperation, would be to waive employer-employee social insurance contributions for minimum wage workers. He says that this would lower wage costs and would increase both the profitability and wages of service workers by 22 percent. The subsidy would be financed through general tax revenues while subsidized employment would reduce welfare state costs (Scharpf 1999: 142–147). Others have made similar proposals, and, as noted, in some countries, reforms in this direction have been undertaken (Supiot 2000: 34–38).

According to Martin Rhodes, reforming labor-market regulation and recasting the welfare states will require in most European countries a "new type of corporatism, a readjustment of the continental model to accommodate market pressures with the preservation of social protection and social consensus." This may require a "more flexible form of 'market' or 'competitive' corporatism. The firm will play a more 'central' role tailoring social intervention more closely with the demands of competition" (Rhodes 1998: 178–203). Rhodes acknowledges that there are counter-pressures to decentralize industrial relations systems. There has to be a high degree of trust between labor and management in order to accomplish flexible specialization and lean production, low levels of hierarchy, high levels of skills – in other words, "'regulated co-operation' to sustain both competitiveness and consensus." Wages have to be restrained to prevent inflationary pressures, maintain competition, and lessen unemployment. He suggests a "dome form" of incomes policy or national wage coordination that allows for flexibility at the firm level – for example, the "centralized decentralization" in the Netherlands. Inevitably there will be more variation and discontinuity in work which will require changes in Social Security systems (Rhodes 1998).

Several countries have attempted to combine a societal form of bargaining alongside lower level flexibility. Rhodes regards the Netherlands as the most advanced example of "competitive corporatism" (Rhodes 1998). In 1982, a national social pact between employers and unions was entered into to re-establish a more flexible corporatism. There would be "decentralized wage bargaining, wage moderation, and re-regulation to contain costs, prevent increasing inequality, and boost employment." In response to a new rise in unemployment, the agreement was consolidated in 1993. There was greater decentralization in bargaining but "concertation with regard to social security contributions, work sharing, training, job enrichment, and the development of entry-level wages." In 1995, there was a "flexicurity accord" – "rights for temporary workers were strengthened in return for loosening of dismissal protections for core workers."[11] Most recently, there was further reform of Social Security. Jelle Visser calls the Dutch system "corporatism and the market" instead of "corporatism against

[11] According to The Economist (2002q), the EU recently "endorsed a new that would give all temporary-agency workers the same rights as full-timers within six weeks of getting their feet under the desk."

markets." By this he refers to "monetary stability, budgetary discipline, and competitiveness while reforming social security, increasing employment and avoiding the social inequality of the UK and the break-down of consensus and the rise of large-scale social unrest as in France" (Visser 2002).

Rhodes thinks that where social pacts are formed around general macroeconomic objectives as well as specific labor objectives, it is more likely that there will be concertation over more general welfare issues and unlikely that there will be an assault on the welfare state as in the United Kingdom. He lists various reforms – "more negotiated regulation rather than legislated or rule-governed labor relations; modifying the protection of full-time workers in return for more protection for temporary, part-time workers; redesigning social security to include women in non-standard employment; providing Social Security coverage for skill acquisition (especially education and training) and social services throughout the life cycle; and more flexible retirement schemes." On the other hand, says Rhodes, a "welfare system should not be so dependent on labor market negotiations that it becomes biased towards organized interests and loses the legitimacy of the democratic government." Where this has happened – he cites Ireland – only the "insiders" benefit and poverty trends are not reversed (Rhodes 1998).

In the meantime, there have been significant changes in labor relations. First, in light of the current economic conditions, including high unemployment, employers will accept new deals only if they support competitiveness and greater flexibility. As a consequence, unions are more willing to modify their traditional position on equal income distribution. Second, in return for effective wage moderation, governments are more willing to offer reductions in taxes and social contributions or to promise to maintain social benefits. Third, increasingly, social partners combine decentralized bargaining with macroeconomic considerations in wage-setting. In Denmark, the Netherlands, and Austria, there is a two-level wage bargaining system. Sectoral or decentralized wages are negotiated within the confines of broader national framework accords (Ferrera et al. 2002b: 14).

As discussed in the section on "soft coordination," there is renewed interest in collective bargaining. According to Alain Supiot, governments are increasingly delegating to the social partners the negotiation and implementation of a wide range of labor laws including commitments to create and maintain jobs, provide training, establish occupational qualifications, reorganize working hours, facilitate

241

worker representation, social benefits and social protection, supplementary pensions (including early retirement), and anti-discrimination measures (especially gender) (Supiot 2000: 187). In many instances, employer organizations have negotiated adjustments and revisions in provisions that would normally be covered by the welfare state (Pierson 2001b: 8). In Ireland, social pacts were developed dealing with taxation, education, health, social welfare, and incomes. Laws explicitly authorize collective bargaining as an alternative to the law, called "derogatory accords," "auxiliary laws," or "provision laws." Management uses collective bargaining for the organization of work, including occupational categories, working hours, the organization of specialties, etc. New subjects, such as health care, have been added. Agreement between the parties is tending to become a precondition for the legitimacy of governing regulations (Supiot 2001: 146). According to Ferrera and his colleagues, the "real surprises" occurred in Italy, Portugal, and Spain, countries which previously experienced a great deal of conflict. Now, income policies have been linked with wider packages of negotiated reform of labor-market, Social Security, and tax systems. In Ireland, Denmark, Italy, the Netherlands, Finland, Spain, and Portugal, unions accepting wage restraint have been rewarded with side payments including work-time reduction, tax cuts, increases for active labor market policies, and vocational training. In these countries, wage bargaining is increasingly about the "social wage" which is broader than nominal gross wages (Ferrera et al. 2002b; Hemerijck 2002).[12]

The decentralization of collective bargaining to the company level enhances the role of worker representatives. At the company level, works councils or elected cooperation committees compete with union representatives. The works councils and cooperation committees have become well-established in a majority of European countries. There can be dual systems of representation, unions and elected representatives, but the practice tends to favor the latter. Company-wide agreements between employers and works councils are similar to collective agreements, but by law, collective agreements take precedence, except when they contain escape clauses which allow for different company-wide provisions (Supiot 2000: 119). An EU Directive recognizes the dual systems of representation (union/elective) in response to the new forms of organization of work, management demands for flexibility, and worker safety (Supiot 2000: 91).

---

[12] Hemerijck, too, points to a "remarkable resurgence of social pacts."

The relationship between industry-wide and company-wide collective agreements varies among the countries. Industry-wide agreements often define the framework. They are usually governed by clear rules – predictable labor costs, a certain degree of wage standardization, a framework for competition. Nevertheless, there are conflicts (e.g., unfair competition, anti-union practices). Company agreements try to evade industry-wide discipline (Supiot 2000: 81). In Germany, there are "escape clauses" – first in the East, now in the West – whereby companies can lower wages, with works council's consent, if the company is in financial straits, to save jobs. Unions are under growing pressure to give consent. These clauses are becoming more widespread (Supiot 2000: 82).

Transnational companies, groups of companies, and regional and networked companies are becoming important as new bargaining units, which can create problems at the national level (Supiot 2000: 107–108). As unemployment has weakened the representative capacity of unions, new organizations are competing with unions – for example, NGOs representing the disadvantaged and the unemployed. It is claimed that unions are completely absorbed by defending those who still have jobs. For example, in France, in 1997, unions protested action by organizations of the unemployed who proposed representatives of the unemployed at the EU level (Supiot 2000: 113).

In the meantime, Supiot argues, since the 1980s, in all member states, "management has recovered the ideological initiative. Management has succeeded in subordinating workers' rights to economic constraints, has demanded greater flexibility, and has marginalized traditional union initiatives. Management has marginalized traditional forms of representation in favor of immediate, direct, and on-going contact with workers." The result is that there are new relationships between capital and labor independent of labor law. He says that this is happening in all the European countries, although forms differ. This has not only significantly weakened unions but employers' associations as well (Supiot 2000: 86).

Some argue that unions will be replaced by new forms of collective representation better suited to reflect the diversity of interests (NGOs, feminist, ecological, the unemployed, charities, consumers, co-ops, etc.). But, thus far, according to Supiot, "these organizations are not in a position to compete with unions because trade unions and employer organizations occupy the key place in the formulation of labor regulations and contribute to social consensus in the broadest sense of the term (i.e., Italy and France)." Like labor unions, regulatory law extends some of their decisions to non-member companies (especially for collective bargaining agreements) (Supiot 2000: 95–96).

He says that two models of collective representation are emerging. First, in France and Germany, there is a shift of representative power to employee-elected representatives. Second, in the Netherlands (and maybe also in the United Kingdom), there is a merging or regrouping of labor and management forces. There is centralized bargaining on security/flexibility and then fine-tuning at the company level. Neither model can work alone. Regrouped unions need company officials to implement top level guidelines. And, representatives at the company level need the coordination of higher level bodies for support (Supiot 2000: 96). The subjects of representation will remain the same – unions will represent workers and employers' associations management but, "labor interests" and "management interests" will become much more complex. Labor can go in either of two directions. The first would be to continue to represent the hard core of workers, or unions can reach out to include those workers presently excluded. With management, the issue is whether dependent companies (subcontractors, services, etc.) will call for specific forms of management representation. There are cases of collective agreements between client companies and subcontractors (Supiot 2000: 97).

In response to these trends, Colin Crouch says that some look to the firm for a "new social contract" (Crouch 1998: 229–243). Workers are increasingly looking at the workplace rather than industry as a whole or the government. In part, due to a lack of confidence in government, firms are coming to be seen as the only acceptable institutions capable of running organizations of many different kinds. "Firms are considered the only organizations sufficiently flexible and close to the market to deal with market uncertainty. This is a return of prior history, that employees should identify with the company" (Crouch 1998). The countertrends are with the Anglo-Saxon firms with changing ownership and the growing casualization of the workforce.

> This extension of the firms is largely unregulated, unnoticed, and unscrutinized. Corporations agree to the social contract only on their terms. And with globalization, power is becoming less constrained and less accountable. In the US, citizens are willing to sue corporations; the Europeans have not yet learned how to do this (but this will still not help the most vulnerable). And now that macroeconomic measures with regard to unemployment have been ruled out, there is almost total

reliance on firms for creating jobs. Thus, firms can demand deregulation. . . . The state, then, loses its capacity to act. Economic fate rests solely with the firm. (Crouch 1998)

With the undermining of labor law, Alain Supiot calls this the "re-feudalization of labor law" (Supiot 2000: 321–345).

What, then, can one expect within the various countries? Paul Pierson says that without a return to significant economic growth, which does not seem likely in the immediate future, the fiscal pressure will create a "context of 'permanent austerity'" which, in turn, will increase the pressure for reform. There will be strong pressure to adopt a centrist position – "those who wish to preserve and modernize key elements of the social contract" – "but without creating large budget demands, that encourage economic productivity. In the current climate, restructuring must be distinguished from retrenchment or dismantling." "The social contract will be 'modernized' to encourage economic productivity. Eligibility will be tightened and benefits reduced thus restricting alternatives to labor market participation. Given the strong resistance to tax increases, spending will be contained or reduced." As Pierson puts it, "Today's politicians . . . act primarily as the bill collectors for yesterday's promises." Then, welfare states will be "recalibrated," which will vary by country. "Re-commodification is most prominent in the liberal states where there have been major cutbacks in unemployment benefits and social assistance, and a sharp rise in income inequality and poverty. In the Social Democratic regimes, the welfare state coalitions remain strong, and women are highly mobilized. Nevertheless, in these countries, there were both welfare cuts and tax increases, and work is expected." Here, the main problem, according to Pierson, is maintaining cross-class solidarity. In the continental regimes, "welfare costs are high and rising because of generous pensions and incentives to leave the labor market. There are high rates of unemployment, especially among the young and unskilled because of the large, fixed labor costs and low women labor force participation. There are significant cleavages between the insiders and outsiders" (Pierson 2001b: 423–424; 425–426; 428–438; 440–443; 445–448).

THOSE WHO REMAIN

Returning to those who remain – the long-term unemployed, the vulnerable populations, the socially excluded – much depends on the various national and global economies; obviously, a healthy economy will facilitate the measures necessary to create good jobs and secure benefits, and provide education and training opportunities and the resources to repair the welfare state. Long- and short-term unemployment will be reduced, the young will more easily enter the labor market, and lone parents will be supported with child care, family leave, and work supports. There will be those who will remain outside of the paid labor market. Significant numbers of people either have various kinds of employment barriers, or family care responsibilities, or otherwise lack the skills and training to earn a living. But, if times are good, one could expect that policies to combat poverty and social exclusion will be more generous; at least that has been the experience of the United States and in Western Europe during the Golden Age. There will be less tension over immigrants and resentment about people who are being perceived as abusing the system. Countries would be more inclined to report progress and "best practices" in combating poverty and social exclusion, and there should be more social activism for reform.

That is the optimistic scenario. At the present time, and for the immediate future, it looks like the economies in several major European countries will remain sluggish or improve slowly. This means that the number of socially excluded will most likely remain high and might well increase the pressures on the welfare state, as summarized by Paul Pierson.

Under either scenario, then, workfare seems likely to continue for those who remain. As discussed in Chapter 3, the moral judgments behind the reforms are complex. To be sure, there is the harshness, the condemnation, the compassion fatigue. There is significant anti-immigrant sentiment. Recall Germany's Chancellor, Gerhard Schröder: "Germans had 'no right to laziness,'" "that those who reject 'a reasonable job' might lose benefits" (The Economist 2001a: 44). In the United Kingdom, New Labour's Minister of State for Social Security, Frank Field, said that the passive benefit system was now " 'broken-backed,' discouraged self improvement, thrift and independence and rewarded 'claimants for being either inactive or deceitful.' " There were political demands for an end to "something for nothing" welfare, to change the culture of dependency (Standing 1999). Labor-market policies should focus more on an active integration or re-integration and less on income support (Ferrera and Rhodes 2000: 4). New Labour began to adopt the rhetoric of "tough love" and "reciprocal" or "mutual" obligation which was popular in the United States and Australia (Finn 1998).

"Tough love" represents the opposite strain. It is in the long history of rehabilitation for the poor. From the earliest days of poverty relief, the "best" people believed that the most effective, most humane way of helping the poor was through rehabilitation – education, training, and work experience. "Money alone is not enough." Today, this ideology has taken hold even in countries, such as Norway and Denmark, with little unemployment and no welfare state crisis. A strongly held view is that the surest road to the re-integration of the socially excluded into society is through the paid labor market. It is now agreed that "welfare-to-work" programs should become a core of welfare systems (Finn 2000: 43–57; Standing 1999: 313). Guy Standing sums up the change: "It may not be hyperbole to describe workfare as the great social experiment of the late twentieth century. Its success or failure will determine social and labour market policy in the early part of the twenty-first century" (Standing 1999: 14; Crespo and Serrano 2001).

The "Third Way" accepts a level of inequality and focuses instead on an "equality of initial endowments, the creation of equal opportunities rather than the de-commodification of labor, on successful market participation rather than market outcomes. Social cohesion is to come about not through equal outcomes but, rather, equal opportunities" (Streeck 1999: 6,10). An active labor market policy gives priority to training, placement, and rehabilitation. Individuals are encouraged to enter the labor market quickly. The emphasis is on improving the labor supply rather than the demand for low-skilled labor.

The capabilities approach reflects the special concern about the socially excluded. The lack of employment, it is argued, leads to a lack of connection with mainstream society. The 1994 EU White Paper (the Delors paper) on *Growth, Competitiveness, Employment*, expressed concern about the development of a dual labor market resulting in a dual society. Those excluded from work are also excluded from the benefits of growth and social protection. A dual standard of treatment discourages new hiring and excludes the jobless from unemployment insurance. The White Paper called for "an economy characterized by solidarity," that is, solidarity between those who have jobs and those who do not, between men and women, between generations, and between more and less developed regions. The growing consensus, according to Hilary Silver, is "to turn a passive and precarious solidarity with excluded people into a contract that offers them real opportunities of both social and economic integration in return for a commitment to make an effort themselves" (Silver 1998a). According to the Third Way, workfare clients have rights and obligations. This is the new social contract.

Contracts in bureaucratic relationships

In Chapter 3, I presented the views of Pierre Rosanvallon as representative of the Third Way. He argued that under the new regime, the socially excluded would be reintegrated back into society through contracts with government services. In return for assistance, the clients would have "rights" to offers of education, training, and work opportunities and "obligations" to accept these offers. The state has the "obligation" to enhance the employability of the clients. The contracts would be tailored to the individual client needs. The government offices would be different from the traditional charity offices because the government workers would have "obligations" and the clients would have "rights." Thus, the existence of client rights and mutual obligations would change the dependency status of the clients. Through contracts, the clients would be *empowered*.

How accurate is this description of workfare contracts? There are lots of "rights" in social welfare but whatever the rhetoric, workfare "rights" are not "rights" as commonly understood in the legal sense. In order for there to be rights *in fact* two conditions have to be satisfied: (1) eligibility has to be fairly clear-cut, with a minimum of field-level discretion; and (2) the benefits have to be infinitely divisible. The clearest example of welfare rights in fact in the United States is Social Security pensions. If an applicant (aged sixty-five) has worked a certain number of quarters in covered employment, he or she is eligible, the amount of benefits is specific, and the benefits are infinitely divisible (as long as the Treasury is solvent). With disability, the benefits (cash) are infinitely divisible but eligibility, in many cases, is not clear-cut. An agency determination has to be made that the disability falls within the prescribed criteria, that is, so severe that the applicant cannot engage in gainful employment for a period of at least one year. In some cases, this would be clear – for example, the loss of a limb – but in many cases, for example, for "soft tissue" injuries, pain, depression, and so forth, the decision would depend on the judgment of the examining and supervising medical administrators.

With public housing, some parts of eligibility are clear-cut – for example, family size – but others are not. Public housing is means-tested. Some elements of the means test are clear-cut (e.g., salary), but others may not be (e.g., assets, other sources of support). But, in any event, the benefits are *rationed*, not divisible. There has to be an available housing unit. Therefore, the "right" to public housing may only be the right to join the queue. A final example involves services – health care, legal services, employment services, social services, etc. Eligibility is not only means-tested but also discretionary with the intake officers – the client's needs or problems have to fit with the organization's requirements. And, the benefits are not divisible. Help will only be given if the organization has the means. Job placements can only be offered if they are available.

"Welfare," the program for single mothers and their children (AFDC, now called TANF) has divisible benefits but discretionary eligibility. Prior to the recent reform (1996), one had a "right" to welfare, an entitlement. What "right" meant with AFDC was that if a client felt that her case was wrongly decided, she had a right to appeal, called a "fair hearing." The right to appeal has been available for a long time. The US Supreme Court held that AFDC was an "entitlement," and therefore, clients had the right to appeal (*Goldberg* v. *Kelly* 397 US 254 (1970)). Clients cannot appeal matters of law – for example, a child is no longer entitled to benefits when he or she reaches eighteen years of age – but can appeal matters of interpretation, factual determinations, or an alleged abuse of discretion, as well as claims of discrimination. The same right to appeal applies to the above example as well – Social Security, disability, public housing, social and legal services.

In practice, the right to appeal is largely ineffective. The system is not proactive. In order for the system to work, there has to be a complaining client. The following conditions have to be met: (1) the client has to realize that she has suffered a wrong; (2) she has to blame the agency for the wrong; (3) she has to have the resources to pursue the remedy; and (4) she has to make a benefit-cost calculation that pursuing the remedy is worth the cost. If there is a failure in *any one* of the conditions, then the right of appeal fails. And all of these conditions are often serious barriers for dependent people.

In order for the client to know that she has been wronged, she has to be aware of the rules and regulations regarding eligibility, benefits, and options. Welfare programs are complex, and now more so with the addition of workfare, and communication is poor. Offices are crowded, the waiting time is long, there are kids to take care of, interviews are usually short and, at least in the United States, are often behind barred windows. In the United Kingdom, interviews were only a few minutes.

Clients complained of interviews in other countries as well. Suppose the worker unlawfully tells the client that her application for aid will not be accepted until she engages in a certain amount of job search. The client has to know that a job search is not required. But ignorance of welfare programs is common.

Then, the client has to blame the agency. Consider, for example, the situation where the client is required to document that she has engaged in job search, i.e., contacted a certain number of employers, asked for a job, and was refused. The worker decides that the documentation is insufficient. The employer did not "sign off" that the client had applied for a job even though the client asked the employer. Does the client blame herself or the worker for refusing to believe that she tried? There are many empirical studies showing that clients internalize wrongs and blame themselves rather than others (Felstiner et al. 1980–81: 631–654). "I messed up," "it's my fault" allows the client to think that she is still in control and will do better the next time rather than engage in a controversy often with a more powerful adversary. For example, victims of employment discrimination will blame themselves rather than confront discrimination (Bumiller 1988). Employees will quit rather than protest. They feel that they are in control (Maranville 2002).

The large majority of welfare recipients are acutely aware of the stigma that attaches to welfare. Moreover, they agree with societal attitudes – that most welfare recipients are morally irresponsible, they do not seriously try to better themselves, and that they manipulate the system. Individual recipients cling to the belief that they personally are different from other recipients and that they are desperately trying to get off of welfare. Nevertheless, they constantly feel the disapproval when they shop or otherwise have to disclose that they are on welfare (Rank 1994: 27–47; Scott et al. 2000: 727).

Workers (and other professionals) often structure the relationship to make the client feel at fault. Selecting, processing, and changing people involve moral judgments. In Chapter 2, I described the process as *moral typification*. Workers classify clients according to preconceptions. The welfare agency will attempt to select those clients who fit organizational needs. They screen in confirming information and ignore conflicting information. Client responses become self-fulfilling prophecies. Programs select and train the most promising and deflect those who may need the services the most. Agencies punish those who fail to comply. Workers apply rules strictly, impose sanctions, minimize errors, and try to get through the day as quickly and painlessly as possible. Requests for change or required change consume scarce administrative time and run the risk of error. Regardless of program demands, the staff response will be survival, and not necessarily service to clients. Because individual field-level decisions are shrouded in factual assessments, supervision is difficult, assuming there is the will to do so (Hasenfeld 1983). There are similar findings in some of the Western European reports.

At the conclusion of Chapter 2, on the US welfare state, I discussed client satisfaction in workfare programs despite the fact that they knew they would only get minimum wage jobs and that they had to get more education and training to improve their employment prospects but that this was not allowed under the "work first" strategy. They expressed satisfaction because the workers had selected them as the better candidates in the pool, the workers reinforced their moral typification (to improve their "success" rates), and the clients could distinguish themselves from those who were rejected and retain feelings of control. Dissatisfaction would mean that they, too, were victims.

Assuming the client can negotiate these two conditions, and that she knows that she has the right to appeal, she then has to have the resources to pursue the remedy. Resources may have to include professional help, and, at least in the United States, legal services are seriously underfunded and in short supply. Clients who try to handle their own appeals are often seriously handicapped. They lack the skills and the information to counter the agency's arguments (Maranville 2002). But there are also the time, social, and psychological costs. The rejected or sanctioned client is a poor person with a family. Her time and energy are devoted to daily survival – pursuing alternative forms of income support, whether through gifts, loans, or an informal job, making sure that she can pay the rent, taking care of her kids, returning favors that relatives and friends have provided. The significant demands on the lives of poor families are well documented (Edin and Lein 1996). When her application is turned down at the welfare office, she may well consider survival as the primary goal.

Then, is it worth challenging the worker and the agency and pursuing the appeal? Here, if the client is in a *continuing relationship*, she has to consider the possibilities of retaliation. In the example of the job search, is it better to challenge the worker – for example, the client did apply to a particular employer but the employer refused to fill out the job search form – and incur the hostility of the worker or "lump it" and try again next month? Does the parent who thinks that the teacher is unfair to her child protest, wondering what will happen to her child the next day, or does she just tell her child, "that's life, get along"? Deborah Maranville documents how low-wage employees either "lump it" or quit rather than challenge an employment decision and jeopardize the chances of a favorable reference when applying for another job (Maranville 2002). Unless the stakes are high enough or there will no longer be a continuing relationship, then the threat or the fear of retaliation may undermine the right to appeal. For all of these reasons, welfare appeals are rarely used in the United States (Handler 1986).

With commercial contracts, the relationship between the parties is horizontal. Contracts envisage two parties, roughly equal, voluntarily entering into a contract which is then enforceable. They are exercising property rights which can be enforced by civil rights. Relationships between government agencies and people are matters of degree; they can range from completely coercive to citizens (e.g., regulated businesses) dominating the agency. There can be a full range of bargaining. In most human service relationships – welfare, health, mental health, education, and so forth – the relationship is vertical. The agency is in the dominant position. It may not be completely dominant – if a worker wants to "cream," the client with employable characteristics has some bargaining leverage – but it clearly has the upper hand. Welfare clients are dependent persons, and dependent persons, in fact as distinguished from theory, do not have rights in bureaucratic relationships. Rosanvallon recognizes the imbalance of power, that the workfare contract is not a "legal contract" and that welfare clients do not have "legal rights." He believes that the relationship is to be made horizontal by virtue of the obligations on the worker. The worker has the obligation to be responsive to the client's individual needs and to treat the client as a subject. In Rosanvallon's words, this will *empower* the clients so that they can meaningfully participate in decisions that affect their lives.

Power and empowerment in human services agencies

It is here that the concern arises. Empowerment is the ability to control one's environment. Before we can consider empowerment, we first have to understand the nature of power in bureaucratic or regulatory settings. As the discussion of rights has shown, the exercise of power by the workers is not always direct and observable; it is often subtle and manipulative. Similarly, empowerment involves not only direct, observable forms of behavior, but also understanding the subtle, psychological reactions of clients. Empowerment involves not only challenge and confrontation but also consciousness-raising. We have seen that there is a large amount of dissatisfaction on the part of clients who nevertheless feel that they have to accept the terms of the contract to get the benefits. We have also seen that most clients seem satisfied. Are these clients empowered? What does consent in a hierarchical relationship mean? If participants are relatively equal and the relationship is voluntary, then agreement is usually not an issue. Agreement or acquiescence, on the other hand, is an issue when power relationships are unequal. It then becomes important to determine why clients acquiesce.

The standard definition of power is: A has power over B to the extent that he can get B to do something that B would not otherwise do (Talcott 1986: 94).[13] At first blush, the definition seems unproblematic, especially in the context of the dependent client. The client, at the price of receiving something that is needed, has to do something that the official insists upon – participate in a work program, reveal a matter of privacy, or engage in other kinds of behaviors. The model assumes an objective conflict of interests; there is a direct exercise of power and a knowing, albeit unwilling, submission.

Suppose, however, that the client willingly submits? Has there been an exercise of power if B *appears* to do what A wants? Now the situation becomes more problematic. Can we take the client's position at face value? Steven Lukes, in *Power: A Radical View* (Lukes 1974), argues that there are three dimensions of power. The one-dimensional approach is the example given above where A gets B to do something he otherwise would not have done. This dimension focuses on observable behavior. As such, it assumes that grievances and conflicts are recognized and acted upon, that participation occurs within decision-making arenas which are assumed to be more-or-less open. Non-participation, or inaction, then, is not a political problem; "the empirical relationship of low socio-economic status to low participation gets explained away as the apathy, political inefficacy, cynicism or alienation of the impoverished" (Gaventa 1980: 7). Quiescence lies in the characteristics of the victims; it is not constrained by power.

---

[13] While this may be a common, and for our purposes useful, definition of power, there is, in fact, no agreement on the various meanings of power. "[I]n our ordinary unreflective judgments and comparisons of power, we normally know what we mean and have little difficulty in understanding one another, yet every attempt at a single general answer to the question has failed and seems likely to fail." (Lukes 1974: 17). For further discussion of power, see, e.g., Clegg (1989); Honneth (1991).

The two-dimensional view of power seeks to meet this last point. Bachrach and Baratz argue that power has a "second face" by which it is not only exercised upon the participants within the decision-making arenas but also operates to exclude participants and issues altogether; that is, power not only involves who gets what, when, and how, but also who gets left out and how (Bachrach and Baratz 1962; Bachrach and Baratz 1970; Bachrach and Botwinick 1992). Some issues never get on the political agenda. Apparent inaction is not related to the lack of grievances. Bachrach and Baratz argue that the study of power also has to include the barriers to even expressing grievances.

Lukes says that the two-dimensional view, while a considerable advance, does not go far enough; it fails to account for how power may affect even the *conception* of grievances. The absence of grievances may be due to a manipulated consensus. Furthermore, the dominant group may be so secure that they are oblivious to anyone challenging their position – "the most effective and insidious use of power is to prevent . . . conflict from arising in the first place" (Lukes 1974: 23). This is the third dimension of power. A exercises power over B not only by getting him to do what he does not want to do, but "he also exercises power over him by influencing, shaping or determining his very wants" (Lukes 1974: 23). "In the two-dimensional approach is the suggestion of barriers that prevent issues from emerging into political arenas – i.e., that constrain conflict. In the three-dimensional approach is the suggestion of the use of power to pre-empt manifest conflict at all, through the shaping of patterns or conceptions of non-conflict" (Lukes 1974: 23). Lukes says that this may happen in the absence of observable conflict even though there is a latent conflict between the interests of A and the "real interests" of B.

The third dimension combines the hegemonic social and historical patterns identified by Antonio Gramsci (1971) and the subjective effects of power identified by Murray Edelman (Edelman 1971: 8; Gaventa 1980: 13).[14] The mechanisms of power include the control of information and socialization processes but also self-deprecation, apathy, and the internalization of dominant values and beliefs – the psychological adaptation of the oppressed to escape the subjective sense of powerlessness. It is the culture of silence which may lend legitimacy to the dominant order (Freire 1985; Gaventa 1980: 15–16).

---

[14] "Political actions chiefly arouse or satisfy people not by granting or withholding their stable, substantive demands but rather by changing their demands and expectations."

Quiescence can be the product of cooptation, symbolic manipulation, or the silent effects of incremental decisions or institutional inaction (Gaventa 1980: 15). Voices become echoes rather than grievances and demands.

While Lukes's three faces of power has been very influential, it has been criticized as presenting a view of power that is overly monolithic, sovereign, top-down – in short, hegemonic. It emphasizes negative, prohibitory power, the denial of sovereignty to sovereign individuals. Building on the work of Foucault, post-structuralists argue that power is not a "thing"; rather it is "property of relations" (Foucault 1980: 98). "Power must be analyzed as something which circulates . . . in a net-like organization. Networks of interest are constituted and reproduced both through conscious strategies and unwitting practices. Over time, individual transactions may be repeated and may become patterned . . . Social actors are thus constrained without knowing from where or whom the constraint derives" (Ewick and Silbey 2002). Stuart Clegg argues that power is never that complete, that there is always a dialectic between agents (Clegg 1989; Honneth 1991: 189).

Because power is relational, there are – or can be – spaces for bargaining, resistance, manipulation, and deceit (Ewick and Silbey 2002). "Variously referred to as secondary adjustments, tactics, or 'weapons' of the weak, these everyday acts of resistance represent the ways relatively powerless persons accommodate to power while simultaneously protecting their interests and identities. Institutional ethnographies – of wards of mental hospitals, assembly lines, classrooms, bureaucratic offices, barracks, prisons and courtrooms – provide us with evidence of the universality of such practices" (Ewick and Silbey 2002: 2–3). In welfare, clients will hide earned income, child support, gifts, and relationships. Workers know this, they know that families cannot survive on the welfare grant, but they choose to look the other way. Investigating and sanctioning just complicates their day, and how is a family to survive? (Gilliom 2001; Edin and Lein 1997). We have seen similar practices in Western Europe, especially with lone mothers.

There is a rich literature on various forms of resistance by dependent people – as mentioned, often referred to as "the weapons of the weak" (Hutchinson 1988; Scott 1990; Ewick and Silbey 1998; Gilliom 2001; White 1990; Winter 1996). And therein lies the problem. While the stories of resistance are moving, and provide a much-needed human dimension to the struggles of dependent people, at the end of the day, they are still dependent. They are still poor, they still exist to a considerable extent on the sufferance of the powerful (Handler 1992: 697–732). Unless challenged, power will automatically reproduce the existing configurations of rules, and domination and will only change when existing practices are challenged. Domination is not challenged that often because clients are embedded within organizations controlled by others. They may not know about the existence of other resources – "they may not know the rules of the game or even recognize the game." They may be aware, but the cost of resistance is too high. When these relational interests are reproduced, when they become fixed or reified, then power tends to be regarded as thinglike, material, concrete. This means that despite possible instability, in practice, power can be "as 'objective' as the policeman's power to arrest" because of the "fixity of stabilized disciplinary powers and discursive practices" (Clegg 1989: 187; Gilliom 2001).

In sum, there appears to be a high degree of convergence as to the characteristics or manifestations of power (Honneth 1991: 173).[15] Whatever the various definitions, power at times can be objectively observed (A getting B to do what B would not ordinarily desire) to the subtle manipulations of the agenda to the construction of ideologies and meaning so that B is not aware of alternatives. Structuralists emphasize the multiple ways in which the powerful dominate. Post-structuralists argue that power is not always total, that there are contradictions and forces of change in society, and that there is often resistance on the part of seemingly powerless people.

Concepts of empowerment mirror the multiple meanings of power – "the ability to act effectively" (Bachrach and Botwinick 1992: 57). Empowerment is both psychological and behavioral. It involves a sense of perceived control, of competence, a critical awareness of one's environment, and involvement in activities that, in fact, exert control (Zimmerman and Rappaport 1988: 725–750; Zimmerman 1993). Charles Keiffer says that empowerment is more than an absence of alienation or sense of helplessness. It involves a sense of connectedness. He emphasizes the importance of the connections between the

---

[15] In describing the evolution of Foucault's theory of power, Honneth says: "Accordingly, he no longer regards individual actors or social groups as the subjects of this developed form of the exercise of power, but instead social institutions such as the school, the prison, or the factory – institutions that he himself must comprehend as highly complex structures of solidified positions of social power. The frame of reference for the concept of power has, therefore, secretly been shifted from a theory of action to an analysis of institutions."

experiences of daily life and perceptions of personal efficacy (Keiffer 1984: 9–36). The contrast is powerlessness which is a sense of loss of control over social relations. "It combines an attitude of self-blame, a sense of generalized distrust, a feeling of alienation from resources for social influence, an experience of disenfranchisement and economic vulnerability, and a sense of hopelessness in socio-political struggle" (Keiffer 1984: 9–36). Keiffer quotes one of his respondents (participants in grass-roots organizations): "It would never have occurred to me to have expressed an opinion on anything . . . It was *inconceivable* that my opinion had any value" (Keiffer 1984: 16).

Empowerment is a long-time learning process. It must be specific; generalized feelings of injustice or consciousness-raising are not sufficient. According to Keiffer's participants, tangible and direct threats to individual or familial self-interests were necessary to provoke responses that would eventually lead to empowerment. There must be a "personally experienced sense of outrage or confrontation" (Keiffer 1984: 19). The next phase is what Keiffer calls the emergence of "participatory competence." By this he means getting over being scared, demystifying the symbols of power and authority, that is, coming to realize that officials do not know everything, and that ordinary people can change things. The process continues with the help of more experienced allies (role models, mentors, instructors, friends), supportive peer relationships, and a more critical understanding of social and political relations. "Action must be reflective. Direct experience is used not only to gain skills, but also to increase understanding and confidence, which, in turn, increases motivation." Eventually, the participants achieve an "increasingly self-conscious awareness of self as a visible and effective actor in the community" and they use their skills to integrate their "new personal knowledge . . . into the reality and structure of their everyday life-worlds" (Keiffer 1984: 23–24).

In discussing the relationship between thought and action, Keiffer is careful to point out that his respondents are not talking about theoretical conceptualization. Rather, thought is used to inform action, to make future activity more effective. There has to be both thought and experience, extending over a period of time. Empowerment as "participatory competence," involves the development of a sense of self-competence, a more critical or analytical understanding of one's social and political environment, and individual and collective resources for social and political activity (Keiffer 1984: 31). Keiffer argues that this definition of empowerment "places the notion of competence and coping within an explicitly political context" (Keiffer 194: 32). Subsequent research confirms Keiffer's conception. Thus, Zimmerman and Rappaport report that studies of participants in a wide variety of settings and organizations suggest that empowerment is a combination of personal beliefs about control, involvement in activities to exert control, and a critical awareness of one's environment. They, too, emphasize *experience* – behaviors designed to exercise control – as well as consciousness-raising (Zimmerman and Rappaport 1988).

The faces of power and empowerment become relevant when considering relationships in human service agencies (this section relies on Hasenfeld 1983; 1992). In Chapter 2, at the conclusion of the discussion of workfare in the United States, I discussed Yeheskel Hasenfeld's analysis of the constraints and strategies of human services officers. The purpose of these organizations is to process or change people. People, in turn, as clients, react to the processing, and thereby affect the work. The very nature of selecting, processing, and changing people conveys a judgment as to the *moral worth* of that client – that the applicant is worth educating or training, that the patient is worth treating, that the poor person is worth helping. How the client is treated also conveys moral decisions. Should the client be consulted or should the client be told what to do? When official decisions are expected to be unchallenged, it is a statement of moral superiority (Hasenfeld 1983).

Cultural beliefs legitimize values which then become "*practice ideologies*" – beliefs as to what is good for clients, and these beliefs provide both the rationale and the justification for the practices. Clients are invested with moral and cultural values that define their status. The agency will attempt to select those clients who fit organizational needs and compartmentalize client needs into "normal" service categories. Other client problems will be considered irrelevant (Hasenfeld 1983; 1992). The practice of "typification" is a pervasive feature in the exercise of field-level discretion. The organization identifies client characteristics in terms of diagnostic labels which then determine the service response. Agency perceptions of the client's moral character are often determinative. Is the client responsible for his or her condition and is the client amenable to change? Is the client morally capable of making decisions? The answers to these questions, in turn, determine the workers' moral responsibility to the client. The social construction of the client's moral character becomes reinforcing (Hasenfeld 1983; Hasenfeld and Abbott 1992).

The principal source of worker power derives from the resources and services controlled by the agency. If the clients want these resources, then they must yield at least some control over their fate. In addition to control over resources, workers have other sources of power: expertise, persuasion, and legitimacy. All of these sources of power are used in various combinations to exercise control over clients. A great deal of the organizational power is exercised through its standard operative procedures – the type of information that is processed, the range of available alternatives, and the decision rules. At the same time, the environment matters; goals represent the interests of those who control the key resources of the agency. In public agencies, which chronically lack the resources to meet demand, social workers are relatively powerless to change the situation; thus, they develop various personal coping mechanisms such as withdrawal and client victimization.

The interests of the client and the agency are determined by their respective positions. Agencies which have a monopoly of services exercise considerable power over clients. On the other hand, clients can exercise considerable power if they possess desirable characteristics. Thus, the exchange relationship between the client and the agency can be voluntary or involuntary depending on the degree of choice that each possesses. However, even in situations where workers possess considerable power, that power may not necessarily be used. There are rules and regulations, and workers, in varying degrees, are influenced by professional norms and values. But in any event, with vulnerable groups, relationships tend to be involuntary. The agency is not dependent on the client for its resources. Demand exceeds resources, and most agencies are in monopoly positions. The clients usually have no alternatives. The more powerful the agency, the more it will use its advantages to maintain its position. To maintain a superior practice, it will select the more desirable clients. Within the agency, the more powerful workers are better able to control the conditions of their work. In this way, the dynamics of power perpetuate the unequal distribution of quality practice. Poor clients tend to receive poor services. This results not only in an inequality of practice, but, Hasenfeld argues, the practice of inequality.

Hasenfeld's description of power in human services agencies tracks the three dimensions of power. The first dimension is the objective observation of an exercise of power. A dependent person applies for welfare; a condition of aid is a behavioral change – for example, a work assignment – which the person would prefer not to do but feels that she has to as the price of receiving assistance. The agency is acting either legally or illegally. In either case, it is a direct, observable exercise of power. Assume that the agency is acting illegally – the woman may be legally exempt from the work requirements, the agency failed to follow required procedures (e.g., evaluation, offers of training, etc.), or legally-required adequate day care was not available. The client knows of the illegality but needs the aid, has no other adequate alternative but lacks the resources to challenge the agency. Or, the client has available competent legal services and does challenge the agency. This is the first dimension of power – there is an objective event – individualized conflict and empirical evidence as to who won what under what circumstances.

Suppose, however, that the client acquiesces in the condition. Why is there acquiescence? Assume that the client is of the same frame of mind – that is, she would prefer not to work. It may be that the agency is acting legally; in this case, the decision has been made legislatively and the agency is not exercising its discretion but is following a rule. The client is now precluded from voicing her grievance, certainly in this forum, and probably also in any other arena as well. This would be a case of the second dimension of power. There is a grievance – the woman feels that she unjustly has to pay a price for the aid – but she has been effectively precluded from contesting the decision.

There are variations on the third dimension of power – where the absence of conflict is due to the manipulation of consensus, where A shapes and determines the very wants of B. Even if the client thinks she is entitled to welfare, there are competing norms. In the discussion of client satisfaction in Chapter 2, we have seen that the obligation to work may be deeply ingrained; many think it perfectly normal and appropriate that an applicant for assistance should work at a public job as the price of the grant; there is very little support for the idea that one is entitled to a minimum level of support without any corresponding obligations (Scott et al. 2000; see also Hartmann 1987). The values of work are reinforced by the client's perception of herself as worthy as contrasted with the other "lazy, immoral" welfare recipients (Scott et al. 2000). To the extent that the applicant for assistance has internalized these values – the mutual obligations of work, responsibility, and welfare – then the dominant group has prevented even the conception of the grievance.

The social and historical patterns and the subjective effects are, of course, much more deeply rooted, much more pervasive than even the complex example of the work obligation. They are manifested in many of the relationships between the dependent citizen seeking services or trying to avoid sanctions and the officer who controls the resources. Both the powerful and the powerless carry into the relationship their respective characters and self-conceptions, their root values, nurtured through immediate as well as past social relationships. Who they are and where they come from – class, race, childhood, education, employment, relations with others, the everyday structures of their lives, their very different social locations – crucially affect their languages, social myths, beliefs, and symbols – how they view themselves, their world, and others – which produce vastly different meanings and patterns in their encounters. How does the staff-professional view herself in its full, deep context and the person sitting across the desk? How does the client view herself, in her context, and the person sitting across from her? The structures of their social life shape their identities and direct their behavior (Molotch and Boden 1985).[16] It is no surprise that the vast majority of clients either fail to pursue their grievances or even to conceptualize a grievance. At a theoretical level, one may argue as to the degree of hegemony of the three faces of power. In human service organizations that deal with the poor and minorities, official power is, for all intents and purposes, just about totalizing. To be sure, there is resistance but it is often quite feeble and at the margins (Handler 1992; Gilliom 2001).

The welfare client in the United States is dependent, not empowered. This, too, is now the challenge facing Western European welfare states implementing workfare. As Rosanvallon and many others pointout, there has to be *individualized* decisions regarding claimants. These discretionary decisions are not made in a vacuum. They are part of political, economic, social, and organizational fields. Jobs, education, and training cannot be offered unless they are available. Then, there is the organization, structure and incentives of the field offices themselves. What are the political and legal environments – at various levels of government? What are the incentives on the agency and the workers? How are they evaluated – the targets they reach? Rosanvallon recognizes the dangers, noting that the welfare offices can resemble old-style charity offices. But he assumes (hopes?) that the welfare officers will treat the

---

[16] There is a large theoretical and empirical literature dealing with the problems of lack of rights consciousness. See, e.g., Felstiner et al. (1980–81), Bumiller (1988) and Handler (1986).

clients with dignity and respect, will help them along their path of social inclusion.

There are examples where Rosanvallon's aspirations are fulfilled.
This would occur when agencies "cream" – that is, where they select
clients that would most likely fulfill the agency's mission. This is a
contract; both sides benefit. Contracts can also occur with dependent
clients – where the agency workers realize that for them to succeed,
the clients have to succeed. But a reconceptualization of the officer's
goals to include the client is not enough. The client has to respond, has
to change behavior, and work to fulfill these goals. In order for the client
to become an active participant, the client not only has to know what
is expected of him or her, but the client has also to *trust* the officer that
the officer has the client's best interests at heart. The officer has to believe that the client understands what is expected, is willing to perform,
and will reliably report back to the officer. In other words, there has to
be reciprocal trust and communication. The client becomes a subject
rather than an object. However, even communication and good inten-
tions are not enough. There has to be what I have elsewhere called
reciprocal concrete incentives. Here, the reciprocal concrete incentives
are that the client gets a job or accomplishes some other project, such
as education and training, and the worker gets rewarded for the client's
success. There are examples of where this occurs – e.g., health care,
long-term care, special education, worker safety, public housing tenants
(Handler 1986; Handler 1990). And there are examples of where this
occurs in workfare – where agency officers listen to clients, work with
them, and share the rewards for success. However, in all of these examples, the relationship is fragile. Over time, the underlying imbalance of
power between the officer and the dependent client threatens, if not
undermines, the reciprocal trust that has developed. In other words, a
horizontal, empowering relationship can never be taken for granted. It
always has to be renewed.

Targeting and exclusion: the failure of accountability

As stated in the introduction, the above-mentioned proposals (some
of which have already been implemented) are complementary to inclusion. At the same time, they may be incomplete or even exclusionary. It
is easy to condemn "hard" law – overly rigid, inappropriate for individual cases, dysfunctional, etc. On the other hand, there are numerous instances where hard law does serve to change values and political ideologies, mobilize grass-roots organizations, and encourage law-abidingness

on the part of field-level officials. Dependent people get rights. In other instances, however, dependent people are unable to enforce their rights. OMC and benchmarking are proposed as an alternative to command-and-control regulation. OMC and benchmarking allow for flexibility and learning. Similar issues are present with OMC and benchmarking. They can highlight best practices, encourage governments and firms to change, and lend support to groups and organizations of the socially excluded. OMC and benchmarking can encourage locally-based groups and organizations. In some cases, these grass-roots organizations have been very effective, but, again, in many instances, the socially excluded are difficult to organize. On the other hand, OMC and benchmarking also allow governments and firms to obscure information, now a serious problem in the United States. A similar analysis applies to the various proposals at the national level. The importance of a full-employment economy, with flexible jobs that are *good* jobs, jobs that provide for a decent income, that accommodate family life, that pay benefits, are essential (Room 2000; Allen 1999). There is no point in having active labor market policies if, at the end of the day, good jobs are not available. The same is true with education and training. There have to be sufficient, relevant slots. On the other hand, good jobs and good education and training may not be enough. There is the problem of creaming, already noted – workers may be under pressure to slot in the most employable, the most trainable. Then, there will be those among the socially excluded who will not be able to accept the jobs or participate in the education and training. These are the people with the multiple handicaps – depression is a large problem among US welfare mothers – or more demanding family responsibilities – caring for a handicapped child or parent. Thus, even if OMC, reforming the labor market and recalibrating the welfare state, succeed, there still is a need for support services.

All of these reforms are subject to myth and ceremony. Whether hard law at the supra- or national level, or OMC and benchmarking, or "recalibrated" labor markets and welfare states, the new policies are promoted as "solutions" to the problem. Regulatory law gives rights, so now welfare recipients have rights. OMC avoids the rigidities of command-and-control regulation and the "legitimacy deficit" of the EU by encouraging cooperation and raising standards through benchmarking. New flexible, recalibrated standards and programs for work, education, and training will include the socially excluded, etc. The myths are that substantial change will happen and that previous problems are solved.

Part-time workers will have security and benefits; workfare recipients will be listened to and will take paths to inclusion. And there are some changes, and some problems are solved, and the proponents of the changes then use the examples to validate the myths. The examples are the ceremony.

These programs are administered in the day-to-day operations at the field level. Activation requires a decentralization of social policies. Local authorities and institutions have more discretion in the interpretation and implementation of rules, regulations, and practices, all of which makes assessment more difficult (Roche 2000: 41–42). There is an emphasis on individual activation plans or contracts which are supposed to specify rights and obligations. Here, too, the practice varies. In Sweden, there apparently was not much negotiation; some participants did not even know that there was a contract, but others said that their views were taken into account. Implementation or the institutional side of activation has to be taken into account – for example, arrangements with the local municipalities and other agencies; the financial responsibilities of the implementing agencies will affect strategies.

I want to emphasize administrative capacity – an issue of critical importance – but which is often ignored or assumed away. The implementation questions that have been discussed in the US system are relevant. The answers are not necessarily the same (indeed, there is considerable variation in the United States), but the questions have to be addressed. How are the local officers, in the individual offices, exercising their discretionary decisions?

Selectivity rules invariably are complex and, in the final analysis, discretionary. In addition to the usual forms of bureaucratic disentitlement – delays, frustrations, unfriendly relationships, errors, typification, and so forth – there are often difficulties in matching legal definitions with social reality. They require local-level interpretation. Means-tested and behavior-tests transfers require officials to interpret, apply, and monitor rules and regulations, benefits and sanctions (Standing 1999: 261; Wright 2001). All organizations at all levels are responsive to their political and social environments for support and cooperation, to avoid hostility, to lessen competition. By actively seeking inclusion, there is inevitably exclusion – those who cannot, for whatever reason, comply with the rules. They may be *a priori* excluded, which is often the case with immigrants and ethnic minorities, or they may be excluded through prejudice and other forms of moral typification. Or they may be excluded because they cannot fulfill the conditions. There can be physical or mental problems, family, child care, or transportation problems. This is the reason why T.H. Marshall, Ralf Dahrendorf and others have argued that citizenship cannot be based on any but the most general obligations (e.g., pay taxes). Otherwise, it is not inclusive (Crespo and Serrano 2001).

Close attention has to be paid to *accountability*. Active labor market policies are individualized, field-level, discretionary decisions. Top-down supervision and control are, at best, limited and, more often than not, counterproductive. The top needs statistical measures of performance – how many interviews conducted, how many work, or training or education "contracts" signed, how many placements, etc. As Dan Finn and others have pointed out, field-level officers are pressured into meeting statistical quotas. Clients with more difficult problems become problems.

Accountability has to be developed at the local level. This is no small task. Over the years, many very promising experiments have been mounted. They are both promising and problematic. They are promising in that they often generate new ideas and valuable information. They are problematic in that they feed the desire for myth and ceremony. Promising experiments are often hard to replicate. Committed, charismatic leaders and staff are the exception, not the rule. Ordinary people staff the usual government agencies.

The cardinal point to keep in mind is the position of the client (recipient, unemployed, lone parent, excluded, etc.). *Most clients are relatively powerless. They are dependent.* As discussed, Mead talks about clients who have been morally weakened by the permissiveness of the welfare state. Rosanvallon views clients differently. He talks about contracts as empowering. Through contracts, there will be mutual obligations and the state's responsibility to the client will be empowering. Contracts assume two equally situated parties, knowing their interests, what they will gain and lose, and *free* to enter or not into the bargain. This is not the case for the vast majority of clients of active labor-market policies. To continue to receive benefits, they must accept the conditions that are offered. In any given situation, the government worker may treat the client as a subject and work with the client as if the client were an empowered individual, but this is at the discretion of the worker. Obvious mistakes can sometimes be corrected, but the ambiguous determinations are difficult to monitor. Rosanvallon recognizes this. He worries about local RMI committees acting like nineteenth century charity offices, and says that clients should be able to appeal and have a speedy

265

determination. But, at least judging by the US experience, the right of appeal is often not very effective with dependent people.[17] As Nanna Kildal states: "The new policy [workfare] is less concerned with 'mutual recognition' than with 'mutual obligation', less concerned with justice than with personal morality. The basic normative challenge of workfare policy is that it ignores the fact that non-humiliating and just institutions matter" (Kildal 2000: 18).

As noted in the last chapter, although workfare is relatively recent and most of the programs are still undergoing significant shifts and changes, there are, however, some disturbing signs (Trickey 2001: 281). Workfare is an individually-based program. To be successful, an individual who applies for assistance has to be accurately assessed and relevant training, education, and/or work opportunities have to be offered, and subsequent behavior (refusing the offer, quitting work, or otherwise not complying) has to be individually and accurately assessed before sanctions are imposed. The target populations are becoming increasingly heterogeneous and with greater barriers to employment. Thus, despite the diversity in strategies, one common element is the use of casework. Workfare programs necessarily involve casework. Benefits are tied to care and control (Lødemel 2001: 308). Accordingly, the demands on line officers are high. They need training, time, and patience, but these officers have little or no control over broader issues that affect client lives – the macroeconomy, housing, transportation, child care, health, tax and benefits ("poverty traps"), and disability. Employers have to be persuaded to employ the target population, when, with slack economies, they have other choices. It is reported that they are becoming increasingly reluctant to employ certain target groups (Trickey 2001: 281–187). Workfare is a move away from the insurance principle of Social Security without strengthening the *right* to work or income security. Targeting and selectivity replace universalism (Standing 1999: 334).

Most policies to help the long-term unemployed, such as training, subsidized work contracts, and insertion in the social economy, have had modest effects on re-employment while offering employer windfalls. Positive outcomes are sometimes counterbalanced by perverse policy effects that contribute to new exclusions (Silver and Miller 2002). The most motivated and skilled workers disproportionately reap the

---

[17] This, as well as other arguments in this section, are more fully discussed in Handler 1986.

benefits of subsidy and training programs. The EU White Paper expressed concern that, of the 10 million new jobs created during the 1980s, only 3 million were taken by those on unemployment registers. New laborforce entrants rather than the socially excluded took the vast majority (Silver and Miller 2002). The French Ministry of Labor reported from a five-year panel study that most policies to help the long-term unemployed – training, subsidized work contracts, and work in the general interest – all had the same modest re-employment rates and stable outcomes over time. Similarly, the OECD reports that discouraged workers – who would like to work but are not actively seeking a job because they think there is no suitable one available – tend to have been unemployed for over three years, and may find re-employment harder than those who never worked (Silver and Miller 2002). Subsidized employment is ineffective in reducing unemployment. The workers who most need income protection – part-timers, services, domestics, home-workers, flexiworkers, the black or shadow economy, etc. – are usually not affected by regulatory schemes (Standing 1999: 293–298; Supiot 2000). To cope with youth unemployment rates, several countries have succeeded in getting youth to stay in school longer, while trying to improve school-to-work transitions. According to the OECD, however, targeted programs, by themselves, such as the apprentice system, do not do much in helping young people – at least as long as unemployment rates remain high (OECD 1999: 8).

While there seems to be a common ideology concerning the general proposition of obligations as well as rights, the considerable variation in the design and implementation of the European programs appears to be related to the perceived characteristics of the target groups. In the more universal and generous programs (e.g., Nordic), groups with more barriers and risks become included, some are stereotyped as more deserving, others not. Recipients of different options within social assistance have different rights and are subject to different attitudes (Lødemel 2001: 324–330). Under this view, Heather Trickey argues that compelling clients to participate in unproven programs is questionable. Under some conditions, compulsory programs can even be more damaging for those who fail; they face even more social exclusion (Trickey 2001: 287–288). While all programs have a range of options, the selection of options, "inevitably mirrors the selectivity of the regular labor market." This leads not only to creaming but also to "exclusion trajectories" or "sink options" where clients are recycled. With the more decentralized programs, most of the disadvantaged who live in the areas of low labor market demand may simply be ignored (Trickey 2001: 288–289). Case management is on the increase, which gives rise to tensions between social work and enforcement, between meeting targets for getting people off the rolls or into work. These tensions become most problematic for clients with multiple barriers. In the Netherlands, research has shown that compulsion has led to an increase in marginalization and social exclusion (Trickey 2001: 289–290).

Thus, although it may seem both efficient and equitable, targeting social and employment policies on the most disadvantaged may further stigmatize those who are already excluded. Universalist welfare state programs enjoy the most political support, while taxpayers suspect that means-tested benefits encourage malingering, even though they now require active contributions by the recipients in return for the benefits. Mandatory workfare programs – because they are stigmatizing – may actually contribute to the loss of motivation to work. Sanctions may thus accomplish the opposite of what is intended, namely, re-integration. Similarly, job creation programs that rely on deregulation also promote labor market dualism, which can contribute to those who lack "real" jobs (Silver and Miller 2002). Yet there are no new anti-exclusion policies. In the Netherlands, a substantial number of the young unemployed, especially those with personal and/or social problems, are not involved even though the policies claim "full-coverage." In time, a "hard core" will be left (Roche 2000: 43). Labor-market insecurity will continue for the foreseeable future – among the employed, those working at the margins of the flexible labor markets, the unemployed, and those outside the laborforce.

Thus far, the social democratic response to the erosion of the legitimacy of the welfare state has been defensive. They have tried to resist the decline in the legitimacy of the welfare state by strengthening the "productivist" or "labourist" character of welfare. They have joined those advocating tougher conditionality in entitlement and less "generosity" for those not in jobs (Standing 1999: 289–290).

These are the holes in the social safety net, even with benchmarking, a reformed labor market, and a recalibrated welfare state.

Reforming social services

There are examples of social services practice where clients are treated as subjects, not objects, where there is, in fact, empowerment (Handler 1996). Incentives have to be created for both the workers and the clients. As noted, the fundamental, underlying condition has to be the

availability of suitable jobs. There cannot be a separation between welfare policy and the economy. There are many obvious reasons why there
have to be jobs for workfare clients. One that I would like to emphasize is that strong demand will reduce the pressures on the government
workfare agencies by facilitating the normal incentives of the clients.
Contrary to the political rhetoric and publicity, the great majority of
US welfare recipients have fairly strong labor market connections, and
are on welfare for relatively short periods. They are virtually indistin-
guishable from the low-wage worker. However, jobs are unstable and
there are child care, transportation, and other family problems. They
are in and out of the labor market and use welfare primarily because
unemployment insurance is not available. Strengthening the low-wage
labor market thus facilitates their exits from welfare and, if the economy
remains strong, keeps them in the labor market.[18]

Would the same attitudes apply in Europe? There is evidence from
several countries that former recipients are very positive about working
rather than being on welfare. This, of course, would vary by the recipient and by benefit program. In the Netherlands, for example, it is hard
to get the older pensioners off benefits. In the United Kingdom, even
though Finn and Blackmore found a dysfunctional workfare system, recipients would still prefer work. The assumption that I make is that
most (but not all) recipients, certainly the younger ones, would prefer
work over welfare. Contrary to Mead, there is a strong work ethic.

If employment demand is strong, then the tasks of the workfare offices
change. They provide information and, if necessary, support services for
those ready, willing, and able to work. They facilitate the movement
back into the paid labor market. They can concentrate on the more
difficult cases. For those who need more assistance, attention has to be
paid to education and training slots. In the United States, welfare agencies contract with existing public or private education and training programs. The problem is that many of these programs are not suitable for
welfare recipients. These programs are primarily geared to adults who
are potentially much more trainable or more employable than the average welfare recipient. For example, in most situations, welfare agencies
refer clients to regular adult education classes. These classes are geared
to adults who are highly motivated and who seek to enroll in these
classes at their own expense. Most welfare recipients, in contrast, are
people who have been unsuccessful in education and are required to

[18] These points are more fully discussed in Handler and Hasenfeld (1997).

attend. The incentives of the programs too often are to take the public money but really to concentrate on the regular clients. It is not surprising that at least in the United States, education and training for welfare recipients is not that successful. There are some notable exceptions. The education and training program in San Diego Country (California) was specifically tailored to welfare recipients, and that program had good results.

The workfare offices must be separated from the benefits office, which has already taken place in some countries.[19] They are performing very different functions. The accountability demands on the payments office are speed and accuracy. The tasks (potentially) can be monitored effectively. The tasks of the workfare office are individualized, judgmental decisions. They require professional experience and, above all, patience. There should not only be a separation, but I have argued that there should be no sanctions.[20] There are several reasons. Many claim (both workers and clients) that sanctions – or the threat of sanctions – are necessary to impress upon the clients the seriousness of the workfare requirements. But so far, the evidence is anecdotal. There is considerable evidence that sanctions (as distinguished from the threat of sanctions) do not change behavior. And there is much evidence (at least in the United States) that sanctions are much abused. It is too easy for the busy worker, who is not that sympathetic with the client to begin with, to impose sanctions too readily. Again, at least in the United States, there are bureaucratic errors, clients have health problems, child care and transportation problems, and many other kinds of things that can trigger sanctions. We have found in our research that government agencies cannot do both – they cannot exercise careful, patient professionalism with sanctions, and that the latter tends to drive out the former. We have found that sanctions are hard to communicate, and many recipients are confused about their responsibilities. Sanctions are symbolic politics. They reassure majoritarian society that those "bums are not going to get something for nothing." But they do cause harm. It must be acknowledged that no matter how good the workfare program, there will be a certain number of people who will not be able to make it in the paid labor market. This will be especially true if workfare agencies do their job and really try to work with the very hard-to-employ. Those who cannot make it should not be held hostage under the

[19] Rosanvallon agrees with this.
[20] This is more fully discussed in Handler and Hasenfeld 1997.

commonly-held but mistaken idea that this is necessary to deter others who might want to choose welfare over work.[21]

Based on research, I believe that the great majority of recipients does want to get off welfare, wants to become independent, and plays by the rules. Most of the hard-to-employ have genuine problems. Without sanctions, agency workers have to work harder with these clients. Here, incentives have to be restructured. Workers have to be rewarded for progress and placements and follow-up. There have to be safeguards against creaming. The goal of restructuring is to redefine the professional task so that fulfillment is more readily accomplished when there is an active, participating, knowledgeable client. When the worker reconceives her professional task in terms of successfully placing the client, especially those with employment barriers, then the client becomes part of the solution, a subject rather than an object. There are several examples where this has happened in human services (Handler 1996).

There should be free-standing, locally-based, multi-service, professional employment service agencies that have close connections with local employers and other monitoring community groups. As noted, in some European countries, local offices have partnership agreements with employers and other groups at the local level. These agencies should be open to all who seek their services, not just workfare recipients. They should have information not only on jobs, and retraining and education placements but also on child care, health care, social services, transportation, and other areas that might impede the successful transition to work. At least in the United States, an important function is post-employment support. We have found that employers of low-wage workers are forgiving when problems arise – e.g., a breakdown in child care or transportation, or family problems – but only up to a point. Post-employment support helps lessen the traffic through the "revolving door." Still, there will be some who cannot negotiate the barriers. Some will stem from the individual. The disabled will be excused, but disability is often not clear-cut. It has just been "discovered" that many US welfare mothers suffer from depression. There are other forms of mental and physical illness which are not readily apparent. There are family problems. Or lack of understanding or will on the part of the recipient. Many of the socially excluded will have suffered – as children in poverty or as adults – and this will take its toll on the ability to function.

[21] The hostage theory of welfare policy comes from Katz (1986).

In the end, it must be recognized – constantly recognized – that restructured programs for the dependent poor will always be fragile. The workers in the programs operate in a climate of pressure, monitoring, and evaluation. They remain powerful. A variety of things can be done to induce the workers to be more professional and more caring, but, in the final analysis, they will continue to hold most of the cards. Thus, even the best programs cannot be taken for granted. There is always the danger that over time, traditional bureaucratic practices will creep in.[22] Programs have to be constantly monitored, constantly renewed. Client and community support groups have to be encouraged to provide strength and encouragement.

Are there ways to make the clients less dependent? As Hasenfeld noted, in the discussion of social service bureaucracies, power can become more equalized if clients have resources that the agency needs – for example, desired skills or other characteristics (e.g., employability) that would increase the success of the worker. Clients may seek power in the community. There has been a rising movement of excluded people who have mobilized against high unemployment. Beginning in France with demonstrations, lobbies, one-day stoppages, and petitions, the movement has spread to Belgium, Germany, and elsewhere. There are associations of the unemployed that have organized actions against plant closures, protests against threats to social welfare, and occupations of public employment offices. There are coalitions with trade unions, social movements, church leaders, and intellectual and political figures. Some think that these movements may foreshadow the formation of a third "social partner" to represent the socially excluded in corporatist institutions and promote full citizenship (Silver 1998a; 1998b). It is argued that policy-makers should foster empowerment, they should move from a "full-employment goal to full engagement." This would require "bottom-up" strategies as well as "top-down strategies" (Roche 2000: 80–91).

A basic income guarantee: from contract back to status
A third alternative, one that is argued for here, is a basic income guarantee. An income guarantee would provide a basic means of subsistence, it would restore social citizenship as a status; but it also gives the client an *exit* option. Thus, the client would no longer be forced to accept what

[22] See my discussion of the Madison (Wisconsin) special education program in Handler 1986.

the social service agency worker offered. Instead, the office would have to make the offer sufficiently attractive that the client would willingly accept. Then, there would be a contract.

Citizenship is our fundamental institution for justice and identity. Social citizenship is one of the essential, core bundles of rights that enable those who are excluded to re-acquire their citizenship rights. Marshall's conception of social citizenship was morally inclusive – "everyone is treated as a full and equal member of society, irrespective of class divisions and market-related achievements" (Kildal 2000: 18). Key aspects of active labor market policies – for example, "flexicurity" – by enhancing the protections of new forms of labor, are a renewal of core social citizenship. But other aspects – especially workfare – have attached conditions and thus selectivity to social citizenship. And conditionality and selectivity *exclude* as well as include. Social citizenship depends on "the scope of moral universalism" (Offe 1993: 219). Selectivity divides society. It creates a society of "us" and "them." It inevitably leads to stigmatization and discrimination.

The conflict between selectivity and inclusion leads one to favor a basic income guarantee. By definition, all are included. But are they? Rosanvallon thinks not. He argues that a basic income, in practice as well as ideology, will subsidize a permanent *excluded* group – those who are not self-sufficient. While there is a strong body of opinion that favors the basic income, in the current ideological climate, it is hard to refute this position – at least confidently. Since the Reagan-Thatcher era, there has been such an ideological shift to center, if not the right. When *The Economist* endorses the re-election of Tony Blair, you know how far the Left has shifted (The Economist 2001d: 12)!

On the other hand, the situation in most of Western Europe is ambiguous. Rosanvallon argues that RMI is revolutionary. Yet, other parts of the French welfare state remain pretty much intact, and despite the pressure to privatize, France seems committed to its large public sector (The Economist 2001e: 50), and, at least rhetorically, to turn the "vices" of the new economy pressures into "virtues" (Levy 2001). Germany is struggling with high unemployment, integrating East Germans, trying to cope with immigrants, and a mixed economic future, at least in the short run. We have discussed some of the pros and cons of the Dutch and Danish experience. There is a major clash between the forces of the new economy and those who favor active labor market policies but at the same time, want to avoid the US and UK employment models.

The Basic Income group believes that the US model of low-wage labor is not the path to follow, not only because of the inequality and poverty, but also because it is unrealistic to think that the labor market will ever provide sufficient jobs, even low-wage jobs; they see massive un- and under-employment in the twenty-first century (Eberle 1996; Lerner 1999; Rifkin 1995). The alternative to spreading poverty, therefore, should not be labor-market reforms, but rather, a broad-based basic income guarantee (BIG) – "an income unconditionally paid to all on an individual basis, without means test or work requirements" (van Parijs 1992). In part, the arguments for BIG are based on lack of credible alternatives – either Keynesian reflation or the unattractiveness of the US low-wage labor market (Jordan 1998; Purdy 1994; Standing 1995; van Parijs 1995).[23] But the more important reasons are to restore social citizenship, alleviate poverty, and provide "real freedom" for people in terms of work, human capital development, and non-paid work, that is, "greater self-control, security and good opportunity" (Standing 1999: 354). This would be:

> a *right* to a basic income for every individual, regardless of work status, marital status, age or other income. It would be given as an *individual* right. It would not require any past or present labour performance, not would it be made conditional on any labour commitment. The thrust of the idea is to give income security that is not based on past or present labouring status but on *citizenship*. It would give income security based not on judgmental decisions about "deserving" and "undeserving" behaviour or status, merely on the need for, and right, to basic security. However, it would be a modest security, so as to give incentives to work and for *sustainable risk-taking*. (Standing 1999: 355; Standing 2002)

But as Guy Standing and others have emphasized, a basic income is not a panacea. Rather, it is part of the package that includes labor-market and welfare reform.

Standing justifies a citizen basic income on two principles: the "Equal Opportunity Principle": each person should have an equal opportunity to pursue a good life; and the "Occupational Security Principle": each person should have an equal, good opportunity to pursue an occupation. At the same time, there are three constraints: not doing harm to others; a citizen income "should not impair sustainable living standards";

---

[23] As an example of BI, Block and Manza (1997) re-open the case for a negative income tax. Their proposed schedule of guarantees would bring all citizens to within 90 percent of the poverty line.

and it "should allow for adequate incentives to work, save and invest" (Standing 1999: 357).

The idea of unconditional basic income has a long history (Widerquist 2001; Wright 2000: 143–156; van Parijs 1995; Standing 1999; Lerner 1999). While there are various names and proposals, the core idea is that no one falls below the minimum whether they work or not, or engage in any other form of participation. The BIG (as distinguished from the Negative Income Tax) is paid to everyone (as individuals, parents would be custodians of their minor children) and all earned income is taxed. Most other redistribution programs (e.g., welfare, family allowances, unemployment insurance) are no longer necessary and are eliminated since the basic income is supposed to provide a decent minimum. Thus, there should be significant savings in administrative costs, although there would be some special needs (e.g., persons with disabilities). It is also argued that there would be no need for a minimum wage since workers would have the option of refusing to take jobs that do not offer decent wages and working conditions.

According to Erik Wright, BIG has the following advantages: It increases the real freedom of workers to refuse objectionable employment, which, in turn, should increase wages and working conditions. Since BIG is universal, poverty is reduced without the stigma of means-tested programs. There are no poverty traps. Earnings are taxed progressively. BIG provides support for uncompensated care-giving as well as voluntary activities. It avoids the need to make distinctions between what is socially useful participation and what is not, which inevitably will be arbitrary (Standing 1999: 366). On the other hand, Wright says, most people must still work in the paid labor force to generate the production and taxes needed to support BIG. The basic grant has to be high enough to significantly reduce poverty but low enough to encourage people to seek paid labor – a difficult empirical question. There is also the possibility of capital flight if a basic income guarantee raises the costs of labor and taxes too high without a commensurate rise in productivity (Wright 2000: 150–151).

The disincentive fear may be exaggerated. There is a long history of strong evidence of a strong work ethic. Contrary to the welfare stereotype, in the United States, most welfare recipients go to great lengths to get off of welfare even when they are worse off. During the "War on Poverty" period, decent training and education programs were always oversubscribed. Today, there has been a sharp (and unfortunate) decline in the use of food stamps among former welfare recipients who are now employed even though they are eligible. There are several reasons for the decline – e.g., inaccessible offices, complex applications – but an important reason is that the welfare leavers do not want to be part of the welfare system (Rank 1994; Scott et al. 2000). Standing reports a strong preference for work even if there were a guaranteed income (Standing 1999: 356). Rosanvallon, in opposing the basic income guarantee, argues that this group would be stigmatized. They would be stigmatized because they would not be working. But if the program were universal, the lines between work and non-work would be blurred, and this would also encourage people to seek work in addition to the basic income guarantee.[24] The basic income guarantee is not proposed as an alternative to the above-mentioned proposals to reform the low-wage labor market and recalibrate the welfare state.

The benefits of a reformed labor market and a basic income guarantee are that they would reduce the levels of income and wealth inequality (Wright 2000: 143). Wright gives the following normative justifications for an equitable distribution in the standards of living: it would alleviate the suffering of those who are now at the bottom of the income distribution; it would reduce generational inequalities in opportunities, especially for poor children; it would reduce the inequalities in what van Parijs calls the "real freedom" of people; it would reduce the inequalities of wealth and income that tend to undermine democracy and the community (see Standing 2002). All of these benefits should not be sacrificed to the specter of the few who choose to remain among the socially excluded.

Under these reforms, the vast majority of people would be working (under better working conditions). With genuine full employment, those who would still be jobless would most likely be people with multiple handicaps or special child care or family care problems. From past experience, we know that many of these people would welcome rehabilitation and other supportive opportunities provided by effective social services, part-time or sheltered work, participation in community-based child and family care, and so forth. These people would not be stigmatized by receiving a basic income guarantee.

There will be some group that will not participate. There may be depression or other forms of mental illness, substance abuse – people who cannot be persuaded to enter into programs. And there will be others who shirk, who abuse the system. It is this group which society

[24] Wright (2000) makes this argument.

demonizes. For over 600 years, Anglo-Saxon welfare policy has been under the shadow of the "sturdy beggar" (Trattner 1999).[25] This shadow has now infected Western Europe (Offe 2002). It is the specter of this group – and the fear that decent, hard-working poor people might slide into this group – that leads to conditions and sanctions in social welfare systems, that creates bureaucracies, and the other pathologies of welfare systems. For centuries the Anglo-Saxon system has tried and failed to separate the "deserving" from the "undeserving" poor. How many working poor would really turn down a job with decent working conditions to join the socially excluded? The disincentives to work are more a function of the available labor-market conditions than welfare benefits.[26]

Marshall acknowledged obligations of citizenship but argued that only a few were really obligatory – the duty to pay taxes, pursue an education, serve in the military. Most citizenship obligations, he felt, were informal, vague responsibilities. Otherwise, social citizenship becomes conditional. Ralf Dahrendorf agrees. Citizenship is a body of rights and duties – a status – that defines full membership of a society; it is a status that by definition is removed from the vagaries of the market. He warns that once rights lose their unconditional quality, the door is open not just for the market but for rules that tell people what to do. Obligations of citizenship must remain general and public. There can be obligations – e.g., obey the law, pay taxes, the military – but they must be strictly circumscribed (Dahrendorf 1994).

Dahrendorf believes that a fundamental challenge comes from the socially excluded. The presence of an underclass is the most tangible evidence of the loss of social citizenship entitlements (Dahrendorf 1994: 10–19). People in this situation have lost regular and guaranteed access to labor markets, to the political community, and to networks of social relations. "The underclass," he says:

> is, technically, not a class. Classes are conflict groups based on common interests. Because there is a mutual dependency among the members, a class generates and presses for its own solutions. In contrast, the "underclass" is a mere category; it is a victim. While the victims have similar

---

[25] The Statute of Laborers (1349), the first welfare statute, prohibited the giving of alms to sturdy beggars.

[26] Van Oorschot (2002: 406), says that "Studies have indeed shown that by far the largest segment of all unemployed individuals is very eager to find a job [citations] and that employers are prejudiced against (long-term) unemployed people."

interests, they are not common interests. Self-organization is unlikely. If change comes about, it will be through outside agents or changes in values. Thus, the underclass does not present a threat; they are politically powerless. Nor is the underclass a status problem. Rather than being at the bottom of the ladder, the underclass is not even on the ladder in the sense that redistribution measures do not reach this group. They are beyond the threshold of basic opportunities of access. They lack entitlements; therefore, they lack citizenship. The challenge of the underclass is to the moral foundations of society.

It is feasible both economically and politically to tolerate the underclass. However, "ignoring the underclass means suspending the basic values of citizenship for one category of people, and thus, weakening the intrinsic universality of citizenship claims. Doubts will then spread to the validity of other claims. The majority will pay a high price for turning away from those who consistently fail to make it, and the fact that the price is intrinsically moral rather than economic should not deceive anyone about its seriousness" (Dahrendorf 1994: 16).

A basic income would bring in the socially excluded, it would restore the status of social citizenship.

REFERENCES

Abraham, Katherine 1983, "Structural/Frictional vs. Deficient Demand Unemployment: Some New Evidence," *American Economic Review* 73: 709–710.

Abramovitz, Mimi 1988, *Regulating the Lives of Women: Social Welfare Policy from Colonial Times to the Present*, Boston, MA.

Adams, Gina and Rohacek, Monica 2002, "Child Care and Welfare Reform," Brookings Institution Policy Brief 14, February.

Adena, Willem, Gray, Donald, and Kahl, Sigrun 2001, *Social Assistance in Germany*, OECD Occasional Papers, Paris.

Ait-Hamadouche, Rabah 2002, "Immigrant Voices in European Politics, France's Estate of Fear," *Le Monde diplomatique*, July 7, 2002.

Allen, Nicolas 1999, *The Employment Guidelines – Are They Working?*, Brussels, BG.

Alstott, Anne 1999, "Work vs. Freedom: A Liberal Challenge to Employment Subsidies," *Yale Law Journal* 108: 967–1058.

Andrews, Edmund 1999, "Sweden, the Welfare State, Basks in a New Prosperity," *New York Times*, October 8, 1999, A1.

2002, "German Face is Blushing: Red Ink Irks its Partners," *New York Times*, February 11, 2002, 5.

Arts, Wil and Gelisson, John 2002, "Three Worlds of Welfare Capitalism or More? A State-of-the-art Report," *Journal of European Social Policy* 12: 137–158.

Atkinson, A.B. 1998, *Poverty in Europe*, Oxford.

1999, *The Economic Consequences of Rolling Back the Welfare State*, Boston, MA.

Atkinson, A.B., Rainwater, Lee, and Smeeding, Timothy 1995, *Income Distribution in Advanced Economies: Evidence from the Luxembourg Income Study*, Syracuse, NY.

Bachrach, Peter and Baratz, Morton 1962, "Two Faces of Power," *American Political Science Review* 56: 947–952.

1970, *Power and Poverty: Theory and Practice*, Oxford.

Bachrach, Peter and Botwinick, Aryeh 1992, *Power and Empowerment: A Radical Theory of Participatory Democracy*, Philadelphia, PA.

Bane, Mary Jo and Ellwood, David 1994, *Welfare Realities: From Rhetoric to Reform*, Cambridge, MA, p.2.

Barbier, Jean-Claude and Théret, Bruno 2001, "Welfare-to-Work or Work-to-Welfare: The French Case," in Neil Gilbert and Rebecca Van Voorhis (eds.), *Activating the Unemployed: A Comparative Appraisal of Work-Oriented Policies*, New Brunswick, NJ, and London, pp.135–183.

Barrell, Ray and Genre, Veronique 1999, "Employment Strategies for Europe: Lessons from Denmark and the Netherlands," *National Institute Economic Review*, pp.82–98.

Becker, Uwe 2000, "Welfare State Development and Employment in the Netherlands in Comparative Perspective," *Journal of European Social Policy* 10(3): 219–239.

Begg, Iain and Berghan, Jos 2002, "Introduction: EU Social (Exclusion) Policy Revisited?," *Journal of European Social Policy* 12(3): 179–194.

Behrendt, Christina 2000, "Do Means-Tested Benefits Alleviate Poverty? Evidence on Germany, Sweden and the United Kingdom from the Luxembourg Income Study," *Journal of European Social Policy* 10(1): 23–41.

Bell, Winifred 1965, *Aid to Dependent Children*, New York.

Belmessous, Hacene 2002, "A Price to Pay for 'Island of Privilege,'" *Le Monde diplomatique*, November 4, 2002, 62.

Bennett, Fran 2002, "Social Policy Digest, Number One Hundred and Twenty Three, November 2001 to January 2002," *International Social Policy* 31(3): 505–536.

Bergmann, Barbara 2001, "Decent Child Care at Decent Wages," *The American Prospect* 12:1.

Berlin, Gordon 2000, *Encouraging Work Reducing Poverty: The Impact of Work Incentive Programs*, Washington, DC.

Bernstein, Nina 2001, "As Welfare Comes to an End, So Do the Jobs," *New York Times*, December 17, 2001, A1.

2002, "Side Effect of Welfare Law: The No-Parent Family," *New York Times*, July 29, 2002, 1.

Berube, Alan, Kim, Anne, Forman, Benjamin, and Burns, Megan 2002, *The Price of Paying Taxes: How Tax Preparation and Refund Loan Fees Erode the Benefits of the EITC*, Washington, DC.

Bhabha, Jacqueline 1998, "Get Back to Where You Once Belonged: Identity, Citizenship, and Exclusion in Europe," *Human Rights Quarterly* 20(3): 592–627.

Biagi, Marco 2000, "The Impact of European Employment Strategy on the Role of Labour Law and Industrial Relations," *International Journal of Comparative Labour Law and Industrial Relations* 16(2): 155–173.

Blank, Rebecca and Schmidt, Lucie 2000, "Work and Wages," Paper presented at the conference on *The New World of Welfare: Shaping a Post-TANF Agenda for Policy*, Washington DC.

Blau, David 2001, "Rethinking U.S. Child Care Policy," *Science and Technology* 18(2): 66–72.

Block, Fred and Manza, Jeff 1997, "Could We Afford to End Poverty? The Case for the Progressive Negative Income Tax," *Politics and Society* 25: 473–510.

Body-Gendrot, Sophie 1995, "Immigration, Marginality, and French Social Policy," in Katherine McFate, Roger Lawson, and William Wilson (eds.), *Poverty, Inequality, and the Future of Social Policy*, New York, pp.571–583.

Boeri, Tito, Layard, Richard, and Nickel, Stephen 2000, "Welfare-to-Work and the Fight Against Long-Term Unemployment," Department for Education and Employment Research Report 206.

Boesby, Doerte, Dahl, Karen, and Ploug, Niels 2002, "Sweden Unemployment Protections and Active Labour Market Policies in the 1990s," in Maurizio Ferrera and Martin Rhodes (eds.), *Welfare Systems and the Management of Economic Risk of Unemployment: Experiences and Prospects for Reform in the European Union*, Rome, Italy.

Bos, Johannes M., Huston, Aletha C., Granger, Robert C., Duncan, Greg J., Brock, Thomas W., and McLoyd, Vonnie C. 1999, *New Hope for People with Low Incomes: Two-Year Results of a Program to Reduce Poverty and Reform Welfare. Executive Summary and Policy Implications*, Washington, DC.

Bosniak, Linda 2000, "Universal Citizenship and the Problem of Alienage," *Northwestern Law Review* 94: 963.

Braudel, Fernand 1979, *The Structures of Everyday Life: The Limits of the Possible*, New York.

Brauner, Sarah and Loprest, Pamela 1999, *Where Are They Now / What States' Studies of People Who Left Welfare Tell Us*, Washington DC, The Urban Institute Series A(32), p.6.

Brito, Tonya 2000, "The Welfarization of Family Law," *Kansas Law Review* 48: 229.

Brodkin Evelyn, Fuqua, Carolyn, and Thoren, Katarina 2002, "Contracting Welfare Reform: Uncertainties of Capacity-Building Within Disjointed Federalism," JCPR: Working Paper of the Project on the Public Economy Work 284, March.

Bulmer, Martin and Rees, Anthony 1996, *Citizenship Today: The Contemporary Relevance of T.H. Marshall*, London.

Bumiller, Kristin 1988, *The Civil Rights Society: The Social Construction of Victims*, Baltimore, MD.

Burtless, Gary 1995, "Employment Prospects of Welfare Recipients," in Demetra Nightingale and Robert Haveman (eds.), *The Work Alternative*, Washington, DC.

   1999, "Growing American Inequality: Sources and Remedies," *Brookings Review* 17(1): 31–35.

Cancian, Maria, Haveman, Robert, Meyer, Daniel, and Wolfe, Barbara 2000, *Before and After TANF: The Economic Well-Being of Women Leaving Welfare*, Institution for Research on Poverty, University of Wisconsin Special Report, p.77.

Carlson, Virginia, and Theodore, Nikolas 1995, *Are There Enough Jobs? Welfare Reform and Labor Market Reality*, Illinois Job Gap Project. Dekalb, IL.

Casey, Bernard 1995, "Apprentice Training in Germany: The Experience of the 1980s," in Katherine McFate, Roger Lawson, and William Wilson (eds.), *Poverty, Inequality, and the Future of Social Policy*, New York, pp.415–437.

Casper, Lynne, Garfinkel, Irwin, and McLanahan, Sara 1994, "The Gender-Poverty Gap: What We Can Learn From Other Countries," *American Social Review* 59: 594–605.

Castles, Francis 2002, "Developing New Measures of Welfare State Change and Reform," *European Journal of Political Research* 41: 613–641.

Children's Defense Fund (CDF) 1998, *New Studies Look at Status of Former Welfare Recipients*, available at www.childrensdefense.org/fairstart_statu

Clark, Sandra and Long, Sharon 1995, *Child Care Prices: A Profile of Six Communities*, Washington, DC, pp.1–2.

Clasen, Jochen 2000, "Motives, Means and Opportunities: Reforming Unemployment Compensation in the 1990s," in Maurizio Ferrera and Martin Rhodes (eds.), *Recasting European Welfare States*, pp.89–112.

   2002, "Managing the Economic Risk of Unemployment in the UK," in Maurizio Ferrera and Martin Rhodes (eds.), *Welfare Systems and the Management of Economic Risk of Unemployment: Experiences and Prospects for Reform in the European Union*, Rome.

Clegg, Stuart 1989, *Frameworks of Power*, London.

Closa, Carlos 1998, "Some Skeptical Reflections on EU Citizenship as the Basis of a New Social Contract," in Martin Rhodes and Yves Mény, *The Future of European Welfare: A New Social Contract?*, New York, pp.266–283.

Cohen, Roger 2000, "For 'New Danes,' Differences Create a Divide," *New York Times*, December 18, 2000, A1.

Commission of the European Communities 2002, "Taking Stock of Five Years of the European Employment Strategy," Communication from the Commission to the Council, the European Parliament, the Economic and Social Committee and the Committee of the Regions, Brussels, Belgium, July 17, 2002, 416 Final.

Coompston, Hugh and Kongshoj Madsen, Per 2001, "Conceptual Innovation and Public Policy: Unemployment and Paid Leave Schemes in Denmark," *Journal of European Social Policy* 11(2): 117–132.

Corbett, Thomas 2002, "The New Face of Welfare: From Income Transfers to Social Assistance?," *Focus* 22(1): 3–10.

Council of Economic Advisors, *The Effects of Welfare Policy and the Economic Expansion on Welfare Caseloads: An Update*, Technical Report, August 3, 1999.

Cowell, Alan 2002, "After Black Teenager Is Slain, Norway Peers Into a Mirror," *New York Times*, January 3, 2001, 1.

Cowell, Alan and Andrews, Edmund 2001, "European Converts to Laissez Fair See the Rush to Intervene as Heresy," *New York Times*, October 25, 2001, C1.

Cox, Robert 1998, "From Safety Net To Trampoline: Labor Market Activation in the Netherlands and Denmark," *Governance, An International Journal of Policy and Administration* 11(4): 397–414.

Crespo, Eduardo and Serrano, Amparo 2001, "The EU's Concept of Activation for Young People: Towards a New Social Contract?," in *European Trade Union Yearbook 2001*, pp.295–322.

Crossetts, Barbara 2000, "The World: It's the American Way: Europe Stares at a Future Built by Immigrants," *New York Times*, January 2, 2000, section 4, 1.

Crouch, Colin 1998, "The Social Contract and the Problem of the Firm," in Martin Rhodes and Yves Mény, *The Future of European Welfare: A New Social Contract?*, New York, pp.229–243.

Daguerre, Anne and Palier, Bruno 2002, "Welfare Systems and the Management of the Economic Risk of Unemployment," in Maurizio Ferrera and Martin Rhodes (eds.), *Welfare Systems and the Management of Economic Risk of Unemployment: Experiences and Prospects for Reform in the European Union*, Rome.

Dahrendorf, Ralf 1994, "The Changing Quality of Citizenship," in Bart van Steenbergen, *The Condition of Citizenship*, London, pp.10–19.

Daly, Emma 2002, "Brutal Death of Immigrant Shakes Faith of Spaniards," *New York Times*, February 13, 2002, A9.

Danziger, Sandra, Corcoran, Mary, Danziger, Sheldon, and Heflin, Colleen 2000, "Work, Income and Material Hardship After Welfare Reform," *Journal of Consumer Affairs* 34(1): 6–30.

Danziger, Sheldon, Smeeding, Timothy, and Rainwater, Lee 1995, *The Western Welfare State in the 1990s: Toward a New Social Model of Anti-Poverty Policy for Families with Children*, LIS Working Paper No.129, Syracuse.

Darnton, Robert 1999, *The Great Car Massacre . . . and Other Episodes in French Cultural History*, New York.

De Parle, Jason 1997, "Lessons Learned: Welfare Reform's First Months – A Special Report: Success, Frustration, as Welfare Rules Change," *New York Times*, December 30, 1997, A16.

1999, "As Benefits Expire, the Experts Worry," *New York Times*, October 10, 1999, 1.

De Schweinitz, Karl 1947, *England's Road to Social Security, 1349–1947*, Pennsylvania, PA.

Desmond, King and Wood, Stewart 1999, "The Political Economy of Neoliberalism: Britain and the United States in the 1980s," in Herbert Kitschelt, Peter Lange, Gary Marks, and John Stephens, *Continuity and Change in Contemporary Capitalism*, New York, pp.371–397.

Diller, Matthew 2000, "The Revolution in Welfare Administration: Rules, Discretion, and Entrepreneurial Government," *N.Y.U. Law Review* 75(5): 1121–1220.

Dixon, Keith 2000, "Third Way, British-Style: Blair's March to Market Modernity," *Le Monde Diplomatique*, January 5, 2000, 2.

Dorf, Michael and Sabel, Charles 1998, "A Constitution of Democratic Experimentalism," *Columbia Law Review* 98(2): 267–473.

Driver, Stephen 1998, "Review," *Journal of Social Policy* 26: 567–569.

Duffy, Katherine 2001, *EAPN Synthesis Report on the 2001–2003 National Action Plans on Social Inclusion*, available at www.eapn.org

Duncan, Greg and Chase-Lansdale, P. Lindsay 2001, *For Better and for Worse: Welfare Reform and the Well-Being of Children and Families*, New York.

Duncan, Greg, Gustafsson, Björn, Hauser, Richard, Schmaus, Günther, Messinger, Hans, Muffels, Ruud et al. 1995, "Poverty and Social-Assistance Dynamics in the United States, Canada, and Europe," in Katherine McFate, Roger Lawson, and William Wilson (eds.), *Poverty, Inequality, and the Future of Social Policy*, New York, pp.67–108.

Eberle, Thomas 1996, "Dislocation Policies in Western Europe: Past, Present and Future," *Annals of the American Academy of Political and Social Science* 544: 127–139.

Economist, The 1999, May 29, 1999.

2000, October 17, 2000.

2001a, "Germany: The Feelbad Factor," *The Economist*, April 21, 2001, 44.

2001b, "The Melting-pot That Isn't," *The Economist*, July 28, 2001, 50–51.

2001c, "Germany's Poor East: More Cash, Please," *The Economist*, May 12, 2001, 55.

2001d, "Britain's Election: The Choice is Clear," *The Economist*, June 2, 2001, 21.

2001e, "France's Public Sector: They Love It," *The Economist*, May 26, 2001, 50.

2002a, "Economic and Financial Indicators," *The Economist*, December 14, 2002, 92.

2002b, "Output, Demand and Jobs," *The Economist*, December 14, 2002, 92.

2002c, "France's Illegal Immigrants. A New Balance," *The Economist*, September 14, 2002, 53.

2002d, "An Uncertain Giant: A Survey of Germany," *The Economist*, December 7, 2002, 3–4.

2002e, "The Politics of Pensions. We Know What's Best for Your Old Age, Why Can't You See It?," *The Economist*, August 3, 2002, 41.

2002f, "Welfare State. The Tender Trap," *The Economist*, August 3, 2002, 45.

2002g, "Asylum. And Stay Out," *The Economist*, May 25, 2002, 57.

2002h, "The European Union and Immigration. Huddled Masses, Please Stay Away," *The Economist*, June 15, 2002, 49.

2002i, "Ireland's New Government. Old Faces, New Headaches," *The Economist*, June 15, 2002, 52.

2002j, "Output, Demand and Jobs," *The Economist*, July 27, 2002, 84.

2002k, "Private Pension Funds in France. Still a Dirty Word," *The Economist*, June 8, 2002, 48.

2002l, "French Politics. The Bermuda Triangle," *The Economist*, September 7, 2002, 49.

2002m, "Output, Demand and Jobs," *The Economist*, December 14, 2002, 92.

2002n, "German Labour-Market Reform. Here are the Ideas. Now for Action?," *The Economist*, June 29, 2002, 51.

2002o, "Is Deutschland AG Kaput? What's Ailing German Industry?," *The Economist*, December 7, 2002, 8.

2002p, "German Politics. Gerhard Schröder's Rocky New Start," *The Economist*, November 16, 2002, 45.

2002q, "The EU Summit on Liberalization. Energy and Lethargy," *The Economist*, March 23, 2002, 49.

Edelman, Murray 1971, *Politics as Symbolic Action: Mass Arousal and Quiescence*, Chicago, IL.

1988, *Constructing the Political Spectacle*, Chicago, IL.

Edin, Kathryn and Lein, Laura 1996, "Work, Welfare, and Single Mothers' Economic Survival Strategies," *American Social Review* 61: 253–266.

1997, *Making Ends Meet: How Single Mothers Survive Welfare and Low-Wage Work*, New York.

Ellwood, David 1988, *Poor Support: Poverty in the American Family*, New York.

1999, "The Impact of the Earned Income Tax Credit and Social Policy Reforms on Work, Marriage, and Living Arrangements," unpublished manuscript.

Elster, Jon 1985, *Making Sense of Marx*, Cambridge, MA.

Enjolras, Bernard, Laville, Jean Louis, Fraisse, Laurent, and Trickey, Heather 2000, "Between Subsidiarity and Social Assistance – the French Republican Route to Activation," in Ivar Lødemel and Heather Trickey, *An Offer You Can't Refuse: Workfare in International Perspective*, Bristol, pp.41–70.

Erlanger, Steven 2002a, "A Jumpy, Anti-Immigrant Europe Is Creeping Rightward," *New York Times*, January 30, 2002, A3.

2002b, "German Unemployment Is Growing Problem for Schröder," *New York Times*, February 7, 2002, A8.

Esping-Andersen, Gøsta 1990, *The Three Worlds of Welfare Capitalism*, Princeton, NJ.

Esping-Andersen, Gøsta and Regini, Marino 2002, *Why Deregulate Labour Markets?*, Oxford.

Estevez-Abe, Margarita, Iversen, Torben, and Soskice David 1999, "Social Protection and the Formation of Skills: A Reinterpretation of the Welfare State," in Peter Hall and David Soskice (eds.), *Varieties of Capitalism: The Challenges Facing Contemporary Economies*, London, pp.145–183.

European Council 2001, *Joint Report on Social Exclusion: Part I – The European Union Executive Summary*.

Evans, Geoffrey (ed.) 1999, *The End of Class Politics? Class Voting Comparative Perspective*, Oxford.

Ewick, Patricia and Silbey, Susan 1998, *The Common Place of Law: Stories from Everyday Life*, Chicago, IL.

2002, "Making Resistance Thinkable: Desired Disturbances of Everyday Legal Transactions," unpublished manuscript.

EXSPRO (Social Exclusion and Social Protection) 2001, *Social Exclusion and Social Protection in the European Union: Policy Issues and Proposals for the Future Role of the European Union*, London.

Fafo Institute for Applied Social Science 2001, *Workfare in Six European Nations: Findings and Evaluations and Recommendations for Future Development*, Oslo.

Falk, Richard 2000, "The Decline of Citizenship in an Era of Globalization," *Citizenship Studies* 4(1): 5–17.

Fein, D.J. and Lee, W.S. 2003, "The Impact of Welfare Reform on Child Maltreatment in Delware," *Children and Youth Services Review* 25: 83–111.

Felstiner, William, Abel, Richard, and Sarat, Austin 1980–1981, "The Emergence and Transformation of Disputes: Naming, Blaming, Claiming . . . ," *Law and Society Review* 15(3–4): 631–654.

Ferrera, Maurizio 1998, "The Four 'Social Europes': Between Universalism and Selectivity," in Martin Rhodes and Yves Mény, *The Future of European Welfare: A New Social Contract?*, New York, pp.81–96.

Ferrera, Maurizio, Hemerijck, Anton, and Rhodes, Martin 2002a, *The Future of Social Europe: Recasting Work and Welfare in the New Economy*, Report for the Portuguese Presidency of the European Union.

Ferrera, Maurizio, Matsaganis, Manos, and Sacchi, Stefano 2002b, "European Briefing: Open Coordination Against Poverty: the New EU 'Social Inclusion' Process," *Journal of European Social Policy* 12(3): 227–239.

Ferrera, Maurizio and Rhodes, Martin 2000, "Building a Sustainable Welfare State" in Maurizio Ferrera and Martin Rhodes (eds.), *Recasting European Welfare States*, Special Issue, *West European Politics* 23(2): 257–282.

Figlio, David and Ziliak, James 1999, "Welfare Reform, the Business Cycle, and the Decline in AFDC Caseloads," in Sheldon Danziger (ed.), *Economic Conditions and Welfare Reform*, Kalamazoo, Michigan, pp.15–48.

Finn, Dan 1998, "Labour's New Deal for the Unemployed and the Stricter Benefit Regime," in Brunsdon et al. (eds.), *Social Policy Review*, pp.105–122.

1999, "From Full Employment to Employability: New Labour and the Unemployed," paper presented at the *European Forum Workshop*, Florence.

2000, "Welfare to Work: The Local Dimension," *Journal of European Social Policy* 10(1): 43–57.

(n.d.), "The 'Employment' First Welfare State: Lessons from the New Deal for Young People," unpublished manuscript.

Finn, Dan and Blackmore, Martin 2001, "Activation: The Point of View of Clients and 'Front Line' Staff," OECD Proceedings: Labour Market Policies and the Public Employment Service. Available at http://www1.oecd.org/publications/e-book/8101051E.PDF

Fix, Michael and Haskins, Ron 2002, "Welfare Benefits for Non-Citizens," The Brookings Institution Policy Brief 15, February 2002.

Flaming, Daniel, Kwon, Patricia, and Burns, Patrick 2002, *Running Out of Time: Voices of Parents Struggling to Move from Welfare to Work*, Los Angeles, CA, pp.1–2.

Forbath, William 2002, "When Jews, Italians, Greeks, and Slavs Belonged to Races Different From 'We, The People': Race, Class, and National Identity in Immigration Law and Policy, 1882–1924," unpublished manuscript.

Förster, Michael 2000, "Labour Market and Social Policy," Occasional Papers No.42: Trends and Driving Factors in Income Distribution and Poverty in the OECD Area, Paris.

Foucault, Michel 1980, *The History of Sexuality: An Introduction*, vol.I, New York.

Fraser, Nancy and Gordon, Linda 1994, "Civil Citizenship Against Social Citizenship? On the Ideology of Contract-Versus-Charity," in van Steenbergen (ed.), *The Condition of Citizenship*, New York, pp.90–122.

Freedman, Stephen, Knab, Jean Tansey, Gennetian, Lisa, and Navarro, David 2000, *The Los Angeles Jobs-First GAIN Evaluation: Final Report on a Work First Program in a Major Urban Center*, New York.

Freeman, Richard 1991, "Employment and Earnings of Disadvantaged Youth in a Labor Shortage Economy," in Christopher Jencks and Paul Peterson (eds.), *The Urban Underclass*, Washington, DC, pp.103–121.

1995, "The Large Welfare State as a System," *American Economic Review* 85(2): 16–21.

2000, "The Rising Tide Lifts . . . ," *Focus* 21(2): 27–37.

Freire, Paulo 1985, *The Politics of Education: Culture, Power, and Liberation*, New York.

Gais, Thomas, Nathan, Richard, Lurie, Irene, and Kaplan, Thomas 2001, "The Implementation of the Personal Responsibility Act of 1996: Commonalities, Variations, and the Challenge of Complexity," paper presented at the conference for *The New World of Welfare: Shaping a Post-TANF Agenda for Policy*, Washington, DC.

Garfinkel, Irwin 2001, "Assuring Child Support in the New World of Welfare," paper presented at the conference for *The New World of Welfare: Shaping a Post-TANF Agenda for Policy*, Washington, DC.

Garfinkel, Irwin and McLanahan, Sara 1986, *Single Mothers and Their Children: A New American Dilemma*, Washington, DC.

Gaventa, John 1980, *Power and Powerlessness: Quiescence and Rebellion in an Appalachian Valley*, Urbana, IL.

General Accounting Office 1997, *Poverty Measurement: Issues in Revising and Updating the Official Definition*, GAO/HEHS-97–38, Washington, DC.

Gerstenberg, Oliver and Sabel, Charles (n.d.), "Directly-Deliberative Polyarchy: An Institutional Ideal for Europe?," manuscript in preparation.

Giddens, Anthony 1998, *The Third Way: The Renewal of Social Democracy*, Cambridge.

Gilens, Martin 1999, *Why Americans Hate Welfare: Race, Media, and the Politics of Antipoverty Policy*, Chicago, IL.

Gilliom, John 2001, *Overseers of the Poor: Surveillance, Resistance, and the Limits of Privacy*, Chicago, IL.

Gladden, Tricia and Taber, Christopher 2000, "Wage Progression Among Less Skilled Workers" in Rebecca Blank and David Card (eds.), *Finding Jobs: Work and Welfare Reform*, New York, pp.160–192.

Gobin, Corinne 1997, "The Mirage of Social Europe," *Le Mond diplomatique*, November.

Goldin, Miriam, Wallerstein, Michael, and Lange, Peter 1999, "Postwar Trade-Union Organization and Industrial Relations in Twelve Countries," in Herbert Kitschelt, Peter Lange, Gary Marks, and John Stephens 1999, *Continuity and Change in Contemporary Capitalism*, New York, pp.94–230.

Golonka, Susan 2001, "The Dynamics of Welfare Reform Implementation," paper presented at the conference on *The New World of Welfare: Shaping a Post-TANF Agenda for Policy*, Washington, DC.

Gong, Jo Ann, Bussiere, Alice, Light, Jennifer, Scharf, Rebecca, Cohan, Marc, and Leiwant, Sherry 1999, "Child Care in the Postwelfare Reform Era: Analysis and Strategies for Advocates," *Clearinghouse Review* (January–February 1999). Available at http://www.welfarelaw.org/chcc.htm

Gordon, Ian 1995, "The Impact of Economic Change on Minorities and Migrants in Western Europe," in Herbert Kitschelt, Peter Lange, Gary Marks, and John Stephens, 1999, *Continuity and Change in Contemporary Capitalism*, New York, pp.521–542.

Gordon, Linda 1988, *Heroes of Their Own Lives: The Politics and History of Family Violence*, New York.

Gormley, William, Jr. 1995, *Everybody's Children: Child Care as Public Problem*, Washington, DC.

Gramsci, Antonio 1971, *Selections from the Prison Notebooks*, London.

Greenberg, Mark 1999, *Beyond Welfare: New Opportunities to Use TANF to Help Low-Income Working Families*, Washington, DC.

Greenberg, Mark and Laracy, Michael 2000, *Welfare Reform: Next Steps Offer New Opportunities: A Role for Philanthropy in Preparing for the Reauthorization of TANF in 2002*, NFG Public Policy Paper 4, pp.1–30.

Greenberg, Mark and Savner, Stuart 1999, *The Final TANF Regulations: A Preliminary Analysis*, Washington, DC.

Greenstein, Robert and Guyer, Jocelyn 2001, "Supporting Work through Medicaid and Food Stamps," in Rebecca Blank and Ron Haskins (eds.), *The New World of Welfare*, Washington, DC.

Grogger, Jeffrey, Karoly, Lynn, and Klerman, Alex 2002, *Consequences of Welfare Reform: A Research Synthesis*, Los Angeles, CA, p.98.

Gustafson, Cynthia and Levine, Phillip 1998, *Less-Skilled Workers, Welfare Reform, and the Unemployment Insurance System*, National Bureau of Economic Research Working Paper 6489.

Gustafsson, Siv 1995, "Single Mothers in Sweden: Why Is Poverty Less Severe?," in Katherine McFate, Roger Lawson, and William Wilson (eds.), *Poverty, Inequality, and the Future of Social Policy*, New York, pp.291–325.

Hadley, Jack 2002, *Sicker and Poorer: The Consequences of Being Uninsured, Executive Summary*, prepared for the Kaiser Commission on Medicaid and the Uninsured, p.6 and pp.8–9.

Hall, Peter 1999, "The Political Economy of Europe in an Era of Interdependence," in Herbert Kitschelt, Peter Lange, Gary Marks, and John Stephens 1999, *Continuity and Change in Contemporary Capitalism*, New York, pp.135–63.

2002, *The Economic Challenges Facing President Jacques Chirac, U.S. France Analysis*, Washington, DC.

Hamilton, Gale 2002, *Moving People from Welfare to Work: Lessons from the National Evaluation of Welfare-to-Work Strategies*, New York.

Handler, Joel 1986, *The Conditions of Discretion: Autonomy, Community, Bureaucracy*, New York.

1990, *Law and the Search for Community*, Philadelphia, PA.

1992, "Postmodernism, Protest, and the New Social Movements," *Law and Society Review* 26(4): 697–732.

1995, *The Poverty of Welfare Reform*, New Haven, CT.

1996, *Down from Bureaucracy: The Ambiguity of Privatization and Empowerment*, Princeton, NJ.

Handler, Joel and Hasenfeld, Yeheskel 1991, *The Moral Construction of Poverty: Welfare Reform in America*, Newbury Park, CA.

1997, *We the Poor People: Work, Poverty, and Welfare*, New York.

Hardiman, Niamh 2000, "Taxing the Poor: The Politics of Income Taxation in Ireland," *Policy Studies Journal* 28(4): 815–842.

Harris, Kathleen 1993, "Work and Welfare Among Single Mothers in Poverty," *American Journal of Sociology* 99: 317–352.

Hartmann, Heidi 1987, "Changes in Women's Economic and Family Roles," in Lourdes Beneria and Catharine Stimpson, *Women, Households, and the Economy*, New Brunswick, NJ, pp.33–64.

Hartog, Joop 1999, "Whither Dutch Corporatism? Or: A Turbulent Tango for Market and State," University of Wisconsin Institute for Research on Poverty Discussion Paper 1197–99.

Hartung, William and Washburn, Jennifer 1998, "Lockheed Martin: From Warfare to Welfare," *The Nation*: 11–16.

Harvey, Philip 1989, *Securing the Right to Employment*, Princeton, NJ.

1994, *Welfare Reform, Human Rights, and the Future of Capitalism*, Milwaukee, WI.

1999, "Liberal Strategies for Combating Joblessness in the Twentieth Century," *Journal of Economic Issues* 33(2): 497–504.

2002, "Taking Economic and Social Rights Seriously," *Human Rights and Economic Policy Discourse* 33: 363–471.

Hasenfeld, Yeheskel 1983, *Human Service Organizations*, Upper Saddle River, NJ.

Hasenfeld, Yeheskel and Abbott, Andrew Delano 1992, *Human Services as Complex Organizations*, Newbury Park, CA.

Hasenfeld, Yeheskel, Ghose, T.J., and Hillesland-Larson, Kandyce 2001, *Characteristics of Sanctioned and Non-Sanctioned Single-Parent CalWORKS Recipients; Preliminary Findings from the First Wave Survey in Four Counties: Alameda, Freson, Kern, and San Diego*, Los Angeles, CA.

Haskins, Ron and Blank, Rebecca 2001, *The New World of Welfare*, Washington, DC.

Haskins, Ron and Primus, Wendell 2001, *Welfare Reform and Poverty, Welfare and Beyond*, Policy Brief 4, p.6.

Healy, Melissa 2000, "Welfare Rolls Fall to Half of '96 Numbers," *Los Angeles Times*, August 23, 2000, A12.

Heclo, Hugh 1994, "Poverty Politics," in Sheldon Danziger, Gary Sandefur, and Daniel Weinberg (eds.), *Confronting Poverty: Prescriptions for Change*, Cambridge, MA, p.420.

Hemerijck, Anton 1999, "Prospects for Inclusive Social Citizenship in an Age of Structural Inactivity," Max Planck Institute for Social Studies Working Paper 99/1.

2002, "The Self-transformation of the European Social Model(s)," in Esping-Andersen et al. (eds.), *Why We Need a New Welfare State*, New York.

Hemerijck, Anton and Visser, Jelle 2000, "Change and Immobility: Three Decades of Policy Adjustment in the Netherlands and Belgium," in Maurizio Ferrera and Martin Rhodes (eds.), *Recasting European Welfare States*, Special Issue, *West European Politics* 23(2): 229–256.

Henly, Julia 1999, "Barriers to Finding and Maintaining Jobs: The Perspectives of Workers and Employers in the Low-Wage Labor Market, " in Joel Handler, and Lucie White (eds.), *Hard Labor: Women and Work in the Post-Welfare Era*, New York, pp.48–75.

Héritier, Adrienne 2001, "New Modes of Governance in Europe: Policy Making Without Legislating?," in Adrienne Héritier (ed.), *Common Goods: Reinventing European and International Governance*, Lanham, MD, pp.1–21.

Hicks, Alexander and Kenworthy, Lane 2003, "Varieties of Welfare Capitalism," *Socio-Economic Review* 1: 27–61.

Higham, John 1988, *Strangers in the Land: Patterns of American Nativism 1869–1925*, New Brunswick, NJ.

Hinrichs, Karl 1995, "Impact of German Health Insurance Reforms on Redistribution and the Culture of Solidarity," *Journal of Health Politics, Policy and Law* 20: 653–687.

Hirst, Paul 2000, *Can the European Welfare State Survive Globalization? Sweden, Denmark, and the Netherlands in Comparative Perspective*, available at: http://polyglot.lss.wisc.edu/eur/works/hirst.html

291

Hodson, Dermot and Maher, Imelda 2001, "The Open Method as a New Mode of Governance: The Case of Soft Economic Policy Coordination," *Journal of Common Market Studies* 39(4): 719–746.

Hoge, Warren 2002, "Swedes Are Out Sick Longer, and Budget Is Ailing," *New York Times*, September 24, 2002, A3.

Honneth, Axel 1991, *Critique of Power: Reflective Stages in a Critical Social Theory*, Boston, MA.

Hooghe, Liesbet and Marks, Gary 1999, "The Making of a Polity: The Struggle over European Integration," in Kitschelt et al. (eds.), *Continuity and Change in Contemporary Capitalism*, pp.70–97.

House Committee on Ways and Means of the 103 US Congress 1998, *Green Book: Background Material and Data on Programs Within the Jurisdiction of the Committee on Ways and Means*, Washington, DC.

Huber, Evelyn and Stephens, John 2001, *Development and Crisis of the Welfare State: Parties and Policies in Global Markets*, Chicago, IL.

Hutchinson, Allan 1988, *Dwelling on the Threshold*, Toronto, Canada.

Institute 1996, "German Wages Have Risen Only Slightly in Real Terms Since 1980," New York.

Jacobsson, Kerstin 2001, "Employment Policy Coordination: A New System of EU Governance," paper presented at the *Scancor Workshop on Transnational Regulation and the Transformation of State*, Palo Alto, CA.

(n.d.), "Soft Regulation and the Subtle Transformation of States: The Case of EU Employment Policy," preliminary version of a book chapter for Bengt Jacobsson and Kerstin Sahlin-Andersson (eds.), *Transnational Regulation and the Transformation of States*.

Johnston, David 1999, "Gap Between Rich and Poor Found Substantially Wider," *New York Times*, September 5, 1999, A14.

2002, "Loans to Poor at Tax Time are Criticized," *New York Times*, May 21, 2002, C1.

Jordan, Bill 1998, "European Social Citizenship: Why a New Social Contract (Probably) Will Not Happen," in Martin Rhodes and Yves Mény, *The Future of European Welfare: A New Social Contract?*, New York, pp.244–265.

Kahl, Sigrun 2002a, "Beyond Workfare: Strategies Towards the Hard to Serve on Social Assistance in the U.S., the UK, Australia, the Netherlands, Norway, Sweden, Finland, Switzerland and Germany," paper presented at the Law and Society Association Meeting, Vancouver, Canada.

2002b, "Social Assistance in Germany," unpublished manuscript.

Kaiser Commission on Medicaid and the Uninsured 2002, *Low-Income Parents' Access to Medicaid Five Years After Welfare Reform*, Policy Brief, June.

Kaplan, Jan 1999, *The Use of Sanctions Under TANF*, Welfare Information Network, Issue Notes 3(3).

Karoly, Lynn, Klerman, Jacob, and Rogowski, Jeanette 2001, "Effects of the 1996 Welfare Reform Changes on the SSI Program," in Rebecca Blank and Ron Haskins (eds.), *The New World of Welfare*, Washington, DC, pp.482–499.

Katz, Bruce and Allen, Katherine 1999, "Help Wanted: Connecting Inner-City Job Seekers with Suburban Jobs," *Brookings Review* 17(4): 31–35.

Katz, Michael 1986, *In the Shadow of the Poorhouse*, New York.

Keiffer, Charles 1984, "Citizen Empowerment: A Developmental Perspective," *Prevention in Human Services* 3: 9–36.

Kenner, Jeff 1999, "The EC Employment Title and the 'Third Way': Making Soft Law Work?," *International Journal of Comparative Labour Law and Industrial Relations* 15(1): 33–60.

Kildal, Nanna 2000, "Workfare Tendencies in Scandinavian Welfare Policies," paper presented at *The European Research Seminar: The Activation Welfare State. New Ways of Fighting Poverty and Social Exclusion in Europe*, Lund.

Kildal, Nanna and Kuhnle, Stein 2002, "The Principle of Universalism: Tracing a Key Idea in the Scandinavian Welfare Model," paper presented at the *BIEN 9th International Congress*, Geneva.

Kitschelt, Herbert, Lange, Peter, Marks, Gary, and Stephens, John 1999, *Continuity and Change in Contemporary Capitalism*, New York.

1999, "Convergence and Divergence in Advanced Capitalist Democracies," in Herbert Kitschelt, Peter Lange, Gary Marks and John Stephens, *Continuity and Change in Contemporary Capitalism*, New York, pp.427–460.

Klausen, Jytte 1999, "The Declining Significance of Male Workers: Trade-Union Responses to Changing Labor Markets," in Herbert Kitschelt, Peter Lange, Gary Marks, and John Stephens 1999, *Continuity and Change in Contemporary Capitalism*, New York, pp.261–290.

Klein, R. and Rafferty, A.M. 1999, "Rorschach Politics: Tony Blair and the Third Way," *American Prospect*, July/August: 44–50.

Knijn, Trudie and van Wel, Frits 2001, "Careful or Lenient: Welfare Reform for Lone Mothers in the Netherlands," *Journal of European Social Policy* 11: 235–251.

Ku, Leighton and Blaney, Shannon 2000, *Health Coverage for Legal Immigrant Children: New Census Data Highlight Importance of Restoring Medicaid and SCHP Coverage*, Washington, DC, manuscript in preparation.

Ku, Leighton and Park, Edwin 2001, *Federal Aid to State Medicaid Programs Is Falling While Economy Weakens*, Washington, DC.

2002, *Improving Transitional Medicaid to Promote Work and Strengthen Health Insurance Coverage*, Washington, DC, p.4.

Ku, Leighton and Rothbaum, Emily 2001, *Many States Are Considering Medicaid Cutbacks in the Midst of the Economic Downturn*, Washington, DC.

Kuhnle, Stein 2000, "The Scandinavian Welfare State in the 1990s: Challenged but Viable," in Maurizio Ferrera and Martin Rhodes (eds.), *Recasting European Welfare States*, Special Issue, *West European Politics* 23(2): 209–228.

Kusmin, Lorin and Gibbs, Robert 2000, "Less-Educated Workers Face Limited Opportunities to Move Up to Good Jobs," *Rural America* 15(3): 33.

Lambert, Susan, Waxman, Elaine, and Haley-Lock, Anna 2001, *Against the Odds: A Study of Instability in Lower-Skilled Jobs*, Chicago, IL.

Lawson, Roger and Wilson, William 1995, "Poverty, Social Rights, and the Quality of Citizenship," in Katherine McFate, Roger Lawson, and William Wilson (eds.), *Poverty, Inequality, and the Future of Social Policy*, New York, pp.693–715.

Layte Richard, Nolan, Brian, and Whelan, Christopher 2000, "Targeting Poverty: Lessons from Monitoring Ireland's National Anti-Poverty Strategy," *Journal of Social Policy* 29(4): 553–576.

Lazere, Ed 1998, *New Findings from Oregon Suggest Minimum Wage Increases Can Boost Wages for Welfare Recipients Moving to Work*, Washington DC.

Lee, Don 1999, "Nature of Work Has Changed," *Los Angeles Times*, September 6, 1999, A1.

Lefaucher, Nadine 1995, "French Policies Towards Lone Parents: Social Categories and Social Policies," in Katherine McFate, Roger Lawson, and William Wilson (eds.), *Poverty, Inequality, and the Future of Social Policy*, New York, pp.257–289.

Lemaigre, Thomas (n.d.), "How are the Employment Guidelines Addressing Long-term Unemployment?," European Anti Poverty Network, Brussels.

Lerman, Robert and Sorenson, Elaine 2001, "Child Support: Interaction Between Private and Public Transfers," National Bureau of Economic Research, NBER Working Paper 8199.

Lerner, Sally 1999, "Arguing for Basic Income in North America: Taking the Dialogue Beyond Value Absolutes," paper presented at *The Society for the Advancement of Socio-Economics (SASE) 11th Annual Meeting*, Madison, WI.

Lester, Gillian 2001, "Unemployment Insurance and Wealth Distribution," *UCLA Law Review* 49: 335–394.

Levy, Jonah 1999, "French Social Policy in the Age of High Unemployment," in Alain Guyomarch et al. (ed.), *Developments in French Politics 2*, London.

    2000, "France: Directing Adjustment?," in Fritz Scharpf and Vivien Schmidt (eds.), *From Vulnerability to Competitiveness: Welfare and Work in the Open Economy*, Oxford, GB.

    2001, "Partisan Politics and Welfare Adjustment: the Case of France," *Journal of European Public Policy* 8(2): 265–285.

Lindbeck, Assar 1995, "The End of the Middle Way? The Large Welfare States of Europe," *American Economic Association Papers and Proceedings*, pp.9–10.

Littlewood, Paul and Herkommer, Sebastian 1999, "Identifying Social Exclusion: Some Problems of Meaning," in Paul Littlewood, Ignace Glorieux, Sebastian Herkommer, and Ingrid Jonsson (eds.), *Social Exclusion in Europe: Problems and Paradigms*, Aldershot, pp.1–21.

Lødemel, Ivar 2001, "National Objectives and Local Implementation of Workfare in Norway," in Ivar Lødemel and Heather Trickey, *An Offer You Can't Refuse: Workfare in International Perspective*, Bristol, pp.133–158.

Lødemel, Ivar and Trickey, Heather 2001, *An Offer You Can't Refuse: Workfare in International Perspective*, Bristol.

Loprest, Pamela 1999, *Families Who Left Welfare: Who Are They and How Are They Doing?*, Urban Institute Discussion Paper 10.

Lukes, Steven 1974, *Power: A Radical View*, London.

Mancur, Olson, Jr. 1995, "The Devolution of the Nordic and Teutonic Economies," *American Economic Review* 85: 22.

Manow, Philip and Seils, Eric 2000, "The Employment Crisis of the German Welfare State," in Maurizio Ferrera and Martin, Rhodes (eds.), *Recasting European Welfare States*, pp.139–160.

Maranville, Deborah 2002, "Workplace Mythologies and Unemployment Insurance: Exit, Voice and Exhausting All Reasonable Alternatives to Quitting," unpublished manuscript.

Marshall, Thomas 1950, *Citizenship and Social Class*, Cambridge.

Maruani, Margaret 1997, "Hard Times for Working Women," Le Mond Diplomatique, September.

Maschino, Maurice 2002, " 'Liberty, Equality, Identity' Do You Eat Couscous at Home? How Often? Are You Sure You're French?," *Le Monde Diplomatique*, June 11, 2002, pp.44–53.

Mayer, Susan 1995, "A Comparison of Poverty and Living Conditions in the United States, Canada, Sweden, and Germany," in Katherine McFate, Roger Lawson, and William Wilson (eds.), *Poverty, Inequality, and the Future of Social Policy*, New York, pp.109–151.

McFate, Katherine 1995, "Introduction: Western States in the New World Order," in Katherine McFate, Roger Lawson, and William Wilson (eds.), *Poverty, Inequality, and the Future of Social Policy*, New York, pp.1–26.

McFate, Katherine, Smeeding, Timothy, and Rainwater, Lee 1995, "Markets and States," in Katherine McFate, Roger Lawson, and William Wilson (eds.), *Poverty, Inequality, and the Future of Social Policy*, New York, pp.29–66.

McKeown, Timothy 1999, "The Global Economy, Post-Fordism, and Trade Policy in Advanced Capitalist States," in Herbert Kitschelt, Peter Lange,

Gary Marks, and John Stephens 1999, *Continuity and Change in Contemporary Capitalism*, New York, pp.11–35.

Mead, Lawrence 1986, *Beyond Entitlement: The Social Obligations of Citizenship*, New York.

  1989, "The Logic of Workfare: The Underclass and Work Policy," *ASPSS* 501: 156–169.

Meyer, Bruce and Rosenbaum, Dan 1999, "Welfare, the Earned Income Tax Credit, and the Labor Supply of Single Mothers," National Bureau of Economic Research Working Paper Series.

Meyer, John and Rowen, Brian 1991, "Institutional Organizations: Formal Structure as Myth and Ceremony," in Walter Powell and Paul DiMaggio (eds.), *The New Institutionalism in Organizational Analysis*, Chicago, IL.

Meyers, Marcia, Han, Wen-Jui, Waldfogel, Jane, and Garfinkel, Irwin 2001, "Child Care in the Wake of Welfare Reform: The Impact of Government Subsidies on the Economic Well-Being of Single-Mother Families," *Social Service Review*, March: 29–59.

Michalopoulos, Charles and Berlin, Gordon 2001, *Financial Work Incentives for Low-Wage Workers: Encouraging Work, Reducing Poverty, and Benefitting Families*, New York.

Michalopoulos, Charles and Schwartz, Christine 2000, *National Evaluation of Welfare-to-Work Strategies. What Works Best For Whom: Impacts of 20 Welfare-to-Work Programs by Subgroup*, New York, pp.4, 7–8.

Miongione, Enzo and Pugliese, Enrico 2000, "Unemployment and Welfare: Two Stories of Migrant and Minority Disadvantage," *Netherlands' Journal of Social Sciences* 36(2): 163–166.

Mishel, Lawrence, Bernstein, Jared, and Schmitt, John 2000, *The State of Working America 1998–99*, Ithaca, NY, pp.134–135.

Molotch, Harvey and Boden, Deirdre 1985, "Talking Social Structure: Discourse, Domination, and the Watergate Hearings," *American Sociological Review* 50: 273–288.

Monroe, Pamela and Tiller, Vicky 2001, "Commitment to Work Among Welfare-Reliant Women," *Journal of Marriage and Family* 63: 816–828.

Morone, James and Goggin, Janice 1995, "Health Policies in Europe: Welfare States in a Market Era," *Journal of Health Politics, Policy, and Law* 20: 558–569.

Murray, Charles 1984, *Losing Ground: American Social Policy, 1950–1980*, New York.

Newman, Katherine 2000, *No Shame in My Game*, New York.

Newman, Katherine and Chauncy, Lennon 1995, "The Job Ghetto," *The American Prospect*: 66–67.

New York Times 2001a, "Denmark Shifts Right in Election Centering on Immigration," *New York Times*, November 21, 2001, A6.

2001b, "After Danish Vote, Anxiety Over the Rightists," *New York Times*, November 22, 2001, A17.

2002, "The Netherlands: New Government Takes Office," *New York Times*, July 23, 2002, A6.

Nickell, Stephen 1997, "Unemployment and Labor Market Rigidities: Europe versus North America," *Journal of Economic Perspectives* 11(3): 55–74.

Nussbaum, Martha 1996, *For Love of Country: Debating the Limits of Patriotism*, Boston, MA.

OECD 1994, *Green Paper on Social Policy*, Brussels, Belgium.

1999, *Employment Outlook*, available at www.oecd.org/pdf/M00028000/M00028142.pdf

2000, Policy Brief *Economic Survey of the Netherlands 2000*, pp.1–6.

2001, "When Money Is Tight: Poverty Dynamics in OECD Countries," in *Economic Outlook*, Brussels, Belgium.

Offe, Claus 1993, *Contradictions of the Welfare State*, Cambridge, MA.

2002, "Wasteful Welfare Transactions: A Critique of Welfare/Workfare as a Strategy to Cope with Income Poverty," paper presented at the 9th Annual BIEN conference, Geneva.

Olsen, Gregg 1996, "Re-Modeling Sweden: The Rise and Demise of the Compromise in a Global Economy," *Social Problems* 43: 1–20.

Ong, Paul 2001, *Car Ownership and Welfare-To-Work*, Los Angeles, CA, UCLA School of Urban Planning, manuscript in preparation.

Ong, Paul and Houston, Douglas 2002a, *Travel Patterns and Welfare to Work*, Los Angeles, CA, UCLA School of Urban Planning, manuscript in preparation.

2002b, "Transit, Employment and Women on Welfare," Los Angeles, CA, UCLA School of Urban Planning, manuscript in preparation.

O'Riain, Sean 2000, "The Flexible Development State: Globalization, Information Technology, and the 'Celtic Tiger,'" *Politics and Society* 28(2): 157–193.

Ormerod, Paul 1998, "Unemployment and Social Exclusion: An Economic View," in Martin Rhodes and Yves Mény, *The Future of European Welfare: A New Social Contract?*, New York, pp.23–40.

Osterman, Paul 1991, "Welfare Participation in a Full Employment Economy," *Social Problems* 38: 475–491.

1995, "Is There a Problem with the Youth Labor Market, and If So, How Should We Fix It?: Lessons for the United States from U.S. and European Experience," in Katherine McFate, Roger Lawson, and William Wilson (eds.), *Poverty, Inequality, and the Future of Social Policy*, New York, pp.387–414.

2001, "Organizing the US Labor Market: National Problems, Community Strategies," paper presented at the conference on *Reconfiguring Work and Welfare in the New Economy: A Transatlantic Dialogue*, Madison, WI, p.7.

Palier, Bruno 2000, "'Defrosting' the French Welfare State," in Maurizio Ferrera and Martin Rhodes (eds.), *Recasting European Welfare States*, Special Issue, *West European Politics* 23(2): 113–136.

Palme, Joakim 2002, "Welfare Trends in Sweden: Balancing the Books for the 1990s," *Journal of European Social Policy* 12(4): 329–346.

Park, Edwin and Broaddus, Matthew 2001a, "OMB Estimates Indicate 400,000 Children Will Lose Health Insurance Due to Reductions in SCHIP Funding," Washington, DC.

  2001b, "Administration Medicaid and SCHIP Waiver Policy Encourages States to Scale Back Benefits Significantly and Increase Cost-Sharing for Low-Income Beneficiaries," Washington, DC.

Paugam, Serge 1998, "Poverty and Social Exclusion: A Sociological View," in Martin Rhodes and Yves Mény, *The Future of European Welfare: A New Social Contract?*, New York, pp.41–62.

Pavetti, La Donna 1999, "How Much More Can Welfare Mothers Work?," *Focus* 20(2): 16–19.

Pavetti, La Donna and Bloom, Dan 2001, "Sanctions and Time Limits: State Policies, Their Implementation, and Outcomes for Families," paper presented at the conference on *The New World of Welfare: Shaping a Post-TANF Agenda for Policy*, Washington, DC.

Pear, Robert 2002, "House Democrats Propose Making the '96 Welfare Law an Antipoverty Weapon," *New York Times*, January 24, 2002, A24.

Philips, Katherin 2001, *Who Knows about the Earned Income Tax Credit*, The Urban Institute Series B (B-27).

Pierson, Paul 1996, "The New Politics of the Welfare State," *World Politics* 48: 143–179.

  2001a, *The New Politics of the Welfare State*, Oxford.

  2001b, "Investigating the Welfare State at Century's End," in Paul Pierson (ed.), *The New Politics of the Welfare State*, New York, pp.1–17.

  2001c, "Coping with Permanent Austerity: Welfare State Restructuring in Affluent Democracies," in Paul Pierson (ed.), *The New Politics of the Welfare State*, Oxford, pp.410–456.

Piven, Frances and Cloward, Richard 1977, *Poor People's Movements: Why They Succeed, How They Fail*, New York.

Polit, Denis, London, Andrew, and Martinez, John 2000, *The Health of Poor Urban Women: Findings from the Urban Change Project*, New York.

Powell, Bill 1996, "Germany's Disease," *Newsweek*, April 8, 1996, p.44.

Primus, Wendell, Rawlings, Lynette, Larin, Kathy, and Porter, Kathryn 1999, *The Initial Impacts of Welfare Reform on the Incomes of Single Mother Families*, Washington, DC.

Procacci, Giovanna 1998, "Against Exclusion: The Poor and the Social Sciences," in Martin Rhodes and Yves Mény, *The Future of European Welfare: A New Social Contract?*, New York, pp. 63–78.

Przeworski, Adam 1999, "How Many Ways Can Be Third?," in Andrew Glyn (ed.), *Economic Policy and Social Democracy*, Oxford.

Purdy, David 1994, "Citizenship, Basic Income, and the State," *New Left Review* 208: 30–48.

Rainwater, Lee 1995, "Poverty and the Income Package of Working Parents: The United States in Comparative Perspective," *Children and Youth Services Review* 17: 11–41.

Rank, Mark 1994, "A View From the Inside Out: Recipients' Perceptions of Welfare," *Journal of Sociology and Social Welfare* 21: 27–47.

Rees, Anthony 1996, "T.H. Marshall and the Progress of Citizenship," in Martin Bulmer and Anthony Rees, *Citizenship Today: The Contemporary Relevance of T.H. Marshall*, London, pp.1–23.

Reissert, Bernd 2001, "Unemployment Protection in Germany: The System and its Changes in the 1990s," unpublished paper, p.11.

Rhodes, Martin 1998, "Globalization, Labour Markets and Welfare States: A Future of 'Competitive Corporatism'?," in Martin Rhodes and Yves Mény, *The Future of European Welfare: A New Social Contract?*, New York, pp.178–203.

    2000, "Desperately Seeking a Solution: Social Democracy, Thatcherism and the 'Third Way' in British Welfare," in Maurizio Ferrera and Martin Rhodes (eds.), *Recasting European Welfare States*, pp.161–186.

Rhodes, Martin and Mény, Yves 1998, *The Future of European Welfare: A New Social Contract?*, New York, pp.157–177.

Rifkin, Jeremy 1995, *The End of Work: The Decline of Global Work-Force and the Dawn of the Post-Market Era*, New York.

Roche, Maurice 2000, *Comparative Social Inclusion Policies and Citizenship in Europe: Towards a New European Social Mode*, SEDEC Network Final Report, Sheffield.

Room, Graham 1999, *Commodification and Decommodification: A Developmental Critique*, Institute for International Policy Analysis Discussion Paper, Bath.

    2000, "Commodification and Decommodification: a Developmental Critique," *Policy and Politics* 28(3): 331–351.

Rosanvallon, Pierre 2000, *The New Social Question: Rethinking the Welfare State*, Princeton, NJ.

Rosdahl, Andres and Weise, Hanne 2001, "When All Must be Active – Workfare in Denmark," in Ivar Lødemel and Heather Trickey, *An Offer You Can't Refuse: Workfare in International Perspective*, Bristol, pp.1–40.

Ross, Fiona 2000, "Interests and Choice in the 'Not Quite So New' Politics of Welfare," in Maurizio Ferrera and Martin Rhodes (eds.), *Recasting European Welfare States*, pp.11–34.

Ryan, Alan 1999, "Britain: Recycling the Third Way," *DISSENT*, Spring.

Sabel, Charles 2000, "The Future of Governance: Technological, Economic, and Social Driving Forces," paper presented at the *EXPO 2000, OECD Forum for the Future Conference on 21st Century Governance: Power in the Global Knowledge Economy and Society*, Hanover, Germany.

Sainsbury, Diane and Morissens, Ann 2002, "Poverty in Europe in the Mid-1990s: the Effectiveness of Means-Tested Benefits," *Journal of European Social Policy* 12(4): 307–327.

Sawhill, Isabel and Thomas, Adam 2001, "A Hand Up for the Bottom Third: Toward a New Agenda for Low-Income Working Families," unpublished manuscript, p.6.

Scharpf, Fritz 1998, "Negative and Positive Integration in the Political Economy of European Welfare States," in Martin Rhodes and Yves Mény, *The Future of European Welfare: A New Social Contract?*, New York, pp.157–177.

1999, *Governing in Europe: Effective and Democratic?*, Oxford.

2000, "Economic Changes, Vulnerabilities, and Institutional Capabilities," in Fritz Scharpf and Vivian Schmidt (eds.), *Welfare and Work in the Open Economy: From Vulnerabilities to Competitiveness*, Oxford.

2001, "Notes Toward a Theory of Multilevel Governing in Europe," *Scandinavian Political Studies* 24(1): 1–26.

Schorr, Alvin 1987, "Welfare Reform, Once (or Twice) Again," *Tikkun*, November–December.

Scott, Ellen, London, Andrew, and Edin, Kathryn 2000, "Looking to the Future: Welfare-Reliant Women Talk About Their Job Aspirations in the Context of Welfare Reform," *Journal of Social Issues* 56(4): 727–746.

Scott, James 1990, *Domination and the Arts of Resistance: Hidden Transcripts*, New Haven, CT.

Scott, Joanne and Trubek, David 2002, "Mind the Gap: Law and New Approaches to Governance in the European Union," European Law Journal 8(1): 1–18.

Seccombe, Karen, Delores, James, and Walters, Kimberly 1998, "They Think You Ain't Much of Nothing: The Social Construction of the Welfare Mother," *Journal of Marriage and the Family* 60(5): 849–865.

Seiden, Danielle 2001, *EITC: The Earned Income Tax Credit*, Los Angeles, CA.

Sengupta, Somini 2000, "No Rise in Child Abuse Seen in Welfare Shift," *New York Times*, August 10, 2000, A1.

Shaviro, Daniel 1999, *Effective Marginal Tax Rates on Low-Income Households*, New York.

Silver, Hilary 1998a, *Modernizing and Improving Social Protection in the European Union*, COM 102 final, Brussels, Belgium.

1998b, "Policies to Reinforce Social Cohesion in Europe," in Arjan de Haan and Jose Burle Figueiredo (eds.), *Social Exclusion: An ILO Exclusive*, Geneva, Switzerland.

Silver, Hilary and Miller, S.M. 2002, "Social Exclusion: The European Approach to Social Disadvantage," *Poverty and Race* 22(5): 1–14.

Simmons, Beth 1999, "The Internationalization of Capital," in Kitschelt et al. (eds.), *Continuity and Change in Contemporary Capitalism*, New York, pp.35–69.

Skopcol, Theda 1992, *Protecting Soldiers and Mothers: The Political Origins of Social Policy in the United States*, Cambridge, MA.

Smith, Roger 1997, *Civic Ideals: Conflicting Visions of Citizenship in US History*, New Haven, CT.

Soskice, David 1999, "Divergent Production Regimes: Coordinated and Uncoordinated Market Economies in the 1980s and 1990s," in Herbert Kitschelt, Peter Lange, Gary Marks, and John Stephens, *Continuity and Change in Contemporary Capitalism*, New York, pp.101–134.

Soss, Joe 2000, *Unwanted Claims: The Politics of Participation in the US Welfare System*, Ann Arbor, MI.

Spies, Henk and van Berkel, Rik 2001, "Workfare in the Netherlands – Young Unemployed People and the Jobseeker's Employment Act," in Ivar Lødemel and Heather Trickey, *An Offer You Can't Refuse: Workfare in International Perspective*, Bristol, pp.105–132.

Standing, Guy 1995, "The Need for a New Social Consensus," in Philippe Van Parijs (ed.), *Arguing for Basic Income. Ethical Foundations for a Radical Reform*, London and New York, pp.47–60.

1999, *Global Labour Flexibility: Seeking Distributive Justice*, New York.

2002, *Beyond the New Paternalism: Basic Security as Equality*, London.

Stapleton, David et al. 2001, *How Well Have Rural and Small Metropolitan Labor Markets Absorbed Welfare Recipients?* The Lewin Group Executive Summary.

Stoll, Michael 2000, "Search, Discrimination, and the Travel to Work," in Larry Bobo, Oliver Melvin, James Johnson, and A. Valenzuela (eds.), *Prismatic Metropolis: Inequality in Los Angeles*, New York, pp.417–452.

Stoll, Michael, Holzer, Harry, and Ihlandfeldt, Keith 2000, "Within Cities and Suburbs: Racial Residential Concentration and the Spatial Distribution of Employment Opportunities across Sub-Metropolitan Areas," *Journal of Policy Analysis and Management* 19(2): 207–231.

Strawn, Julie, Greenberg, Mark, and Savner, Steve 2001, *Improving Employment Outcomes Under TANF*, Washington, DC.

Streeck, Wolfgang 1996, "Neo-Voluntarism: A New European Social Policy Regime?," in Gary Marks, Fritz Scharpf, Philippe Schmitter, and Wolfgang Streek, *Governance in the European Union*, London, pp.64–94.

1998, "The Internationalization of Industrial Relations in Europe: Prospects and Problems," *Politics and Society* 26(4): 429–459.

1999, "Competitive Solidarity: Rethinking the European Social Model," Max Planck Institute for the Study of Societies Working Paper 99/8.

2001, "High Equality, Low Activity: Contribution of the Social Welfare System to the German Collective Bargaining Regime," Robert Schuman Centre for Advanced Studies Working Paper No. 2001/6.

Supiot, Alain 2000, "The Dogmatic Foundations of the Market," *Industrial Law Journal* 29(4): 321–345.

2001, *Beyond Employment: Changes in Work and the Future of Labour Law in Europe*, New York.

Svensson, Mans 1999, *Do Staff Rental Agencies Create a Dual Labor Market in Sweden?*, unpublished manuscript.

Swarns, Rachel 1998, "Stiff Rules Cut Welfare Rolls at Two Offices," *New York Times*, June 22, 1998, AI.

Talcott, Parsons 1986, "Power and the Social System," in Steven Lukes (ed.), *Power: A Radical View*, New York.

Tamas, G.M. 2000, "On Post-Fascism: How Citizenship is Becoming an Exclusive Privilege," *Boston Review*: 42–46.

Taylor-Goodby, Peter 1996, "Paying for Welfare: The View from Europe," The Political Quarterly: 116–126.

2001, "Sustaining State Welfare in Hard Times: Who Will Foot the Bill?," *Journal of European Social Policy* 11(2): 133–147.

Teague, Paul 1999, *Economic Citizenship in the European Union: Employment Relations in the New Europe*, New York.

Torfing, Jacob 1999, "Workfare with Welfare: Recent Reforms of the Danish Welfare State," *Journal of European Social Policy* 9(1): 5–28.

Training and Employment Network (TEN) 1999, "Unemployment Unit and Youthaid," Weekly briefing 71, July.

Trattner, Walter 1999, *From Poor Law to Welfare State: A History of Social Welfare in America*, 6th edn., New York.

Trickey, Heather 2001, "Comparing Welfare Programmes – Features and Implications," in Ivar Lødemel and Heather Trickey, *An Offer You Can't Refuse: Workfare in International Perspective*, Bristol, pp.249–294.

Trickey, Heather and Walker, Robert 2001, "Steps to Compulsion within British Labour Market Programmes," in Ivar Lødemel and Heather Trickey, *An Offer You Can't Refuse: Workfare in International Perspective*, Bristol, pp.181–214.

Trubek, David 2002, "The European Employment Strategy and the Future of EU Governance: An Opportunity for the Baltics and a Challenge for Lawyers," Riga Graduate School of Law Working Paper.

Trubek, David and Mosher, John 2001, *New Governance, EU Employment Policy, and the European Social Model*, available at www.jeanmonnetprogram.org/papers/01/010601.html

Tsakloglou, Panos and Papadopoulos, Fotis 2002, "Aggregate Level and Determining Factors of Social Exclusion in Twelve European Countries," *Journal of European Social Policy* 12(3): 211–225.

Turner, Bryan 1992, "Outline of a Theory of Citizenship," in Mouffe Chantal (ed.), *Dimensions of Radical Democracy. Pluralism, Citizenship, Community*, London, pp.33–63.

Turner, Bryan and Hamilton, Peter (eds.) 1994, *Citizenship: Critical Concepts*, London.

US Bureau of the Census 1998, *Poverty in the United States*, March 1998 Supplement to the Current Population Survey (CPS).

   2001, *Poverty in the United States*, March 2001 Supplement to the Current Population Survey (CPS).

Vaillant, Emmanuel 1997, "The Bounds of Freedom: Making Them Legal," *Le Monde Diplomatique* (November).

van Kersbergen, Kess 1999, "Contemporary Christian Democracy and the Demise of the Politics of Mediation," in Herbert Kitschelt, Peter Lange, Gary Marks, and John Stephens, *Continuity and Change in Contemporary Capitalism*, New York, pp.346–370.

van Oorschot, Wim 2002, "Miracle or Nightmare? A Critical Review of Dutch Activation Policies," *International Social Policy* 31(3): 399–420.

van Parijs, Philippe 1992, *Arguing for Basic Income. Ethical Foundations for a Radical Reform*, London, and New York.

   1995, *Real Freedom for All. What (if Anything) Can Justify Capitalism?*, Oxford.

van Steenbergen, Bart 1994, *The Condition of Citizenship*, London, pp.10–19.

Veenman, Justus 1995, "Ethnic Minorities in the Netherlands," in Katherine McFate, Roger Lawson, and William Wilson (eds.), *Poverty, Inequality, and the Future of Social Policy*, New York, pp.607–628.

Visser, Jelle 2002, "The First Part-Time Economy in the World: A Model to be Followed," *Journal of European Social Policy* 12(1): 23–42.

Visser, Jelle and Hemerijck, Anton 1997, *A "Dutch Miracle" – Job Growth, Welfare Reform and Corporatism in the Netherlands*, Amsterdam.

Voges, Wolfgang, Jacobs, Herbert, and Trickey, Heather 2001, "Uneven Development – Local Authorities and Workfare in Germany," in Ivar Lødemel and Heather Trickey, *An Offer You Can't Refuse: Workfare in International Perspective*, Bristol, pp.71–104.

Wacquant, Loic 1995, "The Comparative Structure and Experience of Urban Exclusion: 'Race,' Class, and Space in Chicago and Paris," in Katherine McFate, Roger Lawson, and William Wilson (eds.), *Poverty, Inequality, and the Future of Social Policy*, New York, pp.543–570.

Walker, Robert 1998, "Does Work Work?," *Journal of Social Policy* 27: 533–542.

Walker, Robert and Wiseman, Michael 2001, *Britain's New Deal and the Next Round of US Welfare Reform*, Madison, WI.

Week in Germany, The 1998, October 23, 1998.

Western, Bruce 1995, "A Comparative Study of Working-Class Disorganization: Union Decline in Eighteen Advanced Capitalist Countries," *American Society Review* 60: 179–201.

Whelan, Christopher, Layte, Richard, and Maitre, Bertrand 2002, "Multiple Deprivation and Persistent Poverty in the EU," *Journal of European Social Policy* 12(2): 91–105.

Whitaker, Barbara 2002, "Spending Up, but California Lacks Day Care," *New York Times*, July 22, 2002, A9.

White, Lucie 1990, "Subordination, Rhetorical Survival Skills, and Sunday Shoes: Notes on the Hearing of Mrs. G.," *Buffalo Law Review* 38(1): 1–58.

1999, "Quality Child Care for Low-Income Families: Despair, Impasse, Improvisation," in Joel Handler and Lucie White (eds.), *Hard Labor: Women and Work in the Post-Welfare Era*, New York, pp.116–142.

Widerquist, Karl 2001, "A Basic Income Guarantee," *Synthesis/Regeneration* 26 (Fall): 26–27.

Williams, Lucy 1999, "Unemployment Insurance and Low-Wage Work," in Joel Handler and Lucie White (eds.), *Hard Labor: Women and Work in the Post-Welfare Era*, New York, pp.158–174.

Wilson, William 1987, *The Truly Disadvantaged: The Inner City, the Underclass, and Public Policy*, Chicago, IL.

Winter, Steven 1996, *The Power Thing*, Durham, NC.

Wolch, Jennifer 1998, "America's New Urban Policy: Welfare Reform and the Fate of American Cities," *Journal of American Planning*: A1.

Wolch, Jennifer, Sommer, Heidi, Handler, Joel, and Stoner, Madeline 1997, "Los Angeles in an Era of Welfare Reform: Implications for Poor People and Community Well-Being," *The Southern California Inter-University Consortium on Homeless and Poverty*, Los Angeles, CA.

Wolfe, Barbara 1994, "Reform of Health Care for the Nonelderly Poor," in Sheldon Danziger, Gary Sandefur, and Daniel Weinberg (eds.), *Confronting Poverty: Prescriptions for Change*, Cambridge, MA, pp.253–288.

Wolfe, Barbara and Hill, Steven 1995, "The Effects of Health on the Work Effort of Single Mothers," Journal of Human Resources 30(1): 42–62.

Wolfe, Barbara and Vandell, Deborah 2002, "Child Care for Low-Income Working Families," *Focus* 22(1): 106–110.

Wong, Yin-Ling Irene, Garfinkel, Irwin, and McLanahan, Sara 1993, *Single-Mother Families in Eight Countries: Economic Status and Social Policy*, Madison, WI.

Wright, Erik 2000, "Reducing Income and Wealth Inequality: Real Utopian Proposals," *Contemporary Sociology*: 143–156.

Wright, Erik and Dwyer, Rachel 2001, "The American Jobs Machine: Is The New Economy Creating Good Jobs?," *The Boston Review* 25(6): 21–26.

Wright, Sharon 2001, "Activating the Unemployed: The Street-Level Implementation of UK Policy," in Jochen Clasen (ed.), *What Future for Social Security? Debates and Reforms in National and Cross-National Perspective*, The Hague, Netherlands, pp.235–249.

Zedlewski, Sheila and Loprest, Pamela 2000, "How Well Does TANF Fit the Needs of the Most Disadvantaged Families," paper presented at *The New World of Welfare: Shaping a Post-TANF Agenda for Policy*, Ann Arbor, MI.

Zeitlin, Jonathan 2002, "The Open Method of Coordination and the Future of the European Employment Strategy," paper presented at the *Mini-Hearing of the Employment and Social Affairs Committee of the European Parliament on the First Five Year Evaluation of the Employment Guidelines*, Madison, WI.

Zimmerman, Marc 1993, "Empowerment Theory: Psychological Organizational and Community Levels of Analysis," in Julian Rappaport and Edward Seidman (eds.), *Handbook of Community Psychology*, New York.

Zimmerman, Marc and Rappaport, Julian 1988, "Citizen Participation, Perceived Control, and Psychological Empowerment," *American Journal of Community Psychology* 16: 725–750.

Zimmerman, Wendy and Tumlin, Karen 1999, "Patchwork Policies: State Assistance for Immigrants under Welfare Reform," Urban Institute, Assessing the New Federalism: Occasional Paper No.24.

INDEX